INSIGHTS ON AMERICAN HISTORY

VOLUME II

INSIGHTS ON AMERICAN HISTORY

VOLUME II

Compiled and Edited
by
Norman K. Risjord

In collaboration with

Thomas J. Archdeacon
Allan G. Bogue
Paul S. Boyer
Charles L. Cohen
John M. Cooper, Jr.
J. Rogers Hollingsworth
Diane Lindstrom
Thomas J. McCormick, Jr.
Stanley K. Schultz
John Sharpless

University of Wisconsin, Madison

Harcourt Brace Jovanovich, Publishers
San Diego New York Chicago Austin Washington, D.C.
London Sydney Tokyo Toronto

Cover:

ISBN: 0-15-541446-1
Library of Congress Catalog Card Number: 87-81169

Printed in the United States of America

PREFACE

This anthology is the product of a cooperative effort by eleven of us at the University of Wisconsin, Madison, who commonly teach the freshman-level American history survey course. A collective teaching experience of more than 200 years informs the effort. The anthology is intended as a supplement to lectures and to a standard textbook in the college-level introductory course in American history.

The choice of materials was based on two criteria: readability and argumentation. We wanted, first of all, to find materials that would catch the attention of students through interesting subject matter and would preserve that attention with smoothly flowing narrative. We held each selection to chapter length, hoping to encourage students to complete each assignment. We felt it equally important, however, that each selection contain enough substance to provoke lively class discussion. While enticing students with readable narrative, we also wanted to challenge them.

We strove for a balance among the various fields of history—political, social/economic, diplomatic—but we also limited the number of selections in each volume to twelve, so the instructor could make additional assignments in fields of special interest or challenge students further with a few full-length monographs. We incorporated a few classic pieces of historical writing, but for the most part we looked for articles and books that were on the cutting edge of historical scholarship, hoping to introduce students to the latest methodologies and interpretations.

In addition to being a cooperative endeavor, this project is an eleemosynary one. All royalties will be turned over to a departmental trust fund managed by the University of Wisconsin Foundation; the proceeds will be used to fund student fellowships. We trust that our numerous friends and alumni, as well as the history profession generally, will respect our motives and appreciate our efforts.

Norman K. Risjord

CONTENTS

1

WORK IDEALS AND THE INDUSTRIAL INVASION

DANIEL T. RODGERS

"No Admission Here Except on Business." This is the motto one nineteenth-century immigrant suggested should be placed over the entrance gates of the United States. American industriousness in the early national period was the wonder of newcomers and visitors. All was bustle, bustle, bustle; no one seemed to have time for leisure. In this essay Daniel T. Rodgers explores the ideological underpinnings of this national obsession with work. From the Puritans, Americans learned that diligence in one's calling was part of God's plan for humankind. From secular moralists like Benjamin Franklin they learned that unremitting work was both a badge of civic virtue and the first rung on the ladder of success. Patriotic writers assured them that the busy labors of millions of individual Americans was the key to national greatness.

But beginning in the 1820s, and accelerating with each passing decade, profound changes in the mode of production fundamentally challenged the national work ethic. With the coming of industrialization, large-scale factories replaced the small shops of an earlier day. The routines of the assembly line supplanted the labor of the skilled craftsman. Work, so long praised as a socially meaningful and morally significant activity, now became for many simply a repetitive routine. How could workers find personal meaning in their labors when they seemed only cogs in a vast impersonal productive apparatus?

In this insightful essay, Rodgers explores the ideological and technological background of the major reassessment of the meaning of work that came in the wake of industrialization—and that continues down to the present day.

—PAUL S. BOYER

Works and days were offered us, and we chose work.

RALPH WALDO EMERSON,
"WORKS AND DAYS" (1857)

"Work, work, work," Henry David Thoreau lectured an audience in the budding factory town of New Bedford in 1854. "It would be glorious to see mankind at leisure for once." Like so many of Thoreau's public activities, his "Getting a Living" was a quixotic gesture, a tilt at one of the most formidable windmills of mid-nineteenth-century opinion. It was the kind of irreverence to be expected of a man who could seriously describe his occupation as inspector of snowstorms and anticipator of sunrises. In a land reared on Franklin's Poor Richard aphorisms and the busy bee of Isaac Watts's poem—a land of railroads and heady ambitions, poised on the edge of a thoroughgoing experiment with industrialization—to doubt the moral preeminence of work was the act of a conscious heretic. But in the longer sweep of time, it was Thoreau who spoke as a conservative and a traditionalist. For the first American dream, before the others shoved it rudely aside, had been one not of work but of leisure. In the Western tradition, in fact, Thoreau's vision was the oldest dream of all.

One could begin with Aristotle's claim that leisure was the only fit life for man—the commonplace of a slave society that passed from there into one of the axioms of Western philosophy. Or one might begin with the fact of slavery itself and the social hierarchies that all through the West had set a man's worth and freedom by his exemption from toil and had made gentility synonymous with leisure. Still closer to the common life was speech, where the ache of toil was fashioned into a tangled etymological relationship between the words "labor" and "pain" that remains deeply embedded in the languages of Western Europe. But it was myth that most clearly gathered up and broadcast the painful indignity of work. Classical and Christian alike,

WORK IDEALS AND THE INDUSTRIAL INVASION From Daniel T. Rodgers, *The Work Ethic in Industrial America, 1850–1920* (Chicago: University of Chicago Press), pp. 1–29. Published 1978. Reprinted by permission of the publisher.

the central fables of the West were shot through with longing for a leisured paradise.

The Greek and Roman poets mined the theme through the legend of a lost, workless past, a golden age at the beginnings of human history when the rivers had flowed with wine and honey and men had lived the effortless life of the gods. "All goods were theirs," Hesiod wrote at the head of the tradition, and "the fruitful grainland yielded its harvest to them of its own accord." And yet somehow, whether through punishment or confusion, man had lost that first innocent state. The age of gold had given way to a poverty-saddled age of want, pain, and endless work. Vergil's lament summed up the centuries of mythmaking: "Toil conquered the world, unrelenting toil, and want that pinches when life is hard."

Where the classical poets had clung to the past, Christian mythology captured the same compound of protest and desire in a more complex design—first in the vision of a garden "eastward in Eden" in which all man's wants had been satisfied, and still more hopefully in what Augustine called the "eternal leisure" of heaven. The biblical tradition was more ambiguous than the classical, and from the beginning it contained seeds of more positive attitudes toward labor. Adam was no idler in Eden, after all, but was placed in the garden to watch and to "till" it, while the Judeo-Christian God himself "worked" and "rested." But Christianity heightened the vision of paradise by pushing it into the reachable future, and the pattern of the Christian myth—in which men fell out of a bounteous harmony into a vale of toil and sorrow, to endure until redeemed to permanent, heavenly rest—reverberated no less strongly than the classical fables with the aching pain of labor. By the end of the Middle Ages, popular versions of the two myths were close enough to coalesce, Christian optimism merging with the sensuousness of the classical golden age as the paradises fused and fused once more with the palpable milk-and-honey Edens that, according to European folk legends, lay hidden somewhere at the ends of the earth for an adventurous explorer to regain. It was a compelling vision, the more so because its roots sank so deeply into the potent stuff of experience. To work was to do something wearisome and painful, scrabbling in the stubborn soil. It was the mark of men entrapped by necessity and thus of men who were not wholly free. At best work was an inescapable necessity, a penance for old sins. Surely not this but leisure was man's first estate, the telltale mark of paradise, the proper focus of men's longings.

The myths waited only for a land to claim them, and with the discovery of America Europeans eagerly turned the hints the new continent offered into visions of a world untouched by the age-old curse of work. Columbus was the first to see the outlines of the ancient fables in the new world, finally giving up his hopes for a passage to the

Indies only to conclude that he had all but reached the gates of Eden itself, perched like the stem end of a pear somewhere in present-day Venezuela. His report was but the first of the images of a land of all but workless plenty, soon inextricably intertwined with stories of the fabulous wealth of Mexico and Peru, which long hovered over the American continents. Exploring the Carolina coast a century after Columbus, Captain Arthur Barlowe found himself in the midst of such "incredible" fruitfulness that, seen through the mists of classical learning and desire, he was certain it was the "golden age" intact—a land where "the earth bringeth forth all things in abundance, as in the first creation, without toil or labor." Even farther to the north the shaping force of desire produced visions only slightly dimmer. Captain John Smith was a veteran of Virginia's first, starvation years by 1614 when he undertook a careful mapping of the New England coast. But he came away convinced that three days' work a week would satisfy any settler in that fruitful land, much of that spent in the "pretty sport" of fishing.

Soberer, disillusioned adventurers often brought back far less flattering reports of America, bearing tales of native savagery and cannibalism and of a coast that turned to barrens and ice as one penetrated northward. But the European imagination fed on stories such as Barlowe's, on the image of an American paradise where the fruitful earth and innocent men lived in the original leisured harmony. As astute a reader of the explorers' reports as Montaigne concluded that the American natives whiled away their days in dancing in an ease far more perfect than the ancient poets had ever imagined. No cares troubled them, he wrote, no poverty, and "no occupations but leisure ones." "All men idle, all," Shakespeare caught the same hopes in *The Tempest*, his "American fable" in Leo Marx's phrase; but

> . . . Nature should bring forth,
> Of its own kind, all foison, all abundance,
> To feed my innocent people.

Not only for those Europeans who stayed at home but for the Englishmen who came to Virginia and the colonies to the south, that dream of a leisured America was to have a long and stubborn history. Here was a new Eden, they claimed of Virginia, "the paradise of the world," "a land even as God made it."

Yet among those Englishmen who settled the country north of the Chesapeake, nothing was more common than to describe their American paradise as a "wilderness"—as a "howling wilderness" during moments of stress. Disappointment figured in the wilderness cry, most clearly in William Bradford's poignant description of Cape Cod in autumn that stands at the head of the tradition. Theology likewise buttressed the idea, for every Puritan minister knew the Book of the

Revelation's promise that when troubles were thickest God would send his church into the "wilderness" for safekeeping. Still, the wilderness image had deeper roots than these, and throughout the seventeenth century, long after the Northern colonists had learned to love their land and prosper in it, it echoed and reechoed in their writings.

In the end the word "wilderness" served as a shorthand for a sense of self and of mission. Unlike the first new world adventurers, the settlers of Puritan New England and Quaker Pennsylvania came with no hopes for prelapsarian ease. They were laborers for their Lord, straighteners of crooked places, engaged in a task filled with hardship, deprivation, and toil. They did not expect to pluck treasures from the land but planned to civilize and tame it, even as they expected to struggle to civilize and tame the wild places in themselves. At times this amounted to a thirst for affliction, a distrust of idly gotten fortune as a snare and a temptation. God's people "must come into, and go through a vast and roaring Wilderness, where they must be bruised with many pressures, [and] humbled under many overbearing difficulties," Thomas Hooker told his Connecticut flock with the same trust in adversity with which other Puritans warned prospective settlers away from the "overflowing riches" of the West Indies. Such men came ready, if not eager, to work in the sweat of their faces and to see, as William Penn wrote, "what sobriety and industry can do in a wilderness against heat, cold, wants, and dangers." They chose to call America a wilderness because it fit the countervision in their minds' eye that the moral life was a matter of hard work and hard-bitten determination. Out of the American Eden they fashioned a land preoccupied with toil.

During the first half of the nineteenth century, when Europeans began to come in numbers to inspect the new American nation, they marveled at the extent of the transformation. Almost without exception, visitors to the Northern states commented on the drawn faces and frantic busyness of Jacksonian Americans and complained of bolted meals, meager opportunities for amusement, and the universal preoccupation with what Charles Dickens damned as the "almighty dollar." The visitors' assessments of the pace of American life are not to be fully trusted. Moving in the company of business and professional men, few of the Europeans actually entered an American workshop or followed a farmer across his fields. There was, moreover, something of a litany to the repeated complaint about the Northerners' compulsive activity; it became a ritual as much a part of the American tour as the Patent Office or Niagara Falls. Yet the Europeans were genuinely perplexed at the absence of an extensive class devoted to the pursuits of leisure. "In the United States," Tocqueville wrote, "a wealthy man thinks that he owes it to public opinion to devote his leisure to some kind of industrial or commercial pursuit or to public business.

He would think himself in bad repute if he employed his life solely in living." After ten years as a resident of Boston, the Viennese immigrant Francis Grund came to the same puzzled conclusion:

> There is, probably, no people on earth with whom business constitutes pleasure, and industry amusement, in an equal degree with the inhabitants of the United States of America. Active occupation is not only the principal source of their happiness, and the foundation of their national greatness, but they are absolutely wretched without it, and instead of the "*dolce far niente*," know but the *horrors* of idleness. Business is the very soul of an American: he pursues it, not as a means of procuring for himself and his family the necessary comforts of life, but as the fountain of all human felicity . . . it is as if all America were but one gigantic workshop, over the entrance of which there is the blazing inscription, "*No admission here, except on business.*"

It was not the pace of work in America that inspired responses like this so much as its universality, its bewilderingly exalted status, the force of the idea itself.

Yet, on the whole, the objects of these complaints were not disturbed at their ignorance of what another visitor, in a distinctly European phrase, called "the difficult art of being gracefully idle." Mid-nineteenth-century politicians and poets alike in the North dwelled expansively on the dignity of labor and the moral worth of those who worked. "Labor, gentlemen, we of the free States acknowledge to be the source of all our wealth, of all our progress, of all our dignity and value," William Evarts told a campaign audience in 1856, in a conviction that, with slightly altered nuances, could be heard at virtually any lyceum series or political rally—Whig, Democrat, or Republican. Amid the paeans to industry and the disrepute of leisure, it was little wonder the Europeans concluded that the Americans had mortgaged the pleasures of life to the wilderness virtues: business, speculation, work, and action.

Ultimately Penn and Hooker and their heirs assaulted the paradise myths themselves, redrawing their moral to suit their revaluation of toil. Like the Puritans before them, nineteenth-century moralists agreed that Adam had worked in Eden or, if not, that his idleness had been all the worse for him. Over and over again, to anyone who would listen, they insisted that work was not a curse, whatever the hints in the Genesis story. Nor was it merely a painful means to moral health and redeeming grace. Labor was a blessing: not "a burden or a bare necessity . . . [but] a privilege, a glory, and a delight." Among academic moralists, the economists held out against the idea that work was natural to man, clinging, by and large, to the older idea that labor was a fragile, irksome habit grafted onto a human nature as lazy as it dared to be. But the weight of moral thinking was against them. Man was "made to labor," the century's orators asserted. "It is his destiny, the law of his nature," placed there by a creator who was himself, as Henry Ward Beecher—mid-nineteenth-century America's most famous preacher—insisted, the most tireless laborer of all.

In the end, even heaven itself—Augustine's "perpetual sabbath"—fell before the onslaught. The idea of an eternity of rest vexed and troubled many nineteenth-century American Protestants, and their most widely read spokesmen answered that uneasiness with promises of more "palpable" and "useful" tasks than mere praise and singing. "Surely there must be work to do in heaven, / Since work is the best thing on earth we know," the mill girl turned poet, Lucy Larcom, wrote toward the end of the century. New York's flamboyant evangelist DeWitt Talmage claimed more confidently that heaven was "the busiest place in the universe." Shunting aside generations of mythmaking, the moralists succeeded in writing the gospel of work not only on the land but on paradise itself. "God sent you not into this world as into a Play-house, but a Work-house," ran a Puritan reminder. It was, in fact, a choice Northerners made for themselves.

In our day we know that perplexing decision as the "work ethic." It is a simplified label, as inviting to abuse as it is convenient, but it points to an important truth: for the elevation of work over leisure involved not an isolated choice but an ethos that permeated life and manners. It reared its head in the nineteenth and early twentieth centuries in the countless warnings against the wiles of idleness and the protean disguises of the idler. It gave a special reverberation to the word "duty" and set an infectious model of active, conscientious doing. Theodore Roosevelt caught its tenor in his thundering insistence that only the strenuous life was worth living, that "nothing in this world is worth having or worth doing unless it means effort, pain, difficulty." That conviction was by no means Roosevelt's alone. The doctrine of the industrious life pervaded churches and children's storybooks, editorial columns and the stump rhetoric of politics. Not least, it transformed the processes of work themselves, energizing, mechanizing, and systematizing them in ways that made those who cared most about the worth of toil at once immensely proud and profoundly uneasy. But in another sense the phrase is misleading, for the work ethic as it stood in the middle of the nineteenth century, at the threshold of industrialization, was not a single conviction but a complex of ideas with roots and branches.

The taproot, as Max Weber suggested long ago, was the Protestant Reformation. Universalizing the obligation to work and methodizing time, the Reformers set in motion convictions that were to reverberate with enormous consequences through American history. At the heart of Protestantism's revaluation of work was the doctrine of the calling, the faith that God had called everyone to some productive vocation, to toil there for the common good and His greater glory. Paul had said as much centuries before, but the Reformers stripped down the list of admissible callings, lopping off not only the beggars and rascals whose idleness cumbered the land but the courtiers and monks who were no better. The medieval *summum bonum*, a life of contemplation and prayer, suddenly was no vocation at all. "True Godliness don't turn men out of the world" into "a *lazy, rusty, unprofitable self-denial*," William Penn insisted, joining the attack on the monasteries; faith set men to work in the occupations of the secular, commonplace world. Nor was their labor there to be seen as an act of penance and mortification, as Christian tradition so long had had it. *Laborare est orare*: work itself was prayer, from the governing duties of kings to the meanest peasant's task. In the end faith, not labor, saved, of course; the Reformers never confused the secular vocation with a believer's primary, spiritual calling. But Protestantism extended and spiritualized toil and turned usefulness into a sacrament. Zwingli's benediction put the point succinctly: "In the things of this life, the laborer is most like to God."

Protestantism tried to turn religion out of the cloisters into the world of work, but it emptied the monasteries only to give everyone the ascetic responsibilities of a monk. This was the side of the Protestant ethic that most interested Weber: the obligation to survey and order the moral life that the Reformation, and English Puritanism in particular, imposed on its adherents. Striking down the Catholic rhythm of sin and confession, folly and remorse, Puritanism required that the believer ceaselessly analyze, rationalize, and forge his life into a systematic service to the Lord. Weber's argument exaggerated the somber, pleasure-destroying side of the Puritans, for they were not nearly the beetle-browed enemies of the spontaneous enjoyment of life he took them for. Even the strictest Calvinist did not object to the "seasonable recreations" that sharpened the wits or exercised the body. But Weber was certainly right in his claim that Puritanism tried to "penetrate . . . [the] daily routine of life with its methodicalness." Puritans methodized the English calendar, throwing out the irregular carnival of saints' days and replacing it with the clocklike rhythm of the weekly Sabbath, when men were to be as tireless and unbending in their rest as they had been during the week at their labors. In the same manner, Puritanism saturated its believers with an acute sense of the dangers of idleness, enjoining them to guard against the misspence of time and to improve the passing moments, each of which, in the end, had to be accounted for in heaven. This was an asceticism of a novel sort, worldly and systematic, looking forward to the time-and-profit calculus of industrial life rather than backward to the flesh-denying torments of the desert hermits. Joined with the doctrine of the calling, it demanded not only that all men work but that they work in a profoundly new way: regularly, conscientiously, and diligently.

Puritans and Quakers carried these injunctions to the new world as articles of faith. Long before Isaac Watts solidified the idea in rhyme, New Englanders spoke of time as "precious" and censured those who used it idly and unprofitably. "Abhor . . . one hour of idleness as you would be ashamed of one hour of drunkenness," Thomas Shepard wrote to his son at Harvard. And from every corner ministers like Shepard broadcast the necessity of a calling. "Away to your business," Cotton Mather charged; "lay out your strength in it, put forth your skill in it." Part of the persistent strength of the work ethic was due to the skill with which the preachers joined the ideal of diligent, productive labor to the demands of faith and gave it the form in which it was to be handed down the generations in homilies and countless Sunday school tracts and carried west on the efforts of revivalists and home mission societies.

Yet the nineteenth-century work ethic was not simply the Protestant ethic in modern dress. In the first place, by the middle of the nineteenth century a good deal of secularization had taken place. The old ideas never completely died out, but gradually the term "calling" faded from common speech and with it the idea that in work one labored in the first instance for the glory of God. Increasingly the moralists talked instead of usefulness. Benjamin Franklin helped set the new tone in his tireless string of maxims and projects for the public good, and by the era of the American Revolution political writing was saturated with the ideal of public usefulness, the common weal filling the place the Reformers had given to God. The legacy persisted well into the nineteenth century. In one of her short stories of the 1830s, Sarah Hale had her Yankee hero try the elegant leisure of a Saratoga resort and come away to conclude that "this trifling away of time when there is so much to be done, so many improvements necessary in our country, is inconsistent with that principle of being useful, which every republican ought to cherish."

So much to be done. Hale's concerns pointed forward as well as backward, for intruding amid the eighteenth-century phrases she placed the idea that increasingly preoccupied nineteenth-century moralists. Not only did immense projects seem to wait at every hand, but with rising conviction, economists, editors, and preachers insisted that a failure to meet them, a slackening of the pace, would send the nation skidding into poverty and decay. The Victorian concern with scarcity, with the economic necessity of constant doing, was evident well before Darwin's *Origin of Species* made its full impact in America. In phrases foreign to the eighteenth century, mid-nineteenth-century writers castigated businessmen who thought to retire and slip out of harness while there was labor left in them. Economics imposed stricter necessities than this. The moralists were loath to call economic life cruel, but they did insist that it demanded constant effort. William Ellery Channing told a Boston mechanics' group in 1840:

> The material world does much for the mind by its beauty and order; but it does more for our minds by the pains it inflicts; by its obstinate resistance, which nothing but patient toil can overcome; by its vast forces, which nothing but unremitting skill and effort can turn to our use; by its perils, which demand continual vigilance; and by its tendencies to decay.

"Life is a stern, hard service," a contributor to the *Atlantic Monthly* wrote a generation later; "it takes a great deal of hard work to keep this world going on." In sentiments like these, scarcity gradually nudged out the common good, just as the ideal of public usefulness had all but nudged out God. Where Puritans had been called to their vocations, nineteenth-century Americans were told that in a world of pressing material demands it was one's social duty to produce.

Working also held one back from the sink of idleness. Despite the gradual dropping away of the theological superstructure of Puritanism, the ascetic injunctions of the Protestant ethic retained and multiplied their force in the mid-nineteenth century. Looking back on her New England childhood years in the 1830s, Lucy Larcom remembered growing up "penetrated through every fibre of thought with the idea that idleness is a disgrace. It was taught with the alphabet and the spelling-book; it was enforced by precept and example, at home and abroad; and it is to be confessed that it did sometimes haunt the childish imagination almost mercilessly." This harrowing of the imagination was often quite deliberate. In his immensely popular *Seven Lectures to Young Men* of 1844, Henry Ward Beecher described the idle mind as an eerie, abandoned castle:

> Its gates sag down and fall; its towers gradually topple over; its windows, beaten in by the tempest, give entrance to birds and reptiles; and its stately halls and capacious chambers are covered with the spider's tapestry, and feebly echo with mimic shrieks of the bat, blinking hither and thither in twilight sports. The indolent mind is not empty, but full of vermin.

There was nothing in this that Thomas Shepard would not have agreed with; idleness was the parent of all sin, the devil's workshop, the Puritans had insisted. But in Beecher's choice of images—the shrieking bats and slithering reptiles—there is more than a hint of the gathering nervousness that were particular to the nineteenth century. Sexuality was one of these, as the metaphors made clear. The imagination of the idler was rank with weeds, Beecher and his contemporaries warned;

it was the haunt of unlawful visitors, a hothouse of "salacious day-dreams . . . rosy at first and distant, [which] deepen every day, darker and darker, to the color of actual evil." In what Carlyle called the "purifying fire" of regular labor, mid-nineteenth-century moralists hoped to consume the sexual passions that seemed increasingly to threaten them. But they hoped for more as well. Work cleared away doubts and vanquished despair; it curbed the animal instincts to violence; it distracted the laborer from the siren call of radicalism; it redeemed the convict prisoner. It did all this in part by character-building, by ingraining habits of fortitude, self-control, and perseverance, and in part by systematic exhaustion. The truly moral man was at once a person of strength and a *perpetuum mobile* of repressing energy, the man "whose days are so crowded full of honest and healthy tasks that he has no room for dreaming." Victorians were somewhat more apt than Puritans to reserve their asceticism for others. But for those who saw their world as beset with temptations and dangers, the sanitizing effects of constant labor offered at once a social panacea and a personal refuge.

The doctrine of usefulness and an intense, nervous fear of idleness were both indirect legacies of the Reformation. The other two ingredients of the mid-nineteenth-century work ethic—the dream of success and a faith in work as a creative act—had other roots and implications. By diligence a man could improve his lot; as the proverbs had it, he could stand before kings. The hope had seeped early into Puritanism, overturning the initially static implications of the "calling." Benjamin Franklin had condensed it into the kind of aphorisms that stuck in one's head and helped shape the axioms of a culture. But none of this was a match for the massive outflow of literature that the nineteenth century produced on behalf of the argument that work was the highroad to independence, wealth, and status. This is a country of "self-made men," where from the humblest beginnings a man with "merit and industry" could rise to the top, Calvin Colton announced in 1844 at the beginning of the flood. Endless repetition—in conduct guides, boys' storybooks, handbooks of business advice, and magazine fillers—ingrained the idea as one of the century's most firmly held commonplaces. In the fluid American economy, hard work, self-control, and dogged persistence were the certain escalators of success. Despite the speculative booms that so conspicuously dotted economic life—despite the financial adventurism and ardent pursuit of the main chance that Twain totted up in *The Gilded Age*—businessmen and moralists stuck to the canon. Even on Wall Street, the "law" of success was "unbending and regular," Matthew Hale Smith wrote in 1873, the year Twain's book appeared: "Industry, honesty, perseverance, sticking to one thing, invariably lead to success." Henry Ward Beecher, who served as the conduit for so many of the presuppositions of mid-nineteenth-century Americans, insisted that the one thing necessary for wealth was "Industry—plain, rugged, brown-faced, homely clad, old-fashioned Industry." By his labor a man worked out the position he deserved on the economic ladder; it was the key to success in the business of living.

Finally, it was urged, through work men impressed something of themselves on the material world. "A small Poet every Worker is," Carlyle wrote. Emerson seconded the idea: "Labor: a man coins himself into his labor; turns his day, his strength, his thoughts, his affection into some product which remains a visible sign of his power." Craft traditions, the legacy of the Renaissance artist-craftsmen, and romanticism all converged on the theme, often with extravagant results. In a poem picked up from the transcendentalist *Harbinger* and passed through the labor papers of the 1840s, Augustine Duganne apotheosized the artisan as "God's high priest," standing "midway / Between the earth and heaven, all things sway / To thy high-working mind!" Perorations of this sort were most common among writers who, like Duganne, stood at the boundary between artisan and literary culture. The more frequent acknowledgment of the creative role of labor was a simpler conviction that "work" was not "drudgery," and that it was room for employment of the mind that told them apart. One stumbles over the distinction again and again. Drudgery was the word the writers recurred to when faced with blind, thoughtless toil—the labor of slaves or the bent, haunting peasant of Millet's famous painting "The Man with the Hoe." In work, they insisted, mind and spirit had a part, transforming "dead" muscle labor into acts of skill. Work was creation. "To become an artist in dealing with tools and materials is not a matter of choice . . . [but] a moral necessity," Hamilton Wright Mabie told the readers of the *Outlook* at the end of the century. "Work is sacred . . . not only because it is the fruit of self-denial, patience, and toil, but because it uncovers the soul of the worker."

Obviously there were tensions within this set of ideals. Work was a creative act and a means of self-repression, a social obligation that paid off in private rewards. The ingredients of the work ethic were not held together by the logical consistency of their premises. The clearest of the tensions lay between the idea of work as ascetic exercise and work as art. The one looked toward system, discipline, and the emerging factory order; the other toward spontaneity, self-expression, and a narrowing of the gulf between work and play. The latter, creative ideal was clearly the weaker of the two in the nineteenth century. For a moment in the 1880s a large number of Americans discarded it altogether and devoured an enormously popular tract entitled "Blessed Be Drudgery," and it was long a half-suspect intruder amid the calls to effort, self-discipline, and ambition.

There was a second, nagging contradiction between the ideals of duty and of success—between the appeal to the dignity of all labor, even the humblest, and the equally universal counsel to work one's way as quickly as possible out of manual toil. Manual workers felt the full force of the contradiction and complained repeatedly of the disjuncture between the grandiloquent rhetoric and the practical disrepute of their occupations. William Dean Howells, who agonized over the point in the 1880s and 1890s, was finally driven to conclude that Americans liked their inconsistencies on a large scale. And yet a man like Beecher, and scores of other writers as well, demonstrably held all these ideas at once: the creative and the ascetic ideals, the rhetoric of an expansive economy and of early Protestantism, a sincere, fervent belief in toil and elitist reservations. The disparate strands all came together to reaffirm the central premise of the work ethic: that work was the core of the moral life. Work made men useful in a world of economic scarcity; it staved off the doubts and temptations that preyed on idleness; it opened the way to deserved wealth and status; it allowed one to put the impress of mind and skill on the material world. At the advent of the factory system, few of the keepers of the Northern moral conscience did not, in some measure, believe in them all.

The Henry Ward Beechers no more spoke for all Northerners, of course, than they spoke for all Americans. There was a sociology to the work ethic as well as an amalgam of ideas. Praise of work in the mid-nineteenth century was strongest among the middling, largely Protestant, property-owning classes: farmers, merchants, ministers and professional men, independent craftsmen, and nascent industrialists. Such groups had formed the backbone of English Puritanism, flinging their gospel of labor at the idle aristocracy and the dissolute mass of laborers that seemed to beset them on either side. The work ethic, too, was largely their creation. The Europeans who marveled at the untiring energy of the Americans were describing not ordinary laborers but their own social counterparts, particularly merchants of moderate means, who in America seemed as hard at work as their junior clerks.

On both ends of the social scale one can readily find other ethics and other styles of life. The ascetic injunctions of Puritanism never penetrated very far into the urban working classes. When Arthur Young wrote that "everyone but an idiot knows that the lower classes must be kept poor or they will never be industrious," he voiced the virtually unanimous conviction of seventeenth- and eighteenth-century English employers. A mass of prejudice obviously entered into statements of this sort, but they were not manufactured wholly out of class bias. In early nineteenth-century America, it is clear that many urban laborers did their best to punctuate work and play in the irregular, clock-defying pattern that is far older than the Protestant ethic. Gambling, rioting, generous drinking habits, and a good deal of boisterous, elbow-shoving, Sabbath-defying amusement played an important part in urban working-class life. If by no means every laborer, journeyman, and apprentice escaped the inner compulsions of the work ethic, enough of them did to make their presence felt in Jacksonian America. Among the very rich, too, the ideal of industriousness met with resistance. Compared with Europe or the American South, in the North the thoroughly idle gentleman was a rarity. The leisured aristocracy there was small, and its resources were relatively limited. But wealthy businessmen like New York City's Philip Hone showed no inclination to chain themselves to their counting tables or to consume their pleasures moderately. Conspicuous leisure was everywhere the identifying mark of the aristocrat, his bastion against the moralistic assaults of the middle classes; and in this regard the North was no exception.

Work was the gospel of the bourgeoisie, above all of the Protestant bourgeoisie, but it was not for that reason simply a subcultural peculiarity. In the American North, as nowhere else in the Western European orbit, the middle classes set the tone and standards for society as a whole. They did so through their hold over the strategic institutions of economics and culture. Business enterprise was theirs. So were the Protestant churches and the myriad agencies of moral reformation they spawned in the nineteenth century to care for the poor, educate the ignorant, and hold the wayward to the path of virtue. So were the institutions of learning: the schools and the colleges, the nation's publishing houses, and the major journals of opinion. It was in the last, in particular, that the ideals of middle-class Protestant respectability were debated, codified, and—with the conservative power of print—preserved. Editors like E. L. Godkin of the *Nation*, J. G. Holland of *Scribner's Monthly*, Howells and Beecher of the *Atlantic* and the *Christian Union*, and Mary Mapes Dodge of the children's *St. Nicholas*—or, after the turn of the century, George H. Lorimer of the *Saturday Evening Post* and Edward Bok of the *Ladies' Home Journal*—oversaw the process with an acute sense of responsibility and self-importance. They opened the pages of the middle-class magazines in a careful and considered way to the organizers of economic and cultural life and to the nation's most prominent writers as well as to a dedicated corps of anonymously conventional scribbles. I have called this interlocking set of persons the "moralists," keepers of their countrymen's moral conscience. They were not the only Northerners who felt keenly about ethics, but, given the institutional structure of their society, their opinions carried uncommon weight and influence.

The work ethic radiated not only from the secular pulpits of journalism but from all the institutional fortresses of the middle class. Campaigns to inculcate the values of industriousness in schoolchildren, and to impose it upon employees and social dependents, gathered and spent their force over and over again in nineteenth-century America, leaving behind a crust of middle-class morality of uncertain but perceptible depth. Still more important, probably, was the subtle contagion of example, aided by the moralists' near-monopoly on the definitions of respectability. In the years after the Civil War, praise of work noisily invaded the South, as its spokesmen turned upon their old "bondage to leisure" to announce their love affair with toil. It officially overrode whatever reservations the bishops of the American Catholic church may have felt about the repressive sobriety of Protestantism and led them, in the midst of the Americanist campaign of the 1880s, to put the weight of their influence behind thrift, industry, temperance, and Protestant Sabbatarianism. Elsewhere, too, potential resistance crumbled. Political aspirants, who presumably knew what they were about, regularly curried the favor of workingmen with orations on the dignity of toil. Frederick W. Taylor's father, a genteel Philadelphia lawyer, retired while still a young man to devote himself to study, public affairs, and the broadening influence of travel; yet the younger Taylor absorbed the work ethic, somehow, into the very marrow of his bones. Over and over again the opposite could be heard, that the old respect for labor was faltering in its paces. But the sense of decay was as indispensable to the moralists' temper as it was to the work ethic itself, a reassurance that there were still urgent tasks to be done and moral wildernesses still to be tamed.

None of the ingredients of the work ethic were unique to America. It was John Locke who announced that all property took its title from labor, Adam Smith who claimed that labor was the ultimate source of wealth, and Henri Bergson who in the phrase *homo faber* made work synonymous with man himself. Samuel Smiles's *Self-Help* dominated nineteenth-century success writing, just as Thomas Carlyle's example loomed over virtually all those in America who wrote in praise of work. But nowhere else than in the American North, with its truncated social structure, was resistance to these claims so limited. The result was an odd creation: a class and sectarian dogma that was at the same time as close to an article of popular faith as the region afforded.

Exactly how busy is a diligent man? It was only after the factories had overrun economic life that Northern industrialists set out to answer that question with any precision and to graft onto their countrymen the time obsession characteristic of modern industrial societies. The work ethic in its mid-nineteenth-century form did not entail a particular pace of activity so much as a manner of thinking, a moral preoccupation with labor. Moreover, the ideas that came together in praise of work took shape and flourished in an era when, by modern standards, time moved at a haphazard gait. First-generation New England ministers might urge their congregations that each moment was precious and that "one grain of time's inestimable sand [was] worth a golden mountain." But in a society in which household clocks were extraordinarily rare and the best of them possessed only a single, marginally accurate hand, such words hardly carried their modern meaning. By the end of the seventeenth century affluent families could purchase pendulum clocks of two and three hands; but large-scale production of brass household clocks did not begin in America until the end of the 1830s, and it was not until the Civil War that the characteristic arbiters of industrial time—cheap, mass-produced pocket watches—began to pour out of the American Watch Company plant at Waltham. "Time is money," Franklin had said, but when so much of time passed by unreckoned it is doubtful that he intended the meanings Frederick W. Taylor was to find in the words two centuries later. There is, in short, a misleading modernity to the phrases of the work ethic. They were rooted in, and creatures of, an economy older than and quite different from that of the factories.

Not only time but work moved in irregular, often leisurely rhythms in preindustrial America. Colonial workers who hired out their labor were generally expected to work the "whole day" six days a week, or from dawn to dusk in winter and from ten to twelve hours a day of actual labor in summer. But work itself was scarcely this even. Farming, the dominant colonial occupation, oscillated between bouts of intense labor and the short, much slower days of winter and was punctuated by country recreations—fishing, horse racing, visiting, and tavern-going—that even in Puritan New England were as much a part of rural life as the aching toil of planting and harvesting. In the same manner, the typical colonial workshop, with its three or four journeymen and apprentices, went through cycles of activity and probably was rarely busy day in and day out. By the early nineteenth century the tempo of economic life had increased perceptibly. In the East, many rural families now filled in the slack periods of farming by turning materials put out to them by nearby wholesale merchants into boot and shoe uppers, woven cloth goods, straw hats, and a variety of other products. The stores and workshops of Jacksonian America were bigger and considerably more bustling than their colonial counterparts. But weather, changes in demand and availability of materials, and poor communication and transportation facilities still conspired to interrupt the steadiness of work. "Incessant toil . . . was not the bane of Philadelphia's antebellum artisans," their most recent historian has concluded, but "the fitful pace of work, the syncopated rhythm of the economy." This context, too, qualified the calls to diligence. For all their intense fears of the idle life, mid-nineteenth-century moralists did not demand that men work with the ceaseless regularity of machines, but merely asked that they keep soberly and steadily to what tasks lay before them. In a world remote from the time clock and the efficiency expert, the work ethic was not a certain rate of busyness but a way of thinking.

Yet the strength of mid-nineteenth-century work ideals was exactly in their mesh with the bustling, irregular economy of the antebellum North. In this regard two characteristics of the antebellum economy were acutely important: its expansive energy and its limited industrial technology. The first is difficult to exaggerate. In the early nineteenth century the North underwent a startling transformation from an essentially agricultural to a commercial economy. Within the generation between 1815 and 1850, Northerners dug a regional transportation system of canals and waterways and started on a railroad network to replace it, dotted the Middle West with new settlements and at the same time burst the institutions of the seaboard cities at the seams, flooded the Patent Office with inventions, and raised the value of manufactures produced severalfold. "Go ahead" was the motto of the age, the European travelers reported, and with good reason.

But, for all the aggressive innovation of the age, as late as 1850 the centers of manufacturing remained the home and the workshop. Home production was not simply a rural phenomenon. The putting-out system flourished in every manufacturing town, employing shoemakers, weavers, tailors, and seamstresses in the traditional hand processes. Moreover, the workshops that threatened the livelihood of the home workers were on the whole far from the factory stage. In Boston, according to a careful enumeration of its factories and workshops in 1832, almost half the workmen were employed in shops of ten or fewer employees, and 80 percent worked in shops of no more than twenty. Philadelphia in the mid-1850s was much further into the industrial revolution, and its two sprawling locomotive works alone employed about 1,600 hands. But even in the nation's preeminent manufacturing center 100 employees was enough to rank an establishment as a major enterprise, and the dozens that reached this size were still surrounded by literally hundreds of tiny one- to five-man workshops.

The cotton textile industry was the great exception. Barn-sized, water-powered spinning mills had begun to appear in southern New England as early as the 1790s. It was the founding of Lowell, Massachusetts, in the early 1820s, however, that marked the real beginning of the new industrial order in America. Lowell was the first of the large-scale mill towns, an unprecedented assemblage of machines, bosses, and operatives. Within a decade there were nineteen textile mills in operation in the city, employing an army of 5,000 factory hands. With its paternalistic regulations and its boarding houses full of Yankee farm girls turned short-term mill hands, Lowell was the marvel of the nation and an obligatory part of the American tour. By the middle of the century, however, rivals had sprung up at Chicopee, Manchester, Manayunk, and a dozen other textile centers. The cotton mills were the first and archetypal factories, set off by their size, discipline, and thorough mechanization. Dwarfing most other enterprises, the largest mid-nineteenth-century textile mills employed a thousand or more workers, operatives for the most part, tied to the power looms and spinning machinery they tended and hemmed in by rigid sets of factory rules. Less dramatically, a few other industries moved in the direction of the cotton mills. Arms manufacturers began extensive use of machinery and subdivision of labor early in the century, ingeniously enough to warrant inspection by an official English delegation in the mid-1850s, which found the same techniques in use in the manufacture of clocks, furniture, and a variety of wood and metal products. In the 1840s iron rolling mills, too, moved swiftly toward factory dimensions. "Stave-machines, planing-machines, reaping-machines, ploughing-machines, thrashing-machines, steam wagons," Walt Whitman chanted in his "Song for Occupations." But this was in 1855, when the shift in manufacturing processes had begun to accelerate rapidly. Outside the textile centers, the home, farm, and workshop still ruled the early nineteenth-century economy. In 1841, in a judgment that comes closer to the truth of the period, a Cincinnati observer claimed: "Our manufacturing establishments, with the exception of a few, . . . are, in the literal sense, manufactures,—*works of the hand.*"

This was an economy in the earliest stages of industrialization—expansive yet simple—and it went hand in hand with the intellectual legacies to fashion the mid-nineteenth-century work ethic. The economic matrix reinforced old assumptions about work, stirred up new ones, and held them all together in a way logic could not. Expansion fueled the command to be up and doing and helped turn the ideal of usefulness out of the religious and political spheres and make it an economic obligation. "The busy world angrily shoves aside / The man who stands with arms akimbo set." James Russell Lowell put the phrase in Oliver Cromwell's mouth, but its accents were those of Lowell's own mid-nineteenth-century generation, impressed by the immensity of the enterprises to be undertaken, the goods to be made, the projects to be done.

Expansion likewise took the hope of upward mobility and screwed it to a new pitch. In a world that seemed to have jumped the old restraining ruts—where a Cornelius Vanderbilt could ride the new transportation systems to a fortune and a skillfull Yankee carpenter such as Thomas Rogers could become one of the nation's leading locomotive manufacturers—the dream of success was hardly to be escaped. It rose in close correlation with economic growth, gathering strength in the 1830s and 1840s and turning into a flood after the middle of the century. But if the promise of mobility was virtually inevitable, it was no less inevitable that the moralists should try to control the unleased promises and turn them, by insistent praise of work and self-control, into safe, familiar channels. Exhilaration and nervousness were both part of mid-nineteenth-century life. Enterprises that boomed hopefully also collapsed spectacularly, and the economy itself fell apart disastrously in 1819, again in 1837, and every twenty years thereafter throughout the nineteenth century. If growth fueled dreams of success, the sudden collapses and paralyses ingrained the lessons of scarcity, heightened anxieties over the disorders of commercial and urban life, and added to the Victorian nervousness. In all, it was a paradoxical society—booming yet fragile, engaged in the march of progress yet adrift in flux, inspiring expansive hope even as it reinforced the fears that encouraged the ascetic, nerve-numbing discipline of diligence. On all counts, even in its contradictions, it helped reinforce the primacy of work.

Finally, the economy of the antebellum North was one in which a certain measure of independence and creativity could be taken for granted. No one directly supervised home workers or farmers, and in the shops and small mills supervision was rarely exacting. The heated political arguments that accompanied the making of shoes or cigars were more than a figment of later, nostalgic imaginations. Pick and shovel labor was a matter of another sort, but in general the hand processes of manufacture, the flexible rhythms of labor, and the absence of strict discipline made it possible for most workers to impress some of their idiosyncrasies on their toil, if not always to love it. Intellectuals have long romanticized the state of things before the coming of the factories. Preindustrial America had ample share of hardships, poverty, and pain. In hindsight, in fact, the degradation of the urban craftsman was well under way by 1850, as artisans found themsleves increasingly caught in dependency to merchants whose capital enabled them to control the supply of raw materials and the marketing of the finished products. In the 1840s, New Englanders likewise peered under the Lowell mills' attractive facade and debated the merits of the factories. But, in the face of an enormous enthusiasm for technology, little of this penetrated far into the consciousness of middle-class Northerners. They thought their society what it seemed to be: a land of bustling farms and workshops where work told; where indeed it was the core of living.

In the second half of the nineteenth century the factory system invaded the antebellum farm and shop economy, overturning not only the familiar patterns of work but the ways Northerners had been accustomed to think of their labor. The speed of the transition to the factory economy varied widely from industry to industry and from place to place. It was an uneven movement—felt not as a shock, as it has often been described, but as a series of shivers, greatest in years of major labor unrest when the nation suddenly reckoned up the extent of change. But in the end the factory system challenged each of the certainties upon which the work ethic had rested and unsettled the easy equation of work and morality in the minds of many perceptive Americans.

Well after 1850 the economy still presented a patchwork array of contrasts. In Philadelphia, handloom weavers worked in their own homes virtually in the shadow of the mechanized textile mills. In New York City, tiny tenement cigar shops competed with factory establishments of several hundred employees. Rural and urban industrial workers differed, the country factory hands often retaining a degree of community power their urban counterparts had lost. The detailed disciplinary codes of the textile mills contrasted with the haphazard management typical of many other mechanized industries. As late as 1889, David A. Wells, one of the nation's leading economists, could depreciate the importance of the factory system altogether and insist that no more than one-tenth of the gainfully employed were properly described as factory hands. Yet for all the variety and confusion, the drift of change was evident. As the century progressed, the mills grew larger, labor discipline more exacting, and the work processes more minutely subdivided and dependent on machinery.

At times and in places, moreover, the transition to the factory economy took place with wrenching, unsettling speed. The shoe industry was for most nineteenth-century Americans the preeminent example of the rate at which the new could obliterate the old. As late as the 1840s the typical New England shoe shop was a 10′ x 10′ cottage housing a handful of skilled workers who made shoes by time-honored hand methods according to their personal, often eccentric, notions of size and fit. Some subdivision of tasks set in during that decade under the pressures of the merchants who controlled the trade, but the real revolution in shoemaking came in the 1860s with a rash of inventions, beginning with a sewing machine capable of stitching soles to uppers. Aggressive subdivision of labor, mechanization, and factory building quickly followed. By the 1870s, the shoemaking cottages were empty, and the men who had once been shoemakers now found themselves factory machine operators: beaters, binders, bottomers, buffers, burnishers, channellers, crimpers, cutters, dressers, edge setters, and so on through some thirty or forty subdivided occupations. Glassmaking was another example of the rapid destruction of a craft. In 1896 the entire output of bottles, jars, and window glass was made by gangs of skilled men and boy helpers, who gathered, blew, and shaped the glass by hand. Twenty years later half the jar and bottle blowers were gone, and the window glass workers were rapidly being replaced with automatic or semiautomatic machines. More commonly than this, the foundations shifted under an entire town. In 1850 Paterson, New Jersey, was a small city with a number of modest manufacturing establishments. Twenty-five years later the city boasted three huge locomotive works, fourteen silk mills, and the largest jute, linen, and mosquito netting factories in the country. The number of inhabitants had trebled; the number of saloons had increased almost sixfold.

Size, discipline, and displacement of skill characterized the factories. The physical growth of the workplace was evident at every hand. The Baldwin locomotive works had been a giant among factories in the mid-1850s with 600 employees. Twenty years later there were 3,000 factory hands at Baldwin, and by 1900 there were more than 8,000. The McCormick reaper plant in Chicago followed the same course, growing from about 150 employees in 1850 to 4,000 in 1900. But the manufacturing colossi of the early twentieth century dwarfed even these. By 1916 the McCormick plant had grown to 15,000 workers; and in that year the payroll at the Ford Motor Company works at Highland Park reached 33,000. Workshops of the size that had characterized the antebellum economy, employing a handful or a score of workers, persisted amid these immense establishments. But they employed a smaller and smaller fraction of the workers. By 1919, in the Northern states between the Mississippi River and the Atlantic Ocean, three-fourths of all wage earners in manufacturing worked in factories of more than 100 employees, and 30 percent in the giants of more than 1,000.

In plants of this size, the informality of the small workshop was an inevitable casualty. From the beginning the great textile mills had laid down extensive regulatory codes and enforced them with heavy fines and the threat of discharge. Other industries adopted such measures more slowly. The Winchester Repeating Arms plant in New Haven, for example, did not begin to insist that employees arrive on time until the 1890s, and in the piecework trades workers clung for a long time to their traditional right to set their own hours of labor. By the 1890s, however, gates were common around factories, supplemented by the exacting eye of the first factory time clocks. Inside the plants the baronial foremen, who had commonly hired, fired, and cajoled the necessary labor out of their workers on their own whim and responsibility, slowly disappeared. In their place the larger factories evolved tighter, more systematic, and more centralized schemes of management. By 1920 personnel departments, rational and precise cost accounting, central planning offices, and production and efficiency engineers had become fixtures of the new factory bureaucracies. Defenders of the new management techniques argued that they were fairer than the old. Certainly by the end of the century there was little to be envied in the lot of the workers left behind in the sweatshops and tenement rooms. But neither qualification lessened the growing distance between a factory hand and his employer or the subordination of the rhythms of work to the increasingly exacting demands of efficiency.

By the same token, skills disappeared in the new factories. Whether owing to such a simple device as the cigar mold—a wooden frame that enabled an untrained worker to bunch cigar tobacco—or the complex, automatic tools of the machine shop, the factories made obsolete a host of carefully preserved hand trades. Tailoring, cabinetmaking, barrel making, felt-hat making, and pottery making all gave way before new inventions and the specialization of labor. The clothing and slaughtering industries were particularly conspicuous examples of the relentless subdivision of tasks. In 1859, less than a decade after the introduction of the sewing machine, a Cincinnati clothing factory had succeeded in dividing the making of a pair of men's pants, formerly the job of a single tailor, into seventeen different occupations. At Smith's packing plant in Chicago at the turn of the century, 150 men, each with his specific mite of butchering to perform, handled each hog on its way from the pen to the cooling room. Dressing the tail of a beef carcass alone occupied the labor of five men: two skinned it, another two cut it off, and a fifth threw the skinned and severed appendage into a box. Nowhere did the pursuit of efficiency go on more aggressively than in the automobile industry, where the jobs were relentlessly morseled before being chained to the assembly line. One of the tasks at Ford's Highland Park plant consisted in joining pistons and rods by driving out, oiling, and replacing a pin, inserting and tightening a screw, and installing a cotter pin. All together the operation took three minutes. The Ford engineers divided the job into four pieces and doubled the output. The automobile had been a triumph of the mechanic's art, but by the second decade of the twentieth century fewer than one job in twelve in the auto plants took more than half a year to learn.

The factories made skills as well as destroyed them. Mule spinners in the textile factories and heaters and rollers in the steel mills worked at highly skilled, factory-created jobs. But the drive toward ever-greater efficiency made every skilled job precarious. A New York City machinist, complaining of the subdivision of labor in his trade in the 1880s, insisted that ten years earlier the machinist had "considered himself a little above the average workingman; he thought himself a mechanic, and felt he belonged to the middle class; but to-day he recognizes the fact that he is simply the same as any other ordinary laborer, no more and no less." Employers did not hesitate to enforce the point. When in 1885 the managers at the McCormick plant found themselves in a dispute with their unionized iron molders, they dismissed the entire force and installed molding machines and unskilled recruits in their places. Despite occasional compensations, all factory jobs increasingly converged toward the semiskilled; the typical factory hand became a machine operator or fractionated workman, toiling at a single bit of the manufacturing process.

How extensive the new modes of work actually were was a matter of some debate. In 1860, one-fifth of the gainfully occupied population of the Northern states worked in what the census defined as a manufacturing establishment; by 1919, when the correlation between factory and "manufacturing establishment" was considerably closer, the proportion had grown to about a third. But the new forms of toil affected not only manufacturing workers but spread out from the factories as well. In the late 1870s, large-scale production methods invaded agriculture in the wake of the rapid mechanization of farm tools. The most famous of the early "food factories," as their critic William G. Moody called them in the 1880s, sprawled over 30,000 acres of Dakota Territory wheat land, and at its peak employed two hundred reapers, thirty steam-powered threshers, and a thousand hands to bring in the crop. Individual bonanza farms like this came and went, and their number grew fairly slowly after the initial spurt of the 1870s. The transformation of coal mining in the early twentieth century was more complete. Between about 1900 and 1910, coal-cutting machinery and subdivision of labor began to enter the bituminous coal mines of the Middle West, remaking the operations and shoving out the hand miners who had once worked at the pit faces virtually as autonomous subcontractors. About the same time the efficiency experts began to turn their attention to the huge new clerical forces employed by firms like Sears and Roebuck. Arrayed behind banks of desks, strictly supervised, paid at times like industrial workers on piecework, many of the new clerical workers differed from factory hands only in status and neatness—just as the big, turn-of-the-century department stores employing several thousand saleswomen and cash girls differed little from fair-sized industrial establishments. In 1850 the job of a clerk or a farmer had been worlds away from that of a mill hand, but slowly, perceptibly, all work grew more and more like factory work.

What industrialization offered in return was a fantastic increase in output. The constantly growing flood of goods impressed and bewildered Northerners. In 1894 Congress instructed the Bureau of Labor to try to compute the savings in time and costs the new methods of manufacture had brought. The two volumes that resulted added nothing to the science of statistics. But the report that the factories were now making ten times as many fine-grade women's shoes and overalls a week as had been possible with the old, hand methods, fourteen times as many hardwood bedsteads, and twenty-two times as many stem-winding watches gave a striking, if impressionistic, suggestion of the economic dividends of the factory system. Modern indexes of production, though they must find approximate ways to equate cotton textile bolts and automobiles, provide a more reliable measure of the change. Between 1860 and 1920, the nation's population a little more than tripled, but the volume of manufactured goods produced increased somewhere between twelve- and fourteenfold. In international terms, the growth of manufactures was just as striking. In 1850 the factory economy was just emerging in America. By the turn of the century the United States had pushed past all other nations in industrial production. By 1910 it had outstripped its nearest rival, Germany, by nearly two to one.

This avalanche of factory-produced goods might have been expected to flow neatly into greater general well-being, but it did not. By the 1880s many businessmen had begun to worry that there were too many factories for the economy to absorb. Excess productive capacity in such diverse industries as steel, stoves, textile machinery, and sewing machines, in fact, troubled the economic waters, driving down prices, encouraging industrial consolidations to jack them up again, and in the process widening still further the gap between the old, workshop economy and the new. Intellectually, too, the phenomenon of more goods than the market could absorb was deeply troubling. Production had long been the chief of the economic virtues, impossible to take to excess. But if the industrial cornucopia could easily spew out far more goods than the nation was able to buy, what then was the place of work?

This was only one of the questions the invasion of the factories posed to those who cared deeply about work. The whole issue was a maze of paradoxes. The industrial economy was in a large part a creature of the intense regional faith in the worth of labor. The work ethic helped impell the restless personal energies of the Northern manufacturers, blessed their enterprises with a sense of mission, and gave them a transcendent sanction. It helped anesthetize employers to the eleven- and twelve-hour days they imposed on their workers and the pace at which the factories drove them. The work ethic provided the language of calculation, system, and diligence into which the efficiency engineers poured their new and stricter meanings, turning the new plants into matchless hives of industriousness. But if the factories were creatures of middle-class work ideals, they devoured those ideals as well. In disturbing ways, the transformation of labor undercut virtually all the mid-nineteenth-century assumptions about the moral preeminence of work.

Industrialization upset the certainty that hard work would bring economic success. Whatever the life chances of a farmer or shop hand had been in the early years of the century, it became troublingly clear that the semiskilled laborer, caught in the anonymity of a late-nineteenth-century textile factory or steel mill, was trapped in his circumstances—that no amount of sheer hard work would open the way to self-employment or wealth. Still more rudely, the factory system overturned the equation of work and art. Amid the subdivided and monotonous tasks, the speed, and the discipline of a box factory or an automobile plant, where was the room for mind or for the impress of individual creativity? Even the successes of the industrial transformation unsettled ideas and values. As the factories poured forth an ever-larger volume of goods into the homes of the middle class, the ascetic legacies of the Protestant ethic slowly and steadily eroded, giving way to a noisy gospel of play and, at the fringes of middle-class thought, to a cultivation of a life free of effort itself. As industrialization shook the idea of the permanence of scarcity, as the measure of economic health turned from how much a society produced to how equitably and conscientiously it consumed, it became harder and harder to insist that compulsive activity, work, and usefulness were the highest goals of life.

The moralists did not perceive these troubling questions all at once. When they did there were always the ancient maxims to fall back on. Work, they continued to insist, was what man was made to do—the foundation of happiness, the condition of existence since the days of Adam's husbandry in the garden. But industrialization could not be stopped from wedging into the preserve of ethics. And as the economy was transformed a deeply rooted set of presumptions cracked and shifted.

DISCUSSION QUESTIONS

1. How did the American work ethic change in the early nineteenth century compared to that of the Puritans?
2. This essay raises a general question: Is ideology an independent force in human affairs, or do our ideas and values simply reflect larger changes in the social and economic order?
3. Does the "work ethic" survive in contemporary America? If so, what value and importance do we find in our work in contrast to the ideologists discussed by Rodgers?

2

WELFARE AND THE WORKER: THE CASE OF BIG STEEL

KATHERINE STONE

The following essay by Katherine Stone focuses on the major changes in labor-management relations in the steel industry at the turn of the century. When the steel industry began in the middle of the nineteenth century, owners of many firms engaged in sub-contracting with skilled artisans. This allowed the workers a good deal of freedom in decision-making, and it allowed them to bargain their own pay-rates. Following the Homestead Strike of 1892, steel firms discontinued this system and began to integrate labor into a hierarchical structure. Increasingly they hired semi-skilled workers, reduced the autonomy of labor over the work process, and centralized control of the steel-making process under the authority of management.

Stone demonstrates that these changes caused a new and sometimes violent cleavage between labor and management. In addition to strikes there were high rates of absenteeism and turnover among employees. In response to these problems, management introduced a variety of programs designed to increase the loyalty of workers to the steel corporations. Among these programs were pensions, health insurance, housing, and stock options. The introduction of these private pension and health insurance programs help to explain why the United States government never adopted national health insurance and why old age pension programs are located predominantly in the private rather than the public sector.

—J. ROGERS HOLLINGSWORTH

1. THE BREAKDOWN OF THE TRADITIONAL LABOR SYSTEM

In 1908 John Fitch, an American journalist who had interviewed hundreds of steel workers and steel officials, described the labor system in the steel industry of his day.

> In every department of mill work, there is a more or less rigid line of promotion. Every man is in a training for the next position above . . . The course would vary in the different styles of mills, as the positions vary in number and character, but the operating principle is everywhere the same. In the open-hearth department the line of promotion runs through common labor, metal wheelers, stock handlers, cinder-pit man, second helper and first helper, to melter foreman. In this way, the companies develop and train their own men. They seldom hire a stranger for a position as roller or heater. Thus the working force is pyramided and is held together by the ambition of the men lower down; and even a serious break in the ranks adjusts itself all but automatically.

Anyone familiar with industry today will recognize this arrangement immediately. It is precisely the type of internal labor market, with orderly promotion hierarchies and limited ports of entry, which economists have recently begun to analyze. When Fitch was writing, it was a new development in American industry. Only 20 years earlier, the steel industry had had a system for organizing production which appears very strange to us today.

Although steel had been produced in this country since colonial times, it was not until after the Civil War that the steel industry reached substantial size. In 1860, there were only 13 establishments producing steel, which employed a total of 748 men to produce less than 12,000 net tons of steel a year. After the Civil War, the industry began to expand rapidly, so that by 1890, there were 110 Bessemer converters and 167 open hearth converters producing 4.8 million net tons of steel per year. This expansion is generally attributed to the protective tariff for steel imports, the increased use of steel for railroads, and to changes in the technology of steel production.

The pivotal period for the U.S. steel industry were the years 1890–1910. During that period, steel replaced iron as the building block of industrial society, and the United States surpassed Great Britain as the

 From Katherine Stone, "The Origins of Job Structures in the Steel Industry," *Review of Radical Political Economics*, Vol. VI, No. 2, (1974), 61–97. Reprinted by permission of the author. Footnotes, references, and citations of authority appearing in the original have been omitted for purposes of this presentation.

world's prime steel producer. Also during the 1890s, Andrew Carnegie completed his vertically integrated empire, the Carnegie Corporation, and captured 25 percent of the nation's steel market. His activities led to a wave of corporate mergers which finally culminated in the creation, in 1901, of the world's first billion dollar corporation, the U.S. Steel Corporation. U.S. Steel was built by the financier J. P. Morgan on the back of the Carnegie Corporation. At its inception, it controlled 80 percent of the United States output of steel. . . .

In the 19th century, the steel industry, like the iron industry from which it grew, had a labor system in which the workers contracted with the steel companies to produce steel. In this labor system, there were two types of workers—"skilled" and "unskilled." Skilled workers did work that required training, experience, dexterity, and judgment; and unskilled workers performed the heavy manual labor—lifting, pushing, carrying, hoisting, and wheeling raw materials from one operation to the next. The skilled workers were highly skilled industrial craftsmen who enjoyed high prestige in their communities. Steel was made by teams of skilled workers with unskilled helpers, who used the companies' equipment and raw materials.

The unskilled workers resembled what we call "workers" today. Some were hired directly by the steel companies, as they are today. The others were hired by the skilled workers, under what was known as the "contract system." Under the contract system, the skilled workers would hire helpers out of their own paychecks. Helpers earned between one-sixth to one-half of what the skilled workers earned.

The contract system was never fully developed in the steel industry. Often the steel companies paid part of the helpers' wage or provided helpers themselves for certain skilled workers, so that a hybrid system was prevalent. For example, in one iron works in Pittsburgh in 1878, puddlers were paid $5.00 per ton, of which one-third went to pay their helper. The helper also received 5 percent of his pay from the company. In the same works, a heater was paid 65¢ per ton and received one helper, paid by the company, with the option of hiring a second helper whom he would pay himself. The number of unskilled workers who were hired and/or paid by the skilled workers was declining in the late 19th century.

The skilled steel workers saw production as a cooperative endeavor, where labor and capital were equal partners. The partnership was reflected in the method of wage payment. Skilled workers were paid a certain sum for each ton of steel they produced. This sum, called the tonnage rate, was governed by the "sliding scale," which made the tonnage rate fluctuate with the market price of iron and steel, above a specified minimum rate below which wages could not fall. The sliding scale was introduced in the iron works of Pittsburgh as early as 1865, and in the 25 years that followed, it spread throughout the industry. The original agreement that established the system read as follows:

> Memorandum of Agreement made this 13th day of February, 1865, between a committee of boilers and a committee from the iron manufacturers appointed to fix a scale of prices to be paid for boiling pig iron, based on the manufacturers' card of prices.

The sliding scale was actually an arrangement for sharing the profits between two partners in production, the skilled workers and the steel masters. It was based on the principle that the workers should share in the risks and the fruits of production, benefitting when prices were high and sacrificing when prices were low. John Jarrett, the president of the iron and steel workers union, referring to another aspect of this partnership, described the system as a

> kind of co-operation offered by the company, in which were certain conditions, the principal of which was that the men agreed to allow the company to retain the first four weeks wages in hand, and also twenty-five percent of all wages earned thereafter, the same to be paid to men at the end of the year, if the profits of the business would justify such payment.

Andrew Carnegie, the largest steel employer of them all, concurred in this view of the sliding scale by saying, "It is the solution of the capital and labor problem because it really makes them partners—alike in prosperity and adversity."

Another effect of the sliding scale was that by pegging tonnage rates directly to market prices, the role of the employer in wage determination was eliminated. Consider, for example, the following account, summarized by David Montgomery from the records of the Amalgamated Association of Iron, Steel and Tin Workers:

> When the Columbus Rolling Mill Company contracted to reheat and roll some railroad tracks in January, 1874, for example, the union elected a committee of four to consult with the plant superintendent about the price the workmen were to receive for the work. They agreed on a scale of $1.13 per ton, which the committee brought back to the lodge for its approval.
>
> There followed an intriguing process. The members soon accepted the company offer, then turned to the major task of dividing the $1.13 among themselves. Each member stated his own price. When they were added up, the total was 3¾ cents higher than the company offer. By a careful revision of the figures, each runback buggyman was cut 2 cents, and the gang buggyman given an extra ¼ of a cent to settle the bill. By the final reckoning, 19¼ cents went to the roller, 13 cents to the rougher up, 10 cents to the rougher down, 9 cents to the catcher, 8¼ cents to each of the four hookers, 5 cents each to the runout hooker and the two runback buggymen, and 13¾ cents to the gang buggyman, half of whose earnings were to be turned over to his nonunion helper.

The employers had relatively little control over the skilled workers' incomes. Nor could they use the wage as an incentive to insure them a desired level of output. Employers could only contract for a job. The price was determined by the market, and the division of labor and the pace of work was decided by the workers themselves. Thus, the sliding scale and the contract system defined the relationship between capital and labor in the nineteenth century.

The skilled steel workers had a union, the Amalgamated Association of Iron, Steel and Tin Workers, which was the strongest union of its day. Formed in 1876 by a merger of the Heaters Union, the Roll Hands Union and the Sons of Vulcan, by 1891, the Amalgamated represented 25 percent of all steel workers. Through their union, they were able to formalize their control over production. For example, at Carnegie's Homestead mill, a contract was won in 1889 that gave the skilled workers authority over every aspect of steel production there. A company historian described it this way:

> Every department and sub-department had its workmen's "committee," with a "chairman" and full corps of officers . . . During the ensuing three years hardly a day passed that a "committee" did not come forward with some demand or grievance. If a man with a desirable job died or left the works, his position could not be filled without the consent and approval of an Amalgamated committee . . . The method of apportioning the work, of regulating the turns, of altering the machinery, in short, every detail of working the great plant was subject to the interference of some busybody representing the Amalgamated Association. Some of this meddling was specified under the agreement that had been signed by the Carnegies, but much of it was not; it was only in line with the general policy of the union . . . The heats of a turn were designated, as were the weights of the various charges constituting a heat. The product per worker was limited; the proportion of scrap that might be used in running a furnace was fixed; the quality of pig-iron was stated; the puddlers' use of brick and fire clay was forbidden, with exceptions; the labor of assistants was defined; the teaching of other workmen was prohibited, nor might one man lend his tools to another except as provided for.

. . . The cooperative relationship between the skilled steel workers and the steel employers became strained in the 1880s. The market for steel products began to expand rapidly. Domestically, the railroads began to generate high levels of demand for steel, and internationally, the U.S. steel industry began to compete successfully with the British and the German steel industry for the world market. (In 1890, for the first time, U.S. steel exports surpassed those of Great Britain.) The effect of this massive increase in demand was to intensify competition in the U.S. industry. What had been a stable market structure was disrupted by the new markets opening up.

Firms competed for the new markets by trying to increase their output and cut their costs. To do that they had to increase the productivity of their workers—but the labor system did not allow them to do that. For example, from 1880 on, the market price for iron and steel products was falling drastically, so that the price for bar iron was below the minimum specified in the union's sliding scale, *even though* the negotiated minimum rates were also declining. As Peter Doeringer says in his essay on the subject, "the negotiated minimum piece rates . . . became the *de facto* standard rates for the organized sector of the industry during most of the period from 1880 to the end of the century." This meant that employers were paying a higher percentage of their income out in wages than they would have were the sliding feature of the sliding scale operative, or had they had the power to reduce wages unilaterally in the face of declining prices.

At the same time that their labor costs as a percentage of revenue were rising, the labor system also prevented employers from increasing their productivity through reorganizing or mechanizing their operations. The workers controlled the plants and decided how the work was to be done. Employers had no way to speed up the workers, nor could they introduce new machinery that eliminated or redefined jobs.

In the past, employers had introduced new machinery, but not labor-saving machinery. The many innovations introduced between 1860 and 1890, of which the most notable was the Bessemer converter, increased the size and capacity of the furnaces and mills, but they generally did not replace men with machines. Sir Lowthian Bill, a British innovator, who toured the U.S. steel industry in 1890, reported that:

> Usually a large make of any commodity is accomplished by a saving of labor, but it may be questioned whether in the case of the modern blast furnace this holds good. To a limited, but a very limited, extent some economy might be effected, but if an account were taken of the weight of material moved in connection with one of our Cleveland furnaces, and the number of men by whom it is handled, much cannot, at all events with us, be hoped for.

However, in the late 1880s and 1890s, the steel companies needed more than just bigger machines and better methods of metallurgy. Bottlenecks were developing in production, so that they needed to mechanize their entire operations. For example, the problem with pig iron production—the first stage of steel-making—was that with increased demand, the larger blast furnaces could produce pig iron faster than the men could load them, so that the use of manual labor became a serious hindrance to expanding output. As one technical authority wrote in 1897:

> The evolution of the blast furnace, especially the American blast furnace, during the last third of a century has indeed been radical, making the question of getting the material to the furnace and the product away from it promptly, cheaply and regularly—the problem once satisfactorily solved by the cart or sled, and wheelbarrow and manual labor—one of great difficulty and importance.

The steel masters needed to replace men with machines, which meant changing the methods of production. To do that, they needed to control production, unilaterally. The social relations of cooperation and partnership had to go if capitalist steel production was to progress. The steel companies understood this well, and decided to break the union. In 1892, Henry Clay Frick, chairman of the Carnegie Steel Company, wrote to Andrew Carnegie that "The mills have never been able to turn out the product they should owing to being held back by the Amalgamated men."

The strongest lodge of the Amalgamated Association was at Carnegie's Homestead mill; it is no wonder that the battle between capital and labor shaped up there. In 1892, just before the contract with the Amalgamated was to expire, Carnegie transferred managing authority of the mill to Frick. Frick was already notorious for his brutal treatment of strikers in the Connellsville coke regions, and he wasted no time making his intentions known at Homestead. He ordered a fence built, three miles long and topped with barbed wire, around the entire Homestead Works; he had platforms for sentinels constructed and holes for rifles put in along the fence; and he had barracks built inside it to house strikebreakers. Thus fortified, Frick ordered 300 guards from the Pinkerton National Detective Agency, closed down the Works, laid off the entire work force, and announced they would henceforth operate non-union. The famous Homestead strike began as a lock-out, with the explicit aim of breaking the union. Dozens of men were killed in the four months that followed, as the Homestead workers fought Pinkertons, scabs, the Sheriff and the State Militia. In the end, the intervention of the state and federal governments on the side of the Carnegie Corporation beat the strikers. The Works were re-opened with strike-breakers, and Frick wrote to Carnegie, "Our victory is now complete and most gratifying. Do not think we will ever have any serious labor trouble again."

The Homestead strike was the turning point for the Amalgamated Associations throughout the country. Other employers, newly invigorated by Frick's performance, took a hard line against the union, and the morale of the members, their strongest local broken, was too low to fight back. Within two years of the Homestead defeat, the Amalgamated had lost 10,000 members. Lodge after lodge was lost in the following years, so that membership, having peaked at 25,000 in 1892, was down to 10,000 by 1898, and most of that was in the iron industry. The union never recovered from these losses. The locals that remained were one by one destroyed by the U.S. Steel Corporation, so that by 1910 the steel industry was entirely non-union.

With the power of the Amalgamated broken, steel employers were left to mechanize as much as they needed. The decade that followed the Homestead defeat brought unprecedented developments in every stage of steelmaking. The rate of innovation in steel has never been equaled. Electric trolleys, the pig casting machine, the Jones mixer, and mechanical ladle cars transformed the blast furnace. Electric traveling cranes in the Bessemer converter, and the Wellman charger in the open hearth did away with almost all the manual aspects of steel production proper. And electric cars and rising-and-falling tables made the rolling mills a continuous operation. These developments led the British Iron and Steel Institute to conclude after its visit in 1903 that:

> the (U.S.) steel industry had made considerable advances in the ten years ending with 1890. It is, however, mainly since that year that the steel manufacture has made its greatest strides in every direction, and it is wholly since that date that costs have been so far reduced as to enable the United States to compete with Great Britain and Germany in the leading markets of the world.

Several visitors to the steel mills around the turn of the century described the new steel-making processes introduced in the wake of the Homestead conflict. One British economist, Frank Poppelwell, was particularly amazed by the degree to which new innovations were labor-saving. He concluded:

> Perhaps the greatest difference between English and American conditions in steel-works practice is the very conspicuous absence of labourers in the American mills. The large and growing employment of every kind of both propelling and directing machinery—electric trolleys, rising and falling tables, live rollers, side-racks, shears, machine stamps, endless chain tables for charging on the cars, overhead travelling cranes—is responsible for this state of things. It is no exaggeration to say that in a mill rolling three thousand tons of rails a day, not a dozen men are to be seen on the mill floor.

A group of British iron-masters from the British Iron and Steel Institute also toured America in 1903, and they, too, were impressed to find in the blast furnaces that

> the bulk of the heavy drudgery has been obviated by the use of machinery. There is no pig-lifting, no hand shovelling of stock, no hauling of charging barrows. All the tedious clay work around the hearth, the incessant changing of tuyeres, is done away with.

They found that in the rolling mills

> the appliances introduced have effected the best results in doing away with manual labor. A tongs or hook is not seen near any of the rail mills visited, and the whole operation is conducted from a platform, where

> levers connected with the various live rollers and lifting tables are collected together.

And as far as the open hearth operations were concerned, perhaps the most vivid description was left by J. H. Bridge, an American journalist who wrote a series of articles about the steel industry for *Everybody's Magazine:*

> It is at Homestead that wonders are performed as amazing as those of the Arabian Nights. Here machines endowed with the strength of a hundred giants move obedient to a touch, opening furnace doors and lifting out of the glowing flames enormous slabs of white-hot steel, much as a child would pick up a match-box from the table. Two of these machines, appropriately named by the men "Leviathan and Behemoth," seem gifted with intelligence. Each is attended by a little trolley car that runs busily to and fro, its movements controlled by the more sluggish monster. This little attendant may be at one end of the long shed and the Leviathan at the other; but no sooner does it seem to see its giant master open a furnace door and put in his great hand for a fresh lump of hot steel, than it runs back like a terrier to its owner and arrives just as the huge fist is withdrawn with a glowing slab. This the Leviathan gently places on its attendant's back; and, to the admiration of all beholders, the little thing trots gayly off with it to the end of the building. Even then the wonder is not ended; for the little fellow gives a shake to his back, and the glittering mass, twice as big as a Saratoga trunk, slides onto a platform of rollers which carry it to the mill. And no human hand is seen in the operation.

In this way, the steel masters succeeded in eliminating the bottlenecks in production by replacing men with machines at every opportunity. This mechanization would not have been possible without the employers' victory over the workers at Homestead. Thus we can see how the prize in the class struggle was control over the production process and the distribution of the benefits of technology. As David Brody summarizes it:

> In the two decades after 1890, the furnace worker's productivity tripled in exchange for an income rise of one-half; the steel workers output doubled in exchange for an income rise of one-fifth . . . At bottom, the remarkable cost reduction of American steel manufacture rested on those figures.
>
> The accomplishment was possible only with a labor force powerless to oppose the decisions of the steel men.

The victory of the employers in 1892 allowed them to destroy the old labor system in the industry. They could then begin to create a new system, one that would reflect and help to perpetuate their ascendancy. Specifically, this meant that they had three separate tasks: to adapt the jobs to the new technology; to motivate workers to perform the new jobs efficiently; and to establish lasting control over the entire production process. The next three sections of this paper will deal with each one of these in turn.

II. EFFECTS OF THE NEW TECHNOLOGY ON JOB STRUCTURE

Unlike earlier innovations in steel-making, the mechanization of the 1890s transformed the tasks involved in steel production. The traditional skills of heating, roughing, catching and rolling were built into the new machines. Machines also moved the raw materials and products through the plants. Thus the new process required neither the heavy laborers nor the highly skilled craftsmen of the past. Rather, they required workers to operate the machines, to feed them and tend them, to start them and stop them. A new class of workers was created to perform these tasks, a class of machine operators known by the label "semi-skilled."

The new machine operators were described by the British Iron and Steel Institute after their visit in 1903 as men who

> have to be attentive to guiding operations, and quick in manipulating levers and similarly easy work . . . the various operations are so much simplified that an experienced man is not required to conduct any part of the process.

Similarly, the U.S. Department of Labor noted the rise of this new type of steel worker in their report of 1910:

> The semi-skilled among the production force consist for the most part of workmen who have been taught to perform relatively complex functions, such as the operation of cranes and other mechanical or metallurgical knowledge . . . This class has been developed largely within recent years along with the growth in the use of machinery and electrical power in the industry. The whole tendency of the industry is to greatly increase the proportion of the production force formed by this semi-skilled class of workmen. They are displacing both the skilled and the unskilled workmen.

The semi-skilled workers were created by the downgrading of the skilled workers and the upgrading of the unskilled. These shifts proceeded throughout the 1890s and early 1900s, as more and more plants were mechanized. Although there are no hard data on these shifts in job categories, they are reflected in the change in relative wage rates. Between 1890 and 1910, the hourly wages of the unskilled steelworkers rose by about 20 percent, while the daily earnings of the skilled workers fell by as much as 70 percent. Also after 1892, the wage differential between the various types of skilled workers narrowed substantially. Thus, the British iron masters reported in 1903

> The tendency in the American steel industry is to reduce by every possible means the number of highly skilled men employed and more and more to establish the general wage on the basis of common unskilled labour. This is not a new thing, but it becomes every year more accentuated as a result of the use of automatic appliances which unskilled labour is usually competent to control.

One consequence of the diminished importance of the skilled workers once their power was broken was the dramatic decline in their earnings. The following table of wage rates for selected positions at the Homestead plant mill between 1892 and 1908 illustrates the fate of skilled workers throughout the industry. Bear in mind that during this interval, their productivity was multiplying and wages throughout the nation were rising. Also, their workday was increased from 8 hours to 12 hours, so that the decline in daily earnings understates their reduction in real wages.

These reductions were part of the steel companies' policy of reducing the wage differentials between the classes of workers to make them more consistent with differentials in skill requirements for the different jobs. An official of one Pittsburgh steel company put it this way:

> It is perfectly true that the tonnage rates, and in some instances the actual daily earnings of skilled laborers, have been largely decreased. The reason for this is, mainly, the tremendous increase in production, due to improved equipment, representing very large capital investment, enabling the men at lower rates to make equal or even higher daily earnings.

He then added, somewhat more straightforwardly:

> At the same time the daily earnings of some of the most highly paid men have been systematically brought down to a level consistent with

TABLE I

WAGES IN PLATE MILLS, HOMESTEAD, 1889–1908

	Decline in Tonnage Rates			Decline in Daily Rates		
Position	1889–92	1908	% decl.	1892	1907	% decl.
Roller	$14.00	$4.75	66.07	$11.84	$8.44	28.72
Heater	11.00	3.99	63.73	8.16	7.21	11.64
Heater's Helpers	7.50	2.09	72.13	5.80	4.09	29.48
Hooker	8.50	2.40	71.76	n.a.	n.a.	n.a.
Shearman	13.00	n.a.	n.a.	9.49	5.58	41.20

TABLE II
PERCENT EMPLOYEES EARNING EACH CLASSIFIED AMOUNT

Hourly Earnings	1900	1905	1910
Under 18 cents	65.0	64.3	41.8
18 and 25 cents	17.4	20.6	32.8
25 cents and over	17.6	15.1	25.4
70 cents and over	1.9	0.9	1.2

the pay of other workers, having in mind skill and training required and a good many other factors.

The other side of the picture was the upgrading effect that the new technology had on the unskilled workers. Their wages were increased considerably during that same period. In part this was accomplished by a raise in the hourly rate for unskilled labor, from 14 cents per hour in 1892 to 17.5 cents in 1910, and in part it was the result of the steel companies putting more men on tonnage rates, enabling them to make higher daily earnings.

Many unskilled workers were put in charge of expensive machinery and made responsible for operating them at full capacity. (It turned out to be very easy to train unskilled workers for these jobs, as will be shown in Part III, Section 2.) Fewer and fewer men were hired just to push wheelbarrows and load ingots, so that, as an official of the Pennsylvania Steel Company said, "While machinery may decrease the number of men, it demands a higher grade of workmen."

Thus, the effects of the new technology was to level the work force and create a new class of workers. The table above shows this process as a whole. The data are based on a survey of 28 steel plants, conducted by the U.S. Commissioner of Labor in 1913. The table reports earnings only of production workers, omitting the earnings of foremen, clerks, timekeepers, weighters, and chemists.

As can be seen from the table, the percentage of workers earning in the middle two categories went from 35% to 58% in the ten-year period.

The existence of the growing group of semi-skilled workers created certain problems for the employers, which will be explored in Part III.

III. SOLVING THE LABOR PROBLEM

In Part I we saw how the market conditions in the industry led employers to destroy the skilled steel workers' union in order to mechanize their operations. Employers therefore became the unilateral controllers of steel production. However, by doing that they created for themselves the problem of labor discipline. When the skilled workers had been partners in production, the problem of worker motivation did not arise. Skilled workers felt that they were working for themselves because they controlled the process of production. They set their own pace and work load without input from the bosses. In the 1890s, however, when the steel masters showed them who was boss, workers lost their stake in production, so that the problem of motivation arose. How hard workers worked became an issue of class struggle.

In Part II we saw how the effect of the new technology introduced in the 1890s was to narrow the skills differentials between the two grades of workers, producing a work force predominantly "semi-skilled." This homogenization of the work force produced another new "problem" for the employers. That is, without the old skilled/unskilled dichotomy and the exclusiveness of the craft unions, the possibility that workers might as a class unite to oppose them was greater than ever. Frederick Winslow Taylor, the renowned management theorist who began his career as a foreman in a steel plant, warned employers of this danger in 1905:

> When employers herd their men together in classes, pay all of each class the same wages, and offer none of them inducements to work harder or do better than the average, the only remedy for the men comes in combination; and frequently the only possible answer to encroachments on the part of the employers is a strike.

Ultimately, however, both the problem of worker motivation and the problem of preventing unified opposition were the same problem. They both revolved around the question of controlling worker behavior. To do that, employers realized they had to control their perceptions of their self-interest. They had to give them the illusion that they had a stake in production, even though they no longer had any real stake in it. This problem was known as "the labor problem."

To solve the labor problem, employers developed strategies to break down the basis for a unity of interest amongst workers, and to convince them that, as individuals, their interests were identical with those of their company.

Out of these efforts, they developed new methods of wage payments and new advancement policies, which relied on stimulating individual ambition. They were designed to create psychological divisions among the workers, to make them perceive their interests as different from, indeed in conflict with, those of their co-workers. Employers also began to use paternalistic welfare policies in order to win the loyalty of their employees. The effect of all these new policies was to establish an internal labor market in the major steel companies, which has lasted, in its essentials, until today. This section will describe the new labor system that was created and the reasons why employers created it.

1. DEVELOPMENT OF WAGE INCENTIVE SCHEMES

With the defeat of the Amalgamated Association, the entire complex traditional system of wage payments collapsed: The sliding scale of wages for paying skilled workers and the contract system for paying their helpers rapidly declined. Employers considered them a vestige of worker power and rooted them out of shop after shop. As the British Iron and Steel Institute noted in 1902:

> Many owners of the works in the United States have set their faces so completely against the contract system that in the opinion of the most experienced authorities, the contractor, as hitherto established, is likely, before long, to entirely disappear.

Thus, the employers had the opportunity to establish unilaterally a new system of wage payment. Initially, they began to pay the new semi-skilled workers. Soon, however, they switched to the system of piece work, paying a fixed sum for each unit the worker produced. The British visitors found, in 1902, "in most of the works and shops visited the piece work is very general in all operations that call for a considerable amount of skill, and, indeed, wherever the work is above the level of unskilled labor."

The most obvious function of piece work was, of course, to increase output by making each worker drive himself to work harder. Employers also contended that the system was in the workers' best interests because it allowed each one to raise his own wages.

However, the employers soon found that straight piece work gave the workers too much control over their wages. That is, when it succeeded in stimulating workers to increase their output, their wages soared above the going rate. Employers would then cut the piece rates to keep the wages in line. Once they did that, however, they had reduced the piece rate system to simple speed-up—a way of getting more work for the same pay. Workers responded to the rate cuts by collectively slowing down their output, so that the system defeated itself, leaving employers back where they had started. An article in *Iron Age*, entitled "Wage Payment Systems: How to Secure the Maximum Efficiency of Labor," gives an interesting account of this process:

> It is in the administration of the piece work system that manufacturers, sooner or later, make their great mistake and over-reach themselves, with the result that the system becomes a mockery and the evil conditions of the old day work system reappears. Regardless of the continually increasing cost of living, the manufacturers decide among themselves, for

> example, that $1.50 for 10 hours is enough for a woman and that $2.50 a day is enough for the ordinary working man and a family. The piece work prices are then adjusted so that the normal day's output will just bring about these wages . . . Immediately throughout the entire shop the news of the cuts is whispered about . . . with the result that there is a general slowing down of all producers.

Thus employers began to experiment with modifications of the piece rate. They developed several new methods of payment at this time, known as "premium" or "bonus" plans. These differed from piece work only in that they gave the workers smaller increments in pay for each additional piece.

The Halsey Premium Plan, developed in 1891, served as a model for most of the others. It called for establishing a base time period for a job, and setting one rate for workers who completed the job in that period. If a worker could finish the job faster, then he received a bonus in addition to the standard rate. The bonus was figured so that only a part of the money saved by the worker's extra productivity went to him, the rest going to the company. Different plans varied according to how they set the base time period and the base wage, and how they decided the more efficient workers' savings between the worker and the company. *Iron Age* recommended one particular variation, called the Half and Half Premium Plan, in which the rule was "to pay the more efficient workman only one-half what he saves in speeding up." The article described one example where under the plan,

> for every extra $1 the man earned by his extra effort, the manufacturers would gain $7. Not a bad investment this premium system. It betters the workingman's condition materially, and, best of all, improves his frame of mind.

Frederick Winslow Taylor's Differential Piece Rate is basically another variation of the Halsey Premium Plan. Under Taylor's system, the employer established two separate rates, a low day rate for the "average workman" and a high piece rate for the "first class workman," with the stipulation that only the fast and efficient workmen were entitled to the higher rate. He suggests setting the high rate to give the worker about 60 percent increase in earnings, and for this, the employer would demand of him a 300–400 percent increase in output. Like the Halsey Plan, it was simply the piece rate system modified to give the worker diminishing returns for his extra effort.

In order for any of the output incentive plans to work, management had to be able to measure each worker's output separately. All of the premium plans stressed the importance of treating each worker individually, but only Taylor gave them a method for doing so. His great contribution was systematic time study—giving employers a yardstick against which to measure an individual's productivity. The emphasis on individual productivity measures reinforced the fragmenting effect of the plans. As Taylor said about his experience implementing the system at the Bethlehem Steel Works:

> Whenever it was practicable, each man's work was measured by itself . . . Only on a few occasions and then upon special permission (. . .) were more than two men allowed to work on gang work, dividing their earnings between them. Gang work almost invariably results in a falling off of earnings and consequent dissatisfaction.

Output incentives were designed to increase individual worker output. Employers understood that to do that, they had to play upon individual worker's ambitions, which meant breaking down workers' collective identity. They gave each worker inducement to work harder, and also divided the workers into different groups, according to their output. They also increased the social distance between the more "efficient" and the less "efficient" workers.

Thus, output incentives served as a lever to prevent workers from taking collective action. As one manufacturer explained in 1928, he had originally adopted output incentives:

> To break up the flat rate for the various classes of workers. That is the surest preventative of strikes and discontent. When all are paid one rate, it is the simplest and almost inevitable thing for all to unite in the support of a common demand. When each worker is paid according to his record there is not the same community of interest. The good worker who is adequately paid does not consider himself aggrieved so willingly nor will he so freely jeopardize his standing by joining with the so-called "Marginal Worker." There are not likely to be union strikes when there is no union of interest.

Taylor, too, boasted in 1985 that

> There has never been a strike by men working under this system, although it has been applied at the Midvale Steel Works for the past ten years; and the steel business has proved during this period the most fruitful field for labor organization . . . I attribute a great part of this success in avoiding strikes to the high wages which the best men were able to earn with the differential rates, and to the pleasant feeling fostered by this system.

An editorial in *Iron Age*, 1905, entitled "Union Restriction of Output," reveals much about employers' views of the incentive plans. It said:

> The premium plan, which has done for the machine shop, and on a smaller scale for the foundry, what the introduction of non-union men did at the Gamble mine—increasing wages and reducing the cost per ton—has been resisted by the molders' union, as it has been steadily opposed by the machinists' union. As grounds for this opposition it is

> urged that the premium plan is only a modification of what the unions regard as the vicious piece price system, and that the union must prevent a greedy scramble for high wages by workmen who take no account of the pace they are setting for the less capable . . .

This article tells us how conscious both the employers and the unions were about effects of the premium plan on the social relations inside the plant. Employers saw it as the equivalent to bringing in scabs to a union shop in its power to break up unity between the workers and advocated it for that reason. The unions opposed it, not because they misunderstood, but because they saw it in precisely the same way.

Quite explicitly, then, the aim of the premium plans was to break up any community of interest that might lead workers to slow their pace (what employers call "restriction of output") or unite in other ways to oppose management. They were a weapon in the psychological war that employers were waging against their workers, and were, at least for a while, quite successful. A survey of plant managers made in 1928 by the National Industrial Conference Board found that:

> There was little dissent from the opinion that the (premium plan) is effective in promoting industrial harmony. The responsibility for low earnings is placed squarely on the shoulders of the worker, leaving no room for complaint of favoritism or neglect on the part of management.

. . . Steel workers opposed the new methods of payment, and the residual unions in the industry raised objections at every opportunity. In one instance, at Bethlehem Steel's South Bethlehem Works, opposition to the bonus system exploded into a major strike in February, 1910. Approximately 5,000 of the 7,000 workers there went out on strike spontaneously. The strike lasted several weeks, during which time one man was killed and many were injured. Strike demands were drawn up separately by each department or group of workers, and every single one called for uniform rates of pay *to be paid by the hour*, and time-and-a-half for overtime. Several added to that an explicit demand for the elimination of piece work and a return to the "day-work" system. A U.S. Senate investigation into the strike found that the "Time-Bonus" System in use was one of its major causes."

However, worker opposition proved ineffective in preventing the use of output incentive schemes. Since 1892, the employers had held the upper hand in the industry, and they used it to perpetuate their power. The wage incentive schemes were aimed at doing just that.

2. NEW PROMOTION POLICIES AND THE DEVELOPMENT OF JOB LADDERS

As we saw in Part II of this paper, the new technology diminished the skill requirements for virtually all the jobs involved in making steel, so that even the most difficult jobs could be learned quickly. The gulf separating the skilled workers from the unskilled workers became virtually meaningless. Charles Schwab himself said in 1902 that he could "take a green hand—say a fairly intelligent agricultural labourer—and make a steel melter of him in six to eight weeks." When we realize that the job of melter was the most highly skilled job in the open hearth department, we can see how narrow the skill range in the industry really was. The employers knew this, and put their knowledge to good use during strikes. For example, during a strike at the Hyde Park Mill in 1901

> it was resolved that the works should be continued with green hands, aided by one or two skilled men who remained loyal. The five mills thus manned were started on the 3rd of August, and up to the date of my visit, near the end of October, they had not lost a single turn.

Around the turn of the century, employers began to recognize the dangers inherent in the homogenization of the work force. They formulated this problem as worker discontent caused by "dead-end jobs." Meyer Bloomfield, an industrial manager who in 1918 wrote a textbook on factory management, summarized their discussion on this subject:

> A good deal of literature has been published within the last dozen years in which scathing criticism is made of what has come to be known as "blind alley" or "dead-end" jobs. By these phrases is meant work of a character which leads to nothing in the way of further interest, opportunity, acquisition of skill, experience, or anything else which makes an appeal to normal human intelligence and ambition. The work itself is not under attack as much as the lack of incentive and appeal in the scheme of management.

Bloomfield says right off, then, that the problem of "dead-end" jobs need not be solved by changing the jobs themselves. The better solution is to change the arrangement of the jobs. To do this, he says,

> a liberal system of promotion and transfer has therefore become one of the most familiar features of a modern personnel plan, and some of the most interesting achievements of management may be traced to the workings of such a system.

Thus, the response of employers to the newly homogenized jobs was to create strictly demarcated job ladders, linking each job to one above and one below it in status and pay to make a chain along which workers could progress. The reason for this response was their view that

> what makes men restless is the inability to move, or to get ahead. This fundamental law of human nature is forgotten frequently, and its neglect

gives rise to situations that are never understood by the employer who looks upon a working force as something rigid.

The establishment of a job ladder had two advantages, from the employers' point of view. First, it gave workers a sense of vertical mobility as they made their way up the ladder, and was an incentive to workers to work harder. Like the premium plan, the promise of advancement was used as a carrot to lure the men to produce more and more. As Charles Hook, the Vice President of the American Rolling Mill Company, a major subsidiary of U.S. Steel, told the Third International Management Congress

> a few general policies govern the selection of all (our employees). One of the most important of these is the policy of promotion within the organization. This is done wherever possible and has several advantages; the most important of which is the stimulating effect upon the ambitions of workers throughout the organization.

The other advantage of the job ladder arrangement was that it gave the employers more leverage with which to maintain discipline. The system pitted each worker against all the others in rivalry for advancement and undercut any feeling of unity which might develop among them. Instead of acting in concert with other workers, workers had to learn to curry favor with their foremen and supervisors, to play by their rules, in order to get ahead. As one steel worker described the effect this had on workers during the 1919 organizing campaign, "Naw, they won't join no union; they're all after every other feller's job." This competition also meant that workers on different ladder rungs had different vested interests, and that those higher up had something to lose by offending their bosses or disrupting production.

As early as 1900, *Iron Age* was advising employers to fill production work vacancies from inside the firm. They advocated a policy of hiring only at the lowest job levels and filling higher jobs by promotion—what contemporary economists refer to as limiting the ports of entry. In one article, titled "Developing Employees," a columnist sharply criticizes a specific employer who

> has very often failed to find the proper qualifications among his employees to promote any one of them to certain higher positions which had become vacant from various causes . . . At such times he usually hired outsiders to fill the positions and thus engendered dissatisfaction among his helpers.

In the following years, the journal suggested that employers issue special employer certificates to their more faithful and efficient employees, which would serve as tickets to advancement when openings became available. By 1905, they concluded that

> The plan is working so well that already employers' certificates are held in higher favor by the industrious well-disposed workmen than a union card could ever be by such a man.

Clearly, the employers' certificates were a gimmick to further the workers' sense of opportunity by holding out the promise of promotions even before there were jobs available. Thus, workers were made to compete with each other for the certificates, as well as for the better jobs. The certificates in themselves did not guarantee anything, they merely improved one's chances—so the "certified" loyal ones still had to compete. . . .

On an aggregate level, the vertical mobility inside the steel industry can be traced through the rise of the various immigrant groups, all of whom entered the industry as common laborers. David Brody, in his book *Steel Workers in America*, gives the following data about one large Pittsburgh mill for the year 1910:

NUMBER OF IMMIGRANTS HOLDING JOBS

Years Service	Unskilled Jobs	Semi-skilled Jobs	Skilled Jobs
Under 2 years	314	56	0
2–5 years	544	243	17
5–10 years	475	441	79
over 10 years	439	398	184

John Fitch also noted that one could chart mobility through the rise of the various groups of immigrants. In the open hearth department, for example, he noted that the newly arrived Slav is

> put to work in the cinder pit; from here he is promoted to be second helper and then first helper. Practically all of the cinder-pit men now are Slavs, and a majority of the second helpers are Slavs, and it would seem to be only a question of time when the first helpers and even the melter foremen will be men of these races promoted from the lower positions.

In this way, the steel companies opened up lines of promotion in the early years of the century by creating job ladders. Employers claimed that each rung of the ladder provided the necessary training for the job above it. But the skilled jobs in the steel industry had been virtually eliminated and production jobs were becoming more homogeneous in their content. If, as Charles Schwab said, one could learn to be a melter in six weeks, then certainly the training required for most jobs was so minimal that no job ladder and only the minimum of job tenure were needed to acquire the necessary skills.

At the time, technological developments made it possible to do away with distinctions between skilled and unskilled workers. Instead of following this trend, they introduced divisions to avoid the consequences of a uniform and homogeneous work force. Therefore, the minutely graded job ladders that developed were a solution to the "labor problem," rather than a necessary input for production itself.

3. THE WELFARE POLICIES

The history of this period also sheds light on another important aspect of the steel industry's labor policies—the welfare programs. U.S. Steel's policy on welfare was formulated during the first few years of the corporation's life, and specific programs were established throughout the early years. These programs included a stock subscription plan for workers and a profit-sharing plan for executives; old-age pensions and accident insurance; a safety and sanitation campaign; and efforts to provide community housing, education and recreation facilities. Indeed, they included most of the functions performed today by the so-called "welfare state." The welfare policies were the most visible and best publicized part of the industry's labor policies. They were set up to serve the interests of the employers as a class, rather than as individual manufacturers.

The stock subscription plan, the first of the welfare measures, went into effect in 1903. It involved the sale of stock at reduced rates to corporation employees, paid for by monthly paycheck deductions. The plan provided the subscribers with a bonus, in addition to the regular dividends, of $5 for each of the first five years that the subscribers remained in the employ of the corporation and retained the stock, provided he showed "a proper interest in its welfare and progress." Also, the deserving subscribers received an extra bonus after owning the stock five years.

The idea of the stock subscription plan was to give employees a share in the growth of the corporation. As such, it was a form of profit-sharing. However, the bonuses and the extra bonuses made the plan something more. They gave employees an incentive to stay with the corporation for five years, and to show "a proper interest" in its welfare. Although it did not specify what showing a "proper interest" involved, certainly joining a union or sabotaging production were not included. The plan was clearly designed to control workers' behavior. One of the workers interviewed by John Fitch saw it simply as ". . . a scheme to keep out unionism and prevent the men from protesting against bad conditions."

The stock subscription plan set the tone for all of the later insurance measures. They all contained clauses and sub-paragraphs stipulating how workers had to behave to be eligible for benefits. For example, the pension fund established in 1911, which was made up solely of corporation contributions, offered retirement benefits at age 60 for employees of 20 years' seniority, *except* "in case of misconduct on the part of the beneficiaries or for other cause sufficient in the judgment of the Board of Trustees." Similarly, a Voluntary Accident Relief Plan was inaugurated in 1910 to pay workers benefits in case of temporary disability, permanent disability, or death resulting from on-the-job injuries. The plan (which was soon superseded by state workmen's compensation laws) was the first of its kind in the United States, and for all of its liberality, was also a device to ward off lawsuits in accident cases caused by company negligence. The plan said explicitly that "No relief will be paid to any employee or his family if suit is brought against the company," and "all employees of the company who accept and receive any of this relief will be required to sign a release to the company."

Other aspects of the welfare program contained more subtle behavior modification devices, aimed at changing behavior indirectly, through changing the attitudes of employees. For example, the steel industry was notorious for its hazardous working conditions and the high accident rate that resulted. The corporation, as part of its welfare program, began a safety propaganda campaign in 1908. They hung safety posters around the plants, distributed safety handbills to all the workers, circulated safety bulletins, and showed safety films—all of which were designed to convince the workers that "workers are solely or partially responsible (for accidents) in ninety percent of the cases." U.S. Steel maintained, and preached, this position despite conclusive statistical evidence published at the time which showed that plant and equipment design were the cause of most work accidents in the steel industry. In other words, the point of the elaborate and highly praised safety campaign was to convince the workers that accidents were their own fault, and so to ward off any blame for the companies' unsafe production practices.

Another part of the corporation's welfare program was to encourage workmen to build houses by giving them low-income loans for that purpose. Although the program benefitted workers, the motives for the program were, at best, mixed. An editorial in *Iron Age* in 1905 praised the corporation's housing program because:

> Workmen will build homes of their own, which is most desirable as bearing upon the permanency of employment and its influence against labor agitation, for the home-owning workman is less apt to be lead astray by the professional agitator than the man whose industrial life is a transient one.

The corporation's welfare efforts in the communities of its employees were extensive and impressive. The corporation by 1924 built 28,000 dwellings, which it rented to its employees, and built entire towns around some of its subsidiaries. Gary, Indiana, for example, was built from scratch by the corporation, and was acclaimed at the time as a model of town planning techniques and modern social services. In these company towns, the corporations built water purification facilities and sewage systems. They employed nurses to visit the families of their employees, instructing them in methods of hygiene, and they employed dentists to visit the children's schools and give them "toothbrush drills." They built emergency hospitals to serve their towns, charging special low rates to families of workers. They helped build the public schools and often supplemented teachers' salaries in order to attract good teachers. They built libraries and club houses for the workers, at which they offered night courses in English, civics, arithmetic, and technical subjects. Every plant had its own glee club, band or orchestra, with instruments provided by the company. Unoccupied company land was turned over to the workers for gardens, where with seed provided by the company, about a million dollars worth of vegetables were produced each year. And for its employees' recreation, the corporation had built, by January 1, 1924, 175 playgrounds, 125 athletic fields, 112 tennis courts, 19 swimming pools, and 21 band stands. Such was the welfare program of the Steel Corporation. The question that remains is, why?

Most writers about the industry treat the welfare work either as a sincere expression of good intentions on the part of the steel management, or as a public relations ploy. Friends of the corporation, such as Arundel Cotter, a personal acquaintance of Judge Gary, argue that the welfare work proved that labor and capital could progress together in harmony, providing better lives for the workmen and higher profits for the corporation at the same time. He sums up his review of the welfare work by saying, "the organization of the U.S. Steel Corporation was the greatest step that has ever been made toward the highest form of socialism." Critics of the corporation like John Garraty and Robert Weibe, both historians of the period, argue that the welfare work was designed to convince the public that the corporation was a "good trust," in order to avoid the furor of the trust-busting sentiment of the times, but that in fact they benefitted very few workers.

A look at the origins of the welfare programs gives a more rounded view of the role they served. The welfare programs were designed by George Perkins, one of J. P. Morgan's top men. Perkins had originally attracted Morgan's attention when, as a Vice President of New York Life Insurance Company, he had developed an extraordinary innovation in labor relations, the NYLIC club. The purpose of the scheme was to reduce employee turnover. Perkins set up the club for all employees who promised never to work for another business. Membership in the NYLIC club gave one monthly bonuses and a life-time pension after twenty years of service. According to Perkins' biographer:

> "The idea of this plan," Perkins told the agents, "is to say to the solicitor . . . that if he will give up . . . any thought of going into any business, or into any other company, no matter what the inducements might be, and will accept . . . the New York Life Insurance Company for his Company, then we will do something for him that is . . . better than any other Company can do."

The plan was enormously successful at reducing turnover, and it made Perkins' career. He went to work for Morgan, and he was put in charge of labor relations for all of Morgan's concerns. He designed welfare policies for Morgan's railroads, the International Harvester Corporation and U.S. Steel, all with the same goal—to bind workers to the company for a long time. Again, Perkins' biographer reports that the stock subscription plan at U.S. Steel

> had certain special features intended to make the employees identify their personal interests with that of U.S. Steel. These features reflected clearly Perkins' experience in the life insurance business, and especially with the NYLIC organization. Just as he had worked to retain his agents on a permanent basis, Perkins was eager to avoid a labor turnover at every level.

The welfare policies caused a bitter dispute within the corporation's Executive Board when they were first proposed. U.S. Steel's original Executive Board was made up of two groups—the Wall Street bankers who had organized the merger, and the presidents of the large steel companies who had been merged. On November 22, 1902, less than a year after the corporation was formed, the financiers on the Board, Judge Elbert Gary and George Perkins, presented the stock-subscription plan. The old-time steel men on the Board immediately opposed the plan. Their labor policy, so effective in the 1890s, was straightforward, out-and-out repression. Charles Schwab, president of the corporation, characterized their attitude by saying, "When a workman raises his head, beat it down." Thus a fight developed between the bankers and the steel men over the labor policy of the new corporation—a fight which was ultimately settled by J. P. Morgan, who threw his support to the bankers. Schwab resigned as president of the corporation soon thereafter, and Gary was made chairman of the Board of Directors. With the victory of the financiers, the welfare programs were begun.

The welfare programs, then, were part of a broader strategy on the part of the finance capitalists to break down the interfirm mobility of workers. The reason for this was not simply that labor turnover was expensive—for indeed turnover was not particularly expensive in those days when there was little on-the-job training and none of the negotiated fringe benefits which make turnover costly today. The reason for reducing turnover was, as Perkins and other managers of the day noted, that changing jobs had an unsettling effect upon the workers. It tended to make them identify with other workers, and to see themselves as a class. All of the major strikes of the 19th century had shown that steel workers were quick to go out in sympathy with striking workers in other companies and other industries. The welfare programs were supposed to combat this tendency, by giving workers both a psychological and an economic motive for remaining loyal to their employer.

The steel companies regarded their welfare work as their greatest contribution to domestic tranquility. They saw welfarism as the way to head off class struggle in society as a whole. For example, during the discussion of welfare work at the 1912 convention of the Iron and Steel Institute, one of the directors of U.S. Steel, Percival Roberts, said:

> We live in an age of discontent and great unrest. It is worldwide, not peculiar to this country at all. And I believe that no body of men is doing more to restore confidence today than those assembled here tonight. It is the one thing which we need today, eliminating all class distinctions, and restoring not only politically, but industrially, good fellowship; and I believe that the Iron and Steel industry is taking a leading position in that work.

The Steel Corporation advertised its welfare work widely. Beginning in 1913, they began an "Iron and Steel Institute Monthly Bulletin" which did nothing but report on the welfare work of the different steel companies. Judge Gary and George Perkins gave many speeches about the welfare work, and encouraged other corporations to follow their example. They sought publicity for the programs in the business press and the popular press. They did this because they saw the programs as more than a labor policy for U.S. Steel. They believed that if all companies followed their example, it would prove to be a solution to the "labor problem" nationally. Welfarism was their answer to the class politics of the Socialist Party, which was making great headway at the time. By increasing the ties between workers and their employer, they hoped to weaken the ties between workers and their class.

Perhaps the best statement of the strategy of the welfare policies was given by Judge Gary, who ended a meeting with the presidents of U.S. Steel subsidiary companies in January, 1919, by saying:

> Above everything else, as we have been talking this morning, satisfy your men if you can that your treatment is fair and reasonable and generous. Make the Steel Corporation a good place for them to work and live. Don't let the families go hungry or cold; give them playgrounds and parks and schools and churches, pure water to drink, and recrea-

> tion, treating the whole thing as a business proposition, drawing the line so that you are just and generous and yet at the same time keeping your position and permitting others to keep theirs, retaining the control and management of your affairs, keeping the whole thing in your own hands.

IV. THE REDIVISION OF LABOR

While employers were developing new systems for managing their work forces, they also altered the definition of jobs and the division of labor between workers and management. They did this by revising the training mechanism for skilled workers, retraining the foremen, and changing their methods of recruiting managers. The result of these changes was to take knowledge about production away from the skilled workers, thus separating "physical work" from "mental work." This further consolidated employers' unilateral control over production, for once all knowledge about production was placed on the side of management, there would be no way for workers to carry on production without them.

Frederick Winslow Taylor was one of the first theorists to discuss the importance of taking all mental skills away from the worker. In his book *Principles of Scientific Management* (1905), he gives a description of the division of knowledge in the recent past:

> Now, in the best of the ordinary types of management, the managers recognize the fact that the 500 to 1000 workmen, included in the twenty or thirty trades, who are under them, possess this mass of traditional knowledge, a large part of which is not in the possession of the management. The management, of course, includes foremen and superintendents, who themselves have been in most cases first-class workers at their trades. And yet these foremen and superintendents know, better than anyone else, that their own knowledge and personal skill falls far short of the combined knowledge and dexterity of all the workmen under them.

Taylor insists that employers must gain control over this knowledge, and take it away from the workers. In his manual *Shop Management*, he says quite simply, "All possible brain work should be removed from the shop and centered in the planning or laying-out department."

Taylor suggested several techniques for accomplishing this. They were all based on the notion that work was a precise science, that there was "one best way" to do every work task, and that the duty of the managers was to discover the best way and force all their workmen to follow it. Taylorites used films of men working to break down each job into its component motions, and used stop watches to find out which was the "one best way" to do them. Taylor also insisted that all work should be programmed in advance, and co-ordinated out of a "planning department." He gives elaborate details for how the planning department should function—using flow charts to program the entire production process and direction cards to communicate with foremen and workmen. These were called "routing" systems. One historian summarizes this aspect of scientific management thus:

> One of the most important general principles of Taylor's system was that the man who did the work could not derive or fully understand its science. The result was a radical separation of thinking from doing. Those who understood were to plan the work and set the procedures; the workmen were simply to carry them into effect.

. . . At the same time that they systematized their own knowledge about production, the steel companies took that knowledge away from steel workers. Previously, the skilled steel workers, acting in teams, possessed all of the skills and know-how necessary to make steel. They also had had authority over their own methods of work. Now employers moved to transfer that authority to the foremen and to transfer that knowledge to a new stratum of managers. This section will describe and document that process, in order to show that this redivision of labor was not a necessary outgrowth of the new technology, but rather was an adaptation of employers to meet their own needs, as capitalists, to maintain discipline and control.

1. THE NEW SKILLED WORKERS

As we saw in Part II, the mechanization of production largely eliminated the role of the traditional skilled worker. However, the steel industry still needed skilled workers. Machines required skilled mechanics to perform maintenance and repair work. Also, certain skills were needed for specialized production processes which had not yet been mechanized. However, these skilled workmen were very different from the skilled workmen of the 19th century, who collectively possessed all of the skills necessary to produce steel. The new skilled workers had skills of a specific nature that enabled them to perform specific tasks, but did not have a general knowledge of the process of production. This new class of skilled workers had to be created by the employers.

One would think that finding skilled men should have been no problem because of the huge numbers of skilled workers who were displaced and downgraded in the 1890s. However, by 1905, employers' associations began to complain about the shortage of skilled men. The reason for this paradox is that when the employers destroyed the unions and the old social relations, they destroyed at the same time the mechanism through which men had received their training.

Previously, the selection, training, and promotion of future skilled steel workers had been controlled by the skilled craftsmen and their unions. The constitution of the Amalgamated Association of Iron, Steel and Tin Workers had a clause that insisted that "all men are to have the privilege of hiring their own helpers without dictation from the management." The men would then train their helpers in their trade. The union also regulated the helpers' advancement. For example, in 1881, it passed a resolution saying "Each puddler helper must help one year and be six months a member of the Association before he be allowed the privilege of boiling a heat." After the union was destroyed, the skilled workers were no longer able to hire and train their own helpers.

Within a few years, employers, realizing that no new men were being trained, began to worry about their future supply of skilled workers. In 1905, *Iron Age* reported that

> The imperative necessity of renewing the apprentice system on a general and comprehensive scale has become apparent to every employer who is dependent on the skilled mechanic (craftsman) for his working force.

. . . In order to create this new class of skilled workers, employers set up a training system that was an alternative to the union-controlled apprenticeship system of the past, known as the "short course." The "short course" involved a manager or superintendent taking a worker who had been in a department for long enough to get a feel for the process, and giving him individualized instruction in some specialized branch of the trade. By using the short course, employers could train men for specific skilled jobs in a limited period of time. The training period varied, according to the skill being taught, from a few weeks to a year. The Secretary of the Milwaukee branch of the National Metal Trades Association described the use of the short course in his district in 1924 as follows:

> The handymen are usually helpers desiring to learn more of the trade—are over 21 years of age and usually limit their training to one special line.

And the chairman of the local association of foundrymen reported that same year that

> In checking up the situation in this community, the committee found that generally most of the foundries were taking on inexperienced help and developing what has come to be known as specialty molders.

In this way, a new class of skilled workers was created during the first two decades of the 20th century. These workers were selected by the employers, trained in a short period of time, and then set to work with their job-specific skill. These workers had skills which were only good for one job. They did not have the independence of the 19th century skilled workmen, whose skills were transferable to other jobs and other plants. Nor did they have the generalized knowledge of the production process that skilled workers previously possessed. The knowledge they had was that which could serve their employer, but not that which could serve themselves.

Thus, the new skilled workers were a dependent class. The employers had created their dependency on purpose, as advice which appeared in *Iron Age* in 1912 reveals:

> Make your own mechanics . . . The mechanics that you will teach will do the work your way. They will stay with you, as they are not sure they could hold jobs outside.

The success of these policies can be judged from the following statement, made by the president of the American Rolling Mill Company in 1927:

> Work has become so specialized in these mills that even men in the regular trades, who have not had mill experience, find it difficult to follow their trade until they have served another apprenticeship, which though not a formal one in the narrow sense is nevertheless a real one. So true is this, that furnace helpers and foremen melters of open hearth furnaces, trained in mills making common grades of steel, are unable to fill similar positions satisfactorily in "quality" mills, and, likewise, men trained for these jobs in "quality" mills have almost equal difficulty in mills where the emphasis is placed upon the making of large tonnage of common steel.

2. THE CHANGING ROLE OF THE FOREMAN

As the employers expanded their control over the process of production, they realized they had to develop an alternative means for exercising control on the shop floor. Just as they had taken knowledge about production away from the skilled workers, they also took away their authority over their own labor and that of their helpers. Now, the task of regulating production was transferred to the foremen, who previously only had authority over the pools of unskilled workers. Foremen were now seen as management's representatives on the shop floor. To do this, employers had to redefine the job of foreman and retrain the men who held those jobs.

In order to transfer authority to the foremen, the employers had to distinguish them from the skilled workers. This distinction had to be created; it did not evolve out of the new technology. Foremen were recruited from the ranks of the skilled workers—foremanship being the highest position to which a blue-collar worker could aspire. Once there, however, steel employers had to re-educate them as to their role in production. This re-education began with convincing them *not* to do manual work, which was no easy task. An editorial in *Iron Age* in 1905 quotes one superintendent lecturing an audience of foremen as saying:

> You men have no business to have your coats off when on duty in your shops unless you are warm. You have no business to take the tools out of a workman's hands to do his work. Your business is to secure results from other men's work.

The editorial goes on to say why this is important:

> A man cannot work with his hands and at the same time give intelligent supervision to a gang of men, and a foreman who does this is apt to lose the control of his men while he is weakening the confidence of his employers in his ability as a general.

The foreman's job was to direct and correct the work, but never to do the work himself. His authority depended upon that. Foremen, as the lowest ranking "mind" workers, had to be made distinct from the manual workers. One steel company official likened the organization of authority to that of the "army, with the necessary distinction between the commissioned officers and ranks. . . ."

Although foreman did little work, they also did little thinking. Most of their training was designed to teach them how to maintain discipline—techniques for handling men, developing "team work," deciding who to discharge and who to promote. They were the company's representative in the shop, and as the companies consolidated their power over the workers, the strategic importance of the foreman increased.

3. NEW TYPES OF MANAGERS

Just as the authority that the skilled workers had previously possessed was transferred to the foreman, their overall knowledge about production was transferred to the managers. By adopting new methods for training skilled workers, steel employers took the generalized knowledge about the production process as a whole away from the skilled workers. In their place, employers began hiring a new class of white-collar employees, recruited from the public and private schools and their own special programs. These workers became the bottom rung of the management hierarchy.

Before 1900, most managers in the steel industry were men who had begun at the bottom and worked their way all the way up. Andrew Carnegie had insisted on using this method to select his junior executives. As he once said, boastingly, "Mr. Morgan buys his partners, I grow my own." Carnegie developed a whole partnership system for the management of his empire based on the principle of limitless upward mobility for every one of his employees. He felt that by "growing his own," he not only found those men who had proven their abilities and loyalty to the firm, but also inspired the others to work that much harder. Thus he wrote to Frick in 1896:

> Every year should be marked by the promotion of one more of our young men. I am perfectly willing to give my interest for this purpose, when the undivided stock is disposed of. There is Miller at Dusquesne, and Brown, both of whom might get a sixth of one percent. It is a very good plan to have all your heads of departments interested, and I should like to vote for the admission of Mr. Corey; and if there is a sixth left, perhaps Mr. Keer of the Edgar Thomson Blast Furnaces deserves it. We cannot have too many of the right sort interested in profits.

This attitude was well known throughout the Carnegie empire, with the result, as Carnegie's biographer puts it, that "just as Napoleon drove his soldiers on with the slogan that every foot soldier carried a marshall's baton in his knapsack, so Carnegie taught his men to believe that every worker carried a partnership in his lunch pail."

Around the turn of the century, employers began to choose college graduates for their management positions. As one prominent steel official told a member of the British Iron and Steel Institute in 1903:

> We want young men who have not had time to wear themselves into a groove, young college men preferably . . . When a college graduate, who shows that he has the right stuff in him, reaches the age of 25 or 30 years, he is ready for a position of trust. When men get older they become more valuable as specialists, but for managers and executives we select young men with brains and education.

This was not mere philosophy; the British visitors found on their tour that, of the 21 blast furnaces they visited, "18 were managed by college graduates, the majority of whom were young men."

Employers used publically-funded technical colleges to train their new managers. Technical colleges were new, established with the support of the business community and over the protest of the labor movement. As Paul Douglas wrote in 1921:

> Employers early welcomed and supported the trade school, both because they believed that it would provide a means of trade-training, and because they believed that it would remove the preparation for the trades from the potential or actual control of unions.

Some steel employers also set up their own schools to train managers in the arts of steel-making. For example, the Carnegie Company opened a technical school in Pittsburgh, in 1905. The purpose of the school was "providing instruction in those studies essential to a technical education" to applicants who were high school graduates.

Technical training alone, however, was not sufficient to produce competent managers for steel factories. The young men also needed to know about steel-making. To meet this need, the steel companies developed a new on-the-job training program to supplement the formal learning of their young college graduates. This program consisted of short rotations in each mill department under the supervision of a foreman or superintendent, which gave the men experience in every aspect of mill work before they were put in managerial positions. This program was called an "apprenticeship," and although it trained managers instead of workers, it was an apprenticeship by the original meaning of the word. It gave the apprentices knowledge of each stage of the production process and how it fit together. A circular describing the Apprenticeship System begun in 1901 at the Baldwin Locomotive Works, which trained both managers and lower-level personnel, stated:

> In view of the fact that in recent years manufacturing has tended so largely toward specialization that young men apprenticed to mechanical trades have been able in most cases only to learn single processes, and, as a result, the general mechanic has threatened to become practically extinct, to the detriment of manufacturing interests generally, the Baldwin Locomotive Works have established a system of apprenticeship on a basis adapted to existing social and business conditions.

The visitors from the British Iron and Steel Institute described the prevalence of the new apprenticeship system in their report of 1903:

> In a number of the leading American (steel) works, the principals attach importance to binding, as apprentices or otherwise, lads and young men who have had the advantage of a first-class education . . . Indeed, in some cases, as at the works of the Midvale Steel Company, at Philadelphia, my attention was specially called to the unusually large number of college graduates that were employed on the premises in various positions.

By the 1920s, such methods were nearly universal throughout the industry. Charles Hook, the vice president of the American Rolling Mill Company, a U.S. Steel subsidiary, described his method for selecting and training managers in a speech of 1927 to the International Management Congress:

> The condition as outlined respecting the selection of the "skilled" employee is quite different from the condition governing the selection of the man with technical education . . . Each year a few second- and third-year (college) men work during the summer vacation, and get a first-hand knowledge of mill conditions. This helps them reach a decision. If, after working with us for a summer, they return the next year, the chances are they will remain permanently . . . Some of our most

> important positions—positions of responsibility requiring men with exceptional technical knowledge—are filled by men selected in this manner.

The prospective managers, in short, were increasingly recruited from the schools and colleges, not from the shops.

In these apprenticeship programs, a distinction was often made between different types of apprentices, distinguished by their years of schooling. Each type was to be trained for positions at different levels of responsibility. For example, at the Baldwin Works, there were three classes of apprentices, such that:

> The first class will include boys seventeen years of age, which have had a good common school (grammar school) education . . . The second class indenture is similar to that of the first class, except that the apprentice must have had an advance grammar school (high school) training, including the mathematical courses usual in such schools . . . The third class indenture is in the form of an agreement made with persons twenty-one years of age or over, who are graduates of colleges, technical schools, or scientific institutions . . .

Similarly, the application for indenture at the steel works of William Sellers and Company, in Philadelphia, read:

> Applications for Indenture as First Class Apprentices will be considered from boys who have had a good common school education . . . Applications for Indenture as Second Class Apprentices will be considered from boys who have had an advanced Grammar or High School training . . . Applicants for a special course of instruction, covering a period of two years, will be considered from young men over twenty-one years of age who are graduates of colleges, technical schools or scientific institutions.

Thus, formal education was beginning to become the criterion for separating different levels of the management hierarchy, as well as separating workers from managers.

During this period, employers redivided the tasks of labor. The knowledge expropriated from the skilled workers was passed on to a new class of college-trained managers. This laid the basis for perpetuating class divisions in the society through the educational system. Recently several scholars have shown how the stratification of the educational system functions to reproduce society's class divisions. It is worth noting that the educational tracking system could not work to maintain the class structure were it not for the educational requirements that were set up at the point of production. These educational requirements came out of the need of employers to consolidate their control over production.

Within management, the discipline function was divided from the task of directing and coordinating the work. This is the basis for today's distinction between "staff" and "line" supervision. We might hypothesize that this division, too, had its origin in the desire of steel employers to maintain control over their low level managerial staff.

The effect of this redivision of labor on the worker was to make his job meaningless and repetitious. He was left with no official right to direct his own actions or his own thinking. In this way, skilled workers lost their status as partners, and became true workers, selling their labor and taking orders for all of their working hours.

DISCUSSION QUESTIONS

1. Why did the steel industry shift to the use of unskilled labor in the nineteenth century?
2. How important were changes in technology in bringing about the alterations in labor-management relations in the steel industry in this period?
3. How acceptable to the workingman were the various efforts at welfare capitalism? Why did much of the welfare program fail to work?

3

LEONARD COVELLO: AN IMMIGRANT'S STORY

DALE R. STEINER

Immigration has been a constant theme in American history, and the importance of the foreign-born and their offspring in shaping the society probably reached its apex in the late nineteenth and early twentieth centuries. Between the late 1880s and the mid-1920s, more than eighteen million immigrants arrived in the United States. The newcomers of that era were pushed by problems and pulled by dreams quite similar to those that had motivated earlier immigrants, but many of them diverged from their predecessors in other respects. The largest blocks of the "New Immigrants" came from the Mediterranean and Slavic areas of southern and eastern Europe rather than from the Anglo-Saxon, Celtic, and Teutonic regions to the north and west. They were even more prone than earlier arrivals to settle in large cities and to engage in work requiring few, if any, skills. Moreover, the representatives of some ethnic groups among the later arrivals were disproportionately young, single men who were migrant workers or who returned home after accumulating a "nest egg" in the United States.

Dale R. Steiner's essay on Leonard Covello treats many of the preceding themes and, by focusing on an individual, makes them personal and concrete rather than anonymous and abstract. Perhaps most important, Steiner illustrates, through Covello, how the psyches of the children of immigrants and of men and women who came to America at a very young age could be pulled between the Old World and the New. Covello's willingness to discard certain aspects of his heritage while retaining others and his ability eventually to appreciate both his past and present cultures make him particularly interesting. Those traits, however, do not necessarily make him a typical individual. For example, relatively few Italian immigrants, or descendants of them, became Protestants. Likewise, the acquisition of advanced education and the emergence of identities secure enough to appreciate being both Italian and American were privileges and accomplishments that usually first appeared among members of the third generation to live in the United States. Covello, therefore, is best understood as a remarkable person whose capacity for squeezing so many stages of assimilation into a single lifetime has made him a symbol of the long-term process by which immigrant nationalities become American ethnic groups.

—THOMAS J. ARCHDEACON

By the uncertain light of a flickering kerosene lamp, the small boy cheerfully wrote out the message which his illiterate mother dictated: "My dear Husband, I am writing these few lines to let you know that we are all well and that we hope you are well too. . . ." Eight-year-old Leonardo Coviello missed his father, although he could barely remember the man. More than four years had passed since Pietro Coviello had departed for New York. Leonardo, his two younger brothers and their mother waited, with hopes that rose and fell, for a message from across the sea, for steamship tickets, for the chance to reunite the family in the promised land of America. Still more months of waiting lay ahead of them, but at last the letter came.

Pietro Coviello's prolonged separation from his family was painful for all concerned, but it was not an unusual situation for Italians to face around the turn of the century. From 1876 to 1914 at least 14,000,000 emigrants left Italy, seeking improved prospects in other European countries, northern Africa, South America, and the United States. But to describe this movement as an exodus of Italians obscures its nature. Prior to its unification in 1861 Italy had been a jigsaw puzzle of independent states, foreign holdings, and territory controlled by the Pope. While not so fragmented as the Germany of Johann Buettner, Italy was divided by regional identifications which endured well past unification.

In Italy a social system had developed which directly mirrored geography and indirectly reflected ethnicity. Northern Italians, often Germanic in appearance, regarded themselves as superior to their shorter, swarthier southern cousins. This prejudice was reinforced by the facts that northern Italy enjoyed a higher standard of living, experienced industrialization earlier, and exhibited more widespread literacy than did the *mezzogiorno*, the southern provinces. The Italian scale of social acceptability declined with each step south: Piedmontese looked down upon Umbrians, who in turn despised Basilicatans, while everyone scorned Sicilians.

Political unification in the 1860s did not alter this situation. Indeed, in some respects it made the problem worse. To a great degree, the new Italian state merely represented an enlargement of the northern kingdom of Piedmont, under whose auspices unification had been accomplished. The government's policies supported northern growth, often at the expense of the more needy south. The earliest and most extensive land reclamation projects were undertaken in the north,

LEONARD COVELLO: AN IMMIGRANT'S STORY From Dale R. Steiner, *Of Thee We Sing: Immigrants and American History*, pp. 176–193.

schools were built, and industrial development encouraged there, while the pressing problems of the *mezzogiorno*—where soil erosion, unemployment, and illiteracy were widespread—went unnoticed. The government imposed a tax on grinding wheat, a largely southern crop, while corn, which was grown in the north, escaped taxation. Understandably, many southerners who had fought for unification in the hope that it would improve their political, economic, and social circumstances were disappointed by the result—power had simply passed from one elite group to another, bypassing them in the process.

Leonardo Coviello was brought up among men—"uncles, cousins, and other relatives"—who had joined in the struggle to unify Italy, and he spent many hours listening to their stories. Living as he did in the mountains of Basilicata—the very heart of the *mezzogiorno*—young Leonardo could not have avoided exposure to their disillusionment. But not all of the problems which plagued the south were man-made. The weather played havoc with the lives of southerners: Winter downpours triggered floods and the unrelenting summer heat severely limited the range of crops which could be grown. "There was suffering enough in the mere business of living," Leonardo recalled many years later. "Torrents of water . . . carried the land away in the spring and the lack of water in summer . . . caked the ground." Because, as he noted, "empty promises of governments and politicians to build dams and create reservoirs were never realized," it was necessary to catch and store rainwater in tubs. One reason for such devastating floods and soil erosion was the deforestation of much of the south. "Wood was scarce and hard to get," according to Leonardo.

The extreme nature of the weather created a severe health problem. Stagnant pools of water in the late spring contributed to deadly outbreaks of malaria. In 1887, the same year that Leonardo Coviello was born, 21,000 Italians died of the disease. The mortality rate from malaria in Basilicata was the highest in Italy, nearly 19 times greater than that of the northern province of Lombardy. A more common health problem was malnutrition, the inevitable result of the meager diet typical of the southern household. Although not of the poorest class, the Coviellos often ate only *acqua sale*, "hard bread soaked in boiling water with a little olive oil and salt added for flavor." Soup afforded an occasional variant in their diet, but the Coviellos rarely tasted meat. Although he never ate breakfast, and carried to school a lunch consisting only of a piece of bread and an onion or a tomato, Leonardo often shared his food with a poorer classmate.

There was not enough food—or too many people. Among Europe's nations only Belgium, the Netherlands, and England had a greater population density than Italy. All three of those nations were highly industrialized, rendering them more capable of sustaining such a burden than was agrarian Italy. In the south particularly, most people were peasants who owned little or no land. Instead, they were victimized by a system which resembled that of Ireland in its viciousness. Absentee landlords resided in Rome or some other distant city, insulated from—and disinterested in—the problems of their tenants. The dual curse of high rents and short leases was amplified by the landowners' refusal to invest any of their profits in improving the land. Fertilizer was rarely utilized and the antiquated techniques and implements employed by nineteenth-century peasants differed little from the standards of Roman times. The combination of exhausted soil and obsolete methods guaranteed a low rate of production.

Toward the close of the nineteenth century things went from bad to worse. Land became increasingly concentrated in the hands of a few wealthy families, while the number of landless peasants living the uncertain existence of day laborers grew. In Basilicata between 1880 and 1900, the number of landowners declined by 5 percent; in neighboring Calabria it dropped 25 percent! By the turn of the century, half the farmers of Basilicata (and two-thirds of those in Calabria and Sicily) were hired laborers. If lucky enough to work regularly, male farm hands might earn from $40 to $60 per year, although they rarely received all their wages in cash. Steady work was uncommon, however, especially during the winter. And because of an excess of workers, wages actually fell as the century drew to a close.

The Italian economy reeled from several severe blows in the last decades of the nineteenth century. In the 1870s, revolutionary advances in production and transportation made wheat from the United States and Russia competitive in Italy. The following decade saw the emergence of the Florida and California citrus industries—and a sharp decline in Italian citrus exports. At the same time, France's imposition of a tariff on wine shut off access to Italy's principal export market, causing further hardship. An interest rate which climbed above 50 percent aggravated the effect of these developments. When Booker T. Washington toured Italy in 1911, the American educator who had been born a slave remarked that the condition of southern Italian peasants was comparable to that of American slaves a half century before.

It is little wonder that the turn of the century witnessed a swelling tide of emigration from Italy. Initially, Italians journeyed to neighboring countries: France, Switzerland, the Austro-Hungarian Empire, Germany. By the 1880s, however, the focus of interest had shifted to the New World, especially Argentina and Brazil. In the late 1880s, Argentina attracted an annual average of 57,000 Italian immigrants, Brazil nearly 69,000, and the United States about 50,000. But the early 1890s saw a crisis in the Brazilian coffee industry, while in Argentina an outbreak of yellow fever which claimed the lives of 9,000 Italians and a disruptive war with Paraguay focused the attention and hopes of prospective emigrants upon the United States.

At virtually the same time that Italian immigration to the United States increased spectacularly, the focus of emigration from Italy shifted from the northern provinces to the south. In 1870, census returns indicated an Italian population in the United States of barely 17,000, most of whom had come from the north. Over the next several decades, Italian immigration mounted dramatically: nearly 56,000 in the 1870s; over 307,000 in the 1880s; 652,000 in the 1890s. From 1901 to 1910, the peak period, 2,046,000 Italians entered the United States, 85 percent of them from the southern provinces.

Tales of success in America as well as dismal conditions in Italy helped shape and magnify this movement. It was "a big event" in Avigliano, the ancient walled town of about 8,000 where the Coviellos lived, when a former resident returned from the United States. Leonardo and the other Aviglianese could not help but be impressed: "Usually the *Americano* had a huge gold chain spread across his vest, at the end of which reposed some masterpiece of the watchmaker's art—tremendous in size." Reflecting upon such events years later, Leonardo concluded, "Everything emanating from America reached [Italy] as a distortion. . . . News was colored, success magnified, comforts and advantages exaggerated beyond all proportions." The result was that the discontented masses "believed what they wanted to believe: that if they were ever fortunate enough to reach America, they would fall into a pile of manure and get up brushing the diamonds out of their hair."

Because he was a member of the artisan class, Pietro Coviello's prospects in Italy were not quite so bleak as those of the peasant majority, but they were dim enough to convince him to seek a better life in America. Arriving in New York in 1890, Coviello found himself within a community of 40,000 Italians. That 22 percent of all Italian immigrants in the United States should live in New York City is not surprising in view of the fact that more than 95 percent of the total entered the nation there. A large proportion of these were, like Pietro Coviello, unaccompanied, working-age males who either intended to send for their families after they had made a start in America, or who planned to stay in the United States for only a few years before returning to Italy. In fact, for most years between 1880 and 1910, males constituted more than 80 percent of the total of Italian immigrants.

This phenomenon often meant terrific hardship—both emotionally and materially—back in Italy. Leonardo heard his mother exclaim, "Cursed be America. Men are lured away." In order to survive she and her three sons were forced to live crowded together in one room of the house belonging to Pietro's brother. Sometimes they went without food, although Leonardo would remember that pride compelled them to conceal their distress: "We bolted the door and rattled kitchen utensils and dishes to give the impression to our close neighbors that the noonday meal was going on as usual." As the oldest child, Leonardo was expected to help out as much as possible. At the age of seven he therefore became an apprentice to his uncle, a shoemaker. Because education was "highly respected" in the Coviello family, Leonardo also managed to find time for school, although "sessions were short and irregular."

At last, after Pietro Coviello had been absent for six years, he sent for his family. Nine-year-old Leonardo and his two younger brothers relished the adventure, but their mother, who had never travelled more than a few miles from Avigliano, found the train ride to Naples and three-week voyage to New York overwhelming. Leonardo sensed the "fear and torment locked in her breast" and realized from her expression how she "longed for familiar scenes . . . and the security of a life she had forever left behind." Their reception at Ellis Island proved even more unsettling. Because of miscommunication, Pietro was unaware of their arrival.

> Two days and two nights we waited, eating the food that was given us, sleeping on hard benches, while my mother hardly closed her eyes for fear of losing us in the confusion. Once during a physical examination men and boys were separated for a short time from the women. My mother was frantic as the guard led me and my two younger brothers away. When we ran back to her, she clutched us convulsively. Still in her eyes was the disbelieving look of a mother who never expected to see her children again.

When the family was finally reunited, Pietro took them to East Harlem, one of several largely Italian neighborhoods known to Americans as "Little Italy." As distinctive as it seemed, this label implied a broader sense of ethnic identification than most Italian immigrants felt. Reflecting the fragmentation of pre-unification Italy, they exhibited an enduring sense of *campanilismo*, loyalty limited to the area within which the village bell can be heard. According to Leonardo, "Anyone who came from outside the town itself was called a *forestiere*, or a foreigner." "With the Aviglianese you are always safe," his father counselled him. "They are your countrymen, *paesani*. They will always stand by you." These loyalties persisted in the New World. The Coviellos lived on 112th Street, surrounded by other displaced Aviglianese. The Accurso and Salvatore families, neighbors from the old country, were also their neighbors in New York. In other of New York's Italian enclaves, Calabrians clustered on Mott Street, Sicilians settled on Prince Street, Genoese claimed Baxter Street, and so on. Ironically, it was only in America that these diverse groups began to acquire the sense that they were *Italian*.

The Coviellos lived in a typical tenement—crowded, dark, airless—with a water pump and toilet in the hall to serve four apartments. As Emma Goldman had noted, congestion was a fact of life in the immigrant ghetto, but among southern Italians, especially Sicilians, it was carried to an extreme. Immigrant families were often large. When the Coviello family grew to include seven children, Leonardo was forced to share a bed with two of his brothers. Many families took boarders into their apartments; for six years before his family arrived Pietro Coviello had lived with the Accursos. In one Italian neighborhood, 3,500 people occupied a single block—the density of 1,100 per acre unsurpassed anywhere in the world. A government investigation failed to discover even a single bathtub on the entire block. The report also indicated that "all halls are cold and dirty the greater part of the time, and most of them are dark." One result of such crowded, unsanitary conditions was a tremendous mortality rate; on a single block 155 children under five years old died in one year.

The congested condition of the ghetto—and the hopelessness which sometimes accompanied it—also contributed to violence and crime. Crime has traditionally represented one of the few avenues out of the slums open to ethnic minorities. It was a route followed by some Irish immigrants in the nineteenth century, by Jews in the early twentieth century, and more recently by Blacks, Puerto Ricans, and Mexicans. But no group has been more closely associated with criminal activities than the Italians—the image of the stiletto-wielding *mafioso* is one of the most durable ethnic stereotypes in American culture. Ironically, the image was fostered in the United States by northern Italians who carried with them their prejudice against and contempt for their southern countrymen.

At the crossroads of the Mediterranean, Sicily was at some point or other in its history attacked and overrun by nearly everyone—Greeks, Spaniards, the French, Turks, Austrians, even Vikings. The recurring chaos undermined respect for authority, loyalty to government, and the power of the law. Instead, feudal lords took matters into their own hands by creating private armies of thugs to protect their estates and control the peasantry. When the feudal system was abandoned these groups persisted, evolving into outlaw bands of *mafiosi* engaged in cattle rustling, extortion, kidnapping, and murder.

These circumstances gave rise to the "Black Hand" conspiracy scare of the 1890s, when large numbers of Sicilians began to arrive in the United States. Ambitious politicians and sensationalist newspapers promoted the fear that a secret, criminal organization—the Black Hand—was being transplanted in the United States by Italian immigrants. Although unsupported by evidence, belief in the Black Hand spread. The late nineteenth century was a tumultuous period characterized by rapid industrialization and the extreme social and economic dislocation which it caused. And it was a violent period, marred by upheavals like the Haymarket Riot and the Homestead Strike. For

Americans who sought an explanation for their nation's climate of violence, it was far easier to assert that it was a foreign importation than to consider that it might result from conditions within the United States. It was less unsettling to blame some shadowy conspiracy than to acknowledge that poverty, hopelessness, and discrimination contributed to criminal behavior.

The violent stereotype attached to Italians represented a rather cruel irony, as they were frequently the *victims* of assault. The worst such incident occurred in 1891 in New Orleans where the Black Hand was accused of murdering the police chief. Although nine Italians were charged with the crime, a jury acquitted six and a mistrial was declared in the case of the other three. Egged on by a local politician, a mob rampaged through the jail and shot ten Italians to death in their cells. An eleventh, wounded, was dragged into the street, hung, and used for target practice. Echoing the public reaction, the *New York Times* applauded the mob, asserting that "these stinking and cowardly Sicilians, the descendants of bandits and assassins, . . . are to us a pest without mitigation." The tragedy in New Orleans was not an isolated incident. In 1894 a mob drove 200 Italians out of Altoona, Pennsylvania. A year later six Italians accused of a murder in Walsenburg, Colorado were lynched. Five Italian storekeepers who had dared to pay blacks the same wages as whites were killed by a Mississippi mob in 1899. There were other, similar assaults.

But in the public view, the image of Italians as the perpetrators of violence rather than its victims was fixed. This stereotype intensified the apprehension with which many Americans regarded the apparently unassimilable, seemingly inferior Italians swarming into the United States. According to one jaundiced observer, the typical Italian dwelling in New York was a "bedlam of sounds, and a combination of odors from garlic, monkeys, and dirty human persons. They were, without exception, the dirtiest population I have met with." Even Jacob Riis, who wrote so sympathetically of New York's immigrants in *How The Other Half Lives*, complained that the Italian immigrant "promptly reproduces conditions of destitution and disorder" like those in his native land, conditions which in "a matter-of-fact American community become its danger and reproach."

The considerable prejudice directed against Italians also reflected the fact that such a high proportion of them were unskilled that they seemed to have little to offer American society. Three quarters of the Italian immigrants in New York in 1880 performed manual labor; more than half were unskilled. A quarter-century later these proportions had diminished a bit, but 42 percent remained unskilled. At the turn of the century the rate of unskilled workers among Italians was twice that of Irish immigrants and nearly four times as high as among Germans. Their lack of skills meant that Italian immigrants commanded lower pay than those other groups did. But that fact, along with their reluctance to join unions, gave them a competitive edge. By 1900 they were beginning to crowd Russian Jews out of the garment industry and challenge Irish longshoremen on the waterfront.

Since so many of the Italian immigrants were unaccompanied by families, they were often employed on railroad construction projects, which placed a premium on mobility. These jobs were frequently secured through an intermediary called a *padrone*. The *padrone* system was common to all turn of the century immigrant groups, although it is most closely connected to Italians. The *padrone* was a labor contractor who, for a commission, secured jobs for immigrants as yet incapable of fending for themselves. Prior to 1885 *padroni* sometimes recruited workers in Italy for jobs in American factories, but passage of the Foran Act that year barred the importation of contract labor. Consequently, the *padroni* worked the New York waterfront, promising new arrivals steady work at good pay. Their need for work, ignorance of English, and suspicion of outsiders made Italian immigrants susceptible to the appeal of the *padrone*. All too often the arrangement proved to be one in which the workers were exploited—shortchanged in their pay, assessed unexpected "transportation charges," or even subjected to physical brutality. But the *padrone* also benefited the immigrant by acting as a translator, locating employment, arranging room and board, writing letters, even serving as a banker who collected savings or sent money overseas.

Pietro Coviello had no need of a *padrone* and, burdened as he was by the presence of a family, he was not inclined to labor at some distant construction site. Although he had worked as a cobbler and had upholstered furniture in Italy, in New York he found employment as a general handyman at a tavern and set pins in a bowling alley beneath it. Coviello made $7–8 per week, plus tips, although as Leonardo noted, he was "often without work for weeks at a time." Coviello's earnings were consistent with the norm; early in the twentieth century immigrant Italian males made an average of $390 per year (even less for southern Italians), well below the $876 which the New York Factory Commission claimed was necessary to maintain a normal family without savings. Clearly other members of the family were required to contribute as well. Women were far more likely to hold jobs among southern Italians than in any other immigrant group, although only a small minority were employed at this time. Children were also expected to do their share. While playing in demolished buildings, Leonardo salvaged lead plumbing and bricks, which he sold to dealers. At the age of twelve he got a job delivering bread several hours each day before school. Although the pay was minimal—$1.75 per week, plus coffee and a roll—it was a vital supplement to his father's wages. A few years later he secured summer work in a factory, earning $3.00 for a 60 hour week, and passed his bakery job to a younger brother. Continuing at the factory beyond summer's end was a tempting possibility; the Coviello family needed all the money its members could earn. But Leonardo was encouraged to remain in school by his father who told him: "In me you see a dog's life. Go to school. Even if it kills you. With the pen and with books you have the chance to live like a man and not like a beast of burden."

Shortly after the family's arrival in America, Leonardo's father had enrolled him in the "Soup School." Run by a Protestant mission group called the American Female Guardian Society, the Soup School derived its name from the bowls of soup served the students every day at noon. It was at the Soup School that Leonardo Coviello became Leonard Covello, his name arbitrarily changed by a teacher who had trouble pronouncing it. In a vain attempt to diminish his father's outrage, Leonard asked, "What difference does it make? It's more American." "Even at that age," he would reflect later, "I was beginning to feel that anything that made a name less foreign was an improvement." After two years at the Soup School, Leonard entered a public elementary school.

Americanization of immigrant children was no less a mission of the public schools than it was of the Soup School. The process was essentially unchanged since John Hughes' time: Americanizing immigrants meant undermining their native culture. In school Leonard Covello was insulated from his past:

> Throughout my whole elementary school career, I do not recall one mention of Italy or the Italian language or what famous Italians had done in the world, with the possible exception of Columbus, who was pretty popular in America. We soon got the idea that "Italian" meant something inferior, and a barrier was erected between children of Italian origin and their parents. This was the accepted process of Americanization. We were becoming Americans by learning how to be ashamed of our parents.

The Americanization of some of its members introduced tension into, or sometimes completely disrupted, the immigrant family. Generally it was the children, more impressionable and less rooted in tradition than their parents, who adapted most readily. Their greater exposure to American society, most notably through attendance at school, furthered this process. Immigrant men usually worked at jobs and engaged in other activities which assured them of at least some contact with the outside world. But immigrant women—especially those with families to care for—were often quite isolated from American society. As a result, they were slow to adjust to American life, clinging tenaciously to tradition. Inevitably this affected the relationships within families. Adults became more dependent upon their English-speaking children and were sometimes transformed from respected figures of authority into sources of shame. Leonard Covello and his classmates were acutely conscious of how "un-American" their parents seemed. Years later he confessed that "we used all our resources to keep our parents away from school—particularly our mothers, because they did not speak English and still dressed in the European way with the inevitable shawl. We didn't want these embarrassing 'differences' paraded before our teachers."

No less important in Leonard's adaptation to American life was the Home Garden mission. Situated in a small brownstone building, the mission offered the youth of East Harlem an alternative to the streets and the waterfront. At Home Garden, children were encouraged to read books, put on plays, and sing songs. Reflecting the religious inclinations of Anna Ruddy, its Protestant director, the mission also offered Sunday school and Bible reading classes. "Miss Ruddy and the Home Garden filled a need we could find nowhere else," Covello acknowledged later. "It was Miss Ruddy who gave me an idea of how important the influence of a teacher can be in the life of a growing boy." He never lost sight of that idea.

Home Garden was typical of the settlement houses established by social workers and middle class idealists shortly before the turn of the century. Designed to relieve the tedium and misery of slum life, settlement houses offered a variety of services and diversions to the disadvantaged—social clubs and hobby shops for children, day care for working mothers, classes in cooking and personal sanitation, libraries, theatrical presentations. Because the slum areas were often populated by immigrants, the settlement houses also functioned as Americanizing agencies where English classes were held and democratic principles imparted.

Under Miss Ruddy's influence Leonard drifted into the Protestant orbit. Like virtually all Italians, his family was Catholic—one uncle was even a priest. But in the United States their loyalty to the Catholic Church was diminished by the fact that it was an institution vastly different from the one which they had known in Italy. In America the Catholic Church was virtually an adjunct to the Irish community, led by Irish immigrants like John Hughes or their descendants. Their cold, austere brand of Catholicism was completely foreign to Italians, who were made to feel less than welcome. One immigrant later remembered that in 1886 at the one Catholic church in East Harlem "we Italians were allowed to worship only in the basement part of the church, a fact which was not altogether to our liking."

Moreover, in Italy the Catholic Church was a part of the power structure, removed from the peasant masses by virtue of its great wealth and its resistance to the unification and liberalization of Italy. As a result, they rarely developed the intensity of commitment to the Church exhibited by Catholics from Ireland, where the Church had shared the misery and oppression of the people.

Recognizing that this distance afforded an opportunity, a variety of Protestant groups and churches mounted a campaign seeking converts among Italian immigrants. Newspapers and pamphlets were published and distributed; Protestant churches and missions were founded in immigrant neighborhoods. The Soup School and Home Garden mission were part of this effort. While most Italians in the United States remained at least nominally Catholic, Leonard Covello left the Church. Years later when he married, the ceremony would be performed in a Presbyterian church; later still, he would teach Sunday school for the Methodists.

The rivalry within the Catholic Church between Irish and Italian immigrants extended into other arenas. The two groups competed with each other for jobs and social standing. And just as Irish domination of the Catholic Church inclined some Italians toward Protestantism, the partisan identification of the Irish influenced the politics of Italian immigrants. Even though the Democratic Party was historically more sensitive to the interests and aspirations of immigrants than was the Republican, Irish domination of the Democratic machines in New York and other northeastern cities persuaded many Italians to join the Republicans.

Political parties functioned as Americanizing agents in much the same fashion as public schools and settlement houses. But the influence which these institutions could exert was limited by the extent to which immigrants were involved in them. For many the daily struggle to survive required so much effort that even a free public education became an unaffordable luxury. Although education might hold out the dim prospect of some future reward, it could hardly compare to the more immediate and tangible benefits offered by a paying job. Compulsory education laws notwithstanding, the rate at which immigrant children dropped out of high school was quite high. A 1911 survey in New York revealed that zero percent of Italian immigrant children received high school diplomas!

Despite an unusual regard for education in his family, Leonard Covello felt the same pressures which terminated the education of all but a few of his fellows. Leonard and two brothers worked after school, adding their earnings to those of their father, but it was not enough to support a family of nine with an ailing mother. So, even though he had but one year left before graduation, Leonard dropped out of high school in 1905. More than economic pressure lay at the root of his decision. Leonard attended Morris High School in the Bronx, away from the familiar surroundings of Italian East Harlem. When he and a few companions had entered Morris, they discovered that the other students "came from better homes in better sections of New York." As a result, Covello noted that "the fear of ridicule, constant with us of foreign birth, was further aggravated."

After working at a variety of jobs for a year, Leonard was persuaded to return to school by Home Garden's Anna Ruddy and Mary Accurso, an interested neighbor. Matured by his experience, Leonard demonstrated new confidence by excelling as a student and an athlete. He became active in the literary club, joined the debate society, and wrote for the school newspaper. His new-found appreciation for learning (as well as his never-ending need for money) led Leonard to offer English lessons to Italian immigrants in the evening and on weekends. His outstanding record and evident promise earned Leonard a full four-year scholarship to Columbia in 1907.

At Columbia Covello majored in French, although his inclination was to study Italian. But as he afterwards acknowledged, "to have prepared myself to teach Italian would have seriously limited my possibilities of earning a living." The subject was simply not offered anywhere. Still, his interest in Italian studies signalled a significant step in Covello's personal growth. In the past he had hidden from his ethnicity, embarrassed and ashamed. At Morris High he and his friends had eaten their lunches—"crusty Italian bread heaped with salami, cheese or Italian sausage"—before they even reached school, so that their classmates "of the white-bread-and-ham upbringing would not laugh" at them. In college Covello "finally came into contact with men of true intellectual caliber" who accepted him for what he was. Their frequent and lengthy discussions encompassed all subjects, including Italians and immigration. In the process, Covello discovered that his ethnicity was no longer something he needed to conceal. It was a liberating experience:

> Across the lunch table the ideas flew. What had been private thoughts and unexpressed ideas in me for years now found words. I could talk with non-Italians about being an Italian, about being an immigrant in America. Something in me was being set free.

Covello had come to recognize that being an American did not mean giving up his Italian heritage. But when he began teaching at DeWitt Clinton High School in 1913, he had difficulty in transmitting this discovery to his students, many of whom were immigrants. Covello taught French and Spanish; no course in Italian existed, despite the city's population of more than 340,000 Italian immigrants. This omission conveyed to Covello's students the same message of inferiority and sense of shame that he had himself struggled with only a few years before. In 1914, he therefore sponsored establishment of *Il Circolo Italiano*, a student Italian club. In explaining its purpose to friends, Covello noted, "It must not be an isolated island interested only in the social or intellectual activities of a group of students of

Italian parentage. . . . The *Circolo* must keep in mind that its members are American citizens in an American school and soon to be active citizens in an American city." The club would help bridge gaps which existed between young Italian-Americans and their parents as well as between the Italian community in the United States and the rest of American society. Within this project lay the seed of the community-centered school, a concept Covello would one day be credited with initiating.

At the same time that his career was being defined in terms of its direction, Covello's personal life was also undergoing significant change. Shortly before he entered Columbia his mother had died. Pietro Coviello had brooded about the loss for two years but then remarried, sending back to Avigliano for a wife. This was *campanilismo* with a vengeance—nearly 20 years had passed since Coviello had seen Italy, but tradition was hard to defy. As Leonard Covello explained, "If someone from Avigliano married a girl from even a neighboring town he was looked upon with disapproval, as if [he thought] the girls of his own *paese* were not good enough for him." These strictures applied not merely to the older generation: when Covello married in 1913 it was to Mary Accurso, long-time New York neighbor and native of Avigliano. Mary died the next year, following a lingering kidney ailment. And when Covello remarried after about 10 years, his new wife was Rose Accurso, Mary's younger sister.

Not long after Covello began teaching at DeWitt Clinton, World War I erupted. The intense anti-German feelings which built up in the United States even before America entered the conflict had a beneficial, if only temporary, impact upon the new immigrant groups from southern and eastern Europe. Objection toward them diminished as nativist passions found an outlet in hostility directed against German-Americans. Because the new immigrants came from Italy and Russia—Allied powers—or were former, unwilling subjects of Germany or Austria, they tended enthusiastically to support the Allied cause, which further raised their standing. When the United States entered the war in 1917, large numbers of immigrants offered tangible evidence of their patriotism by volunteering for military service. Leonard Covello watched with mixed emotions as some of his older students dropped out of school to enlist. Despite the fact that he was 30 years old, Covello concluded that he had to do the same, explaining that "if I sat back . . . and did not enlist I would not be living up to what I was taught to believe."

After a year overseas, Covello returned to New York. A wartime contact led to a job in advertising which paid considerably more than he had made as a teacher. But the emotional rewards were far less, so the beginning of a new school year in 1920 found Covello in the classroom once more, teaching what was perhaps the only Italian course offered by any public school in the nation. To his surprise, Covello and his class were the objects of considerable criticism. He was accused of insulating his students from American culture and retarding their assimilation. As Emma Goldman also discovered, the war had intensified feelings that immigrants should conform. Covello observed that "Americanization meant the casting off of everything that was 'alien,' especially the language and culture of national origin." The Red Scare was in full swing. An early and active leader of the Teachers' Union, Covello felt what he termed "the heavy hand of conformity" descend upon the classroom. Since "to express one's political opinions was sure to result in reprisals," he steered clear of political issues—but he refused to yield on his commitment to a theory of education which acknowledged the immigrant's ethnicity rather than seeking to destroy it.

One axiom which evolved from this line of thinking was that "the unit of education was not merely the child. The unit of education must be the family." Acting on this supposition, he helped organize the Italian Parent-Teachers Association which, in the words of one distinguished educator, "afforded a bridge between the schools and the Italian community." Covello also applied his considerable energy to a newly established East Harlem project called *La Casa del Popolo*—the People's House. Mustering the students from his Italian club at DeWitt Clinton, Covello oversaw the renovation of a building to serve as a center for *La Casa*'s activities. There his students published a weekly bulletin which noted neighborhood problems and items of interest, and organized an after-school recreational program for children. But the principal business of *La Casa del Popolo* was adult education—teaching English to Italian immigrants and preparing them to qualify for citizenship. "If we don't help them, who will?" Covello exhorted his students. "Are we going to allow them to be robbed of their rights as Americans?"

Covello's disciples faced an uphill battle, despite their evident commitment. The rate at which Italians, especially those from the southern provinces, became naturalized citizens was significantly lower than was true for immigrants as a whole. On the eve of World War I fewer than 18 percent of Italian immigrants opted for citizenship, whereas among the general immigrant population the proportion was nearly 46 percent. A dozen or so years later, when *La Casa del Popolo* became a center for the promotion of naturalization, the discrepancy was only slightly less. A major reason for their disinclination to become citizens was the tendency on the part of Italian immigrants to return to Italy. From 1906 through 1915 65 percent as many Italians returned to their homeland from the United States as came to America from Italy! This figure points to the fact that among Italians the "bird of passage"—the temporary immigrant—was a rather common phenomenon. These transients saw no need to become citizens, participate in politics, or even learn English.

But to those who intended to remain in America, Covello felt a sense of almost personal obligation. He rejected offers to teach at colleges, fearing that such a position might isolate him from the Italian-American community. Rather than seeking an escape from East Harlem, Covello immersed himself even more in its rich life. Outside the classroom his spare moments were spent founding, promoting, or otherwise involving himself in a variety of organizations designed to assist Italian immigrants in adapting themselves to American life without sacrificing their ethnic identity or personal pride. Most notable in this regard was Covello's establishment in 1932 of the *Casa Italiana* Educational Bureau. Such an agency was needed, Covello claimed, because "where the Italian immigrant is concerned, the assimilative process has been retarded partly because of lack of intelligent handling on the part of the larger American community and partly by the Italian community itself." Expanding on this, he noted:

> The American community could not, or would not, see the problems that were being created. It is also reasonable to conclude that the Italian, because he considered himself a transient, failed to become conscious of his broader social responsibilities. There was no real development of an immigrant community—it was rather an agglomeration of numerous disjointed groupings. . . .
>
> The need for unification and coordination of all kinds of educational work in Italian-American communities is therefore a pressing matter.

In response to this need, Covello proposed that the *Casa Italiana* Educational Bureau pursue several objectives. It would collect and disseminate "social and educational facts for all agencies and individuals to whom such information may be of value." In addition, the Bureau would function as a focal point of "efforts directed toward social and cultural advancement of the Italian-American." Finally, it would undertake "a promotional program of educational and social activities. To this end it will concern itself with the establishment and guidance of similar organizations throughout the United States."

In a very real sense, the Bureau represented the natural extension of the mutual benefit societies which were so prevalent within the Italian-American community at the time. Initially established to insure proper burial of deceased immigrants and furnish assistance for their survivors, these organizations rapidly enlarged their focus. Groups like the Society for Italian Immigrants, established in New York in 1901, offered their members help in a number of forms—maintaining a library, furnishing interpreters, locating jobs, conducting English classes, in addition to sponsoring a whole range of social and recreational activities. Obviously filling a widely felt need, mutual-benefit societies proliferated wherever Italians settled in the United States. In 1912 estimates placed the number of such societies in Chicago alone at 400, with even more serving New York's larger Italian population. One reason for the prevalence of mutual-benefit societies was the strong sense of *campanilismo* which continued to operate among America's Italians. Most societies were initially established on a regional or even local basis; often they were named for a particular village or for its patron saint.

It was precisely this sort of fragmentation that Leonard Covello hoped to combat when he established the *Casa Italiana* Educational Bureau. Within two years, the Bureau had managed to bring together more than 250 such groups in the Greater New York area to support educational programs, including sponsorship of a scholarship fund for Italian Americans. But his efforts had little lasting effect; the Bureau closed in the early 1940s. Partly the problem lay in the fact that, as Covello later conceded, "the Italian communities . . . never understood educational programs of this character. . . . Such things as educational research and educational programs even for the propaganda of the Italian language never had any financial support." A further explanation might be that another project—more of a mission—commanded increasing amounts of Covello's energy.

In 1934 Leonard Covello was named the principal of newly established Benjamin Franklin High School. His appointment gave Covello an opportunity to assist East Harlem's 90,000 first and second generation Italians more effectively than before. His aim at the time, he would note from the perspective of 35 years later, "was to bring the community into the school, so that our youngsters might better grow into understanding and participatory citizens." The community school concept, which had germinated inside Covello's head since he began teaching 20 years earlier, became a reality.

In addition to the standard educational fare, Benjamin Franklin High School offered night classes for adults, maintained an after-school recreational program for children and functioned as an evening community center. Covello stayed late in his office one night a week, often with some of his teachers, where they "interviewed parents and people of the community who sought our advice on everything from citizenship to childbirth." The school was a beehive of activity:

> Young men and adults who for one reason or another had been unable to graduate from day school were now completing their high-school education at night. In other rooms immigrants of various ages and nationalities struggled with the complexities of the English language, sometimes

> taught by their own sons, while still others prepared for citizenship tests. In the gymnasium a basketball game was in progress. . . . In the library, the Parent-Teachers Association was holding a meeting, while from the auditorium might come the shrill sounds of an argument that meant that the Community Advisory Council was in session.

When Benjamin Franklin High School moved into a new structure in 1942, Covello carried his program one step farther, opening up the school to all members of the community on a 24-hour-per-day, 365-day-per-year basis. Growing with his school, Covello wrote and published articles on immigrants, communities, and schools in a number of educational and sociological journals. This process culminated with his doctoral dissertation, "The Social Background of the Italo-American School Child," for which he received a Ph.D. from New York University in 1944.

Covello's commitment to the community-centered school remained unaltered even as the community itself began to change. The passage of restrictive legislation in the 1920s had greatly reduced the number of new arrivals from Italy. Instead, Blacks and Puerto Ricans flooded into East Harlem, taking over from Italians in much the same fashion that Italian immigrants had previously displaced the Irish. Other than the fact that they were American citizens, these newcomers differed little from the area's earlier occupants in terms of their needs and the problems they faced. Leonard Covello remained in business at Benjamin Franklin.

Upwardly mobile second and third generation Italian-Americans began to fulfill the dreams of their immigrant parents and grandparents by taking better jobs and moving to better neighborhoods. Not until his mandatory retirement in 1957 did the 70-year-old Covello join this exodus, moving to a New Jersey suburb. But he could not altogether sever his ties to the old neighborhood or its new inhabitants. He took the position of Educational Consultant to the Migration Division of the Puerto Rican Department of Labor, drawing upon his years of observation and experience to render valuable service. In 1972, following the death of his wife, Covello responded to the tug of something even more elemental. After more than three quarters of a century in the United States, he journeyed to Sicily where he joined Danilo Dolci, a social activist, at the Center for Study and Action. For a few years Covello assisted Dolci in a campaign against the poverty, unemployment, corruption, and crime that were so much a part of Sicilian life, but at last he retired. Remaining in Sicily, Leonard Covello died in 1982 at the age of 95.

DISCUSSION QUESTIONS

1. Scholars who study immigration often talk of the "push-pull" factors that impel people to move from one country to another. What circumstances helped "push" Leonard Covello's family out of Italy? What "pulled" them to America?
2. The words "typical" and "average" come easily to the pens of historians because they permit generalization. One value of studying the biography of an individual is that it reminds us that no one is truly "typical" or "average." What was there in the experience of Leonard Covello that was atypical or unusual?
3. Describe some of the influences that helped "Americanize" young Leonard Covello. Was becoming an "American" a pleasant experience?

4

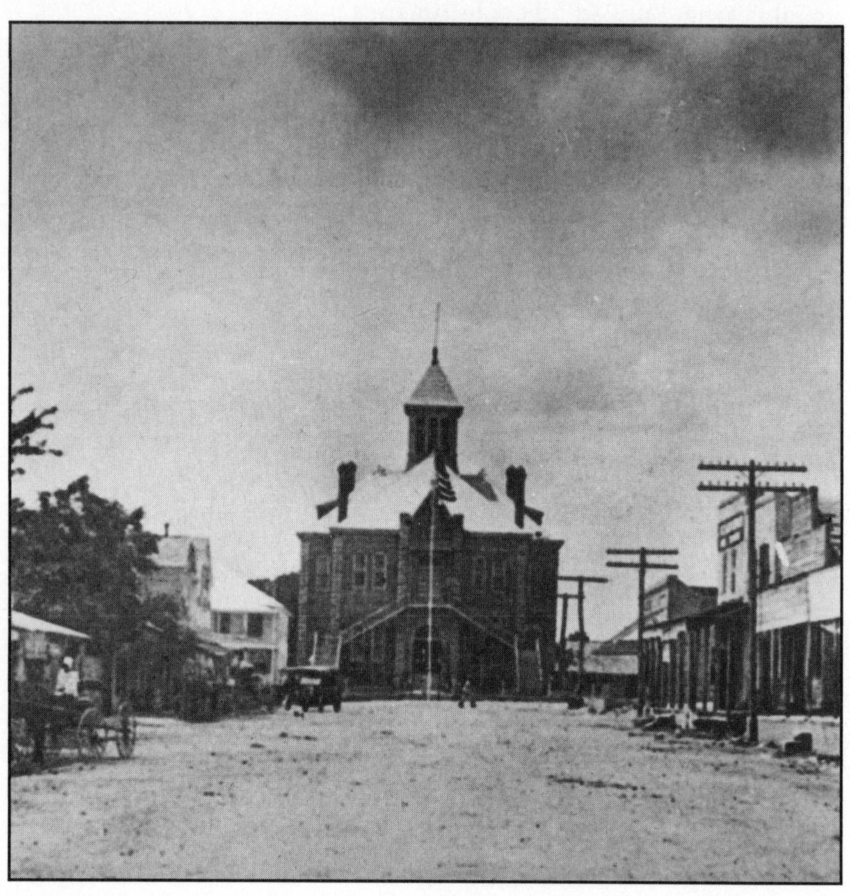

THE MEANING OF POPULISM: BLACK RIGHTS IN A TEXAS TOWN

LAWRENCE C. GOODWYN

The Populist movement remains an historical enigma. For many years the standard interpretation emphasized the fact that the "revolt" was confined essentially to the Great Plains and the South, single-crop farming areas that were at the mercy of an international price depression. If that was so, if Populism was little more than the protest of a financially pressed interest group, why is it accorded such an important place in the history of American "reform"?

The Populists' image suffered further when historians began pointing out that much of the Populists rhetoric was antisemitic and that after the "revolt" died out Populist leaders became some of the most vocal of southern racists. Could such a movement be regarded as democratic and reformist in any sense?

Lawrence C. Goodwyn in the essay below tests these interpretations using an East Texas community as a case study. In an effort to recover the oral traditions about the county's past, Goodwyn's research technique included interviews with persons still living in the area. His mission was to reconstruct the "stuff of life" in a southern community governed by Populists, trying to learn something about both populist insurgency and white conservative orthodoxy. He found a fascinating alliance between the white Populist sheriff and the black community in the county. But he also found that the alliance brought on the ruin of both because white conservative Democrats organized vigilante groups that terrorized the countryside. Populism was driven from the county in a dramatic shoot-out, and white Democrats have controlled it ever since. The story, full of drama and pathos, provides fresh insight into the aspirations of the Populists, as well as their ultimate failure.

—NORMAN K. RISJORD

Nearly a century later the Populist decade lingers in historical memory as an increasingly dim abstraction. The very word "Populism" no longer carries specific political meaning. It is now [1971] invoked to explain George Wallace, as it was used to explain Lyndon Johnson in the sixties, Joe McCarthy in the fifties, and Claude Pepper in the forties. Though afflicting principally the popular mind, this confusion is at least partially traceable to those historians who have insisted on concentrating on Populism as exhortation, so that Ignatius Donnelly's utopian novels or Mary Lease's pronouncements on the respective uses of corn and hell become the explanatory keys to agrarian radicalism. For scholars who mine political movements with a view to extracting cultural nuggets, the focus has been chiefly upon the word, not the deed; in the process the agrarian crusade has become increasingly obscure.

Much of the difficulty centers on the subject of race. There is essential agreement that, on economic issues, Populists were men of the Left, primitive to some; prophetic to others, but leftists to all. But did their banner indicate a highly selective nativist radicalism for whites only, or did they grapple with the inherited legacies of the caste system as part of an effort to create what they considered a more rational social and economic order? The analysis of Populist rhetoric has left us with contradictory answers.

While party platforms can be useful tools in determining professed attitudes, the gap between asserted ideals and performance is sufficiently large to defeat any analysis resting on the implicit assumption that political manifestos have an intrinsic value apart from the milieu in which they existed. In America the distance between assertion and performance is especially evident in matters of race; as a result, on this issue above all, the context of public assertions is central to the task of their political evaluation. An inquiry into the murkiest corner of Populism, interracial politics, should begin not merely with what Populists said but what they did in the course of bidding for power at the local level. What was the stuff of daily life under Populist rule in the rural enclaves where the third party came to exercise all the authority of public office, including police authority? What can we learn not only about Populist insurgency but also about the orthodoxy the third party opposed?

Grimes County, Texas, was one of many counties scattered across the South and West where the People's party achieved a continuing political presence in the latter part of the nineteenth century. Located some sixty miles north of Houston in the heart of what the natives

THE MEANING OF POPULISM: BLACK RIGHTS IN A TEXAS TOWN From Lawrence C. Goodwyn, "Populist Dreams and Negro Rights: East Texas as a Case Study," *American Historical Review*, 76, No. 5 (December, 1971), pp. 1435–1456. Reprinted by permission of the author.

called the Old South part of Texas, Grimes County displayed the cotton-centered economy typical of rural East Texas in 1880. Its largest town, Navasota, contained 1,800 persons in 1890 and its second largest town, Anderson, the county seat, only 574 persons as late as 1900. Farms in Grimes County ranged from plantation size in the rich bottomland country of the Brazos River on the county's western border to small, single-family agricultural units on the poorer land of the northern part of the county. The 1890 census revealed a county population of 21,312, of which 11,664 were black.

Populism in Grimes County is the story of a black-white coalition that had its genesis in Reconstruction and endured for more than a generation. In time this coalition came to be symbolized by its most enduring elected public official, Garrett Scott. The Scotts had roots in Grimes County dating back before the Civil War. Their sons fought for the Confederacy and returned to face a postwar reality by no means unique in the South; possessing moderately large holdings of land but lacking necessary capital to make it productive, the Scotts did not achieve great affluence. During the hard times that continued to afflict undercapitalized Southern agriculture through the 1870s Garrett Scott became a soft-money agrarian radical. His stance was significant in the political climate of Grimes County in the early 1880s. During Reconstruction Negroes in the county had achieved a remarkably stable local Republican organization, headed by a number of resourceful black leaders. When Reconstruction ended and white Democrats regained control of the state governmental machinery in Texas, Grimes County blacks retained local power and sent a succession of black legislators to Austin for the next decade. The local effort to end this Republican rule took the usual postwar Southern form of a political movement of white solidarity under the label of the Democratic party. In supporting the Greenback party Garrett Scott not only was disassociating himself from the politics of white racial solidarity, he was undermining it.

In 1882 a mass meeting of various non-Democratic elements in Grimes County nominated a variegated slate for county offices. Among the candidates were black Republicans, "lily-white" Republicans, and Independent Greenbackers. Garrett Scott was on the ticket as the Independent Greenback candidate for sheriff. Not much is known about the racial climate in Grimes County in 1882, but it must not have been wholly serene, because the "lily-white" nominee for county judge, Lock MacDaniel, withdrew from the ticket rather than publicly associate with black candidates. Garrett Scott did not withdraw, and in November he was elected. Also elected, as district clerk, was a black man who became a lifelong political ally of Scott, Jim Kennard. Thus began an interracial coalition that endured through the years of propagandizing in Texas by the increasingly radical Farmers Alliance and through the ensuing period of the People's party. The success of the coalition varied with the degree of white participation. After the collapse of the Greenback party in the mid-eighties visible white opposition to the Democratic party declined for several years before Grimes County farmers, organized by the Alliance, broke with the Democracy to form the nucleus of the local People's party in 1892. Scott and Kennard were the most visible symbols of the revitalized coalition, but there were others as well. Among them were Morris Carrington, a Negro school principal, and Jack Haynes, both staunch advocates of Populism in the black community, as well as J. W. H. Davis and J. H. Teague, white Populist leaders. These men led the People's party to victory in the county elections of 1896 and again in 1898.

A subtle duality creeps into the narrative of events at this point. To the world outside Grimes County in the 1890s, to both Populists and Democrats, Garrett Scott was simply another Populist officeholder, distinguished for his antimonopoly views and his generally radical approach to monetary policy. To his white supporters within Grimes County he was doubtless respected for the same reasons. But to the Democrats of Grimes County the sheriff symbolized all that was un-Southern and unpatriotic about the third party. Under Populist rule, it was charged, Negro school teachers were paid too much money; furthermore, in Scott's hands the sheriff's office hired Negro deputies. The two Democratic newspapers in Navasota were fond of equating Populist rule with Negro rule and of attributing both evils to Scott. The Navasota *Daily Examiner* asserted that "the Negro has been looking too much to political agitation and legislative enactment. . . . So long as he looks to political agitation for relief, so long will he be simply the means of other men's ambition." To the Navasota *Tablet* Scott was simply "the originator of all the political trouble in Grimes County for years." Both these explanations oversimplify Grimes County politics. The political presence and goals of blacks were definite elements of local Populism, as was, presumably, the personal ambition of Garrett Scott. But the Populists' proposed economic remedies had gained a significant following among the county's white farmers, and this was of crucial importance in inducing white Populists to break with Democrats and ally themselves with blacks. Garrett Scott was a living embodiment of white radicalism; he did not cause it. Beyond this the political cohesion of blacks was a local phenomenon that had preceded Scott's entry into Grimes County politics and had remained relatively stable since the end of the war. The ease with which Democratic partisans saw the fine hand of Garrett Scott in Negro voting was more a reflection of their own racial presumptions than an accurate description of the political dynamics at work in the county.

Through the election of 1898 Democrats in Grimes County had labored in vain to cope with the disease of Populism among the county's white farmers. Finally, in the spring of 1899, the Democrats moved in a new direction. The defeated Democratic candidate for county judge, J. G. McDonald, organized a clandestine meeting with other prominent local citizens and defeated Democratic office seekers. At this meeting a new and—for the time being—covert political institution was created: the White Man's Union. A charter was drawn providing machinery through which the Union could nominate candidates for county offices in elections in which only White Man's Union members could vote. No person could be nominated who was not a member; no person could be a member who did not subscribe to these exclusionary bylaws; in effect, to participate in the organization's activities, so adequately expressed in its formal title, one had to support, as a policy matter, black disfranchisement. Throughout the summer and fall of 1899 the White Man's Union quietly organized.

Writing years later McDonald explained that care was taken not to launch the organization publicly "until the public attitude could be sounded." By January 1900 the covert organizing had been deemed sufficiently successful to permit the public unveiling of the White Man's Union through a long story in the *Examiner*. During the spring the *Examiner*'s political reporting began to reflect a significant change of tone. In April, for example, the *Examiner*'s report of a "quiet election" in nearby Bryan noted that friends of the two mayoral candidates "made a display of force and permitted no Negroes to vote. All white citizens went to the polls, quietly deposited their ballots for whom they pleased and went on about their business." The *Examiner* had progressed from vague suggestions for disfranchisement to approval of its forcible imposition without cover of law.

The first public meetings of the White Man's Union, duly announced in the local press, occupied the spring months of 1900 and were soon augmented by some not-quite-so-public night riding. The chronology of these events may be traced through the denials in the local Democratic press of their occurrence. In July the *Examiner* angrily defended the county's honor against charges by the Negro Baptist State Sunday School Conference that the county had become unsafe for Negroes. The Austin *Herald* reported from the state's capital that the Sunday School Board, "after mature thought and philosophical deliberation," had decided to cancel its annual meeting scheduled for Navasota. The *Examiner* cited as "irresponsible slush" the charge that Negroes were being threatened and told to leave the county, but within weeks reports of just such events began cropping up in the *Examiner* itself. One example of terrorism left no one in doubt, for it occurred in broad daylight on the main street of the county seat: in July Jim Kennard was shot and killed within one hundred yards of the courthouse. His assailant was alleged to be J. G. McDonald.

Intimidation and murder constituted an even more decisive assault on the People's party than had the ominous bylaws of the White

Man's Union. The Populist leadership recognized this clearly enough, and Scott went so far as to attempt to persuade Southern white farmers to shoulder arms in defense of the right of Negroes to vote. Beyond this we know little of the measures attempted by the local Populist constabulary to contain the spreading terrorism. A well-informed member of the Scott family wrote a detailed account of these turbulent months, but the manuscript was subsequently destroyed. In the early autumn of 1900 members of the White Man's Union felt sufficiently strong to initiate visits to white farmers with a known allegiance to the People's party. Under such duress some of these farmers joined the White Man's Union.

In August the Union, aided by a not inconsiderable amount of free publicity in the local press, announced "the Grandest Barbecue of the Year," at which the "workings of the White Man's Union" would be explained to all. The leadership of the People's party objected to announced plans to include the local state guard unit, the Shaw Rifles, in the program. After some discussion the Texas adjutant general, Thomas Scurry, placed at the discretion of the local commander the question of the attendance of the Shaw Rifles in a body. The commander, Captain Hammond Norwood, a leading Navasota Democrat and a member of the White Man's Union, exercised his option, and the Shaw Rifles appeared en masse at the function. Populist objections were brushed aside.

Shortly after this well-attended barbecue had revealed the growing prestige of the White Man's Union as well as the inability of the People's party to cope with the changing power relationships within the county, a black exodus began. People left by train, by horse and cart, by day and by night. The *Examiner,* with obvious respect for the new political climate its own columns had helped engender, suggested elliptically that the exodus could produce complications. Some citizens, said the *Examiner,* "are beginning to feel a little nervous as the thing progresses, and lean to the idea that the action will bring on detrimental complications in the labor market."

The next day, however, the paper printed a public address that it said had been "ordered published by the executive committee of the White Man's Union in order to combat the many reports that are calculated to injure the Union." After reaffirming the Union's intent to end "Negro rule" in the county, the report concluded with a message "to the Negroes":

> Being the weaker race, it is our desire to protect you from the schemes of those men who are now seeking to place you before them. . . . Therefore, the White Man's Union kindly and earnestly requests you to keep hands off in the coming struggle. Do not let impudent men influence you in that pathway which certainly leads to trouble. . . . In the future,

> permit us to show you, and convince you by our action, that we are truly your best friends.

Fourteen days later a black Populist leader, Jack Haynes, was riddled with a shotgun blast by unknown assailants. He died instantly in the fields of his cotton farm.

The White Man's Union held a rally in Navasota two nights later that featured a reading of original poetry by one of the Union's candidates, L. M. Bragg. The verse concluded:

> Twas nature's laws that drew the lines
> Between the Anglo-Saxon and African races,
> And we, the Anglo-Saxons of Grand Old Grimes,
> Must force the African to keep his place.

Another White Man's Union rally held in Plantersville the same week displayed other Union candidates whose conduct won the *Examiner*'s editorial approval: "They are a solid looking body of men and mean business straight from the shoulder." Apparently this characterization of the Plantersville speakers was not restricted to approving Democrats; Populists, too, responded to events initiated by the men who "meant business." In October the Plantersville school superintendent reported that only five white families remained in his school district and that all the Negroes were gone. The superintendent stated that twelve white families had left that week, and "the end is not in sight."

Amid this wave of mounting terror the People's party attempted to go about its business, announcing its nominating conventions in the local press and moving forward with the business of naming election judges and poll watchers. But there were already signs of a fatal crack in Populist morale. The People's party nominee for county commissioner suddenly withdrew from the race. His withdrawal was announced in the *Examiner*, and no explanation was offered.

Throughout the late summer and autumn of 1900 the demonstrated power of the White Man's Union had protected McDonald from prosecution in the Kennard slaying. Nothing short of a war between the Populist police authority and the White Man's Union could break that extralegal shield. An exasperated and perhaps desperate Garrett Scott angrily challenged a White Man's Union official in October to "go and get your Union force, every damn one of them, put them behind rock fences and trees and I'll fight the whole damn set of cowards." That Scott had to use the first person singular to describe the visible opposition to the Union underscores the extent to which terror had triumphed over the institutions of law in Grimes County. By election eve it was clear that the Populist ticket faced certain defeat. The third party had failed to protect its constituency. White Populists as well as black were intimidated. Many would not vote; indeed, many were no longer in the county.

Over 4,500 votes had been cast in Grimes in 1898. On November 6, 1900, only 1,800 persons ventured to the polls. The People's party received exactly 366 votes. The Populist vote in Plantersville fell from 256 in 1898 to 5 in 1900. In the racially mixed, lower-income precinct of south Navasota the Populist vote declined from 636 to 23. The sole exception to this pattern came in a geographically isolated, lower-income precinct in the extreme northern part of the county that contained few Negroes and thus, presumably, fewer acts of terrorism. The Populist vote in this precinct actually increased from 108 to 122 and accounted for one-third of the countywide vote of 366. In north Navasota, also almost all white but not geographically isolated from the terror, the Populist vote declined from 120 to 3. An additional element, nonstatistical in nature, stamped the election as unusual. The underlying philosophy of the South's dominant political institution, the Democratic party, has perhaps never been expressed more nakedly than it was in Grimes County in 1900 when "the party of white supremacy," as C. Vann Woodward has called the Southern Democracy, appeared on the official ballot as the White Man's Union.

On the way to its landslide victory the Union had grown more self-confident in its willingness to carry out acts of intimidation and terrorism in defiance of the local Populist police authority. Now that that authority had been deposed and a sheriff friendly to the White Man's Union had been elected, would terrorism become even more public?

On November 7, 1900, the morning after the election, a strange tableau unfolded on the streets of Anderson, the tiny county seat. Horsemen began arriving in town from every section of the county, tied their horses all along the main street, and occupied the second floor of the courthouse. In a nearby house Garrett Scott's sister, Cornelia, and her husband, John Kelly, watched the buildup of Union supporters on the courthouse square, not fifty yards from the sheriff's official residence on the second floor of the county jail. They decided the situation was too dangerous to permit an adult Populist to venture forth, so the Kellys sent their nine-year-old son with a note to warn Scott not to appear on the street.

At about the same time that this mission was carried out Garrett Scott's younger brother, Emmett Scott, came into town from the family farm, rode past the growing clusters of armed men, and reined up in front of the store belonging to John Bradley, his closest friend in town. Bradley was a Populist but, as befitting a man of trade, a quiet one. His store was adjacent to the courthouse.

Cornelia Kelly's son found the sheriff at Abercrombie's store across the street from the jail and delivered the warning note. As Scott read it an outbreak of gunfire sounded from the direction of Bradley's store. Scott stepped to the street and peered in the direction of the fusillade.

Rifle fire from the second floor of the courthouse immediately cut him down. Upon hearing the gunfire Cornelia Kelly ran out of her house and down the long street toward the courthouse. The gunsights of scores of men tracked her progress. Seeing her brother's body in the street she turned and confronted his attackers. "Why don't you shoot me, too," she yelled, "I'm a Scott." She ran to her brother and, with the assistance of her son, dragged him across the street to the county jail. He was, she found, not dead, though he did have an ugly wound in his hip. Inside Bradley's store, however, three men were dead—Emmett Scott, Bradley, and Will McDonald, the son of a Presbyterian minister and a prominent member of the White Man's Union. McDonald had shot Scott shortly after the latter had entered the store; the two men grappled for the gun, and the fatally wounded Scott fired one shot, killing McDonald. Bradley was killed either by a shot fired from outside the store where Union forces had gathered near the courthouse or by a stray bullet during the struggle inside.

The siege of Anderson continued for five days, with the wounded sheriff and his deputies—black and white—in the jail and the White Man's Union forces in the courthouse. Shots crossed the fifty yards between the two buildings intermittently over the next several days. On the evening of the fatal shooting another member of the Scott clan, Mrs. W. T. Neblett, had left Navasota for Austin to plead with the governor, Joseph D. Sayers, for troops. On Friday she returned, accompanied by the adjutant general of the State of Texas, Thomas Scurry—the same official who had earlier acquiesced in the participation of the state guard in the White Man's Union barbecue. After conferring with the contending forces Scurry pondered various methods to get the wounded Scott out of town and into a hospital; gangrene had set in. For protection, Scurry suggested that he be authorized to select a group of twenty prominent citizens of Navasota to escort the sheriff from the jail to the railroad station. Since most of the "prominent citizens" of Navasota were members of the White Man's Union, it is perhaps understandable that Scott declined this offer. The adjutant general then suggested that the Shaw Rifles be employed as an escort. This idea was respectfully declined for the same reason. Asked what he could consider a trustworthy escort, the wounded sheriff suggested a state guard unit from outside the county.

On Saturday, four days after the shooting, a company of Houston light infantry of the Texas Volunteer State Guard detrained at Navasota and marched the eleven miles to Anderson. On Sunday morning Garrett Scott was placed on a mattress, the mattress put in a wagon, and the procession began. In the wagon train were most of the members of the large Scott clan—Emmett Scott's widow and children, the Kelly family, and the Nebletts, all with their household belongings piled in wagons. A file of infantrymen marched on either side as the procession formed in front of the jail, moved past hundreds of armed men at the courthouse and onto the highway to Navasota, and then boarded a special train bound for Houston.

Thus did Populism leave Grimes County. From that day in 1900 until well after mid-century Negroes were not a factor in Grimes County politics. J. G. McDonald regained his judgeship and served for many years. The White Man's Union continued into the 1950s as the dominant political institution in the county. None of its nominees, selected in advance of the Democratic primary, was ever defeated. The census of 1910 revealed the extent of the Negro exodus. It showed that Grimes County's Negro population had declined by almost thirty per cent from the 1900 total. School census figures for 1901 suggest an even greater exodus.

To this day the White Man's Union, as a memory if no longer as an institution, enjoys an uncontested reputation among Grimes County whites as a civic enterprise for governmental reform. In this white oral tradition the general events of 1900 are vividly recounted. Specific events are, however remembered selectively. The exodus of Negroes from the county is not part of this oral tradition, nor is the night riding of the White Man's Union or the assassination of the Negro Populist leaders.

As for Garrett Scott, he endured a long convalescence in a San Antonio hospital, regained his health, married his nurse, and moved to a farm near Houston. He retired from politics and died in his bed. He is remembered in the oral tradition of the black community as the "best sheriff the county ever had." Kennard and Haynes were killed because they "vouched" for Scott among Negroes. In this black oral tradition the Negro exodus plays a central role. It is perhaps an accurate measure of the distance between the races in Grimes County today that two such contradictory versions of famous events could exist side by side without cross-influence.

To these two oral traditions a third must be added—the Scott tradition. The Scotts were, and are, a proud family. One by one, as they died, they were brought home to be buried in the family plot in the Anderson cemetery, little more than a mile from the site of the bloody events of 1900. Tombstones of female members of the clan bear the Scott middle name, defiantly emblazoned in marble. Edith Hamilton of Richards, Grimes County, was ten years old in November 1900 and remembers vividly the day her nine-year-old brother carried her mother's message to Garrett Scott. She remembers the defiance of her mother, the political commitment of her father, the acts of intimidation by the White Man's Union, the Negro exodus, and what she calls the "intelligence of Uncle Garrett." "They said that Uncle Garrett was a nigger-lover," recalls Mrs. Hamilton. "He wasn't a nigger-lover, or a white-lover, he just believed in being fair to all, in justice."

The Scott oral tradition—similar to the black oral tradition and at odds with the white tradition—is virtually the only legacy of the long years of interracial cooperation in Grimes County. Beyond this the substance of political life that came to an end in Grimes County in 1900 cannot be measured precisely from the available evidence. Very little survives to provide insight into the nature of the personal relationship that existed between Garrett Scott and Jim Kennard, between any of the other Populist leaders of both races, or between their respective constituencies. Scott and his third-party colleagues may have been motivated solely by personal ambition, as the White Man's Union charged; on the other hand, the impulses that made them Populists in the first place may have led them toward public coalition with blacks. It is clear that such stridently white supremacist voices as the Navasota *Tablet* were unable to project any reason other than personal ambition to explain the phenomenon of white men willingly associating themselves politically with black men. To what extent this attitude reflected Populist presumptions is another question. White Populists and black Republicans shared an animosity toward the Southern Democracy that grew in intensity during the bitter election campaigns of the 1890s. Democratic persistence in raising the cry of "Negro domination" to lure Populist-leaning voters back to the "party of the fathers" was effective enough to keep white Populists on the defensive about the race issue throughout the agrarian revolt in the South. The circumstances of a common political foe nevertheless provided Populists and Republicans with a basis for political coalition that was consummated in a bewildering variety of ways—and sometimes not consummated at all. The stability of local black organizations and their demonstrated capacity to withstand Democratic blandishments or acts of intimidation were only two of the factors governing the complex equation of post-Reconstruction interracial politics. A stable, local black political institution existed in Grimes County, and its enduring qualities obviously simplified the organizational task confronting Garrett Scott. What might be regarded as "normal" Bourbon efforts to split blacks from the Populist coalition—mild intimidation, petty bribery, campaign assertions that the Democrats were the Negroes' "best friends," or a combination of all three—failed to achieve the desired results in Grimes County in the 1890s. The precise reasons are not easily specified. The Navasota *Tablet*, seeing the world through lenses tinted with its own racial presumptions, ascribed the credit for Negro political cohesion solely to the white sheriff. In the face of all Democratic stratagems, the third party's continuing appeal to Negroes was, in the *Tablet*'s view, a thing of "magic." A white supremacist view does not automatically exclude its holder from rendering correct political analyses on occasion, and it is possible that the *Tablet*'s assessment of the cause of Negro political solidarity was correct; however, such an analysis does not explain how the Negro Republican organization was able to send a succession of black legislators to Austin in the 1870s and 1880s, before Garrett Scott became politically active. It seems relevant that when Grimes County Democrats decided upon an overt campaign of terrorism, the men they went after first were the leading black spokesmen of Populism in the county rather than the third party's white leadership. To this extent the actions of Democratic leaders contradicted their public analysis of the causal relationships inherent in the continuing Populist majorities.

Before they indulged in terrorism the Democrats already possessed another method of splitting the Populist coalition: regaining the loyalty of white Populists. Against the historic Democratic campaign cry of white supremacy, the People's party had as its most effective defense the economic appeal of its own platform. The persuasiveness of Populism to white farmers in Grimes County was confirmed by newspaper accounts of the public reaction to the Populist-Democratic debates that occurred during the years of the agrarian uprising. While the reports in the *Examiner* were uniformly partisan and invariably concluded that Democratic spokesmen "won" such debates hands down, the papers conceded that Populist speakers also drew enthusiastic responses from white residents. The absence of reliable racial data by precincts renders a statistical analysis of the Populist vote in Grimes County impossible; however, the fragmentary available evidence suggests that the People's party was generally able to hold a minimum of approximately thirty per cent of the county's white voters in the four elections from 1892 to 1898 while at the same time polling approximately eighty to ninety per cent of the Negro electorate. The inability of the Democratic party to "bloc vote" the county's white citizenry, coupled with the party's failure to win black voters by various means or, alternatively, to diminish the size of the Negro electorate, combined to ensure Democratic defeat at the polls. The fact merits emphasis: both the cohesion of black support for the People's party and the maintenance of substantial white support were essential to the local ascendancy of Populism.

This largely deductive analysis, however, reveals little about the internal environment within the third-party coalition during the bitter struggle for power that characterized the decade of Populist-Democratic rivalry. However scrutinized, the bare bones of voting totals do not flesh out the human relationships through which black and white men came together politically in this rural Southern county. In the absence of such crucial evidence, it seems prudent to measure the meaning of 1900 in the most conservative possible terms. Even by this standard, however, a simple recitation of those elements of Grimes County politics that are beyond dispute isolates significant and lasting ramifications.

An indigenous black political structure persisted in Grimes County for thirty-five years following the Civil War. Out of his own needs as a political insurgent against the dominant Southern Democratic party, Garrett Scott decided in 1882 to identify his Greenback cause with the existing local Republican constituency. Once in office as sheriff he found, among other possible motives, that it was in his own self-interest to preserve the coalition that elected him. It is clear that the style of law enforcement in Grimes County under Scott became a persuasive ingredient in the preservation of black support for the People's party. The presence of black deputy sheriffs and Scott's reputation within the black community seem adequate confirmation of both the existence of this style and its practical effect. The salaries paid Negro school teachers constituted another element of third-party appeal. Comparisons with white salaries are not available, but whatever black teachers received, partisans of the White Man's Union publicly denounced it as "too much." It is evident that Grimes County Negroes supported the People's party for reasons that were grounded in legitimate self-interest—an incontestable basis for political conduct. The point is not so much that the county's Negroes had certain needs, but that they possessed the political means to address at least a part of those needs.

From this perspective the decisive political event of 1900 in Grimes County was not the overwhelming defeat of the local People's party but the political elimination of that part of its constituency that was black. Scott was valuable to Negroes in short-run terms because he helped to translate a minority black vote into a majority coalition that possessed the administrative authority to improve the way black people lived in Grimes County. In the long run, however, it was the presence of this black constituency—not the conduct of a single white sheriff nor even the professed principles of his political party—that provided the Negroes of the county with what protection they had from a resurgent caste system. As long as Negroes retained the right to cast ballots in proportion to their numbers they possessed bargaining power that became particularly meaningful on all occasions when whites divided their votes over economic issues. Disfranchisement destroyed the bargaining power essential to this elementary level of protection. Arrayed against these overriding imperatives for Negroes such questions as the sincerity of Garrett Scott's motives fade in importance. Whatever the sheriff's motives, both the political realities that undergirded the majority coalition and Scott's ability to respond to those realities shaped a course of government conduct under the People's party that was demonstrably of more benefit to Negroes than was the conduct of other administrations before or since. The permanent alteration of those realities through black disfranchisement ensured that no other white administration, whether radical, moderate, or opportunistic, would be able to achieve the patterns in education and law enforcement that had come to exist in the county under Populism. Stated as starkly as possible, after 1900 it was no longer in the interest of white politicians to provide minimal guarantees for people who could not help elect them.

Beyond this crucial significance for the county's black people, disfranchisement also institutionalized a fundamental change in the political environment of whites. More than a third party passed from Grimes County in 1900; in real political terms an idea died. Though a new political idea invariably materializes in democratic societies as an expression of the self-interest of a portion of the electorate, the party that adopts the idea in the course of appealing for the votes of that sector of the electorate inevitably is placed in the position of having to rationalize, defend, explain, and eventually promote the idea. If the concept has substance, this process eventually results in the insinuation of the idea into the culture itself. In this sense it is not necessary to know the precise depth of the commitment to Negro rights of the Grimes County People's party to know that the *idea* of Negro rights had a potential constituency among white people in the county as long as black people were able to project its presence through their votes. Given the endurance of this real and potential constituency, one could reasonably intuit that twentieth-century politics in Grimes County would have contained one, or a dozen, or a thousand Garrett Scotts—each more, or less, "sincere" or "ambitious" than the Populist sheriff. Disfranchisement destroyed the political base of this probability. A political party can survive electoral defeat, even continuing defeat, and remain a conveyor of ideas from one generation to the next. But it cannot survive the destruction of its constituency, for the party itself then dies, taking with it the possibility of transmitting its political concepts to those as yet unborn. It is therefore no longer possible to speak of two white political traditions in Grimes County, for the White Man's Union succeeded in establishing a most effective philosophical suzerainty. Seventy years after disfranchisement Mrs. Hamilton can recall the racial unorthodoxy of Uncle Garrett; she cannot participate in such activity herself. "The Negro people here don't want this school integration any more than the whites do," she now says. "They're not ready for it. They don't feel comfortable in the school with white children. I've talked to my maid. I know."

While Garrett Scott's memory has been preserved, the local presence of the creed of his political party died with the destruction of that party. There has been literally no political place to go for subsequent generations of Scotts and Teagues, or Kennards and Carringtons. This absence of an alternative political institution to the Democratic party, the party of white supremacy, has been a continuing and unique factor in Southern politics. The circumstance is based on the race issue, but in its long-term political and social implications it actually transcends that issue.

The Populist era raises a number of questions about the interaction of the two races in the South, both within the third party and in the larger society. It is widely believed, by no means merely by laymen, that after the failure of Reconstruction meaningful experiments with the social order were finished in the South and that the aspirations of blacks were decisively thwarted. The example of Grimes County suggests, however, the existence of a period of time—a decade perhaps, or a generation—when nascent forms of indigenous interracial activity struggled for life in at least parts of the old Confederacy. Was some opportunity missed and, if so, how? How widespread through the South, and the nation, was this opportunity?

The White Man's Union was organized and led by men who considered themselves the "best people" of the South. If this attitude was typical, major adjustments must be made in our understanding of precisely how, and for what reasons, the antebellum caste system, in altered form, was reinstitutionalized in Southern society a generation after the formal ending of slavery. Was the "red-neck" the source of atrocity, or was he swept along by other stronger currents? And what of the Populist role? To what extent was agrarian racial liberalism in Texas traceable to an overall philosophy within the third-party leadership? Through what intuition of self-interest did the radical organizers of the Farmers Alliance, the parent institution of the People's party, accept the political risks of public coalition with blacks? What were their hopes and fears, and where did they falter? And, finally, what does the substance of their effort tell us about the Democrats in the South and the Republicans in the North who opposed them?

Answers to these questions rest, in part, on detailed knowledge of such events as those in Grimes County, but they require more than compilations of local histories, just as they assuredly require more than cultural assessments based on novels, speeches, and party manifestoes considered apart from their organic milieu. These answers will not provide much of a synthesis—Populism was too diverse, too congregational, and too ideologically thin—but they should tell us more about the larger society that, along with the Populists, failed to erect the foundations for a multiracial society in the nineteenth century. As the inquiry proceeds, it should be remembered that Populism perished before developing a mature philosophy—on race, on money, or on socialism. One must generalize, therefore, not only from contradictory evidence but, more important, from incomplete evidence. An analogy, doubtless unfair, could be made with the plight that would face modern historians of Marxism had that movement been abruptly truncated at the time, say, of the Brussels Conference in 1903. Who could have predicted on the evidence available to that date the Stalinist reign of terror that evolved from the mature, victorious revolutionary party of 1917? By the same token sweeping generalizations about what Populist radicalism could have become are not only romantic but historically unsound.

It should be sufficient to observe that in the long post-Reconstruction period—a period not yet ended—during which the social order has been organized hierarchically along racial lines, Populism intruded as a brief, flickering light in parts of the South. For a time some white Southerners threw off the romanticism that has historically been a cover for the region's pessimism and ventured a larger, more hopeful view about the possibilities of man in a free society. Under duress and intimidation this public hope failed of persuasion at the ballot box; under terrorism it vanished completely.

The Grimes County story dramatically illustrates this failure, but in the insight it provides into the underlying politics of black disfranchisement and the achievement of a monolithic one-party political environment in the American South it is not unique. Other Populists in East Texas and across the South—white as well as black—died during the terrorism that preceded formal disfranchisement. In Texas the extraparliamentary institutions formed by white Democrats to help create the political climate for disfranchisement bore a variety of local names: the Citizens White Primary of Marion County; the Tax-Payers Union of Brazoria County; the Jaybird Democratic Association of Fort Bend County; and the White Man's Union of Wharton, Washington, Austin, Matagorda, Grimes, and other counties. The available historical material concerning each of these organizations comes largely from the founders themselves, or their descendants, reflecting an incipient or a mature oral tradition—one oral tradition. The secondary literature based on these accounts, including scholarly works used in graduate schools as well as primary and secondary textbooks, is correspondingly inadequate.

A surprising amount of uninterpreted material from violently partisan white supremacist sources has found its way into scholarly literature. One example from the Grimes experience pertains directly to the scholarly characterization of Negro political meetings during the Populist era. It is worth attention as an illustration of the impact of white supremacist modes of thought on modern scholarship. The sunup-to-sundown work routine of Southern farm labor obviously precluded daytime political meetings. Accordingly, Kennard, Haynes, and Carrington campaigned among their black constituents by holding political meetings in each of the towns and hamlets of the county at night. Democratic partisans termed these rallies "Owl Meetings" and characterized black Populist leaders as " 'fluence men." Drawing upon their own party's time-honored campaign technique with Negroes, Democrats further asserted that owl meetings were more concerned with sumptuous banquets and whisky than with politics. If partisans of white supremacy had difficulty finding reasons for white acceptance of political coalition with blacks, they were culturally incapable of ascribing reasons for Negro support of the third party to causes other than short-run benefits in terms of money and alcohol. The point is not that Democrats were always insincere in their descriptions (as white supremacists they were quite sincere), but that scholars have subsequently accepted such violently partisan accounts at face value. The darkly sinister picture of " 'fluence men" corrupting innocent blacks with whisky at surreptitious owl meetings served to justify, at least to outsiders, the use of terrorism as the ultimate campaign technique of Democratic interracial politics. This sequential recording of events has found its way into scholarly monographs that otherwise demonstrate no inherent hostility to the Populistic inclinations of Southern farmers, black or white. In *The People's Party in Texas* Roscoe Martin precedes his brief allusion to the White Man's Union with a resumé of owl meetings and " 'fluence men" that reflects in detail the bias of white supremacist sources. Other scholars writing broadly about Gilded Age politics have routinely drawn upon such monographs as Martin's, and by this process " 'fluence men" have materialized as an explanation of Negro political insurgency in the nineties. In the heat of local political combat, however, Democratic leaders often were able to face a wholly different set of facts in the course of persuading their followers, and the citizenry as a whole, to adjust to the necessity of terrorism. As the time approached for actual precinct campaigning in Grimes County in the autumn of 1900, the executive board of the White Man's Union published a notice of the Union's intentions, climaxed by a "fair distinct warning" to the county's Negro leadership. The statement is revealing—not only of the transformation visited upon normal campaign practices when they were viewed through the cultural presumptions of white supremacy but also of the dangers of uncritical acceptance of such perspectives by scholars relying upon monoracial sources. The notice read in part:

> The Union is largely composed of the best citizens of the county. . . . They are the tax payers, representing the worth, the patriotism, the intelligence, and the virtues of the county. . . . We are not fighting any political party or individuals, but only those who band together under any name, who seek to perpetuate negro rule in Grimes County. [Good citizens] are astounded at the manner in which the children's money has been expended. Colored teachers with fat salaries and totally incompetent have been appointed for political "fluence." Our white teachers, male and female, enjoy no such fat salaries as these colored politicians or these sweet colored girls. . . . One of the most corrupting practices in the past has been the system of Owl Meetings which has been in vogue for years. . . . This is the school and hot bed where the negro

> politician received his inspiration, and riding from one end of the county to the other as an apostle of his race, corrupting his own people who may be in the honest pathway of duty. We give fair warning that any effort to continue these Owl Meetings—by the appointment of special deputies sheriffs to organize and carry them on—will be prevented. No threat of shotguns will deter us from the discharge of this duty.

Even without recourse to other perspectives this view of the existing political situation in Grimes County contains serious internal contradictions. Black Populist leaders were "incompetent" but as "apostles of their race" they had been so effective that their efforts needed to be stopped. Black teachers were paid "fat salaries" solely for political reasons, but among those receiving such gross patronage were "sweet colored girls," who obviously were not conducting owl meetings. The assertion that black teachers were actually paid more than white teachers must be rejected out of hand. In addition to the compelling fact that such an arrangement would have constituted poor political behavior on the part of a third party strenuously endeavoring to hold a substantial portion of the white vote and the further reality that such expenditures were unnecessary since parity for blacks in itself would have represented a notable accomplishment in the eyes of Negro leaders, Democrats had access to the records of all county expenditures and no such charge was ever leveled, much less documented, at any other time during the Populist decade. Whites complained that Negro teachers received "too much," not that they received more than white teachers. In any case, it seems necessary only to observe that American political parties have routinely utilized night gatherings without having their opponents characterize them as owl meetings and that persons who benefited from incumbency were not presumed to be acting in sinister ways when they campaigned for their party's re-election. The only thing "special" about Garrett Scott's deputies was that some of them were black. Viewed as some sort of black abstraction Jim Kennard might appear convincing as a shadowy " 'fluence man," but as an intelligent and determined voice of the aspirations of Negro people he merits scholarly attention from perspectives not bounded by the horizons of those who murdered him. To an extent that is perhaps not fully appreciated, decades of monoracial scholarship in the South have left a number of Jim Kennards buried under stereotypes of one kind or another. They sometimes intrude anonymously as " 'fluence men," but they simply do not appear as people in books on Southern politics.

This circumstance suggests that not only the broad topic of interracial life and tension but the entire Southern experience culminated by disfranchisement needs to be tested by a methodology that brings both black and white sources to bear on the admittedly intricate problem of interpreting a free society that was not free. At all events, evidence continues to mount that monoracial scholarship, Northern and Southern, has exhausted whatever merit it possessed as an instrument of investigating the variegated past of the American people. The obvious rejoinder—that written black sources do not exist in meaningful quantity—cannot, of course, be explained away; at the same time, this condition suggests the utility of fresh attempts to devise investigatory techniques that offer the possibility of extracting usable historical material from oral sources. The example of the erroneous report in the Navasota *Examiner* of Morris Carrington's death illustrates, perhaps as well as any single piece of evidence, not only the dangers inherent in relying on such "primary sources" for details of interracial tension in the post-Reconstruction South but also the value of received oral traditions in correcting contemporary accounts. Nevertheless, the problem of evaluating such source material remains; white and black versions of the details of racial conflicts are wildly contradictory. When they are measured against other contemporary evidence, however, the interpretive problem becomes considerably less formidable; indeed, the task of penetrating the substance behind partisan contemporary accounts may be lessened through recourse to available oral sources, as I have attempted to demonstrate.

Since much of the *Realpolitik* of the South, from Reconstruction through the modern civil rights movement, rests on legal institutions that, in turn, rest on extralegal methods of intimidation, the sources of political reality may be found less in public debate than in the various forms of intimidation that matured in the region. However determined a historian may be to penetrate the legal forms to reach this extralegal underside of the political culture of the South he is, in our contemporary climate, blocked off from part of his sources by his skin color. For black scholars there are limits to the availability both of courthouse records in the rural South and of responsive white oral sources. There are corresponding limits to the information white scholars can gain from interviews in black communities. Here, then, is fertile ground for scholarly cooperation. Methods of achieving this cooperation need to be explored. In its fullest utilization the subject is not black history or Southern history but American history.

DISCUSSION QUESTIONS

1. How do you explain the support that black voters in Grimes County gave to Sheriff Garrett Scott?

2. Why did the Populists lose the county election of 1900 to the Democrats?

3. What does this case study tell you about the nature of the Populist movement?

5

THE CITY AS MORAL MENACE

PAUL S. BOYER

If there is such a thing as the "American Character," as some historians have alleged, at its core lies a profound sense of morality. From colonial days to the present, American leaders have preached the gospel that public and private moral behavior is essential to the progress of our society. Whatever the advertised goals, nineteenth- and twentieth-century reform campaigns, whether political, economic, social, or cultural in intent, pivoted on the moral betterment of individuals.

Nowhere did that betterment appear more crucial than in rapidly growing industrial cities. Americans traditionally had viewed their cities with suspicion, if not outright hostility. Early in the nineteenth century Thomas Jefferson had labeled cities "boils on the body politic." By century's close, a host of reformers outdid Jefferson in denouncing the great cities as cesspools of political corruption, physical decay, and moral degradation.

By analyzing a variety of urban reform crusades during the depression decade of the 1890s and the following years of so-called "progressivism," Boyer delineates the obvious and the more subtle moralism undergirding such efforts. Relying on either persuasion or coercion, or a mix of both, the critics tried to sanitize urban America. Whichever goal they championed—and most were remarkably single-minded in quest of *the* one campaign that would challenge and change urbanites—the reformers courted the muse of morality. Whether reformers hoped to slay Demon Rum, rehabilitate prostitutes, build play-grounds, clean up slums, purify government, or promote City Beautiful environmental planning practices, at heart they all pursued that most elusive of creatures—the moral American.

—STANLEY K. SCHULTZ

The Coercive Approach: The City as Menace to be Subdued In his 1913 autobiography, with San Juan Hill and the White House behind him, Theodore Roosevelt could still recall with relish the passionate moral atmosphere of 1895–1897 when, as William Strong's police commissioner, he had waged "relentless war" against the "bestial" rulers of "commercialized vice" in "huge, polyglot, pleasure-loving" New York. His only regret was that he had not ordered them horsewhipped! TR is the best known of many urban moral crusaders in this decade who adopted a hostile and coercive tone toward the people they wanted to reform. "It is a dreary old truth," wrote Roosevelt's friend Jacob Riis, "that those who would fight *for* the poor must *fight* the poor to do it." In combating the slum menace, commented the Reverend William S. Rainsford in 1891, "we are but scraping the soil with a harrow, while it needs a steam plow."

When in this coercive mood, the reformers of the 1890s tended to fall back with a vengeance upon the wicked-city stereotype. Unless countermeasures were quickly taken, declared Walter Vrooman, the rising generation of city dwellers would be transformed into "monsters." Charles Sheldon, despite his obvious desire to sympathize with the poor and unemployed, nevertheless described the urban slum as a "cesspool" full of a "vile, debauched . . . , impure, [and] besotted mass of humanity." When one of the reformers in *In His Steps* approaches a drunken prostitute with the intention of reclaiming her, she eyes the "miserable figure" with a feeling "she was afraid would grow into disgust." And in *Civilization's Inferno,* Benjamin Flower warned of slum uprisings that could turn the cities into military garrisons, and conjured up a vision of Boston's moral and social corruption taking the symbolic form of a plague. "Death was everywhere present. I beheld thousands of our people fleeing . . . , but scarcely had they left the city when the wires flashed . . . the fateful news that all cities and towns were quarantined against Boston . . . The plague, impalpable but terrible, seemed omnipresent."

Though often counterbalanced by more hopeful appraisals, this aggressively hostile note was seldom completely absent from this decade's urban-reform literature. Even the generally sunny Washington Gladden was touched by it. Although in *The Cosmopolis City Club* he condemned coercive law-and-order approaches to urban purification, in *Social Facts and Forces,* published two years later, he painted a picture of urban menace so grim as to justify almost any repressive response: "A horror of great darkness rests now upon our cities," he declared; a foe "more powerful and more dangerous" than any "army of invasion . . . is assaulting in overwhelming force the citadel of every one of our municipalities." The danger was "dire and imminent," he continued, and "the man who says that he is too busy to help in fighting these demons surely does not know what he is saying." The stakes were high, and the risks enormous, in this struggle. In *In His Steps*, as the reformers seek to rally the "Christian forces" of their city for the "battle against sin and corruption" (by pushing through a citywide prohibition referendum), they are gripped by a "sickening dread" and even "actual terror."

No urban moralist in this decade was more militantly coercive than Charles Parkhurst. "If it is proper for us to go around cleaning up after the devil," he cried, "it is proper for us to fight the devil"—and fight he did! In this encounter with a "jungle of teeth-gnashing brutes," there was no place for compromise or procedural niceties; it was a struggle to the death. "These things do not go by arithmetic, nor by a show of hands. A man who is held in the grip of the everlasting truth and is not afraid is a young army in himself . . . The incisive edge of bare-bladed righteousness will still cut."

Repressive moralism of the Parkhurst variety is not too far removed, psychologically, from the swift justice of the lynching party, and it is interesting to note that it was in 1887—the year after Haymarket—that California historian Hubert Howe Bancroft published his admiring history of the extralegal bands that had intimidated, expelled, and even hanged evildoers in San Francisco and other California boom towns a generation before. The "storms of public indignation" and "thunderbolts of justice" that had rained down upon California in the 1850s had represented "a grand triumph of the right," insisted Bancroft, contrasting orderly San Francisco of the vigilante period with the "outrages and riots" in New York and other cities. In their more militant phases, the moral reformers of the 1890s seemed to perceive themselves as the latter-day inheritors of this tradition of rough-and-ready social control by an outraged citizenry.

The appeal of the coercive approach in this decade was expressed, too, in the elaborate schemes of moral surveillance and control devised by some reformers. Antiprostitution and antigambling groups had experimented with such an approach in the antebellum period, and more recently the charity organization societies had attempted close moral oversight on a family-by-family basis. Now some would-be moral wardens began to muse about controlling the entire city population. Boston's moral tone could be vastly improved, wrote Unitarian minister Edward Everett Hale in 1890, if her 500 ministers—"the moral guides of this city"—would constitute themselves a "moral police" force, each exercising "personal supervision and responsibility" for a specified area of the city. Parkhurst's City Vigilance League, as we have seen, developed elaborate schemes for the secret investigation and repression of urban vice, and in *Civilization's Inferno*, Benjamin Flower exhorted all who shared his dismay over urban moral conditions to form local bands for "*concerted action.*" Although the effort of these groups might be in part "palliative" and "uplifting," wrote Flower—planning coffeehouses and free concerts in the slums, for example—their "vastly more important" work would be to probe the sources of urban poverty and vice and devise coordinated programs for eradicating them.

Common to all these schemes was the conviction that the "moral forces" of urban America must organize themselves. The City Vigilance League, wrote its secretary in 1895, intended to bring into "*coöperant relations*" that "*great company of earnest young citizens who believe in inoculating foreign-born residents with American impulses.*" Benjamin Flower insisted that his proposed urban reform bands must be tightly organized, with a clear-cut authority structure. To achieve "perfect discipline," he advised, each recruit should pledge "unquestioning obedience to the commands of the superior officers or the governing board"—a pledge "as binding as that of a military organization."

In *In His Steps*, the importance of organization is discussed from a somewhat different angle. Sheldon's middle-class characters—outwardly successful yet plagued by emotional sterility and the lack of strong social ties—resolve these problems by joining the "What Would Jesus Do?" fellowship. Although less authoritarian than Flower might have recommended, this band does give its members emotional warmth and "unspoken comradeship such as they had never known." Whenever they assemble, "a spirit of fellowship . . . flows freely between them," and long-dormant emotions begin to bubble and flow. Most of their meetings end in a good cry. Stronger than the bonds of church or family, the intensity of this close-knit little company becomes almost frightening: "Where would it lead them? . . . They had been living so long on their surface feelings that they had almost forgotten the deeper wells of life."

In insisting on the importance of organized, collective effort, the urban moral reformers of the 1890s revealed not only their sense of the awesomeness of the evils to be subdued but also a profound concern about the viability and spiritual well-being of the middle class. As Robert Wiebe, Richard Sennett, and others have noted, the urban middle class was in a disordered state as the nineteenth century closed. Old patterns of organization had broken down, and new ones were in the process of formation. The uneasiness generated by this situation pervades the literature of the period. Adna F. Weber, for example, in his 1899 study of urbanization, discussed the problem of "city degeneracy" not from the expected angle of the slums, but in terms of the "intellectual, mercantile, [and] employing class." In great detail he reported the theory of the German sociologist George Hansen that the dynamic of urban class mobility was itself "an instrument of social degeneration." In Weber's summary of Hansen's model, the urban elite is continually replenishing itself with fresh recruits who are initially full of "crude vigor and vitality" but who soon find the competitive pace so debilitating and disorienting that they fall by the wayside to join "the ever-increasing number of non-efficients"—and to be replaced by a fresh crop of ambitious newcomers from the hinterlands.

By banding together in a massive moral-control effort, suggested Sheldon and Flower, members of the urban middle class would themselves be strengthened against the kind of disintegrative and devitalizing pressures Hansen had described. This theme was as old as the Jacksonian era, but in the nineties it was vastly broadened. By organizing for a great urban moral purification drive, promised the reform spokesmen, the middle class could not only become a powerful weapon for eradicating vice; it would also achieve a greater degree of internal order and cohesion, and overcome the social isolation and emotional aridity that seemed always to plague it.

The Positive Environmentalist Approach: The City as Moral Habitat

While the coercive impulse loomed large in the 1890s, another strand interwoven with it would ultimately prove equally, if not more, influential: the attempt to elevate the moral character of city dwellers by transforming the physical conditions of their lives. If the brittle moralism of the coercive reformers harks back to the early nineteenth century, the subtler arguments of the environmentalists are recognizably modern. The idea of moral reform through environmental betterment dates to the mid-nineteenth century, but it had always been subordinated to other, more direct strategies. Now, as the century ended, the environmentalist approach began to come into its own. The author of an *Arena* article entitled "Morality and Environment" summed up the central argument: the child born and bred in a slum environment "has no chance but to become wicked. He is not free to choose good from evil . . . [A]ny practical philanthropist . . . will tell you how slight the chances are for children to be virtuous who grow up in that atmosphere."

Slums meant tenements, and in the 1890s a vigorous tenement-reform movement in New York State and elsewhere reflected not only concern about the physical discomforts and public-health hazards of slum overcrowding but its moral consequences as well—an issue Dr. John H. Griscom had raised as early as 1845 in *The Sanitary Condition of the Laboring Population of New York*. But upgrading the tenements was only a preliminary step. The larger task was to replace the demoralizing detritus of years of urban growth with a consciously planned urban environment. The reformers of the 1890s pursued this overall goal on a variety of fronts, including the development of parks and playgrounds; public baths; children's clubs; gymns and swimming pools; and facilities for concerts, lectures, and art exhibits. Slum bathhouses, argued a New York State Tenement House Committee in 1895, would have a "favorable effect . . . upon character; tending to self-respect and decency of life"; more parks and playgrounds, agreed Mayor William Strong's Small Parks Advisory Committee (chaired by the ubiquitous Jacob Riis), would promote both the physical well-being and the "moral health" of the poor; free open-air concerts, suggested Washington Gladden, would counteract the "tendencies to vulgarity and dissipation and immorality" in the cities.

As the foregoing suggests, urban leisure was a special concern of these environmental moralists. In *Civilization's Inferno,* Benjamin Flower's dismay over the few pleasures of slum life was nearly as great as his distress over the hardships. In a saloon in an immigrant section of Boston, he wrote disapprovingly, he had spotted "a company of young men and girls, laughing hilariously over their liquor." Such amusements, Flower pontificated, were actually "counterfeit coins; bearing small resemblance to true enjoyment, whose influence is ever refining and uplifting." Most of the commercialized pleasure available in the city, he added, bore "precisely the relation to its victim that the candle does to the moth." In place of such hellholes, Flower concluded, alternatives must be devised that would not only entertain but also help their patrons to be "pure, just, and noble."

Again in common with the urban moral reformers of earlier decades, the environmentalists of the 1890s looked especially to the children. Benjamin Flower urged the formation of boys' and girls' clubs in which stories embodying "high ideals"; songs emphasizing the "noblest sentiments"; and, of course, the personal example of the club leaders would help impressionable city children avoid vice as a "loathsome contagion" and "give them what, in the nature of things, they have never before enjoyed—correct ideas and a new point of view." The ideas thus implanted in youthful minds would "silently work themselves into the hearts and homes of the unfortunates," Flower added, "becoming a wonderful factor in many lives." (Old-timers who remembered the arguments advanced for urban Sunday schools in the 1830s must have experienced a strong sense of déjà vu upon reading Flower's proposals in 1893!)

One of the more articulate and influential champions of environmental reform in this decade was Josiah Quincy, mayor of Boston from 1895 to 1899. Believing that the duty of a city was to "promote the civilization, in the fullest sense of the word, of all its citizens," Quincy insisted that the playgrounds, bathhouses, swimming pools, gymns, and free concerts he had introduced in Boston's poorer districts represented powerful instruments for "the social and moral development of the masses of the people." Documenting his claim, Quincy asserted that youths who patronized the public swimming pools and gymns were proving "less likely to fall into vicious ways"; that areas around municipal bathhouses had seen a "decrease of juvenile disorder"; and that at city-sponsored concerts attracting as many as 10,000 people, "a very few policemen" had been "quite sufficient to prevent disorder."

Few areas of urban environmental betterment escaped the notice of these late–Gilded Age reformers, and always the moral-control aspect loomed large. Even improved refuse collection (insisted George E. Waring, Jr., street-cleaning commissioner during Mayor Strong's reform administration in New York) would create a more attractive city that would in turn inspire civic loyalty, encourage people to place the public interest above personal concerns, and ultimately raise the moral tone of city life. The slum child who joined a "Juvenile Street Cleaning League," Waring believed, was more likely "to grow up with an increased love for his city" and become "the sturdy, upright citizen which the times demand." Perhaps Benjamin Flower best summed up the larger vision underlying all these efforts and pronouncements. A transformed urban environment, he declared, would give "new and joyous significance" to the lives of multitudes "long exiled from joy, gladness, and comfort." Surely the moral dividends of such a change—in transformed lives and uplifted spirits—could not fail to be enormous!

For all their differences of rhetoric and strategy, most urban reformers of this decade saw the coercive and the environmentalist approaches as simply alternative paths to the same destination. Jacob Riis admired Theodore Roosevelt's repressive stance toward urban vice, and Roosevelt praised Riis's slum playgrounds for taking children from the streets and preventing them from "growing up toughs." Throughout *In His Steps*, Charles Sheldon propagandizes for prohibition—the quintessential coercive reform—while simultaneously advocating more positive environmental reforms such as cooking schools and musical institutes in the slums.

This ambivalence as to strategy found its counterpart in the fluctuating moods of these reformers as they contemplated the urban situation. Sometimes they saw it in the bleakest possible terms, sometimes much more hopefully—and often they expressed both viewpoints simultaneously. "To the superficial observer the outlook may appear discouraging," wrote Walter Vrooman, but "if we probe more deeply we can rest assured of final triumph."

Washington Gladden, despite his fears of an oncoming Armageddon between the forces of good and evil in the city, could also portray urbanization much more hopefully as a manifestation of a divine impulse drawing men together. The Apostle John displayed a "true insight," Gladden declared, when in the Apocalypse he portrayed a "glorified humanity dwelling in a city." In *Civilization's Inferno,* Benjamin Flower's nightmarish fantasy of a Boston decimated by plague is quickly supplanted by a gleaming vision in which vice-ridden slums have been replaced by beautiful, airy apartments and "temple-like" community centers complete with playgrounds, gardens, swimming pools, and lecture halls where "the wonders of other lands and ages" are unfolded with the aid of a "magnificent stereopticon."

For those drawn to this vision of a redeemed city, yet dismayed and discouraged by the actual urban reality, the 1893 World's Columbian Exposition in Chicago—the great "White City"—seemed a portent of enormous significance. "If things looked dark in New York," wrote William Rainsford, "there was another city whose white, classic loveliness stood, for one summer . . . I first saw that city of the ideal as the sun sank behind it . . . , and the utter beauty of it entered my soul."

The World's Fair site, an unpromising swamp on Chicago's lakefront transformed through the efforts of landscaper Frederick Law Olmsted and scores of architects under the general direction of Daniel H. Burnham, included an imposing array of exhibition halls around a majestic reflecting pool and promenade—the "Court of Honor." The overall effect struck millions of visitors with something like religious awe. Transmitted everywhere by photographs, newspaper and magazine stories, and word-of-mouth accounts, the impressive beauty of this ephemeral creation sank deep into the nation's consciousness. "A 'dream city' men called it then," wrote city planner Charles Mulford Robinson a decade later, "but the dream has outlived all else."

For our urban reformers, of course, the fair's moral significance outweighed even its aesthetic satisfactions. A more orderly and uplifting urban environment *could* be achieved, with impressive effects upon human behavior. The moral destiny of a city *could* be influenced by its physical character! "Order reigned everywhere," William Rainsford went on; ". . . no boisterousness, no unseemly merriment. It seemed as though the beauty of the place brought gentleness, happiness, and self-respect to its visitors."

This note was sounded over and over again in contemporary accounts of the fair. "No great multitude of people ever . . . showed more love of order," marveled John C. Adams in the *New England Magazine.* "The restraint and discipline were remarkable," agreed another observer. "Courtiers in . . . Versailles or Fontainebleau could not have been more deferential and observant of the decorum of the place and occasion than these obscure and anonymous myriads of unknown laborers . . . [I]n the presence of the ignorance, vice, poverty, misery, and folly of modern society, . . . pessimism seems the only creed; but doubt is banished here."

The World's Fair, in short, brought a heartening message to the prophets of urban awakening in the 1890s. "The White City . . . is not an apotheosis," insisted a writer in *Cosmopolitan*, "it is a hope." And what was that hope? John C. Adams well summed it up: "The great White City has disappeared," he wrote after the fair's close. "But . . . we shall yet see springing into being throughout the land cities which shall embody in permanent form [its] dignified municipal ideals."

In reading such passages, one is reminded of Robert Wiebe's description of the emotional stance of many reformers in this Depression decade: "Accepting the current signs of disruption, even relishing them in a certain grim fashion, they described an enveloping moral unity to come as the very essence of their visions. In other words, they replaced threats with promise." As Wiebe's observation suggests, the exalted hopes aroused by the White City did not resolve—indeed, they probably exacerbated—the ambivalence with which reformers contemplated the implications of urbanization. Lofty dreams continually gave way to deep apprehension. The tensions inherent in such uncertainty are painfully evident in the effort of the Reverend Lyman Abbott to sum up the moral import of the "bright, beautiful, but awful city": "On the one hand, the city stands for all that is evil—a city that is full of devils, foul and corrupting; and, on the other hand, the city stands for all that is noble, full of the glory of God, and shining with a clear and brilliant light." In terms of moral-reform strategy, the contradictory impulses of the decade were distilled in an 1896 article in the *Congregationalist:* a city, it declared, was "something at once to be feared and loved, to be served and mastered."

But when the afflatus was on them, these urban reformers saw themselves as standing on Mount Pisgah, viewing the Promised Land—a purified, ennobled urban America—that their successors would finally win. "What we have done so far has been practically nothing in actual achievement," wrote one of them in 1902, "but it has raised a little corner of the curtain, given us a glimpse, a foretaste, of what can be done. . . .

COMMON CONCERNS, DIVERGENT STRATEGIES

One century yielded to another, and the flow of humanity cityward continued. In the census of 1920, with sixty-eight cities exceeding the 100,000 figure, America's urban population for the first time surpassed the symbolic 50 percent mark. In the first two decades of the new century, New York City grew by 2.2 million, Chicago by 1 million, Detroit by 425,000—and so on down the roster of established urban giants and fast-growing contenders. Even in the South (historically a laggard in urbanization), though the great surge still lay ahead, the early twentieth century saw a quickened pace of city growth. Foreign immigration continued to account for a large share of this expansion. After a dip in the 1890s, immigration soared to unprecedented levels in these years—over 17 million from 1900 to 1917, with the single-year total exceeding 1 million for the first time in 1905—and most of these millions remained in the cities. By 1920, over 80 percent of all Russian, Irish, Italian, and Polish-born people in the United States were urban residents. Only war and the Immigration Act of 1924 would finally stem the tide.

With such statistics as a backdrop, the familiar warnings persisted. Josiah Strong returned to the fray with *The Challenge of the City* (1907), giving his chapters such lugubrious titles as "The Modern City as Menace to State and Nation," and quoting Shelley's epigram: "Hell is a city much like London." Even those who took a less alarmist view agreed that urban growth was a looming social reality whose full implications America had not yet begun to grasp. The problem of the city, declared the Boston sociologist Frank Parsons, in 1899, was "the problem of civilization." William B. Munro, professor of government at Harvard, agreed that cities were becoming the "controlling factor" in American life. "The modern city marks an epoch in our civilization," wrote Frederic Howe, adviser to Mayor Tom Johnson of Cleveland, in 1906; "Through it, a new society has been created."

As this conviction deepened, the urban social-control impulse, its roots lying deep in the past, assumed fresh urgency. "How to reach the heart of the city and to change its life is, indeed, the question of questions," declared the American Methodist bishops as the new century dawned. William Munro quoted with approval Henry Drummond's challenging aphorism, "He who makes the city makes the world."

Influenced by such battle cries, a large and diverse company of men and women sought a role in shaping the urban moral order. In part, their energies flowed into channels already explored in earlier chapters. More typically, however, they turned to new approaches grounded in assumptions and strategies that had found inchoate expression in the intense urban reform climate of the 1890s.

Whereas the earlier voluntarist movements had concentrated on influencing individuals or families, those of the Progressive era were based on the conviction that the moral destiny of the city would be most decisively influenced through broad programs utilizing a full panoply of governmental power and aimed at a fundamental restructuring of the urban environment.

This central environmentalist assumption, however, led in two radically different directions. The divergent and even contradictory approaches that in the 1890s had coexisted under the capacious rhetorical umbrella of "urban awakening" now widened into two quite distinct branches of reform activity. On one hand, some reformers—"negative environmentalists," we might call them—pursued a coercive and moralistic approach, concentrating on eradicating two institutions that for them had come to epitomize urban moral and social breakdown: the brothel and the saloon. The other category of reformers—the "positive environmentalists"—took their cue from the more hopeful and visionary side of the late-nineteenth-century urban reformism. Their goal was to create in the city the kind of physical environment that would gently but irresistibly mold a population of cultivated, moral, and socially responsible city dwellers.

Despite profound differences, however, these two approaches shared certain fundamental moral-control purposes: the elevation of character, the inculcation of a "higher" standard of individual behavior, the placing of social duty above private desire, the re-creation of the urban masses in the reformers' own image. At this basic level, both remained firmly linked to an urban social-control tradition extending back to the Jacksonian period. . . .

Moralism and Expertise: The Links between the Great Coercive Crusades and Progressivism Historians have engaged in a lively debate over whether prohibition—and, by implication, the antiprostitution crusade—should be included within the canon of legitimate Progressive reforms. Writing in 1955, Richard Hofstadter said no. Prohibition, he contended, was "a ludicrous caricature of the reforming impulse"—a "pinched, parochial substitute" for genuine reform, imposed by spiteful rural folk upon the more tolerant and urbane cities. In the same vein, Egal Feldman in 1967 described the coercive aspects of the antiprostitution crusade as "irrational, evangelical, uncompromising, and completely divorced from the humanitarianism of the early twentieth century." Other historians have challenged this thesis. Demonstrating the close connections—in terms of personnel, mutual affirmations of support, and overlapping organizational commitments—that can be established between the moral-control crusades and other strands of progressivism, they argue that the former must be considered an authentic expression of the broader Progressive impulse.

Interestingly, the Progressives themselves had trouble reaching a consensus on this question. Although some reformers and ideologues welcomed the prohibition and antiprostitution campaigns, other denied any kinship between what *they* stood for and the coercive moral-control crusades. Walter Lippmann, for example, ridiculed the "raucous purity" of some antivice campaigners, and Charles A. Beard in 1912 criticized the "moral enthusiasts" who were "pushing through legislation which they are not willing to uphold by concentrated and persistent action." Herbert Croly in *The Promise of American Life* declared that reformers who functioned merely as "moral protestants and purifiers'' were engaged in a fundamentally "misdirected effort." Only "personal self-stultification," he insisted, could result from such an "illiberal puritanism." True reform, Croly characteristically added, involved "an intellectual as well as a moral challenge."

The answer depends in large part, of course, on where one looks on the Progressive spectrum and, indeed, on how one defines progressivism, and that, as Peter Filene has reminded us, can be a difficult task. But one trait common to most reformers of these years—and one which helped establish a bond between the coercive reformers and other Progressives—was an infinite capacity for moral indignation. For Progressives of all stripes, as for their predecessors in the 1890s, questions of social injustice, corporate wrongdoing, governmental corruption, and personal morality were inextricably linked. Almost every Progressive cause had its moral dimension; almost every condition Progressives set out to change was seen as contributing to a debilitating social environment that made it easier for people to go wrong and harder for them to go right. Child labor and the exploitation of women workers were evil not only because they were physically harmful, but also because they stunted the moral and spiritual development of their victims. (Society had the right to limit the hours of women in industry, Louis D. Brandeis argued before the United States Supreme Court in 1908, because the fatigue of long hours was undermining their moral fiber and driving them to "alcoholic stimulants and other excesses.") Urban graft and misgovernment were evil not only because they wasted taxpayers' money but also because they debased the moral climate of the city. ("The influence and example of bad municipal government . . . , of public servants dishonest with impunity and profit," cried an officer of the National Municipal League in 1904, echoing his reform predecessors of the Gilded Age, "constitutes a disease against which we have greater need of a quarantine than we ever had against yellow fever.") As Stanley K. Schultz has written of progressivism's journalistic advance guard the muckrakers, their writings often "assumed the nature of a moral crusade, . . . because ultimately their search was a moral endeavor."

The moral substratum of progressivism is heavily underscored in the autobiography of Frederic C. Howe, in many respects a prototypical Progressive, in which he describes his intensely evangelical upbringing and its shaping influence on his later reform career: "Physical escape from the embraces of evangelical religion did not mean moral escape. From that religion my reason was never emancipated. By it I was conformed to my generation and made to share its moral standards and ideals . . . Early assumptions as to virtue and vice, goodness and evil remained in my mind long after I had tried to discard them. This is, I think, the most characteristic influence of my generation."

Some historians have drawn sharp distinctions between progressivism's various facets, opposing the economic and political reforms to those that were explicitly moralistic. Such an approach, if too literally applied, does violence to the powerful moral thrust underlying *all* these reforms. For the Progressives, society had the right—indeed the duty!—to intervene at *any* point where the well-being of its members was threatened, since every such threat had its moral aspect. A 1914 article in a reform journal edited by Josiah Strong and W. D. P. Bliss put the matter plainly: "We are no longer frightened by that ancient bogy—'paternalism in government.' We affirm boldly, it is the business of government to be just that—paternal . . . *Nothing human can be foreign to a true government.*"

Within this intensely moralistic ambience, it was easy to see the coercive social-control crusades as simply one piece in the larger reform mosaic. In *The Shame of the Cities* (1904), for example, muckraker Lincoln Steffens frequently called attention to organized gambling and prostitution as byproducts of municipal political corruption. Similarly, a leading San Francisco Progressive, newspaper editor Fremont Older, in fighting boss Abraham Ruef in 1907–1909, revealed many seamy details of Ruef's involvement with organized vice.

Those who were seeking to rid urban America of these vices, for their part, never doubted that they were in the mainstream of the era's broader reform current. "We are tired of poverty, of squalor, of ignorance . . . , of the wretchedness of women and the degradation of men," wrote a prohibition leader in 1908. "Our hearts bleed when we look upon the misery of child life." Convinced that intolerable conditions of work and habitation were driving men into the saloons and women into the streets, they supported such Progressive reforms as wage-and-hour laws, tenement codes, and factory-safety legislation. "Is it any wonder," asked the Chicago Vice Commission rhetorically, "that a tempted girl who receives only six dollars per week working with her hands sells her body for twenty-five dollars per week when she learns there is a demand for it and men are willing to pay the price?"

A second important respect in which the coercive moral reformers were closely attuned to the broader Progressive impulse was in their reliance on statistics, sociological investigation, and "objective" social analysis to buttress their cause—a strategy characteristic of many otherwise quite disparate Progressive reforms. For the antisaloon and antiprostitution forces, this represented a significant shift from earlier approaches. Through much of the Gilded Age, the temperance and social purity enthusiasts had concentrated on moral appeals to the individual, assuming that they and the objects of their benevolent attention shared, at some level, a common body of values and standards. (There were exceptions to this personalistic approach—the state drives to raise the legal age of consent, the quadrennial electoral campaigns of the Prohibition party—but in general the personal moral appeal was the preferred strategy.)

By the end of the century, as the old assumptions faded, overtly moralistic personal appeals were being supplanted by a more generalized emphasis on the reformers' technical expertise and superior factual grasp of urban issues. Moral reform must be rooted in careful investigation and social analysis, insisted Benjamin Flower in *Civilization's Inferno.* "Mere sentimentality will not answer. We must have incontrovertible data upon which to base our arguments." The first step of a prestigious Committee of Fifty for the Investigation of the Liquor Problem formed in New York City in 1893 was to "secure a body of facts which may serve as a basis for intelligent public and private actions." Even the WCTU established a Department of Scientific Temperance Instruction that lobbied for alcohol-education programs in the public schools.

In the Progressive years this shift accelerated and the personalistic approach was largely abandoned. Now, by contrast, intemperance and sexual deviation came to be viewed less as personal failings than as products of an urban environment that needed to be purified—by force of law if necessary. The Chicago Vice Commission expressed the prevailing view when it dismissed as "naive" those who looked for the sources of prostitution in the individual prostitute's flaws of character. The emphasis was now on eliminating from the urban environment those *institutions* that undermined individual moral resistence—especially the saloon and the brothel.

With this development, the "scientific" aura of urban moral reform intensified. A *Scientific Temperance Journal* was established in Boston in 1906 by Cora Frances Stoddard. Muckraking journalists like George Kibbe Turner marshaled facts, statistics, dates, and names to buttress their indictment of the saloon, and the antiprostitution crusaders similarly strove for a tone of objective expertise as remote as possible from the thundering moral denunciations of earlier years. Indeed, in a number of cities the antiprostitution groups called themselves "Morals Efficiency Commissions." The 1902 report of New York's Committee of Fifteen exuded the scholarly aura appropriate to what its secretary called in the preface "a valuable scientific contribution," and *The Social Evil in Chicago,* a forbiddingly dry compendium of charts, statistics, appendixes, medical data, and analyses of interviews with 2,420 prostitutes, was similarly described by its sponsors as a "scientific study" based on the findings of "experts and trained investigators. . . ."

To be sure, these reforms ultimately depended on the moral energy of Protestant America, and denominational agencies like the Methodist Board of Temperance and Morals played an important role in rallying support. Yet appeals to the evangelical moral code do not figure strongly in either the prohibition or the antiprostitution movements, and the organizations promoting these reforms were not by any means overweighed with clergymen. The top ASL men were ministers, to be sure, but during the prohibition struggle they functioned almost entirely as secularized managers, lobbyists, and propagandists rather than as latter-day Jeremiahs pronouncing God's judgment on the saloon. The lower echelons of ASL administration were even more completely secular. The organization's general superintendent, Purley A. Baker, set the tone. "The narrow, acrimonious and emotional appeal is giving way," he declared in 1915, "to a rational, determined conviction that the [liquor] traffic . . . has no rightful place in our modern civilization."

The antiprostitution movement, despite the prominence of an occasional cleric like Chicago's Dean Sumner, was even more completely divorced from the Protestant establishment. Indeed, by around 1910, antivice zealots among the clergy had become a distinct embarrassment. The Chicago Vice Commission roundly condemned an evangelist who was conducting prayer meetings in front of the city's leading brothels. An *Arena* writer in 1909 urged that the cause be pursued "sanely and scientifically" and not through " 'moral' rant from the pulpits." The local vice commissions usually had only token ministerial representation, and many delegated the actual investigative work to the team of New York–based researchers originally put together by George Kneeland for the Committee of Fifteen. As an older generation of urban moral reformers passed from the scene, the movement came to exude more of the aura of the laboratory, law library, and university lecture hall than the pulpit.

Indeed, the very shift in terminology in the antiprostitution movement, from "social *purity*" to "social *hygiene*," is significant. The entire urban moral-control effort in these years was suffused with public-health terminology and rhetoric. A writer in *Social Hygiene* in 1917 predicted that New Orleans would soon conquer prostitution just as she had eradicated yellow fever, and in *The Challenge of the City*, Josiah Strong suggested that the polluters of the city's "moral atmosphere" should be considered as deadly as the "vermin of an Egyptian plague." In Boston, the Watch and Ward Society won praise in these years from Harvard professor Francis G. Peabody for "unobtrusively working underground, guarding us from the pestiferous evil which at any time may come up into our faces, into our homes, into our children's lives." Picking up on these cues, the Watch and Ward, like similar moral-control agencies elsewhere, increasingly defined its mission in public-health terms. "The old idea of 'charity' . . . has gradually given way to a larger conception," it declared in 1915, "to prevent . . . the moral diseases which lead to misery and crime."

The fullest elaboration of the public-health analogy in this period was probably that offered by the Massachusetts prohibitionist Newton M. Hall in *Civic Righteousness and Civic Pride* (1914). "The moral evil of the community does not remain in the foul pools in which it is bred," he wrote. "A moral miasma arises from those pools, and . . . enters not the poorest homes of the city alone, but the most carefully guarded, and leaves its trail of sorrow and despair . . . Why should the community have any more sympathy for the saloon . . . than . . . for a typhoid-breeding pool of filthy water, . . . a swarm of deadly mosquitoes, or . . . a nest of rats infected with the bubonic plague?" For Hall, the logic of the analogy was irresistible: "Cut off the impure water and the typhoid epidemic is conquered"; destroy the saloon and the urban "moral epidemic" would vanish.

The ubiquitous medical terminology in the utterances of these reformers had more than rhetorical significance, because recent advances in venereal disease research had made clear the ravages of the disease's advanced stages, the process of transmission, and the clear link with sexual promiscuity. For the antiprostitution reformers, the moral implications of these findings were no less important than the medical. "In all previous efforts to safeguard the morality of youth," wrote one reformer in *Social Hygiene*, "the ethical barrier was alone available," and "the situation seemed . . . hopeless"; now, happily, the "ethical ideal" could be "grounded upon the most convincing facts." Jane Addams welcomed these findings as a powerful force in the emergence of a "new conscience" on prostitution, and Dr. Prince A. Morrow expressed his pleasure that "punishment for sexual sin" no longer need be "reserved for the hereafter."

Through lectures, tracts, posters, exhibits, and graphic films, the antiprostitution reformers warned of promiscuity's grim consequences—for the wrongdoer and his innocent progeny alike. The Chicago Vice Commission vividly spelled out VD's long-range effects—"the blinded eyes of little babes, the twisted limbs of deformed children, degradation, physical rot and mental decay"—and demanded that every brothel be quarantined forthwith as a "house of contagious disease." The control of sexual expression, in short, was simply another of the social constraints essential to modern urban life. Just as "the storage of gasoline and other combustibles is controlled by the city," argued the Louisville Vice Commission, so dance halls and other "vice combustibles" had to be "carefully watched and controlled. . . ."

POSITIVE ENVIRONMENTALISM

THE IDEOLOGICAL UNDERPINNINGS

It was 1914, and Newton D. Baker had a problem. He had been mayor of Cleveland for two years, and among such reform objectives as lower transit fares, municipal ownership of utilities, and the other familiar goals of municipal progressivism was the desire to achieve in this great industrial city, with its diverse immigrant population, at least an approximation of the moral order he remembered from his own West Virginia boyhood.

Focusing his attention on Cleveland's numerous dance halls, with their drunkenness, sexual laxity, and general ribaldry, he had first tried the familiar approach: denunciation and repression. But police surveillance, arrests, and padlocking all proved ineffective. The dance halls seemed only to grow more popular and more brazen.

In desperation, Baker tried a different tack. Instead of fighting the dance halls head-on, he opened several municipal dance pavilions in the city parks, seeing to it that they were attractive, well lit, alcohol-free, and "chaperoned by carefully selected men and women." Soon the disreputable private establishments were standing practically empty, outdistanced by the more wholesome publicly sponsored alternative. Early in 1918, Baker took time from his massive duties as secretary of war to recount this instructive experience of the American Social Hygiene Association.

For Baker, as for many of his generation, the lesson was clear: the most promising long-range strategy of urban moral control was not repression but a more subtle and complex process of influencing behavior and molding character through a transformed, consciously planned urban environment. Growing from the positive-environmentalist initiatives of the 1890s, this conviction found expression not only in muncipally sponsored amusements like Baker's dance pavilions but also in tenement reform, in park and playground development, in civic pageants and municipal art, and ultimately in the city-planning movement. While the crusades against the saloon and the brothel have traditionally shaped our image of urban moral reform in the Progressive era, these other efforts had an important moral-control dimension as well.

The positive environmentalists often shared the underlying moral assumptions of the coercive crusaders, but they differed fundamentally on basic strategy. Their aim (as they constantly stressed), was not to destroy urban vice through denunciatory rhetoric or legal repression, but by creating the kind of city where objectionable patterns of behavior, finding no nurture, would gradually wither away. In an influential 1904 work, *The American City,* Delos F. Wilcox yielded to no one in portraying urban immorality and vice as dire social threats "preying upon the vitals of municipal democracy," but with equal firmness he rejected coercive solutions to the problem. Instead of "repression" and "puritanic legislation," he called for "other and more effective weapons of warfare" to create in city dwellers "a wider social consciousness, a heartier spirit of cooperation, [and] a keener sense of responsibility to the future."

Even the coercive moral reformers, implicitly conceding the drawbacks of their approach, occasionally endorsed positive environmentalist strategies. In *Substitutes for the Saloon*, for example, Raymond Calkins insisted that the answer to the saloon and other urban vices did not lie in forcing the masses into a rigid moral straitjacket. Instead, he argued, reformers must study the social needs met by the saloon, the dance hall, and so forth, and develop alternatives to meet those needs without the evil side effects. Among Calkins's "substitutes" were parks, playgrounds, municipal theaters, and "temperance saloons" offering camaraderie but not alcohol. (In one experimental temperance saloon, Calkins reported hopefully in 1919, the patrons were as convivial as ever, but instead of beer mugs at their tables, one now saw "milk chocolate, a peanut candy bar, or perhaps a soda or iced drink.") As such changes were effected in the city, Calkins concluded, "the coarser elements of the environment" would "exert a gradually diminishing influence."

Among the antiprostitution crusaders, the Louisville Vice Commission contended that one way to produce "vice-proof or vice resisting young people" was to encourage "the wholesome use of their leisure hours." Similarly, Hartford's vice investigators, noting that one thoroughfare had been "cleansed of prostitutes in 1908 when it was broadened [and] paved," urged further environmental improvements as a means toward their city's moral purification. From its founding in 1914, the American Social Hygiene Association insisted that "remedial and constructive measures" were as important in the antiprostitution struggle as legal repression. "Legislation is essential . . . , but we must go deeper," argued an ASHA spokesman. "The ideal is to so mould the interests, activities, and organized volitions of youth, that it will put the brothel out of business through lack of patronage."

The conviction that the most enduring moral advance would come through a gradual reshaping and enrichment of the urban environment found strong support among Social Gospel spokesmen in these years. In the ethical realm, argued Walter Rauschenbusch in *Christianity and the Social Crisis* (1907), "physical compulsion" was "impotent" unless it rested upon a "diffused, spontaneous moral impulse in the community." The law might represent the "stiff skeleton of public morality," but the "finer tissues . . . must be deposited by other forces." Even Josiah Strong, who continued to paint the urban menace in lurid colors, now concluded that the challenge was not to engage urban vice in frontal combat through "Draconian law," but to nurture the "awakening social conscience" of the urban masses and thereby "overcome evil with good."

Among settlement leaders, Jane Addams emerged as a persuasive champion of the environmentalist outlook—an outlook which grew naturally from the settlements' emphasis on the role of environmental factors in shaping the lives of the immigrant masses. Although in *The*

Spirit of Youth and the City Streets (1909) and other writings of the period Addams made no effort to conceal her distaste for the moral ambience of the modern city with its "vicious excitements and trivial amusements," she rejected preurban modes of social control as "totally unsuited to modern city conditions." If public authorities were to "intelligently foster social morality," they must offer municipally sponsored alternatives to the exploitative and debasing commercial amusements. Warming to her theme, Addams described a transformed city in which publicly supported recreational and leisure activities would become the social cement of a cohesive urban community. "We are only beginning to understand," she wrote, "what might be done through the festival, the street procession, the band of marching musicians, orchestral music in public squares or parks." In the urban future she envisioned, the stroller in the city would encounter not the jangling distraction of raucous commercialized entertainment, but "spontaneous laughter, snatches of lyric song, the recovered forms of old dances, and the traditional rondels of merry games." The "delicious sensation to be found in a swimming pool" would surely outweigh the temptation "to play craps in a foul and stuffy alley, even with the unnatural excitement which gambling offers."

In her 1912 work on prostitution, *A New Conscience and an Ancient Evil,* despite a fleeting nostalgia for the days when the village gossip kept people in line, Addams conceded that the new social reality demanded a rethinking of the entire question of urban morality. The "new conscience" she envisioned was rooted not in the coercive enforcement of a rigid moral code but in a gradually maturing popular awareness that the imperatives of urban life required the subordination of individual gratification to the larger social good. "Fortunately . . . for our moral progress. . . , a new form of social control is slowly establishing itself. . . . This new and more vigorous development. . . , while reflecting something of that wholesome fear of public opinion which the intimacies of a small community maintain, is much more closely allied to the old communal restraints and mutual protections to which the human will first yielded." This new urban moral consciousness could not be artificially imposed, Addams insisted; it would emerge only slowly, through careful nurture, from sources within individual city dwellers. In contrast to "the forced submission that characterized the older forms of social restraint," the "new control" would be "based upon the voluntary cooperation of self-directed individuals. . . ."

POSITIVE ENVIRONMENTALISM IN ACTION

Jacob Riis was, above all, a journalist; he knew the value of the dramatic and the concrete. Thus, when he sought to sum up the complex reality of New York's immigrant slums in his 1890 exposé *How the Other Half Lives*, he chose a single vivid example—Mulberry Bend near the infamous Five Points on the Lower East Side—and devoted an entire chapter to this "foul core of New York's slums."

It was, therefore, of considerable symbolic significance when the municipal authorities in 1894 announced plans to raze the moldering tenements and criminal-infested alleys of Mulberry Bend and create a *park* in their place. Degeneracy and vice would yield to sunlight an fresh air; profanity and drunken brawling to the laughter of children at play! Where generations of tract distributors, Sunday school teachers, city missionaries, Children's Aid agents, and friendly visitors had trudged on their weary rounds of uplift, trees and green grass would flourish.

Bureaucratic delays held things up, but then tragedy struck: a collapsing wall in an abandoned building in the district Riis had made famous killed several children who had been playing inside. Here was epitomized the heartlessness of the urban environment, snuffing out not only the moral spark but now even the very lives of its innocent victims. The plans were pushed with fresh urgency, and by 1897 Mulberry Bend had, indeed, become a park.

Such transformations were taking place in cities all over the country in the late nineteenth and early twentieth centuries, as Progressive reformers pursued the practical implications of the ideas explored in the last chapter. The most important of these positive-environmentalist efforts—tenement reform, the park and playground movements, and city planning—are familiar enough in broad outline. But viewed from the perspective of the larger urban moral-control movement, they take on interesting new dimensions and reveal some unexpected interconnections. Indeed, they might be viewed as a set of concentric circles, moving outward from the tenement all the way to the city itself, each circle in turn involving an enlarged conception of the scope of the environmentalist approach and its potential for reshaping the urban moral climate. . . .

The conviction that an intimate link existed between a city's physical appearance and its moral state—and that America's cities were sadly deficient on this score—was central to the "city beautiful" movement, a surge of interest in civic betterment and beautification that began in the mid-1890s and crested in the first two or three years of the twentieth century. The city beautiful enthusiasm has proved difficult for historians to deal with, because its structure and objectives were so diffuse. By 1905, according to one partisan's happy report, no fewer than 2,426 "improvement societies" of various description were at work in cities throughout the land. Even mention of the leading organizations can quickly turn into a chronicle: the Municipal Art Society of New York (1893), the American Park and Outdoor Art Association (1897), the Architectural League of America and its National Committee on Municipal Improvements and Civic Embellishments (1899), the American League for Civic Improvement (1900), the American Civic Association (1904)—on and on the list could go. In periodicals like the *American City, Charities and the Commons*, the *Survey*, and *Municipal Affairs* (founded in 1897 by the Reform Club of New York), these groups kept in touch and traded improvement ideas. Superficially, their betterment projects seem impossibly diverse. Some campaigned to eliminate factory pollution, ugly billboards, unsightly fences, overhead electrical wires, and street refuse. (The latter goal seemed more attainable as horses were replaced by motorized vehicles.) Others planted trees, shrubs, and flower beds along city streets, cleaned up alleys and vacant lots, and sponsored home beautification contests. Still other groups, particularly those established by artists, called for the adornment of public buildings and squares with statuary, fountains, and murals, and the commissioning of more aesthetically pleasing boulevards, bridges, streetlights, and even trash cans. Around 1902, as city beautiful enthusiasm shifted toward the more comprehensive city-planning movement, many of these organizations began to propagandize for civic centers and other more ambitious undertakings. But though the specific projects were piecemeal and particularistic in nature, the long-range goal of the city beautiful evangelists was no less than the physical transformation of the city.

The motivations underlying the city beautiful movement are nearly as difficult to sort out as its varied manifestations. The president of the American Civic Association saw it simply as a "bubbling and uprising of the desire for better things" and compared it to an irresistible natural phenomenon. "It takes a snowball to start an avalanche, and we have a thousand such snowballs gathering force in a thousand communities! With a little help we can have these associated avalanches roll in whitening purity over ten thousand dirt spots in America." Accepting such contemporary assessments at face value, historians have typically portrayed this movement as the unselfish work of "public spirited citizens [who] gradually became aware of the gross deficiencies in their environment and determined to remedy matters."

If a disinterested philanthropic impulse led some reformers into the city beautiful movement, the issue for others was primarily aesthetic: billboards, belching smokestacks, and filthy streets were ugly; sparkling fountains, wide boulevards, and gleaming marble public buildings were deeply gratifying to the senses. For still others, a nagging feeling of national inferiority and backwardness in the arts—a pained awareness of the squat plainness of the average American city in contrast to the great centers of Europe—played a role. Under the leadership of important figures in the arts such as the sculptor Augustus Saint-Gaudens and the architects Charles McKim and Richard M. Hunt, turn-of-the-century American artists organized to remedy this situation and "convert city government to art patronage."

Boosterism and status considerations played a part as well: the desire to enhance one's own self-image by enhancing the beauty of one's city. Thorstein Veblen, predictably, saw this as *the* motive. In *The Theory of the Leisure Class* [1899], Veblen dismissed Chicago's park programs and incipient city-planning projects as merely illustrative of the "great cultural principle of conspicuous waste."

And for some capitalists, the appeal of the city beautiful lay no deeper than their pocketbooks: ugliness, dirt, and disorder were bad for business; a more attractive and orderly city would surely attract more customers and investors. In 1899, after a violence-plagued transit workers' strike in Cleveland, a local businessman called for accelerated work on a new civic center to counteract the city's image as a place of "rioting, bloodshed, and anarchy." Even Chicago architect Daniel H. Burnham, whose commitment to civic beautification had complex sources, was not above bald appeals to the profit motive. "Beauty has always paid better than any other commodity," he told the Chicago Commercial Club in 1907, "and always will."

But none of these motives goes to the heart of the city beautiful movement. Fundamentally, it sprang from the conviction that a more livable and attractive urban environment would call forth an answering surge of civic loyalty from the urban populace, and that this in turn would retard or even reverse the decay of social and moral cohesiveness which seemed so inevitable a concomitant of the rise of cities. As an editorial in the Dayton, Ohio, *Daily Journal* put it in 1901, a more beautiful city would surely be a place of superior "moral development."

If a tradition-laden urban past could not be summoned up, the city of today could be made more attractive, and thus a more compelling symbol of the moral authority of the civic ideal. A Boston University law professor developed the argument in very explicit terms in these years. "An important result of these city movements is the development of civic interest and pride on the part of the people. A city which does nothing except to police and clean the streets means little. But, when it adds schools, libraries, galleries, parks, baths, lights, heat, homes and transportation, it awakens interest in itself. The citizen cares for the city which shows some care for him. He looks upon it as his city, and not as a thing apart from him; and he becomes a good citizen because it is his city." The motto of the New York Municipal Art Society conveyed the same point in twelve words: "To make us love our city, we must make our city lovely." Or, as Robert A. Pope, a New York City landscape architect put it in 1909, "The beautiful city . . . makes possible a more beautiful life. . . ."

From the City Beautiful to City Planning: The Moral Dimension Remains Central As the city beautiful movement evolved, many of its partisans became persuaded that piecemeal beautification and improvement must give way to more comprehensive, integrated approaches. A degree of planning had characterized American urban development since the eighteenth century, and in the 1840s Robert Fleming Gourlay had produced a plan for Boston involving a succession of circumferential streets radiating concentrically outward from the center. (Gourlay included eight such streets in his plan, beginning with Washington and ending with Van Buren, presumably believing that Boston's further growth and the accession of new president's would proceed at an exactly equal pace.)

It was in the early twentieth century, however, that the movement attracted public notice, gained professional stature, and took on a heavy freight of social meaning. The immediate impetus was the creation by Congress in 1901 of a prestigious commission of architects, artists, and landscape designers to draw up plans for the completion of Pierre L'Enfant's 1791 design for Washington, D.C. Olmsted's great nineteenth-century parks played a role, as did the Chicago World's Fair, contemporary city-planning advances in Germany, and the writings of the Britishers Ebenezer Howard and Patrick Geddes. In *Tomorrow: The Peaceful Path to Real Reform* (1898), Howard set forth his vision of a network of "garden cities" to house the English working class. As orderly and symmetrical as compass and ruler could make them, Howard's ideal cities featured greenbelts alternating with residential and business sections, and rapid transit to the factory. (Howard's ideals found partial expression in Letchworth, a planned community established near London in 1903.) A United States Garden City Association was founded in 1906 by W. D. P. Bliss, but the movement's American influence was less in inspiring the creation of new towns than in heightening interest in transforming existing ones. Geddes, a Scottish biologist with a gifted amateur's interest in city planning, influenced American thought through a series of lectures in Boston in 1899 and still more through his 1904 work *City Development*. . . .

Like the city beautiful vogue from which it sprang, the city-planning movement must be viewed against a background of profound apprehension about the moral fate of the city. It was, in fact, the culminating expression of the positive environmentalists' effort to achieve moral and social ends through environmental means. As Benjamin Marsh put it in 1909, "A city without a plan is like a ship without a rudder."

The movement's moral significance, heavily emphasized in its literature and at the 1909 city-planning conference in Washington, was nowhere more pointedly underscored than in *What of the City* (1919), a hymn in praise of city planning by Walter D. Moody of the Chicago

Plan Commission. For decades, he wrote, American cities had "stunted" the moral development of their inhabitants, and now—with newcomers pouring in and the maintenance of "good order" becoming increasingly problematic—they faced the threatening consequences. The answer was as obvious as it was urgent: "The remedy must be found in planning." (Displaying the usual cavalier attitude toward earlier urban moral-control efforts, Moody insisted that before the advent of city planning, "practically nothing" had been done for the "moral, sociological, and physical upbuilding" of city dwellers.) For Moody, as for Charles Mulford Robinson, the importance of planning lay not primarily in the physical transformation it promised, but in its effect upon the "conflict between the opposing elements of good and evil" raging in every great city.

San Francisco offers a particularly graphic illustration of the way city planning could function as an alternative strategy for pursuing traditional moral-reform objectives. The Association for the Improvement and Adornment of San Francisco, sponsor of Daniel Burnham's city plan of 1905, was almost identical in composition to the group that had supported Mayor James D. Phelan's reform administration (1897–1901) in its crusades against prostitution, gambling, and other forms of urban vice. Defeated in 1901 by boss Abraham Ruef and his handpicked choice for mayor, the reformers turned to city planning as an alternative avenue to the kind of morally pure city they sought.

At times, the moral-control objective was acknowledged quite openly. One of the advantages of the civic center proposed for Cleveland in 1903, its planners noted, was that it would require the razing of an area notorious for its brothels and saloons. In a speech at the Washington city-planning conference in 1909, New York banker and real-estate figure Henry Morgenthau (father of the future treasury secretary) declared that the planners' primary assignment should be to wipe out the slums that were the breeding places of "disease, moral depravity, discontent, and socialism." In 1910, presenting a city plan for New Haven, Connecticut—a Yankee bastion reeling under the impact of immigration—Frederick Law Olmsted, Jr., spoke bluntly of the project's class basis and social objectives. "People of the old New England stock still to a large extent control the city, and if they want New Haven to be a fit and worthy place for their descendants it behooves them to establish conditions about the lives of *all* the people that will make the best fellow-citizens of them and of their children."

Generally, however, the movement's social objectives were cast in terms that were both more hopeful and more artfully imprecise. The aim, wrote one enthusiast in 1909, was to create "a new sense of citizenship," and arouse "a new and vital interest in the city as our common heritage." The plan proposed for New York, declared that city's planning commission, would give it "monuments worthy of its importance," thereby enhancing "the civic pride of its citizens." Joseph Lee, welcoming city planning as a natural extension of the playground reform, defined its objectives in similarly lofty and generalized terms. "The child should be helped to carry his city and his country with him in imagination," Lee wrote in 1915; "to this end we must make much use of symbols . . . We must preserve and dignify our monuments, erect our public buildings in a spirit of reverence for the Commonwealth." Even Olmsted retreated from his 1910 candor into the blander rhetoric of civic harmony. The modern city was "one great social organism," he wrote in 1916, and city planning was simply an effort to express that organic unity and the "interdependence" of all its elements.

But whether expressed baldly or obliquely, such comments offer a revealing insight into the thinking of this first generation of city planners. Over the decades, a succession of reformers—Bible and tract distributors, Sunday school teachers, YMCA secretaries, charity organization workers, and the others who have passed through these pages—had seen themselves as indispensable instruments in controlling the moral and social development of the urban masses. Now, under the altered circumstances of the early twentieth century, the city planners translated familiar social-control objectives into the idiom of environmental improvement. "The making of the new city will mean the making of a new citizen," declared a confident Charles Zueblin of the University of Chicago in 1903, "and the process is in no sense visionary." Ten years before, in a poem celebrating the Chicago World's Fair and the decorum its buildings seemed to inspire in the fairgoers, Richard Watson Gilder had anticipated some of the messianic spirit which soon would suffuse the city-planning movement:

> Ah, silent multitudes, ye are a part,
> Of the wise architect's supreme and glorious art.

But it was the president of the New York City board of aldermen in the Progressive years, a staunch city-planning advocate, who perhaps best summed up the movement's social-control dimension as the planners preferred to view it. "City planning . . . is the guidance into proper channels of a community's impulses towards a larger and broader life. On the face it has to do with things physical . . . , [b]ut its real significance is far deeper; a proper city has a powerful influence for good upon the mental and moral development of the people."

Few careers better illuminate the social outlook of the early city-planning movement than that of the man mainly responsible for the White City of 1893 that Gilder found so inspiring: Daniel Hudson Burnham. Sharing with his contemporary William James a deep mystical strain (perhaps, like James's, the product of a childhood saturated in Swedenborgianism), Burnham brought to all his projects an outlook summed up in his oft-quoted motto: "Make no little plans; they have no magic to stir men's blood." This power to "stir men's blood" was, for him, what gave city planning its high moral significance.

Born in 1846 in upstate New York, Burnham's earliest social experiences beyond the family were, as for so many urban moral reformers, those of the country village. Soon, however, he came with his parents to Chicago where his father prospered in the wholesale drug business. Here, in 1873, after a period of drift and uncertainty, Daniel joined with John W. Root in the practice of architecture. For the next eighteen years, until Root's death in 1891, the two were heavily engaged in designing the mansions, churches, banks, and office buildings of the emergent commercial elites in the major cities. Burnham and Root played an important role in the development of the skyscraper in these years, in keeping with their underlying objective: to create an urban architecture that would "convey in some large elemental sense an idea of the great stable, conserving forces of modern civilization."

Never veering from that objective, Burnham, after his partner's death, pursued it increasingly through public architecture and civic design. Clearly a decisive factor in this shift was his achievement as chief of construction for the Chicago World's Fair. The triumph of 1893 convinced Burnham of the social possibilities of municipal architecture, and from that year onward he turned his energies to a succession of large-scale civic design projects: in Washington, Cleveland, San Francisco, and, finally, his own Chicago. His perodic exhortations to Chicagoans—especially the commercial elite—to translate the ephemeral achievement of 1893 into a permanent reshaping of their city met with little response at first, but if the businessmen of Chicago were slower than their brethren elsewhere to catch the city-planning vision, their conversion, when it came, was complete. In 1906 the Merchants' Club retained Burnham to prepare a city plan, and with the merger of the Merchants' Club and the older Commercial Club a short time later, the organized business interests of Chicago were lined up solidly behind the idea. This, then, was the background for the publication, on the Fourth of July, 1909, of the *Plan of Chicago*, in many respects the quintessential expression of the social vision underlying the Progressive city-planning movement.

No dry technical treatise, the *Plan of Chicago* was designed to persuade, and it still remains seductive after the passage of many chastening years. A beautifully crafted quarto volume, enhanced by delicate architectural drawings, sepia photographs, and dreamlike watercolor renderings by the muralist Jules Guérin, this is a quietly passionate visual and verbal evocation of Burnham's vision of the city of the future.

Like Edward Bellamy and William T. Stead, Burnham effectively contrasted his dream city with the bleak reality of Chicago as it was: a city almost overwhelmed by rampant industrial expansion and a ceaseless influx of immigrants. Years of "formless growth" had spawned the familiar array of urban evils: poverty, congestion, immorality, ugliness, and "the frequent outbreaks against law and order which result from narrow and pleasureless lives." The "disorder, vice, and disease" among Chicago's poor, warned Burnham, menaced the "moral and physical health" of the population and indeed "the well-being of the city itself."

But, happily, the period of drift was ending. The World's Fair had revealed that "the soul of Chicago" was "vital and dominant," and now at last the city's "practical men of affairs" had recognized that Chicago's larger problems could be mastered by a comparably determined effort. "Chicago, in common with other great cities, realizes that the time has come to bring order out of the chaos incident to rapid growth, and . . . the influx of people of many nationalities without common traditions or habits of life."

How, precisely, did Burnham propose to deal with the social, moral, and physical challenges facing the city? In part, he hoped to combat them through direct and open social control stratagems: "cutting . . . broad thoroughfares through the unwholesome district," for example, or, as a last resort, forcibly relocating those city dwellers "so degraded by long life in the slums that they have lost all power of caring for themselves." He also planned to enlarge Chicago's park system, in the spirit of Frederick Law Olmsted's belief in the moral power of grass and trees. The person who maintained "close contact with nature," Burnham contended, would develop "saner methods of thought" than one exposed only to "the artificiality of the city." Through the beneficent influence of parks, he believed, "mind and body are restored to a normal condition, and we are enabled to take up the burden of life in our crowded streets and endless stretches of buildings with renewed vigor and hopefulness."

But Burnham's conception of the social mission of city planning was more subtle than the above might suggest. The idea was not just to build more parks or to uproot the slums. The fundamental object of Burnham's vast plan was to restore to the city a lost visual and aesthetic harmony, thereby creating the physical prerequisite for the emergence of a harmonious social order. The city planner's great opportunity—and solemn obligation—was to wage battle against the external physical disorder that was both a symptom and a cause of the city's deeper spiritual malaise.

The disarray and inharmoniousness of the city, observed Burnham in a striking passage, intruded even into the habitation of the dead. In the villages of bygone days, he wrote, "the old churchyards, with their serried ranks of slate headstones, their cypresses and weeping willows, and their rows of tombs, made a direct appeal to the deepest feelings of the human heart." In the city, by contrast, "the disorder of the modern . . . cemetery would seem to carry the idea of turbulence even to the grave itself."

Burnham's ideal city was, above all, one that would foster the "love of good order." Indeed, the word *order*—along with *harmony* and *dignity*—runs like a leitmotif through the *Plan of Chicago*. Making the city more orderly meant beginning with its public areas: the parks, squares, boulevards, and especially the public buildings. Like Charles Mulford Robinson, Burnham viewed the design and arrangement of municipal edifices as the heart of city planning. It is hard to convey the enthusiasm and eloquence with which he described the great civic complexes that loomed over the Chicago of his dreams and discussed their role in the city's social and moral evolution.

Struck by the awe the human mind experiences in "contemplating orderly architectural arrangements of great magnitude," Burnham saw in this instinctive response an important instrument of social and moral leverage: "the city has a dignity to be maintained; and good order is essential to material advancement," and "impressive groupings of public buildings" would promote those objectives. In their magnitude, orderliness, and symmetry, these structures would express Chicago's "unity and dignity," and symbolize "in concrete form the feeling of loyalty to and pride in the city." When constructed, they would represent "a long step toward cementing together the [city's] heterogeneous elements."

Furthermore—and most important—this "cementing together" of Chicago's diverse population would be achieved not by coercion or exhortation, but through a pervasive visual appeal to the "higher emotions of the human mind." Only in this way could a city "truly exercise dominion" over its inhabitants.

This insistence on the importance of reinforcing architecturally the social values of order and dignity was no new theme for Burnham in 1909. Immediately before the Chicago project, he had designed an administrative capital for the Philippine Islands—newly acquired by the United States in the aftermath of the Spanish-American War—and in the *Plan of Chicago* he suggested that just as that design had symbolized the "power and dignity" of imperial America, so Chicago's municipal structures should express the superiority of the civic claim over personal interests or wants.

In the *Plan of Chicago*, the reiteration of these themes becomes almost hypnotic: the complex of cultural institutions envisioned for

Grant Park must be "impressive and dignified"; the design of the county courthouse must symbolize the "dignity, majesty and impartiality of justice"; a straightened and widened Michigan Avenue "would be to the city what the backbone is to the body"; the civic center must express the "dignity and importance of the city from the administrative point of view."

The building on which Burnham lavished the greatest attention in the *Plan of Chicago* was the imposing and majestic city hall, the focal point of his proposal civic-center complex and the keystone of the whole plan. "The central building is planned not only to dominate the place in front of it, but also to mark the center of the city from afar and [to be] a monument to the spirit of civic unity . . . [I]n the center of all the varied activities of Chicago will rise the towering dome . . . , vivifying and unifying the entire composition." Burnham gave his imagination full rein in evoking the awesomeness of his projected city hall: "Rising from the plain upon which Chicago rests, its effect may be compared to that of the dome of St. Peter's at Rome."

Daniel Burnham's vast conception was well served by the brush of Jules Guérin. His delicate and tranquil paintings, with their softened light, muted colors, and subordination of technical exactitude to overall impression, exude the essential spirit of the *Plan of Chicago*. In Guérin's vision of Chicago, as in Burnham's, there is no hint of congestion, of discordant elements, or even of human diversity. The city he portrayed was large to be sure, but what catches the eye is not the undifferentiated blur of private structures stretching into the horizon, but the great primary civic elements: the sweeping boulevards, the imposing squares, the breathtaking lakefront development, and above all the overmastering civic center with its soaring city hall dominating a city that almost literally lies prostrate at its base.

Burnham and the plan in which he took such pride have not fared well at the hands of city-planning historians. John W. Reps faults his obsession with "monumental structures" and his neglect of the city's "more pressing social and economic ills." In the same vein, Mel Scott dismisses his "American Paris on the shores of Lake Michigan" as "an essentially aristocratic city, pleasing to the merchant princes who participated in its conception but not meeting some of the basic economic and human needs." George F. Chadwick sees the *Plan of Chicago* as a mere exercise in aestheticism—"an architect's conception; an ordering of the city to visual ends." Burnham's projected city hall, scoffs Vincent Scully, was "a dome on a drum . . . attenuated to skyscraper proportions." The Cleveland civic-center plan of which he was principal author, write John Burchard and Albert Bush-Brown, was "an empty, lifeless memorial to the City Beautiful idea." And Burnham's most recent biographer notes the "paradoxical" contrast between his willingness to take on the architectural challenge of the modern industrial city and the "antique academic formulas" with which he answered that challenge. Particularly puzzling has been Burnham's proposal to limit all private structures in Chicago to some twenty stories: a limitation which he of all men had reason to know was hopelessly unrealistic in the era of the skyscraper.

In accounting for the impracticality, archaic classicism, and seeming aesthetic megalomania of the *Plan of Chicago*, city-planning historians have placed the blame variously on the philistinism of Burnham's business sponsors, on his compulsion to re-create the success of the 1893 World's Fair, on the early removal of John W. Root's creative influence and Burnham's subsequent reliance on sterile classical models, and even on his supposed ambition to duplicate Baron Georges Haussmann's rebuilding of Paris along classical lines in the 1850s. As for the height limitation on private structures, Burnham's biographer can attribute it only to some deep and inexplicable revulsion against tall buildings. (Why, then, a city hall that soared into the clouds?)

If *The Plan of Chicago* is viewed not from a narrow perspective, but as yet another product of the long-standing impulse to devise an effective mechanism of urban social control, its apparent contradictions and paradoxes begin to make sense. Burnham, after all, did not perceive his plan as anachronistic or irrelevant. He believed it to be a creative response to the moral challenge of the city, and, indeed, on one level it was. Like the Saint Louis Pageant and Masque of 1914, the *Plan of Chicago* was a daring effort to convey in compelling tangible form the city's moral claim upon its inhabitants. It was the supreme expression of some Progressives' dream of transforming the behavior and moral outlook of America's urban masses by transforming the cities in which they lived.

This was the vision—not misguided classicism or a sycophant's desire to flatter Chicago's meat packers and grain merchants—that shaped Burnham's conception. His insistence that the city hall dwarf every other building in the city may have been outlandish in practical architectural terms, but it makes sense as an expression of his belief in the moral potential of civic idealism. "After all has been said," he wrote, "good citizenship is the prime object of good city planning." To contribute to the transformation of "the intellectual, social, moral, and aesthetic conditions" of the city—this was the long-range goal of the city planner's efforts. In terms of architectural history, Burnham's ideological affinities were perhaps closest to those Enlightenment figures, especially Giambattista Piranesi, who saw in their urban designs a means of imposing a rational order on the city. Indeed, one could apply to the *Plan of Chicago* Manfredo Tafuri's characterization of Piranesi's 1761 plan for Rome as an epic expression of "the struggle between architecture and the city, between the demand for order and the will to formlessness."

During the final stages of the preparation of the *Plan of Chicago*, after several bedside visits with the ailing Burnham, his young assistant Edward Bennett noted in his diary: "We talked of Swedenborg or rather I listened . . . and came away strengthened in purpose . . . We talked of the plan, but more of the philosophy of life—and his belief in the infinite possibilities of material expression of the spiritual." The man who perpetrated the leaden dictum "Beauty has always paid better than any other commodity, and always will" could also muse that "children must grow up dreaming of a beautiful city." To understand the meaning of the *Plan of Chicago*, one must probe the implications of both comments.

Daniel Burnham was already mortally ill when the *Plan of Chicago* was published, and he lived for only three years more. But his dream found other champions whose zeal helps us gauge the depth of its appeal. A quasi-official Chicago Plan Commission, made up of 300 "representative citizens" was established under the direction of the merchant and brewery heir Charles H. Wacker. A booklet promoting the *Plan* was published in an edition of 165,000 copies, and a simplified version was adopted as a civics text in Chicago's schools.

The publicists dwelt less on the plan's practical and aesthetic aspects than on the social vision underlying it. "Every generation has its burdens," declared one advocate; "to this is given the duty of curbing the individualism and establishing the collectivism of Democracy." The "noble character" of Burnham's proposed city hall, proclaimed Charles H. Wacker, would epitomize "the intellectual and moral quality of the city"; here Chicago's "best impulses" would "crystallize," and here her people would be "inspired . . . into devoted action for the public good." The physical transformation of Chicago envisioned by Burnham, added another supporter, would go far toward reversing the "physical and moral deterioration of the human race under bad conditions of city life" that was "one of the great problems of the age."

But although Chicago spent $300 million on projects related to the Burnham plan in the fifteen years following its publication, the belief in the moral potential of city planning that found such passionate expression in the *Plan of Chicago* proved short-lived. In the 1920s bureaucratization set in, the focus narrowed to such matters as zoning, and city planners offered assurances that they had abandoned the sweeping pretensions of their predecessors and were now dealing with matters that were "ninety nine percent technical." This development simply reflected a larger shift in post-World War I thinking about the city, but it must have been dismaying to the shade of Daniel Hudson Burnham. In his day, when city planning was in its infancy, its aspirations had been incomparably grander.

DISCUSSION QUESTIONS

1. Do you believe, as some of the urban reformers argued, that the nature and quality of the physical environment in which one lives strongly influences or even determines an individual's willingness or capacity to behave as a moral human being?
2. Which conditions of life in the city do you think most affect the ways in which individuals behave toward one another individually and toward their society at large? Are these conditions peculiar to society in the city, or are they more general in American society today?
3. If you had to list the qualities and characteristics that mark an individual as "moral" or "immoral," which ones would you choose? Are those habits of thought and behavior most easily exemplified in those people living in a large city, a suburb, a town, or on the countryside? Why did you make that choice?

6

ANGUISHED DECISION: WOODROW WILSON AND WORLD WAR I

JOHN M. COOPER, JR.

The following selection focuses on two related questions. Why did Europe go to war with itself in 1914, and why did the United States enter that war in 1917? The author's answer to the first question stresses long-term structural facts: destabilizing tendencies in the world system and class conflict within each major European society. His answer to the second question emphasizes specific events and individuals: German blunders over its submarine warfare policy and the unique personality and presidential leadership of Woodrow Wilson.

It is the latter question of American intervention that has preoccupied most American scholars for over a half-century. Some have argued that economic factors prompted an intervention to protect American commercial profits and prosperity from disruption by the German submarine blockade. Others have contended that geopolitical considerations ordained that the United States could not permit any one power (in this case, Germany) to dominate the European land mass. Some scholars have stressed idealistic motives that reinforced the moral revulsion against submarine technology and produced a liberal crusade to "make the world safe for democracy," while others have pointed to the cultural and political affinity between the two great English-speaking peoples that made Americans susceptible to British wartime propaganda.

Cooper's essay suggests that all these prior explanations err in placing too much emphasis on underlying forces, while paying too little heed to the nuances and historical specificity of individual policies and individual leaders. Especially provocative are his conclusions that the United States would not have entered the war if Germany (quite unnecessarily) had not resumed submarine warfare in early 1917, and that the decision to intervene was Wilson's and his alone.

—THOMAS J. MCCORMICK

One day in July 1955 the ground around the town of Messines, Belgium, trembled from an underground shock. It was not an earthquake. It was the explosion of a cache of munitions buried nearly 40 nears before. For eleven months, during 1916 and 1917, British troops had dug 21 mineshafts deep under the German lines in that part of Flanders and had filled them with five hundred tons of explosives. Early in the morning of June 7, 1917, the British had detonated the charges, causing a blast that had awakened people as far away as London, 130 miles distant. Only 19 of the loaded mineshafts had blown up, however. The rumbling in 1955 signaled the explosion of one of the two remaining charges. The other lies somewhere in the Flemish earth, still unexploded but practically certain to go off someday.

That incident of the explosives planted deep and their continuing after-effects is emblematic of the impact of World War I both on its own time and on the subsequent history of the 20th century. The war appeared to many contemporaries as a gigantic explosion or earthquake; those were two of the most popular terms used to describe the conflict. In longer perspective, too, the war looks like an explosion or earthquake in a metaphorical sense. It undermined an international dispensation under which European nations dominated among the world's major powers and ruled over much of the globe through their colonial empires. Likewise, the war shattered the domestic stability of those nations, sapping the authority of traditionally dominant groups and giving rise to violent extremism at both ends of the political spectrum. The shocks generated by the crumbling of that international and domestic order have precipitated the greatest events of the last 60 years, since the end of the war, and their final tremors are yet to be felt.

From its outbreak, nearly everyone recognized the momentousness of World War I. The suddenness and magnitude of the conflict that erupted in August 1914 tended to throw imaginations out of kilter. Observers instinctively grasped for non-human terms to describe it. Natural catastrophes, like an explosion or earthquake, came readily to mind. Henry James called the war "the plunge of civilization into this abyss of blood and darkness." Theodore Roosevelt believed that it was "on a giant scale like the disaster to the Titanic." Others resorted to supernatural terms. In the United States, which was so strongly influenced by Bible-reading Protestantism, the most widely used name for the war came to be "Armageddon," the nation-shattering miracle

ANGUISHED DECISION: WOODROW WILSON AND WORLD WAR I From John M. Cooper, Jr., "World War I: European Origins and American Intervention," *Virginia Quarterly Review*, 56, No. 1 (Winter, 1980), pp. 1–18, reprinted by permission; and John M. Cooper, Jr., *The Warrior and the Priest: Woodrow Wilson and Theodore Roosevelt* (Cambridge, MA: Harvard University Press, 1983), pp. 318–323.

preceding the Last Judgment in the book of Revelation. "Now Armageddon has a real meaning," announced one American magazine. ". . . If this be not Armageddon, we shall never suffer the final death grip of nations." Those who have witnessed later occurrences in this century may balk at that assertion, but no one can doubt that people at the time of World War I knew that they were living through one of history's greatest events.

Such knowledge was not an unalloyed advantage to the participants. The ready comparison of the war to events that did not have human origins betokened an attitude that the war was also beyond human control. That attitude, not the destruction and carnage, was what made World War I so profoundly disheartening. World War II claimed more lives, laid waste more land and cities, and introduced more terrible weapons. Yet that later war has legitimately exciting, hopeful, and noble aspects. The difference between the world wars involved more than the fixity of the first versus the movement of the second. Rather it is a question of why they differed in that way, and the answer lies less in the technology or art of war and more in the imagination and grasp of the civilian and military leaders of the belligerent powers.

"The Second World War in some ways gave birth to less novelty and genius that the First," writes Sir Isaiah Berlin, who compares the literary production of the two wars. "Yet," Berlin adds, "perhaps there is one respect in which the Second World War did outshine its predecessor: the leaders of the nations involved in it were, with the significant exception of France, men of greater stature, psychologically more interesting than their prototypes." One does not have to agree with all of Berlin's judgements of individual leaders to concede the truth of his observation. H. H. Asquith, Sir Douglas Haig, Erich Ludendorff, and Kaiser Wilhelm, for example, contrast so hollowly with Winston Churchill, George S. Patton, Erwin Rommel, and even Adolf Hitler, because those earlier figures made themselves captives rather than masters of events. World War I produced only two authentic world leaders, Woodrow Wilson and Vladimir Lenin, because they alone of all the national leaders grappled with the task of controlling the war itself. In their conflicting ways, Wilson and Lenin offered the only lights in the drab field of leadership in World War I.

What really made the war so staggering to people's sensibilities was its human origin: for the first time in history the deeds of men seemed to match the accidents of nature and the acts of God. World War I sprang from two related breakdowns in mankind's proudest creations at the beginning of the 20th century—the highly civilized nation-states of Europe. One breakdown, which was immediate and obvious, lay in relations among those nation-states. Although Europe had not experienced a general conflict for a hundred years before 1914, its state system had shown unmistakable signs of instability for at least a generation. All the main European powers except Great Britain held grudges against each other, and their grudges involved such intractable matters as control of territories and populations and assertions of political and economic influence that were considered vital. The relative detachment of the British afforded no safety, either, since the general instability also threatened them. Imperial expansion during the generation before the war had sometimes deflected rivalries from European concerns, but in the end controversies over colonies and spheres of influence in Africa and Asia had exacerbated tensions among the home countries. Moreover, the colonial and naval dimensions of the European rivalries had alarmed the British and drawn them into the struggle in ways that strictly continental controversies probably would not have done.

It seems clear now that of all the instigators of the war which broke out in 1914 Germany bore the heaviest responsibility. During the preceding ten years Europe had witnessed a series of crises initially occasioned by conflicts in the Far East, North Africa, or the Balkans. The Germans had either fomented those crises or rushed into them, each time in hopes of sowing discord among their rivals and reaping gains for themselves and their client states. Those German actions had reflected more than a normal but reckless desire to get ahead at the expense of adversaries. As Fritz Fischer and other German historians have shown, an expansionist consensus had grown up since the 1890's behind the proposition that Germany must become a "world state" with a "world mission." Further, a number of German leaders had become convinced that their nation's destiny could be fulfilled only through what the Foreign Minister in 1913 called "the coming world war." By 1914, diplomatic setbacks in the Balkans and the Near East and foreign economic uncertainties had created what Fischer terms a "crisis of German imperialism." The government in Berlin therefore greeted the dispute following the Austrian Archduke's assassination at Sarajevo in a mood of desperate hope. The Germans not only gave the Austrians a "blank check" in their dealings with Serbia, but they encouraged their ally to go to war. As Fischer concludes, "It is impossible to speak seriously either of Germany's being 'towed in Austria's wake' or of her being 'coerced.' "

Laying such responsibility at the Germans' door does not mean that they should once more be arraigned for "war guilt," as the victorious Allies did in 1919 in the Treaty of Versailles. No one has yet examined British, French, or Russian moves with the same access and assiduity that Fischer has studied the German role in the coming of the war. It seems likely that closer examination of French or, if it were possible, Russian sources might uncover at least a few comparable actions in goading Germany toward confrontation. Some elements in

France did seek and welcome war in 1914. There, too, a nationalist revival had been flourishing, with increasingly shrill assertions of French destiny and revanchism toward Alsace and Lorraine. Even Britain, which was the last and most reluctant major power to enter the war in 1914, does not appear entirely blameless. For a number of years the British Foreign Secretary, Sir Edward Grey, had been giving assurances to the French of backing in the event of war. Grey had kept those assurances secret not only from Parliament but also from the full Cabinet, and though he had never explicitly promised British intervention, he had made commitments to the French that could not realistically be honored without fighting at their side. As events transpired, the German violation of Belgian neutrality averted a political crisis over Britain's entry into World War I. Defending "brave little Belgium" forestalled debate and rallied people to the colors in Britain in 1914 much as Pearl Harbor did in America in 1941.

Responsibility for the war was also generalized among the European nations in another way besides their diplomatic conduct. The second breakdown that contributed to the outbreak of World War I lay in the internal affairs of the countries involved. Foreign policy never exists in a vacuum, and in 1914 the actions of all the nations that became belligerents reflected domestic conditions. The Kaiser's regime ruled Germany in a mood of constant, though often exaggerated, insecurity. A plethora of proscriptions and legal disadvantages had not availed to prevent the Social Democrats from emerging as the strongest single party, and in 1913 and 1914 some conservative spokesmen had advocated war as a means of curbing rising Socialist strength. In France socialism and nationalism had competed for the allegiance of the working classes, and only the fortuitous assassination of the eloquent Jean Jaurès in July 1914 had removed a potential rallying point for Socialist opposition to the war. British internal discord stemmed not only from the growing strength and militancy of the Labour Party but also from woman suffrage agitation and, most gravely, from incipient civil war over autonomy for Ireland. Ironically, of all the major European powers, only backward, despotic, chronically troubled Russia seemed to be gaining in internal stability, thanks to massive industrialization and sweeping land reform.

By 1914, the breakdown that became so evident in Europe after World War I was already well advanced. The war undoubtedly accelerated the process, and in the case of Russia it may well have paved the way for a revolution that might not otherwise have occurred. But the war did not cause that internal breakdown. Instead, the breakdown contributed to the war. The dominant mood of the leaders of the nations that took up arms in 1914 was relief. British, French, and German leaders all seemed glad to lay aside their troubles at home and fight a foreign foe. David Lloyd George, the strongest figure in the

British government, told one friend in August 1914, "In a week or two it might be good fun to be the advance guard of an expeditionary force to the coast of France, and run the risk of capture by a German ship!" The masses of men who went to war briefly shared such summer holiday sentiments, but their euphoria soon gave way to gloom and despair. Among thoughtful European observers, World War I almost at once instilled doubts about human nature and the progress of civilization. For men in the trenches and reflective onlookers, it was understandable that the war might seem beyond human control. For their leaders, however, the abdication of responsibility seems to have stemmed from their original relief at having escaped unpleasant domestic conditions. It would seem that European leaders did not try harder to control the war because they did not want to. They evidently preferred the carnage of the war to the upheavals which they knew would meet its end if they did not emerge somehow triumphant.

II

Viewed from America, many aspects of World War I appeared different. Observers in the United States also immediately marveled at the immensity of the conflict, and they used the same nonhuman descriptions and bemoaned the setback to human progress. But other elements entered into reactions on this side of the Atlantic. Where Europeans initially thrilled to the adventure of war, Americans expressed relief at not being in it. Later, when the United States did enter the war, the most popular description for it would be "over there"; that phrase also expressed the basic American attitude toward World War I at its outbreak. From the American standpoint, the war was a terrible catastrophe that had befallen somebody else, far way. "Again and ever I thank Heaven for the Atlantic Ocean," wrote the American ambassador in London at the end of July 1914. People in the United States felt not only geographically but also morally removed from the war. It appeared to offer spectacular confirmation of longstanding notions about New World innocence and purity in opposition to Old World sin and decadence. In August 1914, the *New York Times*, usually a sober newspaper, contrasted the opening of the Panama Canal with the outbreak of the war by gloating, "The European ideal bears its full fruit of ruin and savagery just at the moment when the American ideal lays before the world a great work of peace, goodwill, and fair play." In short, many Americans reacted to the outbreak of World War I by figuratively repeating the Pharisee's prayer, "Thank God I am not as other men are."

That pervasive sense of removal from the war presented the most formidable barrier to eventual American intervention. But any thoughts of intervention lay well in the future. When President Wilson admonished his countrymen in August 1914 to remain "neutral in fact as well as in name," he simply seemed to be voicing the prevailing popular attitude. The following December he reiterated such sentiments when he dubbed the European conflict "a war with which we have nothing to do, whose causes can not touch us. . . ." Actually, Wilson meant to do more than convey soothing reassurance, since he had early come to fear the potential impact of the conflict on the United States. The mood of detachment lasted for the better part of the first year of the war. By the spring of 1915—despite some expressions of sympathy for the Allies, despite frictions with the British over their blockade of the Central Powers, and despite jitters at the German submarine proclamation—people appeared less concerned than ever about World War I. "Americans regard the war either as a bore," reported the British ambassador in Washington in April 1915, "or as an immensely interesting spectacle provided for their entertainment, of which they are commencing to be rather tired."

The great majority of Americans' attitudes toward World War I changed suddenly and dramatically on the afternoon of May 7, 1915. That was when the news reached the United States that a German submarine had sunk the British liner *Lusitania,* the world's largest passenger ship, killing 1,198 men, women, and children, 198 of whom were Americans. Ten years later the journalist Mark Sullivan discovered that all the people he interviewed could remember exactly where they had been when they had learned of the sinking of the *Lusitania,* what they had thought and felt, and what they had done for the rest of the day. The event left an indelible memory not only because it was another great catastrophe but also because it raised the threat of involvement in the war. Although many spokesmen fumed with outrage over the *Lusitania,* few raised cries for war. Out of 1,000 newspaper editors asked to telegraph their views to New York newspapers, six called for war. President Wilson caught the dominant public reaction when he stated a month after the sinking of the *Lusitania,* "I wish with all my heart I saw a way to carry out the double wish of our people, to maintain a firm front in respect of what we demand of Germany and yet do nothing that might by any possibility involve us in the war."

That statement defined the diplomatic dilemma that persisted until the United States entered World War I in April 1917. German-American relations did not begin a long slide toward war. A grave but polite diplomatic duel persisted between the two countries for nearly a year, until an American ultimatum forced the Germans to restrain their submarines in the spring of 1916. Thereafter, the threat of war receded for several months, and most of the friction between the United States and European belligerents involved the Allies, particularly Britain. Only Germany's launching of an expanded submarine offensive at the end of January 1917 brought the final crisis that plunged America into the war. Yet behind the ebb and flow of German-American relations lay the same conditions that Wilson had described after the sinking of the *Lusitania*. From mid-1915 onward two basic requisites existed for American intervention. Those requisites were the German use of the submarine and the presence of Woodrow Wilson in the White House.

For the last 40 years nearly all American interpreters have portrayed their nation's entry into World War I as a well-nigh inevitable event. Deploring "revisionists" and applauding "realists" have alike viewed intervention in 1917 as an outcome virtually foreordained by the machinations of great political, economic, and strategic forces. By contrast, most British interpreters and Arthur S. Link in this country have emphasized the twists and turns of specific events and the roles of individual actors. Although the two perspectives can be complementary, whether to stress the weight of over-arching forces or the actions of contemporaries poses an inescapable choice in assessing American entry into World War I. Of the two perspectives, the second—the stress on specific men and events—is the correct one. When due account has been given to the influences of culture, trade, political sympathies, and strategic reckoning that may have affected the course of American policy, two incontrovertible facts remain. First, the United States would almost certainly never have entered World War I if Germany had not resorted to submarine warfare. Second, the vehicle through which the United States did enter the war was Woodrow Wilson.

The German decision to use the submarine represented one of the most fateful moves of the war. It also involved two great blunders. The first blunder occurred with the initial submarine proclamation in February 1915, when Germany threatened to sink without warning all merchant shipping in a zone surrounding the British and French coasts. By issuing that proclamation, the Germans were, as Ernest May has pointed out, doing the only thing that could have caused meaningful hostility with the Americans. British control of the seas had curtailed contacts between the United States and Germany so thoroughly that no other occasion for war or even much diplomatic friction could have arisen without the submarine. Worse, the Germans were risking a wider war for doubtful military advantage. Not only were Germany's World War I submarines small, vulnerable craft which carried few torpedoes and had a short cruising range, but in 1915 there were so few of them that they could inflict at most minimal shipping losses. Why the Germans took such a bad risk and then clung stubbornly to their intentions in the face of American protests sprang in part from tense, complicated civil-military relations within the Kaiser's regime. But the submarine policy also reflected a new and disheartening development in the history of warfare. The German submarine advocates' claims in 1915 offered the earliest example of what has become a familiar 20th-century faith in military "hardware"—the notion that some new piece of technology will bring victory that is both quick and cheap in one's own expenditure of manpower and resources. Air power and nuclear weapons would offer later fields for this faith which the submarine had first occasioned.

The second even greater submarine blunder was the decision in January 1917 to resume and widen the undersea war. The German government made that decision in full knowledge and expectation of likely American intervention. They were taking the calculated risk that their submarines could knock the Allies out of the war by cutting off their overseas supplies of munitions and food long before any American contribution could swing the balance against them. This risk in 1917 seemed considerably better than the earlier one, inasmuch as German shipyards had by then built enough submarines to make serious inroads in Allied shipping. The rate of tonnage losses inflicted in the spring of 1917 nearly crippled the British war effort. Only the timely adoption of the convoy system cut those losses to an acceptable level by providing an effective defense against the submarine.

III

The German error in 1917 lay in believing that the submarine offered the sole means to victory. By the beginning of that year, the Allies had fallen into desperate financial straits. The impending collapse of their credit in the United States was about to accomplish the same result as the German submarine offensive—cutting the Allies' overseas supply lifeline—with no risk of American intervention. In fact, the Allied financial position had deteriorated so badly that nothing could save them short of the rapid, massive infusion of money that would require American co-belligerency as a precondition. By resuming and broadening submarine warfare in January 1917 the Germans were doing the one thing that could save the Allies from collapse. To use a recent phrase, Germany was snatching defeat from the jaws of victory. Why the Germans made this blunder evidently stemmed from two considerations. One was a simple, though inexcusable failure of intelligence. "So far as I know the Germans were totally unaware of our financial difficulty," wrote the British Treasury expert John Maynard Keynes, who talked with his German opposite numbers after the war. Such ignorance seems incredible, particularly because much of the information about the Allied financial predicament was public knowledge and a few hours of simple intelligence gathering in New York and Washington would have yielded further, convincing evidence.

A second, deeper consideration also underlay the German blunder. As the German historian Gerhard Ritter has observed, indications abounded in Berlin not only that the best chance to win the war lay in waiting to let Allied troubles mount but also that a more cautious submarine policy might keep the United States neutral. Despite those signs, the Germans went ahead with the submarine campaign because nothing less than swift decisive military victory seemed acceptable to the men in power. That decision sprang in part, as Ritter suggests, from the ascendancy of the military, which had transformed the Kaiser's government into a dictatorship by General Ludendorff behind the figurehead of Field Marshal Paul von Hindenburg. Even more, the decision reflected the abdication by both military and civilian leaders to what they regarded as the larger than human requirements of the World War. They were simply unable to conceive of any course except riding the war through to total victory. It seems likely, therefore, as the British historian Patrick, Lord Devlin has speculated, that the German leaders would have chosen to unleash their submarines even if they had known more about the Allies' financial peril. If that were so, then the German choice of the submarine campaign was, as Edmund Burke described the French Revolution, "a fond election of evil."

The second incontrovertible fact about American intervention in World War I is what Winston Churchill recognized more than 50 years ago when he wrote of Woodrow Wilson, "It seems no exaggeration to pronounce that the actions of the world depended, during the awful period Armageddon, upon the workings of this man's mind and spirit to the exclusion of almost every other factor; and that he played a part in the fate of nations incomparably more direct and personal than any other man." Wilson's role was the opposite of that of the German submarine. If the United States would not have entered World War I except for the submarine, no one besides Wilson would have done so much to keep the country out of the war. No major American statesman of the time equaled Wilson either in representing majority opinion or in grasping basic problems. His principal rivals and critics all leaned too far toward the belligerent half of the people's "double wish," as with Theodore Roosevelt, Elihu Root, and Henry Cabot Lodge, or toward the pacific half, as with William Jennings Bryan and Robert M. La Follette. William Howard Taft and Charles Evans Hughes came closer to Wilson's middle ground, and Taft also looked beyond the immediate controversies, but they lacked Wilson's boldness and perception.

From the war's outbreak, Wilson had apprehended that his fundamental task lay in attempting to end the conflict and prevent the recurrence of anything like it. His early admonitions about neutrality and remoteness from the war had also contained urgings to remain self-controlled in order to be ready to perform great international services. That vision of service owed less to any Presbyterian idealism of

Wilson's than to his convictions about the indivisibility of world peace and security. In this regard, he resembled his fellow, deeply religious Southerner, Jimmy Carter, with whom he has been compared, rather than a more worldly operator like Franklin Roosevelt. In his handling of the submarine troubles with Germany in 1915 and 1916, Wilson proved highly resourceful in hewing to the middle way between war and submission when so many others were falling away, including his successive Secretaries of State, Bryan and Robert M. Lansing, and his main confidant, Colonel Edward M. House. Moreover, all the while he was preparing for an effort to end the war and lay the basis for a new international order.

Wilson's finest hour during World War I came in the two-and-a-half months following his re-election in November 1916, when he moved simultaneously on several fronts to mediate the conflict and create a structure for peace. Shortly after the election, Wilson exercised America's financial leverage over the Allies by backing and strengthening a Federal Reserve Board warning against excessive foreign loans. Then in December 1916 he dispatched a circular note to the belligerent powers, asking them to state their peace terms and pledging American participation in a future international body empowered to maintain peace. The note went first through diplomatic channels and was made public two days afterward. Finally, on Jan. 22, 1917, after receiving various replies from the warring nations, Wilson delivered a speech to the Senate in which he called for "a peace without victory. . . . Only a peace among equals can last. Only a peace the very principle of which is equality and a common benefit." In that speech he also laid down the specific principles for the war's settlement which he reiterated a year later in the Fourteen Points, and he again pledged American participation in an international concert to keep the peace.

Wilson gave an extraordinary performance. He moved deftly and calmly amid suspicions, jealousies, and recriminations abroad and at home. The Germans and the Allies responded to the American initiative by executing labyrinthine, often deceitful, maneuvers which reflected internal strains as well as mutual enmity. The mediation effort drew fire in the United States from pro-Allied stalwarts like Lodge and Roosevelt, who charged Wilson with playing Germany's game. His proposal for American membership in an international peacekeeping organization earned denunciations both from pacific isolationists, who feared involvement in foreign conflicts, and from nationalists, who rejected any abridgment of sovereignty and self-interest. Those attacks in December 1916 and January 1917, which were spearheaded by Senators Henry Cabot Lodge and William E. Borah, offered a foretaste of the postwar debate over joining the League of Nations. Besides outright opposition, Wilson also had to brook disloyalty from his top lieutenants, as Secretary Lansing and Colonel House each in his own way tried to sabotage the mediation venture. Whether Wilson's attempt to gain control of the international situation at the beginning of 1917 would have succeeded if Germany had not reopened submarine warfare is doubtful. Too many factors seem to have been working against it. Yet, merely by making the attempt, Wilson had staked his claim to world leadership.

Doubts about whether the United States would enter the World War were well founded. Contrary to the hopes of Roosevelt and others like him, public pressure did not prod Wilson toward intervention. Outrage again flared as Americans died in submarine attacks on British liners and, for the first time since early in 1915, on American vessels. Some previously uncommitted politicians and newspapers came out for war at the end of February and beginning of March 1917. Interventionist sentiment rose particularly after publication of the Zimmermann Telegram, in which Germany promised Mexico restoration of the "lost provinces" of Texas, New Mexico, and Arizona if, in the event of war between Germany and the United States, Mexico fought against the United States. But most contemporary estimates and subsequent studies of public opinion have shown that substantial anti-interventionist sentiment persisted in March and April. The great majority of Americans apparently still clung to their "double wish" to uphold national honor and stay out of the war. Congressional opinion reflected the public uncertainty. Several independent observers noted that large majorities in both houses remained undecided about intervention right up to the night of April 2.

The decision to go into or stay out of the World War fell upon Wilson alone. His decision has remained mysterious for three reasons. First, Wilson made it in his usual solitary way; second, he expressed doubts about the wisdom and likely consequences of entering the war; and finally, both his choice of and his justification for intervention seemed out of character.

None of those considerations should cast unnecessary shadows over Wilson's thought and action. His solitariness as president was never so great a handicap as some critics claimed, and it probably affected his performance between February and April 1917 even less than at other times. Wilson frequently discussed the matters that were uppermost in his thinking. The cabinet considered submarine issues at four meetings during February and March, and Wilson talked about those issues several times individually with the members most concerned, the secretaries of state, war, and the navy. Wilson also bared some of his deepest qualms about the choice to Frank Cobb, editor of the New York *World*. He revealed his thoughts in public as well. On February 3 Wilson told a joint session of Congress that a diplomatic break with Germany was the only "alternative consistent with the dignity and honor of the United States," but he wanted "merely to stand true alike to the immemorial principles of our people which I sought to express in my [peace without victory] address to the Senate only two weeks ago." On February 26 he told another joint session that the United States sought simply to defend "those rights of humanity without which there is no civilization." On March 5, in his second inaugural address, he urged Americans to persevere in bringing "calm counsel" to the issues of war and peace. "The shadows that now lie dark upon our paths will soon be dispelled and we shall walk with the light all about us," he maintained, "if we be but true to ourselves—to ourselves as we have wished to be known in the counsels of the world and in the thought of all who love liberty and justice and the right exalted."

Wilson often sounded like a mystic when he portrayed himself as a representative and instrument of popular opinion, but no leading politician in 1917 was better attuned to the sentiment of the majority. It was Wilson's attunement to the pacific side of the public's "double wish" that fostered much of the doubt he expressed about the wisdom and consequences of intervention. That doubt has, in turn, formed the second reason for finding mystery in his choice of war. In February and March Wilson expressed repugnance toward entering the World War on two grounds. One was an odd combination of international concerns. At one cabinet meeting, the president reportedly asked what effect "the depletion of manpower" caused by American intervention might "have upon the relations between the white and yellow races?" But Wilson's greatest international concern was about abandoning "peace without victory." According to Frank Cobb's recollection, Wilson argued "that so long as we remained out there was a preponderance of neutrality, but that if we joined the Allies the world would be off a peace basis and onto a war basis." Intervention would change everything, Cobb recalled Wilson asserting. "It means an attempt to reconstruct a peace-time civilization with war standards, and at the end of the war there will be no bystanders with sufficient power to influence the terms. There won't be any peace standards to work with. There will be only war standards." As Wilson stated in his speeches and as others have repeatedly observed, his basic foreign policy problem was how to pursue "peace without victory" through war.

Wilson's second ground for fearing the consequences of intervention was domestic. He also reportedly asserted to Cobb, "Once lead this people into war, and they'll forget there ever was such a thing as tolerance. To fight you must be brutal and ruthless, and the spirit of ruthless brutality will enter into the very fibre of our national life, infecting Congress, the courts, the policeman on the beat, the man in the street." Much of that prediction did come true after the United States went to war, and the later curtailment of civil liberties has raised questions about whether Wilson really feared those consequences. It is indisputable, however, that he viewed the likely political impact of the war with misgivings. "Daniels, if this country goes into war," he reportedly also said in March 1917, "you and I will live to see the day when the big interests will be in the saddle." Since the beginning of his presidency, Wilson had expressed similar fears, in connection with threats of war in Mexico, that the nation would be distracted from reform and that conservatives and big business would gain political advantage.

Wilson's fears of the foreign and domestic consequences of intervention have helped lend the note of mystery to his choice of war. If Wilson knew that intervention would have so many evil consequences at home and abroad, how could he choose to fight? Much of the mystery has stemmed from viewing those utterances as isolated from other ideas expressed by Wilson. He gave equal weight to the other side of the "double wish." He did not hesitate to break relations with Germany or to arm American ships against the submarines. "We may even be drawn on, by circumstances, not by our own purpose or desire," he warned in March in his inaugural address, "to a more active assertion of our rights as we see them and a more immediate association with the great struggle itself." In none of his doubts about entering the war did Wilson speak as a diehard anti-interventionist. For him, evil consequences were realities to be faced and dangers to be recognized, not necessarily insuperable obstacles. Most of his doubts amounted to factors to be weighed in the scales of circumstance, interest, and strategy as he decided how to address the situation.

Wilson also felt deep personal anguish over his decision. In April 1914 the deaths of American servicemen at Veracruz had shaken him, and he had understandably recoiled from the mass slaughter on the western front. "Think what it was they were applauding," Wilson reportedly said to Tumulty after asking Congress for the declaration of war on April 2. "My message to-day was a message of death for our young men. How strange it seems to applaud that." Such evidence of emotional involvement has raised a persistent question about Wilson's decision to intervene. If he felt so deeply against the war and such a personal burden of guilt for the deaths of young Americans, how could he still choose to fight? The most common answer to that question, aside from confessions of bewilderment, has been the contention that only an idealistic crusade to reform the world—making the world "safe for democracy" and fighting "a war to end all wars"—could justify such sacrifices and assuage the guilt that plagued Wilson.

That interpretation, based upon two errors, is wrong. One error is a mistaken view of Wilson's political personality; the other is a misreading of his war address. The mistaken view of Wilson's personality has derived from a depiction of him, albeit usually unconsciously, as a Nietzschean Priest. From that perspective, with its pejorative stress on a reluctance to wield power, nothing short of a holy war involving eternal principles of right and wrong could have reconciled Wilson to intervention in World War I. Actually the only correct element in the Nietzschean categorization of Wilson has been the recognition that he was not a Warrior. But neither was he a Priest. Instead, Wilson's beliefs in self-control and in realization of ideals through self-interest made him resemble more the figure who embodied Nietzsche's ideal of self-overcoming and creative expression of the will-to-power—not the Warrior, but the Superman.

A second, closely related error in interpretations of Wilson's choice of intervention has been the misreading of his speech of April 2 as an endorsement of an idealistic crusade. The address is a work of somber beauty, which lays major stress on uncertainty, limitation, and inescapability. "We must put excited feeling away," Wilson declared early in the speech. "Our motive will not be revenge or the victorious assertion of the physical might of the nation, but only the vindication of right, of human right, of which we are only a single champion." For himself, Wilson added, he felt "a profound sense of the solemn and even tragical character of the step I am taking." Wilson was casting himself and his country in a tragic role.

The tragedy lay in having to pursue good ends through evil means. "I have exactly the same things in mind now that I had in mind when I addressed the Senate on the twenty-second of January last," Wilson avowed. ". . . Our object now, as then, is to vindicate the principles of peace and justice in the life of the world as against selfish and autocratic power and to set amongst the really free and self-governed peoples such a concert of purpose as will henceforth insure the observance of these principles." Yet he urged that Americans must "fight without rancor . . . without passion and ourselves observe with proud punctilio the principles of right and of fair play we profess to be fighting for." In closing, Wilson again acknowledged, "It is a fearful thing to lead this great peaceful people into war, into the most terrible and disastrous of all wars, civilization itself seeming to be in the balance. But the right is more precious than the peace, and we shall fight for the things which we have always carried nearest our hearts—" and, after reciting once more the objects that he had named earlier for the United States to pursue, he ended—"God helping her, she can do no other."

Those last words, as many recognized, paraphrased and echoed Martin Luther's declaration to the Diet of Worms, "God helping me, I can do no other." The words were probably a chance combination, but it seems doubtful that Wilson did not know he was imitating Luther's declaration. Although Wilson often admitted that he was no theologian, his origins and upbringing among highly educated Protestant clergymen made it almost certain that he grasped, at least in a general way, the philosophical implication of invoking Luther. Next to his role in the Reformation, Luther's best-known contribution to Christianity was his dictum, "Sin boldly." Luther had held that inasmuch as Christians lived in a sinful world and were themselves sinners, they could not avoid sin but must, in seeking to follow God's will, "sin boldly."

Wilson's basic argument in the war address was analogous to Luther's contention. In trying to make the world freer, more just, and more peaceful, both he and the United States confronted the sin of the World War. Yet, as he argued, continued armed neutrality would result in much of the destruction of war without the advantage of being able to influence the war's conduct and aims. Wilson's choice, therefore, was not the possibly lesser, but also less promising, evil of staying out. Rather, for the sake of greater leverage in pursuing his international program, he would "sin boldly" by going into the war. He made the decision, not as a Nietzschean Priest or Superman, but as the protagonist in a Christian tragedy.

In one way, Wilson's tragedy began as he delivered the war address. Applause interrupted him after his most belligerent statements, particularly when he uttered the phrase "safe for democracy." This time Lodge led the applauding senators. He rushed up afterward to shake Wilson's hand and tell him, "Mr. President, you have expressed in the loftiest manner the sentiments of the American people." La Follette, who sat grimly through the address with his arms tightly folded, led the senatorial opposition. On April 4 the Senate approved a declaration of war with six members voting against—La Follette, two other insurgent Republicans, and three Bryanite Democrats. Two days later the House followed suit, with fifty-four representatives voting or announced in opposition—thirty-five Republicans, a majority of whom were insurgents; eighteen Democrats, all Bryanite stalwarts, including Majority Leader Kitchin, and the lone Socialist. The congressional opposition reflected some likely influence from German-American constituencies and a clear sectional bias toward the Middle West and West, but its strongest characteristic was a reformist inclination. As in the preparedness and submarine policy controversies a year before, Wilson was bending his side of the political spectrum toward an uncongenial foreign policy, and he was once more accepting support from the other side. As before, he succeeded overwhelmingly for the time being, but he was sowing more seeds of future trouble.

American intervention revolutionized World War I. It saved the Allies from financial collapse, which, together with the other reverses they suffered in 1917, would have insured their defeat. It gave the British and French the morale boost that allowed them to hold out on the Western Front in the spring of 1918 against the last great German offensive. It supplied fresh manpower for the counteroffensive that ended the war on Nov. 11, 1918. Moreover, American intervention made the war for the first time a global conflict. Before April 1917, it had involved mostly European nations and had had ramifications elsewhere largely through their colonial possessions. The entry of the United States drew in the Western Hemisphere and extended connections into the Pacific. Also, because of Wilson's efforts, the war came to be about more than territorial appetites and imperial designs. Now it involved world-wide aspirations to self-government, new ways of conducting relations among nations, and attempts to create a different international order. Without Wilson and without the United States, it would have been a far different war.

Woodrow Wilson never forgot that he might be making a tragic mistake by entering World War I, and he may have. Certainly his justification for intervention helped implant the habits of glib globalizing and facile homogenizing of disparate parts of the world which have been besetting sins of American foreign policy since World War I. Similarly, despite Wilson's intentions, the war did turn into a self-righteous crusade for many Americans, thereby confirming another dangerous predilection in the nation's conduct in world affairs. The international and the domestic orders of Europe lay in ruins, and instability was going to reign there no matter who won the war. Perhaps, as the isolationists always insisted, America might have done better to have left that unhappy continent alone and might have done more for the world by setting an example of restraint. But that was not what Woodrow Wilson chose to do, and that has not been America's role in the 20th-century world. Thanks to him and to the long-running after-effects of World War I, the United States has tried again and again to shape events that have seemed to others beyond human control. That has been America's glory and tragedy.

DISCUSSION QUESTIONS

1. If the author is correct that the United States would not have entered World War I if Germany had not resumed submarine warfare, why didn't the United States limit its response to a naval war on German submarines? Does the author's analysis of Wilson suggest why the President found it necessary to fight a land war on the European continent?

2. The author stresses Wilson's ability to guage complex popular feelings and respond to those feelings with strong presidential leadership. Was this peculiar to Wilson or did it presage a continuing phenomenon sometimes called the Imperial Presidency? Recent examples of the Imperial Presidency are Franklin Roosevelt's role in American entry into World War II, President Truman's intervention in Korea, and President Lyndon Johnson's escalation of the Vietnam War.
3. The guiding principle of Wilson's foreign policy can be described as "internationalism." The author calls the continuing efforts to implement that principle "America's glory and tragedy." In what sense might that be so?

7

THE MEANING OF THE "MONKEY TRIAL"

LAWRENCE W. LEVINE

The United States in the 1920s was torn by social and cultural tensions. The automobile, movies, and radio were transforming the lives of millions. Small-town America eyed the immigrant cities with suspicion; city sophisticates ridiculed country folk as "hicks" and "hayseeds." The reaction against the exalted idealism of the war years left a bitter aftertaste of disillusionment.

In this stressful cultural environment, some Americans sought to reassert traditional values by symbolic means. Millions joined the Ku Klux Klan which asserted the dominance of white Protestant America and its rigorous moral code. Others, called Fundamentalists, rejected religious liberalism and affirmed what they viewed as the fundamentals of Christianity, including the literal truth, or "inerrancy," of every word in the Bible.

One part of the Fundamentalist project was to ban the teaching of the theory of evolution in the public schools. Charles Darwin's original formulation of this theory, *The Origin of Species*, had appeared as long ago as 1859 and in the intervening years had won wide acceptance among scientists and religious leaders alike. But in the volatile cultural climate of the 1920s, Fundamentalists focused their fire on evolutionary theory as a basic threat to the embattled traditional order.

In 1925, when Tennessee prohibited the teaching of evolution in the public schools of the state, the American Civil Liberties Union of New York offered to defend any teacher who would challenge the law. John T. Scopes, a young biology teacher in Dayton, Tennessee, encouraged by local boosters who saw a chance to put Dayton on the map, took up the offer. To defend Scopes, the ACLU brought in Clarence Darrow of Chicago, a famous trial lawyer.

The prosecution team recruited William Jennings Bryan, three times Democratic presidential candidate, former secretary of state, and a prominent champion of Fundamentalism. Bryan arrived in Dayton confident that he could persuade a jury to convict Scopes, uphold Tennessee's anti-evolution law, and thereby win a great symbolic victory for Fundamentalism. But the outcome, as Lawrence Levine makes clear in his interpretation of this endlessly fascinating episode, was very different from what Bryan and his supporters had anticipated.

—PAUL S. BOYER

By the beginning of 1925 neither Bryan nor any of his fellow fundamentalists could feel that their efforts had been in vain. Although no other state immediately followed Florida in declaring officially against the teaching of evolution, fundamentalist pressure in a number of states caused officials to ban textbooks which included Darwinian theories; the number of college professors and secondary school teachers who were forced to resign because of their belief in evolution was steadily increasing; and throughout the South and Midwest local school boards were ordering their teachers to ignore the new biological theories.

This type of pressure and intimidation, because it was so difficult to isolate and combat openly, was unquestionably the most effective tactic the fundamentalists could have employed. Yet the leaders of that movement were not satisfied; they thirsted for statutes which would settle for all time the question of how man was created. Early in 1925 the lower house of the North Carolina Legislature defeated an anti-evolution measure by a vote of 67 to 46. During the struggle the presidents of the state university and of Wake Forest College had taken the lead in combating the proposed legislation. This kind of opposition was lacking in the neighboring state of Tennessee, where the fundamentalists now focused their attention.

In 1924, W. B. Marr, a Nashville attorney, had invited Bryan to speak in Nashville. Impressed by his lecture "Is the Bible True?" Marr and his associates had several thousand copies printed and distributed throughout the state. Shortly after the 1925 session of the Tennessee General Assembly opened, Senator John A. Shelton introduced an anti-evolution statute. Marr quickly sent five hundred copies of Bryan's speech to members of both houses in order to "guide" them during the deliberations. The Senate Judiciary Committee, however, recommended rejection of Shelton's bill on the ground that "it would not be the part of wisdom for the legislature to make laws that even remotely affected the question of religious belief." It was not Shelton but John Washington Butler, an obscure member of the Tennessee House of Representatives, who was destined to make his name immortal by attaching it to a statute prohibiting the teaching of evolution. Butler, a farmer from highly rural Macon County and a member of the Primitive Baptist Church, had first been elected to the House in 1922 on a platform stressing his belief in the literal Bible and his opposition to the teaching of evolution in the schools.

It was not until his second term that Butler decided to embody his convictions in a bill. Once his decision was made, he did not consult Bryan or anyone else. On his forty-ninth birthday he sat down and drafted a bill which made it unlawful for a teacher in any school supported in whole or part by state funds "to teach any theory that denies the story of the divine creation of man as taught in the Bible, and to teach instead that man has descended from a lower order of animals." Butler's bill, which was submitted to the House on January 21, 1925, one day after Shelton's was introduced in the Senate, was accorded a happier reception. Two days after its introduction the House Committee on Education recommended its passage, and four days later the House adopted it overwhelmingly by a vote of 71 to 5.

The Butler bill was then sent on to the Senate, where Senator Shelton threw his support behind it. He quickly solicited Bryan's suggestions for improving the measure, writing: "If necessary we can defer final action for a few days longer in order to have the benefit of your advice." "The special thing I want to suggest," Bryan responded immediately, "is that it is better not to have a penalty." Upon first consideration the Senate Judiciary Committee recommended rejection of the statute but following a month's recess, during which public opinion made itself felt, the committee reversed itself and by a vote of 7 to 4 reported the law favorably. The debate in the Senate produced slightly more opposition to the proposed statute than it had faced in the House. One Senator tried to laugh it out of the legislature, as similar bills had been in other states, by proposing an amendment to "prohibit the teaching that the earth is round." But all such attempts—and there were relatively few of them—failed, and the Senate approved the measure 24 to 6. The bill now found its way to the desk of the state's able governor, Austin Peay. Peay's dilemma was a real one. Although he was reputed to have privately felt it to be an absurd bill, Peay found no ground swell of opposition to which he could appeal. During the debate in the legislature not one word of protest was heard from any of the state's leading citizens, from the State Department of Education, from the University of Tennessee, or from any other major educational institution in the state. No aspirant to martyrdom, Peay signed the bill and defended his action by writing: "Right or wrong, there is a widespread belief that something is shaking the fundamentals of the country, both in religion and in morals. It is the opinion of many that an abandonment of the old-fashioned faith and belief in the Bible is our trouble in large degree. It is my own belief."

Although Bryan was not pleased at the inclusion of fines from $100 to $500 for offenders of the statute, he hailed its enactment. "The Christian parents of the State owe you a debt of gratitude for saving their children from the poisonous influence of an unproven hypothesis," he wired the Governor. ". . . The South is now leading the Nation in the defense of Bible Christianity. Other states North and South will follow the example of Tennessee." It was precisely this expectation that prompted the American Civil Liberties Union to make a *cause célèbre* out of a statute which was, in reality, merely one more small ripple in the wave of prohibitory legislation that engulfed the nation during the Twenties.

As far as the Governor of Tennessee was concerned, the law to which he had just appended his signature was not intended to be an active statute. "After a careful examination," he wrote in a message to the legislature, "I can find nothing of consequence in the books now being taught in our schools with which this bill will interfere in the slightest manner. Therefore, it will not put our teachers in any jeopardy. Probably the law will never be applied." All that the framers of the legislation intended, Peay insisted, was to lodge "a distinct protest against an irreligious tendency to exalt so-called science, and deny the Bible in some schools and quarters . . ." Peay, of course, was attempting to justify his own action, yet there is a certain validity in his interpretation of the law. During the period between its enactment and the beginning of the Scopes Trial, no attempt was made on the part of state officials to translate it into action. The contents of science courses and texts were not investigated, and students continued to learn biology from teachers and texts that accepted Darwin and his theories.

The sole attempt to enforce the Tennessee "monkey-bill" was due not to the actions of its friends but of its foes. Shortly after the law was passed, the officers of the American Civil Liberties Union deliberated and decided to sponsor a test case. In the closing days of April the organization began its search for a plaintiff by informing Tennessee newspapers of its willingness to guarantee legal and financial assistance to any teacher who would test the anti-evolution law.

One of those who read of the Union's offer was George Rappelyea, a young mining engineer in Dayton, Tennessee, who had opposed the law since its passage and who now decided that Dayton was the very place to test it. Calling in the town's 24-year-old science teacher, John Thomas Scopes, Rappelyea asked him if he could teach biology without teaching evolution. When Scopes answered in the negative, F. E. Robinson, the head of the county board of education, in whose drug store the interview was being held, accused him of violating the law. "So has every other teacher," Scopes replied and then explained that Hunter's *Civic Biology*, the state-approved textbook, taught from an evolutionary standpoint. "Let's take this thing to court and test the legality of it," Rappelyea suggested almost casually. It took some doing to overcome Scopes's understandable reluctance, but the glib-tongued engineer, appealing to Scopes's duty as an American and as an educator, finally prevailed. "He therefore consented to the arrest and the plans were drafted," Rappelyea has recorded. "I wired the American Civil Liberties Union that the stage was set and that if they could defray the expenses of production the play could open at once. They agreed."

All that remained was the selection of the principal actors. On May 7, Scopes was arrested. Five days later, Bryan, who was in Pittsburgh delivering a series of lectures, received a wire from the executive committee of the World's Christian Fundamentals Association informing him of his selection as their attorney at the trial. "I shall be pleased to act for your great religious organizations and without compensation assist in the enforcement of the Tennessee law provided of course it is agreeable to the Law Department of the State," Bryan replied. It was more than agreeable, as Bryan learned a few days later when he received the following letter from Sue Hicks, one of the prosecuting attorneys:

> We have been trying to get in touch with you by wire to ask you to become associated with us in the prosecution of the case of the State against J. T. Scopes . . . but our wires did not reach you.
>
> We will consider it a great honor to have you with us in this prosecution.

Almost immediately Clarence Darrow and Dudley Field Malone offered their services to John Randolph Neal, Scopes's local attorney. Scopes and Neal, acting on their own, accepted the offer, and the American Civil Liberties Union, which had planned to secure politically conservative and religiously orthodox attorneys to defend Scopes, found itself saddled with an outspoken skeptic and a prominent divorce lawyer.

William Jennings Bryan, Jr., a Los Angeles attorney who had long been desirous of assuming an active role in the fundamentalist crusade and who, after his father's death, was to become president of the Anti-Evolution League of America, took his place alongside the elder Bryan as a member of the prosecution. The appearance of the two Bryans for the state and of Darrow, Malone, and the American Civil Liberties Union's attorney, Arthur Garfield Hays, for the defense, converted the trial into a free-for-all in which the fundamental issues at stake were often in danger of being forgotten. The Scopes Trial, occupying the center of national attention, offered the friends of academic freedom a rare opportunity to proclaim the essentials of their creed and to point out that while local communities had the unquestionable legal authority to regulate education, there were moral as well as legal limitations to the curb that could be placed upon free speech and thought in the classroom. This point, of course, was made more than once, but its applicability to other parts of the nation and to issues other than evolution was blurred by the cultural and sectional struggle which was being waged simultaneously.

At the very outset Bryan seemed to have a clear idea of what the trial was all about. "I have been explaining the case to audiences," he reported to Sue Hicks in May. "It is the *easiest* case to explain I have ever found. While I am perfectly willing to go into the question of evolution, I am not sure that it is involved. The *right* of the *people* speaking through the legislature, to control the schools which they *create* and *support* is the real issue as I see it." "The first question to be decided," he announced in June, "is who shall control our public schools?" If not the people speaking through their legislatures, then who? The scientists? But there was only one scientist for every ten thousand people, "a pretty little oligarchy to put in control of the education of all the children." The teachers themselves? That proposition, Bryan felt, needed only to be stated to be rejected as absurd. "The teacher is an employee and receives a salary; employees take directions from their employers, and the teacher is no exception to the rule. No teacher would be permitted to teach the students that a monarchy is the only good government and kings the only good chief executives."

While on the one hand Bryan spoke as if he was willing to see the trial waged on the issue of how far the community could go in imposing limitations upon learning, on the other he acted as if the trial was to be a "duel to the death" between religion and evolution. "I greatly appreciate the opportunity the Fundamentalists have given me to defend the faith," he wrote one of his colleagues in the beginning of June. Some days later he informed a supporter that "The American people do not know what a menace evolution is—I am expecting a tremendous reaction as the result of the information which will go out from Dayton . . ."

During that brief period when he controlled the defense strategy, John Randolph Neal echoed Bryan's initial statements. "The question is not whether evolution is true or untrue," he asserted, "but involves the freedom of teaching, or what is more important, the freedom of learning." His new associates, however, did not share his opinion. Their attitude was best summed up by their scientific ally Henry Fairfield Osborn, who observed on the eve of the trial: "The facts in this great case are that William Jennings Bryan is the man on trial; John Thomas Scopes is not the man on trial. If the case is properly set before the jury, Scopes will be the real plaintiff, Bryan will be the real defendant." This was precisely what Darrow himself had in mind. In explaining his courtroom strategy, years after the trial, Darrow wrote: "My object, and my only object, was to focus the attention of the country on the programme of Mr. Bryan and the other fundamentalists in America." To Arthur Garfield Hays the issue was even more clear-cut. The trial, he wrote, "was a battle between two types of mind—the rigid, orthodox, accepting, unyielding, narrow, conventional mind, and the broad liberal, critical, cynical, skeptical and tolerant mind."

The days before the trial were busy ones for Bryan. In May he was in Columbus, Ohio, attending the 1925 General Assembly of his church. The situation at the Presbyterian conclave was confused since all of the leading candidates were fundamentalists. Bryan tried to ply the middle of the road by refusing to support either Dr. L. E. MacAfee, the candidate of the extreme fundamentalists or Dr. Charles R. Erdman a moderate fundamentalist whose candidacy was being advanced by the liberals. Instead Bryan backed Dr. W. O. Thompson the retiring president of Ohio State University. On the day of the balloting Dr. Thompson withdrew from the race and Bryan, who had helped to break the ranks of the extreme fundamentalists, had to sit unhappily by and watch Dr. Erdman's election.

During this period Bryan began to modify his earlier stand on religion and the schools. If the spiritual foundations of the nation were being undermined by the teaching of evolution, were they not being weakened equally by the absence of any religious teachings in the schools? As early as 1914 he had suggested to Rabbi Wise and Cardinal Gibbons that "there should be some way of utilizing a part of the school time in the teaching of morals, and believing that morals rest upon religion, I know of no way of teaching them except under religious supervision."

More than ten years later, in April 1925, Bryan wrote to Representative Taylor of the Florida lower house, proposing a law making the reading of the Bible compulsory in the public schools with a provision allowing parents to have their children excused if they so desired. "But I would go farther than this," he added. "We are interested in the religious development of young Jews and of young Catholics as well as young Protestants, and the law could, and in my judgment should, provide that any religious denomination or group of denominations shall have the privilege of using the school rooms on equal terms . . . for religious teaching."

When the Florida Legislature passed a law providing for the reading of the Scriptures in the public schools, Bryan congratulated it but made it clear that he was not satisfied: ". . . the reading of the Bible a few minutes each day is not sufficient. The Bible needs to be taught, as school lessons are taught, by teachers who are free to interpret, explain and illustrate them." This is as far as Bryan was prepared to go up to the time of his death, though his opponents charged that his plans were far more grandiose. During the Scopes Trial a *New York Times* correspondent informed the public that Bryan was planning to "put God in the Constitution," an assertion which Bryan angrily denied. And eight months after Bryan's death, Augustus Thomas, the playwright, who had nominated Bryan for President in 1908, claimed that he saw the actual wording of an amendment drawn up by Bryan which would have established the United States as a Christian nation. Though it is possible that Bryan might have been driven to make such proposals had he lived, there is no evidence that he did so before his death.

In the beginning of June Bryan stopped at Nashville on his way home to Florida to confer with three fellow members of the prosecution, Wallace C. Haggard and the Hicks brothers. At the end of the conference the four men announced that they had come to a "clear understanding of the lines of the prosecution." Nonetheless, Bryan continued to keep in close touch with the Tennessee prosecution. The one point upon which Bryan was adamant from the beginning of his association with the prosecution was the question of punishment. ". . . I don't think we should insist on more [than] the minimum fine," he informed Sue Hicks, "and I will let the defendant have the money to pay if he needs it. It is a test case and will end all controversy."

"The unbelievers are evidently very much worried about the case," Bryan wrote Hicks on June 10. The defense, he noted, was frantically searching for big-name attorneys. "They seem to realize they are in for a real fight." Bryan himself, however, seemed a bit nervous. While he assured Hicks of his confidence that the prosecution as it was presently constituted could "meet their attack without any outside aid," he felt that the case was too important to take any chances, and he suggested that they too invite some prominent attorneys to join them. "The biggest lawyer I know of is Samuel Untermyer of New York. He has had large experience in big cases and is a match for any of the men on the other side. Being a Jew, he ought to be interested in defending Moses from the Darwinites. He has been my personal and political friend for twenty-five years and I am sure he will be glad to join us." Anxious to have as united a religious front as possible, Bryan also felt it might be useful to seek the aid of a prominent Catholic such as Senator Thomas Walsh of Montana or Senator David Walsh of Massachusetts.

Without waiting to hear from Hicks, Bryan invited Untermyer to assist in the prosecution. Hicks's first response was not encouraging. He had talked over Bryan's suggestion with Attorney General Stewart, Ben McKenzie, and other members of the prosecution, and they were of the opinion that the prosecution should stand pat. Stewart felt that it would be a greater victory to convict Scopes in spite of the talent he had representing him. "Knowing the sentiment of the court (who by the way is somewhat indiscreet in discussing the merits of the case with the Attorney General), General Stewart is confident their motion to quash the indictment will be over-ruled and all evidence will be admitted at the trial."

The very next day Hicks and his associates had a change of heart and agreed that it might be useful to have additional counsel, "although, we some what doubt the advisability of having a Jew in the case for the reason that they reject part of the Bible and do not believe in the Divinity of Christ. However we are willing to leave this matter to your judgment and accept the attorneys you advise." It was now Bryan's turn to be inconstant. Untermyer had gone to Europe and probably would not be able to help in any case, he informed Hicks. "I recognize the force of the objection you make to him and Walsh. . . . After reading your letter, I am inclined to think we shall not need any additional attorneys." "It is interesting to note the growing interest in the case," he added. "Am preparing myself on all imaginable points."

When Bryan finally did hear from Untermyer, his suspicions were confirmed. The New York attorney would be in Europe throughout the month of July and thus could not aid in the prosecution of Scopes. He did, however, have some prophetic advice to give Bryan. He urged him to confine the issue strictly. "I would seek to exclude all discussions by experts or otherwise on the subject of Evolution (which to my mind has nothing whatever to do with the case . . .), and rest squarely on the proposition that the plain letter and spirit of the law have been violated, and that the burden rests upon the Defence to establish the unconstitutionality of that law not by introduction of evidence, but by discussion of the legal problem involved." "I am fearful however that there is so much of 'grand-stand play' involved in this prosecution and so great a desire on the part of the local influences to convert it into a sensational controversy instead of adhering closely to the issues involved, that it will not be easy to keep the trial within the legal limits."

Toward the end of June, Darrow, Malone, and Bainbridge Colby, who was then associated with the defense, traveled to Dayton to look over the scene of the impending trial. Hicks and Wallace Haggard were quick to report the event to Bryan. Both men found Darrow an impressive figure, and both thought he was surprised at the cordiality of his reception. "Darrow at one time said that some of the Northern people had the idea that they would be in bodily danger if they came down here among the fundamentalists," Hicks wrote. The Progressive Club of Dayton held a banquet in Darrow's honor, at which the Chicago lawyer spoke for over an hour. Haggard described the reaction of the audience for Bryan: "Those in attendance seemed to shudder and even abhor the woe and despair that crept through his various thoughts and was even written on his countenance. . . . there can be no doubt, despite his intelligence and his magnetism, he cannot prevail upon our people."

Bryan read these letters with interest. Darrow, he agreed, "is an able man, and, I think, an honest man." As the opening day of the trial approached, Bryan seemed more convinced than ever that it would serve a great purpose. "There is no reason why the Scopes Trial should not be conducted on a high plane without the least personal feeling," he wrote one of his neighbors. ". . . The trial will be a success in proportion as it enables the public to understand the two sides and the reasons on both sides. Every question has to be settled at last by the public and the sooner it is understood the sooner it can be settled."

The environment in which the Scopes Trial took place has been described too often to require repetition here. The little town of Dayton in the Tennessee hill country, the meetings of the Holy Rollers from surrounding areas, the sudden invasion of cranks of all sorts vying with one another to attract attention, the garish exhibits and banners enjoining the people to read their Bible and avoid damnation, the fundamentalist judge from Gizzard's Cove, Tennessee, who was to rule over the proceedings—all provided an unusually rich feast for the army of journalists, few of whom were able to restrain themselves. "The thing is genuinely fabulous," exulted H. L. Mencken. "I have stored up enough material to last me twenty years."

Bryan left his home in Miami on Monday, July 6, and arrived in Dayton the next day. As he descended from his train he was cheered by three hundred residents. After an automobile procession down the main street, Bryan, in his shirt sleeves and with a pith helmet protecting him from the blazing sun, spent the afternoon strolling through the town getting acquainted. He really did not have to, of course. He had been in hundreds of towns like it before, and he knew it and its people well. In a speech before the Dayton Progressive Club that night Bryan threw down the gauntlet to his opponents. "The contest between evolution and Christianity is a duel to the death. . . . If evolution wins in Dayton Christianity goes—not suddenly of course, but gradually—for the two cannot stand together. . . . The atheists, agnostics and all other opponents of Christianity understand the character of the struggle, hence this interest in this case. From this time forth the Christians will understand the character of the struggle also. In an open fight the truth will triumph."

The following night Bryan and his party drove six miles straight up into the mountains to keep a speaking engagement at the Morgan Springs Hotel. After dinner Bryan stepped out onto the veranda overlooking the Tennessee valley, and began to speak to the two hundred hill folk sitting on the railings and steps around him. Directly in front of him sat an old man in a wheelchair who looked up at Bryan "with the rapt countenance of one who listens to someone inspired." Next to him stood a tall mountaineer who remained immobile throughout the speech, one hand grasping a glass of water if Bryan should want it. As he stood in the darkness, his figure silhouetted by a thin ray of light from the hotel door, an occasional flash of lightning and rumble of thunder made the scene seem almost contrived. Bryan spoke softly of his pride in the South and predicted the coming of a great religious revival which would begin in the South and sweep across the nation. His final words were met with a reverential hush. "His voice, always a beautiful instrument, vibrated with feeling," wrote the *Times* correspondent, "his whole being was synchronized into a graceful machine for driving home his word . . ." This night convinced the journalist that Bryan "is more than a great politician, more than a lawyer in a trial, more even than one of our greatest orators, he is a symbol of their simple religious faith."

The trial opened on Friday, July 10, 1925, and after a jury was selected court adjourned until Monday. Bryan found himself in great demand as a speaker during that first weekend. In these talks he explained the reasons for his participation in the trial. "The people of Tennessee," he said on Saturday, "have a right to protect the Bible as they understand it. They are not compelled to consider the interpretations placed upon it by people from other states." Speaking from the pulpit of the Methodist Episcopal Church the next morning he declared: "While God does not despise the learned, he does not give them a monopoly of His attention. The unlearned in this country are much more numerous than the learned. . . . Thank God I am going to spend the latter years of my life in a locality where there is a belief in God, and in the Son of God, and in a civilization to be based on salvation through blood." Speaking to a large gathering on the courthouse lawn in the afternoon, Bryan denied the widely circulated statement which quoted him as having said that he intended to "put God into the Constitution." "Our purpose and our only purpose," he assured his listeners, "is to vindicate the right of parents to guard the religion of their children against efforts made in the name of science to undermine faith in supernatural religion. There is no attack on free speech, or freedom of the press, or freedom of thought, or freedom of knowledge, but surely parents have a right to guard the religious welfare of their children."

The opening days of the trial were glorious days for Bryan. Everywhere he went he was met by throngs of devoted and admiring followers. H. L. Mencken in his characteristically hyperbolic style remarked: "There were many . . . who believed that Bryan was no longer merely human, but had lifted himself up to some level or other of the celestial angels. . . . It would have surprised no one if he had suddenly begun to perform miracles. . . . I saw plenty of his customers approach him stealthily to touch his garments. . . . Those with whom he shook hands were made men." When the court reconvened on Monday morning most of the one thousand spectators who crowded into the Dayton courtroom had hopes of hearing their champion rise and defend the faith, but Bryan was in no hurry. During the first four days of the trial he sat in the stifling courthouse in his shirt sleeves waving a large fan, and except for one or two brief statements he remained silent as the defense made a futile attempt to quash the indictment against Scopes on legal grounds. Nor did he break his silence as his fellow attorneys for the prosecution opened and closed their exceptionally brief case which consisted merely of calling four witnesses all of whom testified to the fact that Scopes had based his lectures in biology upon Darwin's teachings.

As soon as the prosecution rested its case the defense announced that it would introduce fifteen scientists and clergymen who had journeyed to Dayton from all sections of the country and who would endeavor to show that there was no conflict between the Biblical and scientific accounts of creation. As Darrow was examining the first of these fifteen, Dr. Maynard M. Metcalf, a zoologist from Johns Hopkins University, Attorney General A. T. Stewart, and former Attorney General McKenzie objected to the introduction of such testimony. The ensuing debate over the admissibility of scientific evidence, which consumed the entire fifth day of the proceedings, was the occasion of Bryan's first and last major speech of the trial. "We do not need any expert to tell us what the law means," he said in opening, "an expert cannot be permitted to come in here and try to defeat the enforcement of a law . . . This is not the place to try to prove that the law ought never to have been passed. The place to prove that was at the legislature."

As Bryan spoke, the eyes of all the spectators were upon him. The residents of Dayton had been waiting for precisely this moment. They leaned forward expectantly to hear their champion demolish the opponents of their faith with words of derision and scorn, and Bryan, forgetting Untermyer's advice, did not disappoint them. Holding up a copy of Hunter's *Civic Biology,* the text from which Scopes had taught, Bryan turned to a diagram on page 194 which classified all the animal species:

> Of course it [the diagram] is only a guess, and I don't suppose it is carried to a one or even to ten. I see they are in round numbers, and I don't think all the animals breed in round numbers, and so I think it must be a generalization of them. (Laughter).
>
> 8,000 protozoa, 35,000 sponges. I am satisfied from some I have seen there must be more than 35,000 sponges. (Laughter.)
>
> . . . Then there are the amphibia. I don't know whether they have not yet decided to come out, or have almost decided to go back. (Laughter.)
>
> . . . And then we have mammals, 3,500, and there is a little circle, and a man is in the circle. Find him; find man.
>
> There is the book. There is the book they were teaching your chil-

> dren; teaching that man was a mammal and so indistinguishable among the mammals that they leave him there with other mammals. (Laughter and applause.) Including elephants. (Laughter.)
>
> Talk about putting Daniel in the lion's den! How dare those scientists put man in a little ring like that with lions and tigers and everything that is bad?
>
> Tell me that the parents of this day have not any right to declare that children are not to be taught this doctrine—shall not be taken down from the high plane upon which God put man? Shall we be detached from the throne of God and be compelled to link our ancestors with the jungle—tell that to these children?

Bryan next picked up a copy of Darwin's *Descent of Man* and began to quote from it, after first apologizing "if I have to use some of these long words—I have been trying all my life to use short words, and it is kind of hard to turn scientist for a moment (Laughter) and try to express myself in their language." Drawing more laughter still by taking Darwin to task for having man descend "Not even from American monkeys but from Old World monkeys," Bryan grew more serious and militant. Pointing to Dr. Metcalf, he thundered: "I suppose this distinguished scholar who came here shamed them all by his number of degrees. He did not shame me, for I have more than he has. . . . Did he tell you where life began? Did he tell you that back of all there was a God? Not a word about it. Did he tell you how life began? Not a word and not one of them can tell you how life began. . . . They want to come in with their little padded-up evolution that commences with nothing and ends nowhere." He held up Nietzsche and the young Chicago murderers, Leopold and Loeb, as products of evolutionary teachings, and pointed out that in his defense of Leopold and Loeb, Darrow had argued that the professors who taught Nietzsche's doctrines to the young, impressionable Leopold were just as responsible for the murder as Leopold himself. When Darrow denied this, Bryan read verbatim extracts from Darrow's arguments to prove his point.

Bryan ended as he had begun, by defending the right of a state to enforce its own statutes without outside interference. ". . . I think we ought to confine ourselves to the law and to the evidence that can be admitted in accordance with the law," he said in closing. ". . . The facts are simple, the case is plain, and if these gentlemen want to enter upon a larger field of educational work on the subject of evolution, let us get through with this case and then convene a mock court. . . . (Prolonged applause.)" "Papa spoke," Mrs. Bryan wrote her daughter Grace, "and I never saw him quite so agitated. He trembled when he stood up, and it has alarmed William and me very much. His speech was very well received."

The differences—and similarities—between the two sides were

perhaps brought out most forcibly in the speeches delivered by Darrow and Attorney General Stewart. Both men spoke with deep fervor, both used similar arguments to bolster their case, and both tried to convince their audience that even one concession to their opponents would open wide the floodgates of disaster. The banning of evolution was only the first step, Darrow warned on the second day of the trial. Next "you may ban books and the newspapers. Soon you may set Catholic against Protestant, and Protestant against Protestant, and try to foist your own religion on the minds of men. . . . Today it is the public school teachers, tomorrow the private, the next day the preachers and the lecturers, the magazines, the books, the newspapers." Stewart, in his speech a few days later, hailed Darrow as one of the greatest lawyers in America and remarked: "Great God! the good that a man of his ability could have done if he had aligned himself with the forces of right instead of aligning himself with that which strikes its poisonous fangs at the very bosom of Christianity." If evolution won this battle the next step would be to deprive Christians of their right to believe in the Virgin Birth, then in the Resurrection, "until finally that precious Book and its glorious teachings upon which this civilization has been built will be taken from us."

It was not Bryan or Darrow or Stewart, but Dudley Field Malone who delivered the most eloquent speech of the trial. Malone had served under Bryan in the State Department and still referred to him as "my old chief and friend." Malone reminded his "old chief," however, that whether he knew it or not "he is a mammal, he is an animal, and he is a man." "Mr. Bryan," he thundered, "is not the only one who has spoken for the Bible. . . . There are other people in this country who have given their whole lives to God." "There is never a duel with truth," he said in his stirring peroration, "the truth always wins. . . . The truth does not need the forces of Government. The truth does not need Mr. Bryan. . . . We feel we stand with progress. . . . We feel we stand with fundamental freedom in America. We are not afraid. Where is the fear? We defy it!"

"Dayton thundered her verdict at the end of the speech of Malone," wrote the correspondent for the Memphis *Commercial-Appeal*, ". . . Women shrieked their approval. Men, unmoved even by Darrow, could not restrain their cheers. . . . People climbed over the rails to greet the New Yorker. Crowds surged into the aisle. It was a quarter of an hour before the room could be quieted." The Daytonians showed unmistakably that despite their faith they could appreciate eloquence for its own sake. The reception accorded Malone was doubtless disquieting to Bryan, but it failed to make him more cautious. It failed also to move the Judge. When court opened on Friday morning, Judge Raulston read his ruling barring scientific testimony, though he dismissed the jury in order to allow the testimony to be read into the record in the event that the case was appealed to a higher court. The court then adjourned until Monday.

Though the court was not in session the opposing attorneys continued to hammer away at one another throughout the weekend. On Saturday morning Darrow stated that although Bryan had been instrumental in precipitating the Scopes Trial and had called for a "battle to the death," his unwillingness to allow scientific testimony betrayed a lack of confidence in his own position and a fear of testing his views against those of eminent educators and scientists. Bryan, Darrow announced, "has fled from the field, his forces disorganized and his pretensions exposed." On Sunday evening, addressing an outdoor meeting in nearby Pikesville, Bryan spoke of "a gigantic conspiracy among atheists and agnostics against the Christian religion." He also took this occasion to strike back at the reporters who throughout the trial had been vilifying him and his followers. "These men," he told his listeners, "who come from another state to call you yokels and bigots, I wish I had them here to set them face to face with a humanity they cannot imitate. But in the end every critic you have will be rotted and forgotten."

With the ruling out of scientific testimony it seemed that the trial was at an end. Darrow and his colleagues had based their entire case upon the testimony of the fifteen experts they had brought to Dayton, and there was apparently no one else they could call. H. L. Mencken was so positive that the trial was over that he packed his bags during the weekend and left the torrid Tennessee climate behind him, remarking that nothing remained to be done except "the formal business of bumping off the defendant." With the end of the trial in sight the unusually large crowds that had been packing the courtroom grew larger still, for with such eloquent lawyers on both sides no one in or around Dayton wanted to miss the final arguments. Bryan had been waiting for this moment. For weeks he had been working on his final speech; a speech which he described as "the mountain peak of my life's effort."

When the court reconvened on Monday morning Judge Raulston allowed the scientific experts to finish reading their testimony into the record, and then ordered the court to adjourn to the courthouse lawn for the danger of the building collapsing had increased with the crowd. This move was an extremely popular one, since it allowed almost anyone who so desired to view the proceedings. The scene could not have been more propitious for the delivery of Bryan's final summation had he arranged it himself, but the defense had other ideas. As soon as the court was settled in its new surroundings Arthur Garfield Hays rose and asked Bryan to take the stand. This request, which according to Hays took even Darrow and Malone by surprise, was vigorously opposed by Attorney General Stewart. Convinced as always of the righteousness of his cause, Bryan consented to testify despite Stewart's objections.

As Bryan took the stand, Darrow, clad in a blue shirt and blue suspenders, moved forward to examine him. Darrow, who had been an active supporter of Bryan in his earlier political battles, was nonetheless the perfect antithesis of Bryan in temperament and training. Raised on a diet of Darwin, Lyell, Buckle, Tyndall, and Spencer, Darrow was an iconoclast, an agnostic, and in many respects a cynic, whose active, searching mind, unlike Bryan's, conceived of truth not as merely a possession to be defended but as a prize to be discovered. For the next two hours Darrow pursued Bryan relentlessly.

Darrow began by questioning Bryan on his literal acceptance of the Scriptures. Did Bryan believe that the whale swallowed Jonah, that Joshua made the sun stand still, that the flood actually took place, that the different languages of the world really dated from the Tower of Babel, that Adam and Eve were the first people? To all of these questions Bryan answered in the affirmative, stating at one point that he would believe that Jonah swallowed the whale if the Bible said so for "one miracle is just as easy to believe as another." Darrow also endeavored to show Bryan's extremely narrow fund of knowledge. Bryan admitted that he knew little or nothing about ancient civilization, that he had never read a book on philology, that he never thought about how long man had been inhabiting the earth, or how old the earth itself was, that he knew nothing about Buddha or Confucius or Zoroaster, and that the entire subject of comparative religion was a vast wasteland to him.

Paradoxically, it was Bryan's more enlightened views rather than his narrower ones that probably led to his diminished popularity during the course of the trial. During their discussion of Joshua, Darrow forced Bryan to state reluctantly that he believed the earth moved around the sun and that in describing Joshua as having made the sun stand still the Bible was merely using language which the people of that time with their limited knowledge could understand. Similarly, in discussing the creation, Bryan admitted that the six days described in the Bible were probably not literal days but periods which might have encompassed millions of years. For the first time it became evident to many of Bryan's followers that their leader did not accept the Bible literally at all times. As we have seen, Bryan did not enter the fundamentalist movement primarily to defend the literal word of the Bible; his motives were far more complex than that. Bryan, in fact, seems to have been concerned about an absolutely literal reading of the Scriptures only in those areas where such an interpretation could help close the door upon a theory which he felt would have pernicious results for mankind. His literal acceptance of the Bible did not lead to his rejection of evolution so much as his rejection of evolution led to his willingness to accept literally certain portions of the Bible in the face of the educated portion of the community. Nevertheless, Bryan unquestionably committed a serious blunder in revealing his actual attitudes toward the creation and the story of Joshua on the stand, and it is probable that he regretted having done so.

During the examination Attorney General Stewart rose time and again to point out the irrelevancy of the proceedings and to demand that they be halted, but each time Bryan indicated his willingness to continue. "These gentlemen," he told Stewart at one point, "have not had much chance. They did not come here to try this case. They came here to try revealed religion. I am here to defend it, and they can ask me any questions they please." The nature of most of this much-heralded examination is illustrated by the following example:

Darrow: Mr. Bryan, do you believe that the first woman was Eve?
Bryan: Yes.
Darrow: Do you believe she was literally made out of Adam's rib?
Bryan: I do.
Darrow: Did you ever discover where Cain got his wife?
Bryan: No, sir; I leave the agnostics to hunt for her.
Darrow: . . . The Bible says he got one, doesn't it? Were there other people on the earth at that time?
Bryan: I cannot say.
Darrow: You cannot say? Did that ever enter into your consideration?
Bryan: Never bothered me.

As questioning of this sort continued, the tempers of both men began to wear thin, and when Darrow returned to the question of Adam and Eve and demanded to know how the snake moved before God commanded him to crawl on his belly, Bryan grew angry and the following exchange took place.

Bryan: Your Honor, I think I can shorten this testimony. The only purpose Mr. Darrow has is to slur at the Bible, but I will answer his questions . . . and I have no objection in the world. I want the world to know that this man, who does not believe in God, is trying to use a court in Tennessee—
Darrow: I object to that.
Bryan: to slur at it, and, while it will require time I am willing to take it.
Darrow: I object to your statement. I am examining you on your fool ideas that no intelligent Christian on earth believes.

At this point both men were on their feet shaking their fists at one another. Judge Raulston banging his gavel promptly adjourned court until the next morning.

Bryan had hoped to put Darrow on the stand the next day, but that night Stewart, who had opposed the cross-examination from the start and who had spoken to Judge Raulston immediately after court had adjourned, informed him that there would be no further examination of counsel on either side. When the court reconvened on Tuesday morning Judge Raulston ordered Bryan's testimony of the previous day expunged from the records. The time had now come for the final arguments, but the defense in declining to sum up their case dealt Bryan a final blow by depriving him of the opportunity of delivering the speech which he had labored on for so long. In later years Darrow admitted that the defense had feared the effect that Bryan's oratory might have on the "assembled multitudes" and had felt that "by not making a closing argument on our side we could cut him down."

The jury's verdict of guilty, which was arrived at after eight minutes of deliberation, surprised no one. Nor did it really disappoint anyone since Darrow and his colleagues had desired such a verdict so that they might appeal the case to a higher court. Bryan in his few words of thanks to the court said: "This case will stimulate investigation and investigation will bring out information. The facts will be known, and upon the facts as ascertained the decision will be rendered. I think, my friends and your Honor, that if we are actuated by the spirit that should actuate every one of us, no matter what our views may be, we ought not only desire but pray that that which is right will prevail, whether it be our way or somebody else's."

It was obvious that the Scopes Trial had done neither Bryan nor his cause any good, but it is doubtful if Bryan ever realized just how much harm it had done. He could not have been unaware that the fundamentalists had received an enormous amount of bad publicity, that in the eight days of the trial he and his followers had been the objects of more scorn and derision than the supporters of most causes generally receive in a lifetime. He also must have been aware that while Darrow, Malone, and their colleagues had converted few Daytonians to evolution, the force of their personalities and eloquence had won the respect and even the friendship of many of the local residents.* Nonetheless, Bryan took comfort in the knowledge that the anti-evolution statute had been upheld.

Nor was the trial a complete victory for the defense. In 1933, eight years after the Scopes Trial, Professor Howard K. Beale submitted a questionnaire to a cross-sampling of American teachers. One-third to

*It has been too easily assumed that the increased esteem in which Darrow and Malone were held at the end of the trial was the result of the impact of their ideas. In reality, theirs was largely a personal victory. They won friends but not followers. There is no evidence to substantiate the view that the cause of scientific freedom won many adherents in Dayton and the surrounding area at the close of the Scopes Trial. The Tennessee anti-evolution statute has remained in force to this day. Several years ago when Senator Z. Carter Patten of that state tried to have the law repealed he found only four supporters of his repeal bill in both houses of the state legislature and could not even get the bill out of committee. If Bryan lost popularity among some of Dayton's residents due to the trial, it was not because they had been converted to Darrow's side, but because they were deeply disappointed at the concessions Bryan made under Darrow's questioning.

one-half of them revealed that they were still afraid to express acceptance of the theory of evolution. But their inhibitions did not end here. One-fourth of the teachers polled felt it was unsafe to favor the abandonment of the Monroe Doctrine, criticize American actions in the Mexican War, or defend Britain's position in the American Revolution. One-third feared to disturb the aura of sanctity surrounding the heroes of American history. Large numbers felt it was dangerous to question the profit system or express disapproval of local businessmen. One-third were afraid to criticize President Hoover for using force to dispel the Bonus Army. Between one-third and one-half thought it the better part of discretion to avoid criticism of the Ku Klux Klan, the Daughters of the American Revolution, the American Legion, or the Confederate Veterans. Hardly any teachers felt it was safe to admit disbelief in God.

Beale's study pointed out what should have been clear in 1925, but what, in fact, is still not entirely clear today—that the Scopes Trial was not unique; it was not merely an aberration of a backward part of the populace. "Try teaching communism in the schools of a community that denounced Tennesseean intolerance," Beale suggested. The fact was that every American community had its sacred beliefs which no teacher could question with impunity. The "hired-man" theory for teachers was not restricted to any one section of the country. When Bryan proclaimed: "The hand that writes the pay check rules the school," he was not speaking for the fundamentalist South alone. The community whose teachers were not governed by this dictum was a rare one. Men, however, are always reluctant to look too closely at their own back yards. To view the Scopes Trial as symptomatic of the evils in American education as a whole would have been too painful an experience. The American people wanted to be amused not perplexed by the trial, and they were not disappointed. They read with incredulity the lurid accounts of the primitive hill folk of Tennessee; they chuckled with self-satisfaction at the biting comments Mencken made at the expense of the "Babbitts," "morons," "peasants," "hillbillies," and "yokels" of Dayton; they shuddered with righteous indignation at the shameful lack of tolerance exhibited by the people of the South; and they conveniently and comfortably forgot that the teachers in their own communities wore muzzles hardly less restraining than the one placed on John Thomas Scopes by the state of Tennessee.

To say this is not to deny the importance of the trial. The prosecution, by dealing Bryan and his fellow fundamentalists some heavy blows and by helping to check the spread of the anti-evolution movement, unquestionably aided the cause of academic freedom. Unfortunately, for too many Americans the Scopes Trial was an end in itself. If Bryan and his followers were being simplistic in pointing to evolution as the root cause of Christianity's ills, what can be said of their fellow Americans who fastened upon fundamentalism as the only real threat to education in the nation? It was important that the battle in Dayton should have been waged, but it was no less important to continue the struggle in the hundreds of communities throughout the country where academic freedom still rested upon the shaky foundation of local prejudice and whim. This simple fact was forgotten in the wave of jubilation that followed Bryan's humiliation in the Tennessee courtroom.

If Bryan left the Scopes Trial "an exhausted and broken man," as one writer has recently maintained, he did a masterly job of concealing it during the five days of life remaining to him. The trial ended on Tuesday. Bryan spent Wednesday and Thursday in Dayton dictating his undelivered speech to his secretary, who typed it. Friday he traveled to Chattanooga to confer with George Fort Milton and arranged for the publication of his speech. The manuscript was taken to the Chattanooga Printing Company, and that evening Bryan began to read the first proof sheets. Early Saturday morning Mrs. Bryan drove down from Dayton, and she and her husband traveled to Winchester, Tennessee, the home of Judge Raulston and Attorney General Stewart, where Bryan was scheduled to speak.

Before the Scopes Trial Bryan had announced his intention of retiring from the platform to devote his time to completing his memoirs and caring for his wife. Subsequently, however, he made plans to lead a pilgrimage to Palestine during the coming winter, and on his trip to Winchester he apparently indicated to his wife that he was going to carry on his fundamentalist crusade in the United States. Mrs. Bryan reminded him that care must be taken to prevent "the perfectly legitimate work" of protecting religion from degenerating into an encroachment upon individual religious beliefs; religious zeal must not become intolerance. Bryan responded: " 'Well, Mama, I have not made that mistake yet, have I.' And I replied, 'You are all right so far, but will you be able to keep to this narrow path?' With a happy smile, he said, 'I think I can.' 'But,' said I, 'can you control your followers?' and more gravely he said, 'I think I can.' And I knew he was adding mentally, 'by the help of God.' "

After his address in Winchester, Bryan returned to Chattanooga, where he spent the night reading proof. Sunday morning at 9 A.M. he was back in Dayton and according to his wife he was in an ebullient mood. He was pleased with the progress the printers were making with his speech, he praised his son's performance at the recent trial, he read a letter from his oldest grandson that touched him, he was thankful for the kindness of the people in Dayton. At eleven o'clock he went to church and, asked to offer the prayer, he spoke for the last time in public. At Sunday dinner he informed his wife of a recent physical examination which indicated that he had at least several more years to live.

After dinner he made a few telephone calls to arrange for a vacation in the Smoky Mountains for himself and his wife. At three o'clock he phoned Milton in Chattanooga to discuss his speech. "I want you to study this speech," he told the editor. "I think it answers all the arguments of the evolutionists. . . . I am particularly hopeful that my speech will be printed in full and distributed all over the country." He then laid down to take a nap from which he never arose.*

If Bryan's soul was, as his wife believed, still marching on "just beyond our mortal vision," it unquestionably enjoyed the final scenes—the thousands of letters of sympathy that poured in upon the widow; the funeral train speeding through the countryside on its way to Washington, D.C.; the crowds of farmers and their wives and children gathering at every little junction and station, even in the dead of night, to catch a glimpse of the train; the long lines of silent mourners who filed past the still body in Dayton, Chattanooga, Nashville, and Washington; the simple Christian eulogy spoken by a minister who as a young man had decided for the ministry after hearing Bryan lecture on religion. In death, as in life, William Jennings Bryan was tugging at the heartstrings of the people he loved so well.

DISCUSSION QUESTIONS

1. Did the cause of "science" win a victory at Dayton?
2. Apart from the truth or falsity of the theory of evolution, what larger public-policy issues emerged in the Dayton trial?
3. How much authority should state officials or local school boards have in determining the content of schools courses and textbooks?
4. What public events in contemporary America have had a symbolic significance comparable to the "monkey trial" of 1925?

---

*The precise cause of Bryan's death is still a bit obscure. The newspapers reported that he died of apoplexy. See *New York Times*, July 27, 1925. Even his death, however, became the object of an attack by his enemies. Throughout most of his life Bryan had had a voracious appetite and his critics immediately accused him of having eaten himself to death. Clarence Darrow, for instance, upon being told that Bryan died of a broken heart is supposed to have mumbled: "Broken heart nothing; he died of a busted belly." Stone, *Clarence Darrow*, p. 64. In 1931, Bryan's daughter Grace, apparently still unsure of the nature of her father's death, wrote a letter of inquiry to his personal physician, Dr. J. Thomas Kelly. Although Kelly was not present when Bryan died and did not examine the body, his reply is the closest thing we have to a first-hand medical report. "In March 1914," he wrote, "at Mrs. Bryan's solicitation I examined the urine of Mr. Bryan and found it loaded with sugar, in other words, he had diabetes. He was immediately put on an anti-diabetic diet *and continued on the diet up to the time of his death*. I saw Mr. Bryan at frequent intervals, examined his urine and changed his diet as seen fit. . . . I saw many newspaper pictures of Mr. Bryan while he was in Tennessee and felt very apprehensive for him. You will remember it was very warm and *he was looking very thin*. Mr. Bryan died of diabetes melitis, the immediate cause being the fatigue incident to the heat and his extraordinary exertions due to the Scopes Trial." J. Thomas Kelly to Grace Bryan Hargreaves, June 25, 1931, Bryan Papers. Italics added.

8

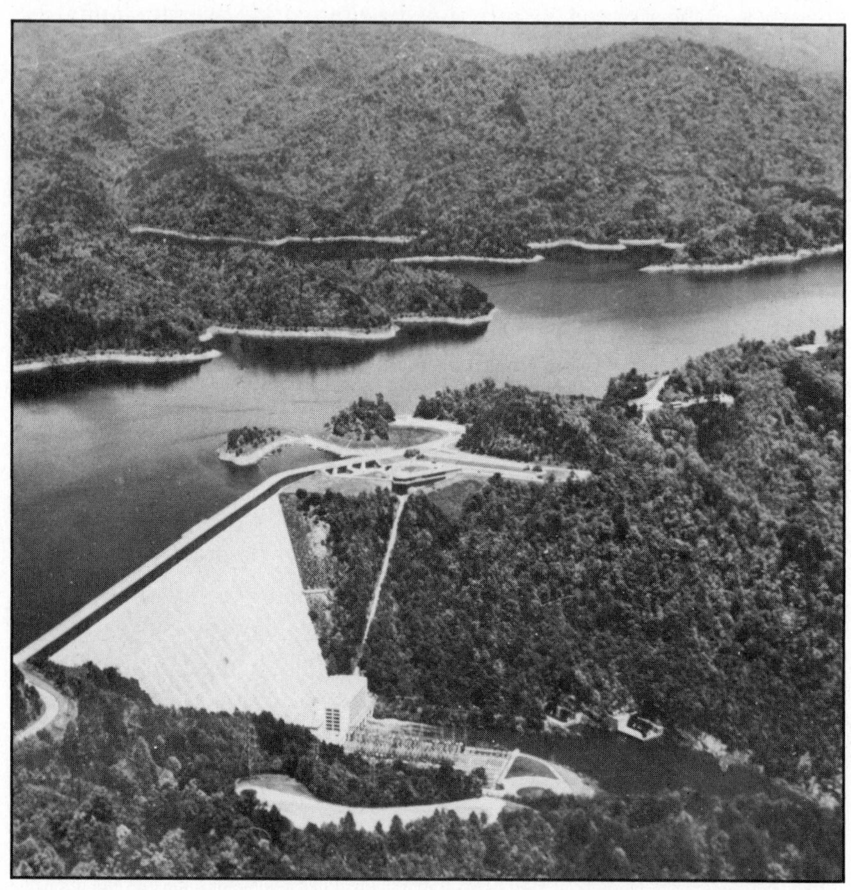

THE ACHIEVEMENT OF THE NEW DEAL

WILLIAM E. LEUCHTENBURG

Franklin Roosevelt's New Deal set the tone and the agenda for American liberalism for nearly a generation after Roosevelt died. By the 1960s, however, political radicals began to perceive it as an inadequate model for reform. Historians of the "new left" criticized Roosevelt for being in league with big business. They pointed out that his most lasting accomplishments were in areas like banking reform and energy production that benefited businessmen more than anyone else. They also faulted Roosevelt for responding to the demands of skilled workers and middle-class farmers while virtually ignoring the needs of unskilled labor, farm tenants, and southern sharecroppers. Most importantly, they accused Roosevelt of failing to fight for civil rights for blacks and of doing little for women.

Radicals thought Roosevelt ought to have done more to redistribute wealth through selective taxes, to experiment more with cooperative business enterprises, and to develop training programs for the unskilled and unlettered. Instead of seizing up the opportunity to reform the system from top to bottom, said the radicals, Roosevelt merely reinforced the system by patching up its most glaring faults.

With this last point historian William Leuchtenburg, author of a well-known book on the New Deal, would probably not disagree. But he would argue that Roosevelt's achievements went far beyond a mere rescue mission for American capitalism. In the following essay, which was presented to a conference summoned in 1983 to examine the New Deal from the perspective of fifty years, Leuchtenburg stresses the many innovations of the New Deal that created new opportunities for thousands and brought hope to millions.

—NORMAN K. RISJORD

The fiftieth anniversary of the New Deal, launched on March 4, 1933, comes at a time when it has been going altogether out of fashion. Writers on the left, convinced that the Roosevelt experiment was either worthless or pernicious, have assigned it to the dustbin of history. Commentators on the right, though far less conspicuous, see in the New Deal the origins of the centralized state they seek to dismantle. Indeed, the half-century of the age of Roosevelt is being commemorated in the presidency of Ronald Reagan, who, while never tiring of quoting FDR, insists that the New Deal derived from Italian fascism.

To be sure, the New Deal has always had its critics. In Roosevelt's own day Marxists said that the New Deal had not done anything for agriculture that an earthquake could not have done better at the same time that conservatives were saying that FDR was unprincipled. Hoover even called him "a chameleon on plaid." Most historians have long since accepted the fact that New Deal policies were sometimes inconsistent, that Roosevelt failed to grasp countercyclical fiscal theory, that recovery did not come until armaments orders fueled the economy, that the President was credited with certain reforms like insurance of bank deposits that he, in fact, opposed, that a number of New Deal programs, notably aid for the marginal farmer, were inadequately financed, and that some New Deal agencies discriminated against blacks.

During the 1960s historians not only dressed up these objections as though they were new revelations but carried their disappointment with contemporary liberalism to the point of arguing either that the New Deal was not just inadequate but actually malign or that the New Deal was so negligible as to constitute a meaningless episode. This estimate derived in large part from disaffection with the welfare state, which Herbert Marcuse in *One-Dimensional Man* characterized as "a state of unfreedom," and which, as one critic noted, some considered "the ultimate form of repressive super-ego." The New Deal was now perceived to be elitist, since it had neglected to consult the poor about what legislation they wanted, or to encourage the participation of ghetto-dwellers in decision-making. Roosevelt's politics, historians maintained, redounded to the benefit of those who already had advantages—wealthier staple farmers, organized workers, business corporations, the "deserving poor"—while displacing sharecroppers and neglecting the powerless. An "antirevolutionary response to a situation that had revolutionary potentialities," the New Deal, it was said,

THE ACHIEVEMENT OF THE NEW DEAL From William E. Leuchtenburg, "The Achievement of the New Deal," in Harvard Sitkoff, ed., *Fifty Years Later: The New Deal Evaluated* (New York: Alfred A. Knopf, 1985), pp. 211–230.

missed opportunities to nationalize the banks and restructure the social order. Even "providing assistance to the needy and . . . rescuing them from starvation" served conservative ends, historians complained, for these efforts "sapped organized radicalism of its waning strength and of its potential constituency among the unorganized and discontented." The Roosevelt Administration, it has been asserted, failed to achieve more than it did not as a result of the strength of conservative opposition but because of the intellectual deficiencies of the New Dealers and because Roosevelt deliberately sought to save "large-scale corporate capitalism." In *Towards a New Past*, the New Left historian Barton Bernstein summed up this point of view: "The New Deal failed to solve the problem of depression, it failed to raise the impoverished, it failed to redistribute income, it failed to extend equality and generally countenanced racial discrimination and segregation."

Although the characterization of Bernstein as "New Left" suggests that he represents a deviant persuasion, the New Left perspective has, in fact, all but become the new orthodoxy, even though there is not yet any New Left survey of the domestic history of the United States in the 1930s. This emphasis has so permeated writing on the New Deal in the past generation that an instructor who wishes to assign the latest thought on the age of Roosevelt has a wide choice of articles and anthologies that document the errors of the New Deal but no assessment of recent vintage that explores its accomplishments.

The fiftieth anniversary of the New Deal provides the occasion for a modest proposal—that we reintroduce some tension into the argument over the interpretation of the Roosevelt years. If historians are to develop a credible synthesis, it is important to regain a sense of the achievement of the New Deal. As it now stands, we have a dialectic that is all antithesis with no thesis. The so-called "debate" about the New Deal is not truly a debate, for even some of the historians who dispute the New Left assertions agree that one can only take a melancholy view of the period. The single question asked is whether the failure of the New Deal was the fault of the Roosevelt Administration or the result of the strength of conservative forces beyond the government's control; the fact of failure is taken as the basic postulate. As a first step toward a more considered evaluation, one has to remind one's self not only of what the New Deal did not do, but of what it achieved.

NEW DEAL CHANGES

Above all, one needs to recognize how markedly the New Deal altered the character of the State in America. Indeed, though for decades past European theorists had been talking about *der Staat*, there can hardly be said to have been a State in America in the full meaning of the term before the New Deal. If you had walked into an American town in 1932, you would have had a hard time detecting any sign of a federal presence, save perhaps for the post office and even many of today's post offices date from the 1930s. Washington rarely affected people's lives directly. There was no national old-age pension system, no federal unemployment compensation, no aid to dependent children, no federal housing, no regulation of the stock market, no withholding tax, no federal school lunch, no farm subsidy, no national minimum wage law, no welfare state. As late as Herbert Hoover's presidency, it was regarded as axiomatic that government activity should be minimal. In the pre-Roosevelt era, even organized labor and the National Conference of Social Workers opposed federal action on behalf of the unemployed. The New Deal sharply challenged these shibboleths. From 1933 to 1938, the government intervened in a myriad of ways from energizing the economy to fostering unionization.

In the First Hundred Days of 1933, the New Deal reversed the familiar assumptions in an electrifying manner. André Maurois has commented:

> One cannot help calling to mind, as one writes the history of these three crowded months, the Biblical account of the Creation. The first day, the Brain Trust put an embargo on gold; the second day, it peopled the forests; the third day, it created three point two beer; the fourth day, it broke the bonds that tied the dollar to gold; the fifth day, it set the farmers free; the sixth day, it created General Johnson, and then, looking upon what it had made of America, it saw that it was good.
>
> But it could not rest on the seventh day.

This vast expansion of government led inevitably to the concentration of much greater power in the presidency, whose authority was greatly augmented under FDR. Rexford Tugwell has written of Roosevelt: "No monarch, . . . unless it may have been Elizabeth or her magnificent Tudor father, or maybe Alexander or Augustus Caesar, can have given quite that sense of serene presiding, of gathering up into himself, of really representing, a whole people." The President became, in Sidney Hyman's words, "the chief economic engineer," to whom Congress naturally turned for the setting of economic policy. Roosevelt stimulated interest in public affairs by his fireside chats and freewheeling press conferences, shifted the balance between the White House and Capitol Hill by assuming the role of Chief Legislator, and eluded the routinized traditional departments by creating emergency agencies. In 1939 he established the Executive Office of the President, giving the Chief Executive a central staff office for the first time. "The verdict of history," wrote Clinton Rossiter, "will surely be that he left the Presidency a more splendid instrument of democracy than he found it."

To staff the national agencies, Roosevelt turned to a new class of people: the university-trained experts. Before FDR, professors had not had an important role in the national government, save briefly in World War I, but when Roosevelt ran for president in 1932, he recruited advisers, most of them from Columbia University, who supplied him with ideas and helped write his speeches. During the First Hundred Days, large numbers of professors, encouraged by FDR's reliance on the Brain Trust, flocked to Washington to draft New Deal legislation and to administer New Deal agencies. The radical literary critic Edmund Wilson wrote, "Everywhere in the streets and offices you run into old acquaintances: the editors and writers of the liberal press, the 'progressive' young instructors from the colleges, the intelligent foundation workers, the practical idealists of settlement houses." He added: "The bright boys of the Eastern universities, instead of being obliged to choose, as they were twenty years ago, between business, the bond-selling game and the field of foreign missions, can come on and get jobs in Washington."

The capital had hitherto thought of government workers largely as civil service employees awaiting the rise in grade that would permit them to buy a house in Chevy Chase and it scarcely knew what to make of the invasion of eager newcomers. Everybody wanted to know the professors, reported one magazine: "Office-seekers dog their footsteps. Hostesses vie to land them as guest of honor. Professors are the fad." "On a routine administration matter you go to a Cabinet member," observed a reporter, "but on matters of policy and the higher statesmanship you consult the professoriat." "All Washington is going to school to the professors," he noted. "Debutantes hang on their exposition of the quantitative theory of money, the law of diminishing returns, and the intricacies of foreign exchange. Bookstores are selling their books like hot cakes. Their works are not available at the Library of Congress, the volumes having been withdrawn by the Senators and Congressmen."

Some may doubt today whether it is always an unmitigated good to have "the best and the brightest" in seats of power, but in the 1930s this infusion of talent gave an élan to the national government that had been sorely missing in the past. The *New Republic* commented: "We have in Washington not a soggy and insensitive mass of dough, as in some previous administrations, but a nervous, alert and hard-working group who are doing their level best to effectuate a program." Friends of Roosevelt's, like Felix Frankfurter, sent to Washington a cadre of brilliant young lawyers—men like David Lilienthal and Jerome Frank—who, immensely confident of their ability, generated new ideas, tested novel methods, and conveyed an infectious enthusiasm for the possibilities of government.

This corps of administrators made it possible for Roosevelt to carry out a major change in the role of the federal government. Although the New Deal always operated within a capitalist matrix and the government sought to enhance profitmaking, Roosevelt and his lieutenants rejected the traditional view that government was the handmaiden of business or that government and business were coequal sovereigns. As a consequence, they adopted measures to discipline corporations, to require a sharing of authority with government and unions, and to hold businessmen accountable. In the early days of the National Recovery Administration, the novelist Sherwood Anderson wrote:

> I went to several code hearings. No one has quite got their significance. Here for the first time you see these men of business, little ones and big ones, . . . coming up on the platform to give an accounting. It does seem the death knell of the old idea that a man owning a factory, office or store has a right to run it in his own way.
>
> There is at least an effort to relate it now to the whole thing, man's relations with his fellow men etc. Of course it is crude and there will be no end to crookedness, objections, etc. but I do think an entire new principle in American life is being established.

Through a series of edicts and statutes, the administration invaded the realm of the banker by establishing control over the nation's money supply. The government clamped an embargo on gold, took the United States off the gold standard, and nullified the requirement for the payment of gold in private contracts. In 1935 a resentful Supreme Court sustained this authority, although a dissenting justice said that this was Nero at his worst. The Glass-Steagall Banking Act (1933) stripped commercial banks of the privilege of engaging in investment banking, and established federal insurance of bank deposits, an innovation which the leading monetary historians have called "the structural change most conducive to monetary stability since bank notes were taxed out of existence immediately after the Civil War." The Banking Act of 1935 gave the United States what other industrial nations had long had, but America lacked—central banking. This series of changes transformed the relationship between the government and the financial community from what it had been when Grover Cleveland had gone, hat in hand, to beseech J. P. Morgan for help. As Charles Beard observed: "Having lost their gold coins and bullion to the Federal Government and having filled their vaults with federal bonds and other paper, bankers have become in a large measure mere agents of the Government in Washington. No longer do these powerful interests stand, so to speak, 'outside the Government' and in a position to control or dictate to it."

A number of other enactments helped transfer authority from Wall Street to Washington. The Securities Act of 1933 established government supervision of the issue of securities, and made company directors civilly and criminally liable for misinformation on the statements they were required to file with each new issue. The Securities and Exchange Act of 1934 initiated federal supervision of the stock exchanges, which to this day operate under the lens of the Securities and Exchange Commission (SEC). The Holding Company Act of 1935 levelled some of the utility pyramids, dissolving all utility holding companies that were more than twice removed from their operating companies, and increased the regulatory powers of the SEC over public utilities. Robert Sobel has concluded that the 1934 law marked "a shift of economic power from the lower part of Manhattan, where it had been for over a century, to Washington." To be sure, financiers continued to make important policy choices, but they never again operated in the uninhibited universe of the Great Bull Market. By the spring of 1934, one writer was already reporting:

> Financial news no longer originates in Wall Street. . . . News of a financial nature in Wall Street now is merely an echo of events which take place in Washington. . . . The pace of the ticker is determined now in Washington not in company boardrooms or in brokerage offices. . . . In Wall Street it is no longer asked what some big trader is doing, what some important banker thinks, what opinion some eminent lawyer holds about some pressing question of the day. The query in Wall Street has become: "What's the news from Washington?"

The age of Roosevelt focused attention on Washington, too, by initiatives in fields that had been regarded as exclusively within the private orbit, notably in housing. The Home Owners' Loan Corporation, created in 1933, saved tens of thousands of homes from foreclosure by refinancing mortgages. In 1934 the Federal Housing Administration (FHA) began its program of insuring loans for the construction and renovation of private homes, and over the next generation more than 10 million FHA-financed units were built. Before the New Deal, the national government had never engaged in public housing, except for the World War I emergency, but agencies like the Public Works Administration now broke precedent. The Tennessee Valley Authority laid out the model town of Norris, the Federal Emergency Relief Administration (FERA) experimented with subsistence homesteads, and the Resettlement Administration created greenbelt communities, entirely new towns girdled by green countryside. When in 1937 the Wagner-Steagall Act created the U.S. Housing Authority, it assured public housing a permanent place in American life.

A NEW DEAL FOR THE COMMON MAN

The New Deal profoundly altered industrial relations by throwing the weight of government behind efforts to unionize workers. At the outset of the Great Depression, the American labor movement was "an anachronism in the world," for only a tiny minority of factory workers were unionized. Employers hired and fired and imposed punishments at will, used thugs as strikebreakers and private police, stockpiled industrial munitions, and ran company towns as feudal fiefs. In an astonishingly short period in the Roosevelt years a very different pattern emerged. Under the umbrella of Section 7(a) of the National Industrial Recovery Act of 1933 and of the far-reaching Wagner Act of 1935, union organizers gained millions of recruits in such open-shop strongholds as steel, automobiles, and textiles. Employees won wage rises, reductions in hours, greater job security, freedom from the tyranny of company guards, and protection against arbitrary punishment. Thanks to the National Recovery Administration and the Guffey acts, coal miners achieved the outlawing of compulsory company houses and stores. Steel workers, who in 1920 labored twelve-hour shifts seven days a week at the blast furnaces, were to become so powerful that in the postwar era they would win not merely paid vacations but sabbatical leaves. A British analyst has concluded: "From one of the most restrictive among industrially advanced nations, the labour code of the United States (insofar as it could be said to exist before 1933) was rapidly transformed into one of the most liberal," and these reforms, he adds, "were not the harvest of long-sustained agitation by trade unions, but were forced upon a partly sceptical labor movement by a government which led or carried it into maturity."

Years later, when David E. Lilienthal, the director of the Tennessee Valley Authority, was being driven to the airport to fly to Roosevelt's funeral, the TVA driver said to him:

> I won't forget what he did for me. . . . I spent the best years of my life working at the Appalachian Mills . . . and they didn't even treat us like humans. If you didn't do like they said, they always told you there was someone else to take your job. I had my mother and my sister to take care of. Sixteen cents an hour was what we got; a fellow can't live on that, and you had to get production even to get that, this Bedaux system; some fellows only got twelve cents. If you asked to get off on a Sunday, the foreman would say, "All right you stay away Sunday, but when you come back Monday someone else will have your job." No, sir, I won't forget what he done for us.

Helen Lynd has observed that the history of the United States is that of England fifty years later, and a half century after the welfare state had come to Western Europe, the New Deal brought it to America. The NRA wiped out sweatshops, and removed some 150,000 child laborers from factories. The Walsh-Healey Act of 1936 and the Fair Labor Standards Act of 1938 established the principle of a federally imposed minimal level of working conditions, and added further sanctions against child labor. If the New Deal did not do enough for the "one-third of a nation" to whom Roosevelt called attention, it at least made a beginning, through agencies like the Farm Security Administration, toward helping sharecroppers, tenant farmers, and migrants like John Steinbeck's Joads. Most important, it originated a new system of social rights to replace the dependence on private charity. The Social Security Act of 1935 created America's first national system of old-age pensions and initiated a federal-state program of unemployment insurance. It also authorized grants for the blind, for the incapacitated, and for dependent children, a feature that would have unimaginable long-range consequences.

The veteran social worker Grace Abbott, in explaining why, as a lifelong Republican, she was voting for Roosevelt in 1936, said that greater progress has been made in security for children "during the past three years than the previous thirty years." She added: "The support of the Child Labor Amendment by the President and his cabinet, the raising of Child Labor standards under the N.R.A., the inclusion of the sugar beet children in the benefits of the Costigan Sugar Act and the President's own pet project—the C.C.C. Camps—now so largely filled by young men and boys are also concrete evidence that the President considers the welfare of children of national importance."

Roosevelt himself affirmed the newly assumed attitudes in Washington in his annual message to Congress in 1938 when he declared: "Government has a final responsibility for the well-being of its citizenship. If private co-operative endeavor fails to provide work for willing hands and relief for the unfortunate, those suffering hardship from no fault of their own have a right to call upon the Government for aid; and a government worthy of its name must make fitting response."

A NEW DEAL FOR THE UNEMPLOYED

Nothing revealed this approach so well as the New Deal's attention to the plight of the millions of unemployed. During the ten years between 1929 and 1939, one scholar has written, "more progress was made in public welfare and relief than in the three hundred years after this country was first settled." A series of alphabet agencies—the FERA, the CWA, the WPA—provided government work for the jobless, while the National Youth Administration (NYA) employed college students in museums, libraries, and laboratories, enabled high school students to remain in school, and set up a program of apprentice training. In Texas, the twenty-seven-year-old NYA director Lyndon Johnson put penniless young men like John Connally to work building roadside parks, and in North Carolina, the NYA employed, at 35 cents an hour, a Duke University law student, Richard Nixon.

In an address in Los Angeles in 1936, the head of FDR's relief operations, Harry Hopkins, conveyed the attitude of the New Deal towards those who were down and out:

> I am getting sick and tired of these people on the W.P.A. and local relief rolls being called chiselers and cheats. . . . These people . . . are just like the rest of us. They don't drink any more than us, they don't lie any more, they're no lazier than the rest of us—they're pretty much a cross section of the American people. . . . I have never believed that with our capitalistic system people have to be poor. I think it is an outrage that we should permit hundreds and hundreds of thousands of people to be ill clad, to live in miserable homes, not to have enough to eat; not to be able to send their children to school for the only reason that they are poor. I don't believe ever again in America we are going to permit the things to happen that have happened in the past to people. We are never going back . . . to the days of putting the old people in the alms houses, when a decent dignified pension at home will keep them there. We are coming to the day when we are going to have decent houses for the poor, when there is genuine and real security for everybody. I have gone all over the moral hurdles that people are poor because they are bad. I don't believe it. A system of government on that basis is fallacious.

Under the leadership of men like Hopkins, "Santa Claus incomparable and privy-builder without peer," projects of relief agencies and of the Public Works Administration (PWA) changed the face of the land. The PWA built thoroughfares like the Skyline Drive in Virginia and the Overseas Highway from Miami to Key West, constructed the Medical Center in Jersey City, burrowed Chicago's new subway, and gave Natchez, Mississippi, a new bridge, and Denver a modern water-supply system. Few New Yorkers today realize the long reach of the New Deal. If they cross the Triborough Bridge, they are driving on a bridge the PWA built. If they fly into La Guardia Airport, they are landing at an airfield laid out by the WPA. If they get caught in a traffic jam on the FDR Drive, they are using yet another artery built by the WPA. Even the animal cages in the Central Park Zoo were reconstructed by WPA workers. In New York City, the WPA built or renovated hundreds of school buildings; gave Orchard Beach a bathhouse, a mall, and a lagoon; landscaped Bryant Park and the campus of Hunter College in the Bronx; conducted examinations for venereal disease, filled teeth, operated pollen count stations, and performed puppet shows for disturbed children; it built dioramas for the Brooklyn Museum; ran street dances in Harlem and an open-air night club in Central Park; and, by combing neglected archives, turned up forgotten documents like the court proceedings in the Aaron Burr libel case and the marriage license issued to Captain Kidd. In New York City alone the WPA employed more people than the entire War Department.

Though much of the network inevitably concentrated on operations like road building, the Roosevelt government proved ingenious in devising other activities. Years later, John Steinbeck recalled:

> When W.P.A. came, we were delighted, because it offered work. . . . I was given the project of taking a census of all the dogs on the Monterey Peninsula, their breeds, weight and characters. I did it very thoroughly and, since I knew my reports were not likely to get to the hands of the mighty, I wrote some pretty searching character studies of poodles, and beagles and hounds. If such records were kept, somewhere in Washington, there will be a complete dog record of the Monterey Peninsula in the early Thirties.

The New Deal showed unusual sensitivity toward jobless white-collar workers, notably those in aesthetic fields. The Public Works of Art Project gave an opportunity to muralists eager for a chance to work in the style of Rivera, Orozco, and Siqueiros. The Federal Art Project fostered the careers of painters like Stuart Davis, Raphael Soyer, Yasuo Kuniyoshi, and Jackson Pollock. Out of the same project came a network of community art centers and the notable *Index of American Design*. A generation later the sculptor Louise Nevelson, summed up what it meant:

> When I came back from Germany where I studied with Hans Hoffman . . . I got on the WPA. Now that gave me a certain kind of freedom and I think that our great artists like Rothko, de Kooning, Frank Kline, all these people that have promise today and are creative, had that moment of peace . . . to continue with their work. So, I feel that that was a great benefit, a great contribution to our creative people and very important in the history of art. And not only in the visual arts but in the theater, and the folk arts, there wasn't a thing that they didn't touch on. . . . At that period, people in our country didn't have jobs and the head of government was able so intelligently to use mankind and manpower. I think it's a high-light of our American history.

The Federal Writers' Project provided support for scores of talented novelists and poets, editors and literary critics, men like Ralph Ellison and Nelson Algren, John Cheever and Saul Bellow. These writers turned out an exceptional set of state guides, with such features as Conrad Aiken's carefully delineated portrayal of Deerfield, Massachusetts, and special volumes like *These Are Our Lives*, a graphic portfolio of life histories in North Carolina, and *Panorama*, in which Vincent McHugh depicts "the infinite pueblo of the Bronx." Project workers transcribed chain-gang blues songs, recovered folklore that would otherwise have been lost, and collected the narratives of elderly former slaves, an invaluable archive later published in *Lay My Burden Down*. When the magazine *Story* conducted a contest for the best contribution by a Project employee, the prize was won by an unpublished 29-year-old black who had been working on the essay on the Negro for the Illinois guide. With the prize money for his stories, subsequently published as *Uncle Tom's Children*, Richard Wright gained the time to complete his remarkable first novel, *Native Son*.

Some thought it an ill omen that the Federal Theatre Project's first production was Shakespeare's *Comedy of Errors,* but that agency not only gave employment to actors and stage technicians but offered many communities their first glimpse of live drama. The "boy wonder" Orson Welles directed and acted in the Federal Theatre, which also discovered such unknowns as Joseph Cotten. Its Dance Group revealed the virtuosity of Katherine Dunham, Doris Humphrey, and Charles Weidman. The Federal Theatre sponsored the first U.S. presentation of T. S. Eliot's *Murder in the Cathedral,* and its Detroit unit staged the original professional production of Arthur Miller's first play.

If the creation of America's first state theatre was an unusual departure, the New Deal's ventures in documentary films seemed no less surprising. With Resettlement Administration funds, Pare Lorentz produced *The Plow That Broke the Plains* in 1936 and the classic *The River* in 1937. He engaged cameramen like Paul Strand, who had won acclaim for his movie on a fisherman's strike in Mexico; invited the young composer Virgil Thomson, who had just scored Gertrude Stein's *Four Saints in Three Acts,* to compose the background music; and employed Thomas Chalmers, who had sung at the Metropolitan Opera in the era of Caruso, to read the narration. Lorentz's films were eye-openers. American government documentaries before the New Deal had been limited to short subjects on topics like the love life of the honeybee. *The River,* which won first prize in Venice at the International Exposition of Cinematographic Art in 1938, proved that there was an audience in the United States for well-wrought documentaries. By 1940 it had drawn more than 10 million people, while *The Plow That Broke the Plains,* said one critic, made "the rape of millions of acres . . . more moving than the downfall of a Hollywood blonde."

Lorentz's films suggest the concern of the New Deal for the American land. Roosevelt, it has been said, had a "proprietary interest in the nation's estate," and this helps account for the fact that the 1930s accomplished for soil conservation and river valley development what the era of Theodore Roosevelt had done for the forests. The Tennessee Valley Authority, which drew admirers from all over the world, put the national government in the business of generating electric power, controlled floods, terraced hillsides, and gave new hope to the people of the valley. In the Pacific Northwest the PWA constructed mammoth dams, Grand Coulee and Bonneville. Roosevelt's "tree army," the Civilian Conservation Corps, planted millions of trees, cleared forest trails, laid out picnic sites and campgrounds, and aided the Forest Service in the vast undertaking of establishing a shelterbelt—a windbreak of trees and shrubs: green ash and Chinese elm, apricot and blackberry, buffalo berry and Osage orange from the Canadian border to the Texas panhandle. Government agencies came to the aid of drought-stricken farmers in the Dust Bowl, and the Soil Conservation Service, another New Deal creation, instructed growers in methods of cultivation to save the land. As Alistair Cooke later said, the favorite of the New Dealers was the farmer with the will to "take up contour plowing late in life."

These services to farmers represented only a small part of the government's program, for in the New Deal years, the business of agriculture was revolutionized. Roosevelt came to power at a time of mounting desperation for American farmers. Each month in 1932 another 20,000 farmers had lost their land because of inability to meet their debts in a period of collapsing prices. On a single day in May 1932, one-fourth of the state of Mississippi went under the sheriff's hammer. The Farm Credit Administration of 1933 came to the aid of the beleaguered farmer, and within eighteen months, it had refinanced one-fifth of all farm mortgages in the United States. In the Roosevelt years, too, the Rural Electrification Administration literally brought rural America out of darkness. At the beginning of the Roosevelt era, only one farm in nine had electricity; at the end, only one in nine did not have it. But more important than any of these developments was the progression of enactments starting with the first AAA (the Agricultural Adjustment Act) of 1933, which began the process of granting large-scale subsidies to growers. As William Faulkner later said, "Our economy is not agricultural any longer. Our economy is the federal government. We no longer farm in Mississippi cotton fields. We farm now in Washington corridors and Congressional committee rooms."

GOVERNMENT OF AND FOR MORE OF THE PEOPLE

At the same time that its realm was being expanded under the New Deal, the national government changed the composition of its personnel and of its beneficiaries. Before 1933, the government had paid heed primarily to a single group—white Anglo-Saxon Protestant males. The Roosevelt Administration, however, recruited from a more ethnically diverse group, and the prominence of Catholics and Jews among the President's advisers is suggested by the scintillating team of the Second Hundred Days, Corcoran and Cohen. The Federal Writers' Project turned out books on Italians and Albanians, and the Federal Theatre staged productions in Yiddish and wrote a history of the Chinese stage in Los Angeles. In the 1930s women played a more prominent role in government than they ever had before, as the result of such appointments as that of Frances Perkins as the first female cabinet member, while the influence of Eleanor Roosevelt was pervasive.

Before Eleanor Roosevelt, First Ladies had been content to preside over the social functions of the White House. But by 1940 Mrs. Roosevelt had travelled more than 250,000 miles, written 1 million words, and became the leading advocate within the administration for the underprivileged, especially blacks and unemployed youth. No one knew where she would turn up next. In the most famous cartoon of the decade, a begrimed coal miner in the bowels of the earth cries out in astonishment to a fellow miner, "For gosh sakes, here comes Mrs. Roosevelt." Admiral Byrd, it was said, always set up two places for dinner at the South Pole "in case Eleanor should drop in." She was renowned for her informality. When the King and Queen of England visited America, she served them hot dogs and beer, and when during World War II, she travelled to Australia and New Zealand, she greeted her Maori guide by rubbing noses. No one captured the goals of the New Deal better than Eleanor Roosevelt. "As I have said all along," she remarked, "you have got to have the kind of country in which people's daily chance convinces them that democracy is a good thing."

Although in some respects the New Deal's performance with regard to blacks added to the sorry record of racial discrimination in America, important gains were also registered in the 1930s. Blacks, who had often been excluded from relief in the past, now received a share of WPA jobs considerably greater than their proportion of the population. Blacks moved into federal housing projects; federal funds went to schools and hospitals in black neighborhoods; and New Deal agencies like the Farm Security Administration (FSA) enabled 50,000 Negro tenant farmers and sharecroppers to become proprietors. "Indeed," one historian has written, "there is a high correlation between the location of extensive FSA operations in the 1930s and the rapidity of political modernization in black communities in the South in the 1960s." Roosevelt appointed a number of blacks, including William Hastie, Mary McLeod Bethune, and Robert Weaver, to high posts in the government. Negroes in the South who were disfranchised in white primaries voted in AAA crop referenda and in National Labor Relations Board plant elections, and a step was taken toward restoring their constitutional rights when Attorney General Frank Murphy set up a Civil Liberties Unit in the Department of Justice. The reign of Jim Crow in Washington offices, which had begun under Roosevelt's Democratic predecessor, Woodrow Wilson, was terminated by Secretary of the Interior Harold Ickes who desegregated cafeterias in his department. Ickes also had a role in the most dramatic episode of the times, for when the Daughters of the American Revolution (DAR) denied the use of their concert hall to the black contralto Marian Anderson, he made it possible for her to sing before thousands from the steps of Lincoln Memorial; and Mrs. Roosevelt joined in the rebuke to the DAR. Anderson's concert on Easter Sunday 1939 was heard by thousands at the Memorial, and three networks carried her voice to millions more. Blacks delivered their own verdict on the New Deal at the polling places. Committed to the party of Lincoln as late as 1932, when they voted overwhelmingly for Hoover, they shifted in large numbers to the party of FDR during Roosevelt's first term. This was a change of allegiance that many whites were also making in those years.

THE DURABLE LEGACY OF THE NEW DEAL

The Great Depression and the New Deal brought about a significant political realignment of the sort that occurs only rarely in America. The Depression wrenched many lifelong Republican voters from their moorings. In 1928, one couple christened their newborn son "Herbert Hoover Jones." Four years later they petitioned the court, "desiring to relieve the young man from the chagrin and mortification which he is suffering and will suffer," and asked that his name be changed to Franklin D. Roosevelt Jones. In 1932 FDR became the first Democrat to enter the White House with as much as 50 percent of the popular vote in eighty years—since Franklin K. Pierce in 1852. Roosevelt took advantage of this opportunity to mold "the FDR coalition," an alliance centered in the low-income districts of the great cities and, as recently as the 1980 election, the contours of the New Deal coalition could still be discerned. Indeed, over the past half-century, the once overpowering Republicans have won control of Congress only twice, for a total of four years. No less important was the shift in the character of the Democratic party from the conservative organization of John W. Davis and John J. Raskob to the country's main political instrumentality for reform. "One political result of the Roosevelt years," Robert Burke has observed," was a basic change in the nature of the typical Congressional liberal." He was no longer a maverick, who made a fetish of orneriness, no longer one of the men Senator Moses called "the sons of the wild jackass," but "a party Democrat, labor-oriented, urban, and internationalist-minded."

Furthermore, the New Deal drastically altered the agenda of American politics. When Arthur Krock of the *New York Times* listed the main programmatic questions before the 1932 Democratic convention, he wrote: "What would be said about the repeal of prohibition that had split the Republicans? What would be said about tariffs?" By 1936, these concerns seemed altogether old fashioned, as campaigners discussed the Tennessee Valley Authority and industrial relations, slum clearance and aid to the jobless. That year, a Little Rock newspaper commented: "Such matters as tax and tariff laws have given way to universally human things, the living problems and opportunities of the average man and the average family."

The Roosevelt years changed the conception of the role of government not just in Washington but in the states, where a series of "Little New Deals"—under governors like Herbert Lehman in New York—added a thick sheaf of social legislation, and in the cities. In Boston, Charles Trout has observed, city council members in 1929 "devoted endless hours to street paving." After the coming of the New Deal, they were absorbed with NRA campaigns, public housing, and WPA allotments. "A year after the crash the council thought 5,000 dollars an excessive appropriation for the municipal employment bureau," but during the 1930s "the unemployed drained Boston's treasury of not less than 100,000,000 dollars in direct benefits, and the federal government spent even more."

In a cluster of pathbreaking decisions in 1937, the Supreme Court legitimized this vast exercise of authority by government at all levels. As late as 1936, the Supreme Court still denied the power of the United States government to regulate agriculture, even though crops were sold in a world market, or coal mining, a vital component of a national economy, and struck down a minimum wage law as beyond the authority of the state of New York. Roosevelt responded with a plan to "pack" the Court with as many as six additional Justices, and in short order the Court, in what has been called "the Constitutional Revolution of 1937," sounded retreat. Before 1937 the Supreme Court stood as a formidable barrier to social reform. Since 1937 not one piece of significant social legislation has been invalidated, and the Court has shifted its docket instead to civil rights and civil liberties.

What then did the New Deal do? It gave far greater amplitude to the national state, expanded the authority of the presidency, recruited university-trained administrators, won control of the money supply, established central banking, imposed regulation on Wall Street, rescued the debt-ridden farmer and homeowner, built model communities, financed the Federal Housing Administration, made federal housing a permanent feature, fostered unionization of the factories, reduced child labor, ended the tyranny of company towns, wiped out many sweatshops, mandated minimal working standards, enabled tenants to buy their own farms, built camps for migrants, introduced the welfare state with old-age pensions, unemployment insurance, and aid for dependent children, provided jobs for millions of unemployed, created a special program for the jobless young and for students, covered the American landscape with new edifices, subsidized painters and novelists, composers and ballet dancers, founded America's first state theater, created documentary films, gave birth to the impressive Tennessee Valley Authority, generated electrical power, sent the Civilian Conservation Corps boys into the forests, initiated the Soil Conservation Service, transformed the economy of agriculture, lighted up rural America, gave women greater recognition, made a start toward breaking the pattern of racial discrimination and segregation, put together a liberal party coalition, changed the agenda of American politics, and brought about a Constitutional Revolution.

But even this summary does not account for the full range of its activities. The New Deal offered the American Indian new opportunities for self-government and established the Indian Arts and Crafts Board, sponsored vaudeville troupes and circuses, taught counterpoint and *solfeggio,* was responsible for the founding of the Buffalo Philarmonic, the Oklahoma Symphony, and the Utah State Symphony, served hot lunches to school children and set up hundreds of nursery schools, sent bookmobiles into isolated communities, and where there were no roads, had books carried in by packhorses. And only a truly merciful and farsighted government would have taken such special pains to find jobs for unemployed historians.

The New Deal accomplished all of this at a critical time, when many were insisting that fascism was the wave of the future and denying that democracy could be effective. For those throughout the world who heard such jeremiads with foreboding, the American experience was enormously inspiriting. A decade after the end of the age of Roosevelt, Sir Isaiah Berlin wrote:

> When I say that some men occupy one's imagination for many years, this is literally true of Mr. Roosevelt and the young men of my own generation in England, and probably in many parts of Europe, and indeed the entire world. If one was young in the thirties, and lived in a democracy, then, whatever one's politics, if one had human feelings at all, the faintest spark of social idealism, or any love of life whatever, one must have felt very much as young men in Continental Europe probably felt after the defeat of Napoleon during the years of the Restoration: that all was dark and quiet, a great reaction was abroad, and little stirred, and nothing resisted.

In these "dark and leaden thirties," Professor Berlin continued, "the only light in the darkness that was left was the administration of Mr. Roosevelt and the New Deal in the United States. At a time of weakness and mounting despair in the democratic world Mr. Roosevelt radiated confidence and strength. . . . Even to-day, upon him alone, of all the statesmen of the thirties, no cloud rested neither on him nor on the New Deal, which to European eyes still looks a bright chapter in the history of mankind."

For the past generation, America has lived off the legacy of the New Deal. Successive administrations extended the provisions of statutes like the Social Security Act, adopted New Deal attitudes toward intervention in the economy to cope with recessions, and put New Deal ideas to modern purposes, as when the Civilian Conservation Corps served as the basis for both the Peace Corps and the VISTA program of the War on Poverty. Harry Truman performed under the shadow of FDR, Lyndon Johnson consciously patterned his administration on Roosevelt's, Jimmy Carter launched his first presidential campaign at Warm Springs, and Ronald Reagan has manifested an almost obsessive need to summon FDR to his side. Carl Degler has observed:

> Conventionally the end of the New Deal is dated with the enactment of the Wages and Hours Act of 1938. But in a fundamental sense the New Deal did not end then at all. Americans still live in the era of the New

> Deal, for its achievements are now the base mark below which no conservative government may go and from which all new reform now starts. . . . The reform efforts of the Democratic Truman, Kennedy, and Johnson administrations have been little more than fulfillments of the New Deal.

The British historian David K. Adams has pointed out that the philosophy of the New Frontier has "conscious overtones of the New Deal" and indeed that John Kennedy's "New Frontier" address of 1960 was "almost a paraphrase" of an FDR speech of 1935. Theodore White has commented that both John and Robert Kennedy shared sentences from a Roosevelt address that reporters called the "Dante sequence." When at a loss for words, each was wont to quote a favorite passage from Franklin Roosevelt: "Governments can err, Presidents do make mistakes, but the immortal Dante tells us that Divine Justice weighs the sins of the cold-blooded and the sins of the warm-hearted on a different scale. Better the occasional faults of a government living in the spirit of charity, than the consistent omissions of a government frozen in the ice of its own indifference."

By restoring to the debate over the significance of the New Deal acknowledgment of its achievements, we may hope to produce a more judicious estimate of where it succeeded and where it failed. For it unquestionably did fail in a number of respects. There were experiments of the 1930s which miscarried, opportunities that were fumbled, groups who were neglected, and power that was arrogantly used. Over the whole performance lies the dark cloud of the persistence of hard times. The shortcomings of the New Deal are formidable, and they must be recognized. But I am not persuaded that the New Deal experience was negligible. Indeed, it is hard to think of another period in the whole history of the republic that was so fruitful or of a crisis that was met with as much imagination.

DISCUSSION QUESTIONS

1. In the light of the achievements listed by Professor Leuchtenburg, how valid is the "new left" contention that Roosevelt was merely a middle-class reformer intent on salvaging the free enterprise system?
2. Of the numerous achievements discussed, which strikes you as the most significant? Why?
3. If the achievements of the New Deal are a model for twentieth century liberal reform, what would you say is the agenda for liberalism today?

9

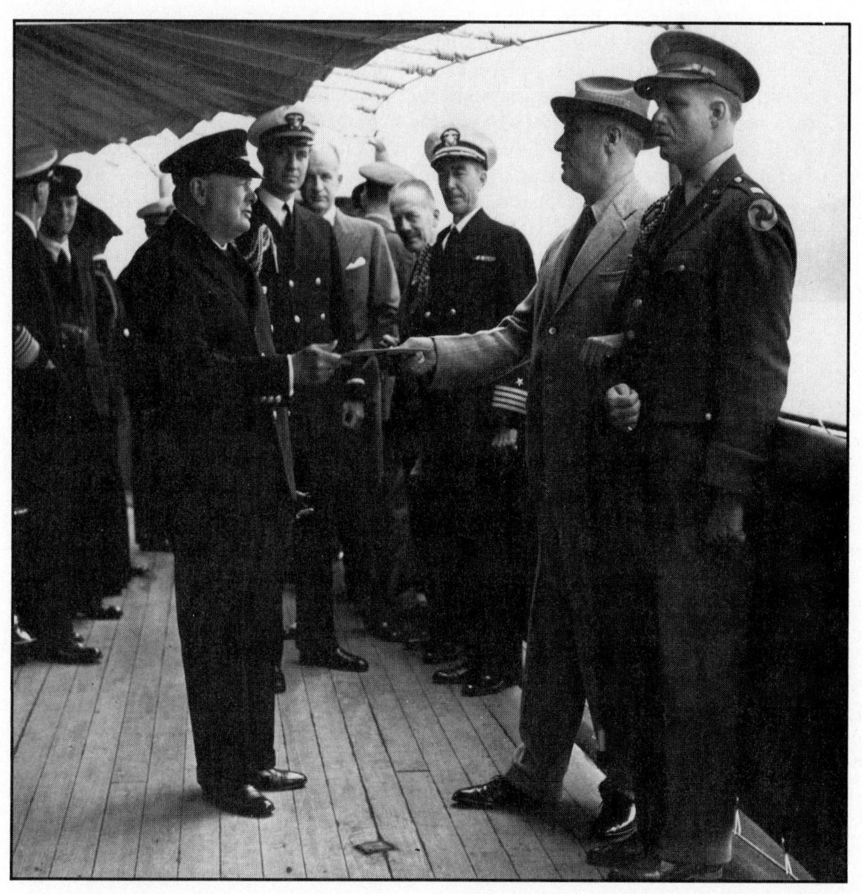

THE "LESSONS" OF THE PAST: SECOND THOUGHTS ABOUT WORLD WAR II

MELVIN SMALL

Americans have always viewed World War II as "the good war," as journalist Studs Terkel has labeled it. American leaders have made use of that conviction to derive "lessons" for the guidance of American policy. The lesson most commonly cited is the Munich analogy: that is, if the western democracies had opposed Hitler's expansionist demands, rather than appeasing Hitler at the Munich conference and elsewhere, German ambitions could have been contained and World War II might have been avoided. The corollary is that peace depends on collective security and the containment of totalitarian forces; appeasement only whets the appetite of an aggressor and thus endangers world peace. Throughout the Cold War this "lesson" has been used to justify American policy in Europe, Asia, Central America, and the Middle East, and it was the underlying rationale for both the Korean intervention and the Vietnam War.

Melvin Small's essay takes exception to the notion that World War II was a "good war," and he casts doubt on the "lessons" that can be derived from it. He points out that neither Germany nor Japan presented a threat to America's national security in 1941. American policy was governed not by the need for self-defense but rather by a blend of emotion, morality, and the antecedents of the past. Small reminds us that Hitler did not want war with the United States in 1941; with Britain and the Soviet Union he had enough enemies already. He was forced to declare war on the United States because of the activities of the Roosevelt administration, which had done everything it could to aid Britain except send American troops to Europe.

With respect to Japan, Small concedes that a contest for supremacy in the Pacific had been brewing between the United States and Japan for many years. Because of this historic rivalry a fight of some kind may have been inevitable. But he argues that it could have been avoided in 1941—or at least delayed as the American military wanted—if Roosevelt had been willing to cut a deal with Japan over China. Given our historic relationship with China, Small concedes that such a bargain would have been "amoral."

War with both Germany and Japan may have been morally justified. But moral and emotional justifications should not be confused with national security. Nor do they provide much guidance for us in the present.

—THOMAS J. MCCORMICK

Where to begin the epic story of the origins of World War II? Some would look to the Treaty of Versailles that ended World War I, a treaty "purple with revenge" whose sweeping financial and spiritual claims on Germany made the survival of the democratic Weimar Republic problematic. Others might choose that day in Geneva in 1920 when the League of Nations first convened and a shadow fell across the empty chair of the United States. Still others would look to China in the spring of 1915 when Japan's Twenty-One Demands were assailed by Washington and the handwriting on the wall became clear—the Open Door could not coexist with Japanese programs for Asia.

Though we might go back even further, there is general agreement that the first substantial marker on the road to Pearl Harbor was the Manchurian Incident of 1931–1933. From that point on, few doubted that Japanese and Americans would one day clash in the Pacific. The seizure of the important Chinese province of Manchuria by a Japanese army operating independent of civilian authorities in Tokyo provoked a strong rhetorical response heard time and again through the next decade. We condemned Japanese aggression, urged them to withdraw, and refused to accept any alteration in the Asian status quo brought about by force. All of our notes, threats, and appeals to international law and League of Nations resolutions did not deter the Japanese either in Manchuria in 1931 or in the rest of China in 1937. Some day, it was expected, they would go too far and we would finally have to put some muscle behind the Open Door notes of John Hay that had guided our policy for almost two generations.

Our reactions to the European markers on the road to World War II were more restrained. To be sure, we disapproved of Mussolini's attack upon the Ethiopians in 1935 and Germany's seizure of Austria in 1938 and Czechoslovakia in 1939. France and England, however, protected our interests in Europe, or so we thought.

When war finally did come to the continent in the first days of September in 1939, we were ready for it, although not for Hitler's blitzkrieg in Poland. Supported by the vast majority of the American population, Roosevelt prepared to assist the Allies as much as possible consistent with the conviction that we did not belong in the war. His speech to the nation on September 3 was realistic. After proclaiming our neutrality, he broke with Wilson's precedent when he did not "ask that every American remain neutral in thought as well. Even a neutral has a right to take account of the facts. Even a neutral cannot be asked to close his mind or conscience."

THE "LESSONS" OF THE PAST: SECOND THOUGHTS ABOUT WORLD WAR II From Melvin Small, "World War II," pp. 223–265 in *Was War Necessary? National Security and U.S. Entry into War*.

Almost everyone in America echoed those sentiments. Over 80% of those polled thought the Allied coalition would defeat Hitler and well over 90% hoped they would. Our commitment to the British and French was signaled by the easy victory of neutrality law revision in Congress. After November 4, 1939, merchants were permitted to sell arms and other war materials to belligerents, as long as they picked them up here on a cash-and-carry basis. Since the British, as usual, controlled the seas, our neutrality revision helped only one side in the conflict.

It is instructive to contrast our policies with those of 1914. Throughout our period as a neutral during World War II, we were not bothered by torpedo attacks. Even though the Germans possessed a first-rate U-boat fleet that harassed Allied shipping, Hitler was reluctant to provoke the United States. The neutrality act barring American vessels from the war zone made his job easier. On the other hand, when the British surface fleet instituted its blockade of German-controlled territories, the same sort of sweeping and extralegal blockade that drew our wrath in 1807 and 1914, Roosevelt offered a mild protest for the record, and then proceeded to cooperate with the Admiralty.

After a certain point, perhaps the spring of 1940, most Americans were convinced that war was inevitable. Each new escalation from the Japanese or Germans brought a corresponding escalation from us. Even though we maintained dialogues with the Axis, especially the Japanese, throughout the months preceding our entry, there was no turning back from our acknowledged drift toward belligerency. And unlike other wars, this scenario had nothing to do with defensive responses to challenges to our neutrality. Our reactions to Axis activities were only remotely connected to affronts to our flag or rights. We made no attempts to be even-handed; there was no talk of total embargoes or Gore-McLemore resolutions to keep us out of the way of Germany or Japan.

At the same time, each advance toward belligerency was made cautiously and only with the knowledge that the other side would not issue a declaration of war. As things turned out, our military was not ready in December of 1941. They would have liked another six months or a year to prepare themselves. In this case, the civilians in Washington were more anxious for war than the army and navy. Still, even the hawkish civilians knew that a declaration of war would have to be preceded by an attack upon our territory. Even though we were ready for war and expected it sooner or later, we told pollsters that we would not declare war without sufficient provocation. Perhaps this reluctance to go to war was illusory and reflected the normal response anyone would give to the question, "Do you want to go to war *now*?" Be that as it may, few opposed our neutral policies or lack of them—

our role as a passive belligerent in the British camp stands in sharp contrast to our strained, yet generally successful attempts to maintain legal neutrality from 1914 to 1917.

THE LIGHTS GO OUT ALL OVER EUROPE

With western Poland occupied by the Germans and eastern Poland "liberated from capitalist exploitation" by the Russians, the principals settled down for the Phony War during the amazingly peaceful winter of 1939–1940. All eyes were fixed on France where the next blow would surely fall. Surprisingly, it did not fall in the west nor did it involve any of the major belligerents. On the last day of November, Russia invaded Finland. (The American *Daily Worker* saw it differently in a story headlined "Red Army Hurls Back Invaders.") Although the origins of the bloody Winter War are beyond our purview, American reactions were illustrative of the nature of isolationist thought.

As news of the Soviet invasion reached these shores—a modern David-Goliath story—our hearts went out to the Finns even more than they had to the Poles, British, and French. After paying their World War I debts and producing a record-shattering Olympic athlete, the democratic Finns were now fighting the Bolsheviks. Herbert Hoover, who was slow to embrace the Allies earlier, took up his traditional role when he became head of the Finnish Relief Fund. The editor of the isolationist *Chicago Tribune* joined internationalists such as Secretary of the Interior Harold Ickes in support of the Finnish cause. Many isolationists were among the first to leap aboard the Save Finland bandwagon, although they called for private, not official aid. Such a turnabout suggests a linkage between anticommunists and isolationists. Some anticommunists had been unhappy about aid to the Allies because whatever Hitler may have been, he was the enemy of the anti-Christ in the Kremlin. Now that someone else had taken up the battle against communism, we had to help with money and material.

The Winter War, with its tragic denouement for the Finns, was quietly forgotten when the Western Front heated up in the spring of 1940. First the Germans took over Denmark and Norway in April and then, in May, attacked the Low Countries and the allegedly impregnable French Maginot Line. During this phase of the war, Roosevelt put us firmly on record as partners in the Allied camp, a camp made more attractive when that uninspiring appeaser, Neville Chamberlain, was replaced by the indomitable Winston Churchill.

In several stirring speeches and letters, the President committed our moral, spiritual, and economic resources to the cause of the fast-failing French. When the French Prime Minister asked for clouds of American planes to save the day, however, Roosevelt came up empty-handed. During this same period, the President delivered his famous "hand that held the dagger has struck it into the back of its neighbor" address. Despite Roosevelt's pleas, Mussolini entered the war to pick up his piece of France.

The fall of France and the arrival of the Nazis on the Atlantic Coast quickened the pace of our preparedness movement. Many who had heretofore viewed the development of a large military establishment as costly, unnecessary, and provocative became frightened. Such relatively isolationist organizations as the National Association of Manufacturers and the National Chamber of Commerce soon began to support the official policy of all possible aid to Britain, our last line of defense on the continent. This new cooperation between business and reforming New Dealer was helped along by the President's eager acceptance of capitalist leadership in wartime agencies that sprung up every place in Washington where land could be found to erect a quonset hut. The businessmen might not have been so compliant had they known that Roosevelt was preparing new policies that almost dared the Germans to mix with us.

Churchill had asked Roosevelt for overage destroyers. Losing an increasing number of destroyers to Germany's ravenous submarine wolfpacks, the Admiralty desperately needed more vessels to assure delivery of our war materials. Despite a rare personal plea from King George, the President was fearful of taking up such a proposal in the summer of 1940. An election was near, an election in which he was going to try to shatter American tradition and win a third term.

Fortunately for Roosevelt (and Churchill), the Republicans offered the electorate an echo and not a choice. Wendell Willkie was a liberal internationalist who eventually approved the substance of the Destroyer Deal, as it came to be called. In September, the political coast was clear for Roosevelt to trade a bunch of useless, old, leaky white elephants, as they were described, for naval bases in Newfoundland and the West Indies. It seemed like a sharp Yankee bargain, especially when one compared some allegedly worthless ships to Bermuda. Republicans did complain about Roosevelt's employment of an executive order to effect the unprecedented transaction. Even Willkie, who did not oppose the deal itself, spoke out against its questionable constitutionality. Most of Roosevelt's other opponents remained silent since the public overwhelmingly applauded the deal.

Americans had other things on their minds as the nation prepared for the climax of our quadrennial exercise in invective and bunkum. The electorate was unaware of a September policy paper from the military chiefs reporting: that sooner or later the Japanese would attack our possessions in the Pacific; that in the ensuring war we had to concentrate on Hitler first (no clues were given as to how we were going to get into a war with Germany); and that we needed to work even more quickly on the development of a defense capability second to none. The Joint Chiefs predicted that war would break out within a year or two. Naturally no one expected the President to reveal the military game plan during the campaign, but his public position bore no resemblance to his advisors' secret policy. Perhaps we should not blame him for his deception. He was encouraged by Willkie's campaign rhetoric.

At the start of the campaign, the two candidates tacitly agreed to keep foreign policy out of the debate for national security reasons. Willkie approved of Roosevelt's program of aid to Britain and cautious interventionism. However, with election day approaching and the polls offering no solace for Republicans, Willkie violated the gentleman's agreement and took the low road. He began to say that a vote for the Democratic standard-bearer was a vote for war. This new approach, which appeared to be effective, scared Roosevelt. Backed into what he perceived to be a corner, the President came out fighting with categorical promises that he would keep America out of war and that American boys would not be sent to fight in foreign wars. Repeatedly, during the waning days of the campaign, he assured his listeners that his policies would keep us out of war. Privately, of course, he thought that we might have to go to war against Germany and Japan. Had he leveled with the American people and told them that although he found war abhorrent, the world situation was such that we might find ourselves swept into the maelstrom, he could have lost the election. Although not very happy about it, Roosevelt lied, or at the very least distorted the truth in order to win the election. Contributing to the unrealistic expectations of the public, he unwittingly increased his postelection problems.

His defenders contend that the President deceived the people for their own good. Because voters could never understand the heady issues of national security and military technology, they had to be dealt with simplistically and emotionally. When Willkie demagogically threatened that a vote for Roosevelt was a vote for war, Roosevelt responded equally demagogically. He was like the doctor who wants his or her patient to swallow awful tasting medicine. The patient might reject the medicine if the doctor told him the truth, so he or she tells him a white lie, the patient drinks the concoction and recovers, in the eternal debt of his doctor. A white lie was told, the President was reelected, and the country was saved.

Some have tried to distinguish between similar historical cases. Roosevelt's deceit is considered permissible because the cause was noble while comparable deceit from Lyndon Johnson and Richard Nixon is not. Not an isolated incident, Roosevelt's lauded deceit does not speak well for our system. Something is wrong when the person who speaks the honest, pessimistic truth will lose to the person who tells the dishonest, comforting lie.

TO THE BRINK

Although to determine why people vote for certain candidates is always difficult, Roosevelt's foreign policy was apparently endorsed by the American people. Of course, he did not offer them a candid view of that policy. Nevertheless, Roosevelt's electoral success emboldened Churchill to ask for even more from the self-proclaimed Arsenal of Democracy. The British needed planes, ships, ammunition, and every other kind of material imaginable. There was one catch. The once-bottomless British Exchequer was empty. In polite phrases, couched in eloquent Churchillian prose, the Prime Minister asked for a handout from that same Uncle Shylock who had proven to be such a heartless creditor during the interwar period.

From our point of view, the British were serving as surrogate soldiers in the war against fascism. Their purchases also helped keep our economy going. After some deliberation, the President decided to do away with the "silly foolish old dollar sign." If his neighbor's house was on fire, he would lend him our hose and not ask for a rental fee. If the fire was put out, we might expect to have our hose returned but that was of secondary importance. In a brilliant public relations gambit, the Lend Lease Bill was assigned the number House Resolution 1776. Roosevelt told a receptive American audience that Britain's defense was vital to our own. Since they were making unparalleled sacrifices, standing alone against the Nazis who had conquered almost all of Western Europe, the least we could do would be to lend them the material necessary for their survival. The Lend Lease Bill eventually sailed through Congress by a two-to-one margin in the Senate and better than four to one in the House. The margins accurately reflected the national consensus on the policy to aid the British however possible. Lend Lease was unprecedented for a neutral. Throughout 1941, we *gave away* material one side used against the other. And still the Germans maintained their cautious posture, unwilling to challenge the United States again. During previous centuries, such a blatant violation of the spirit, if not the letter, of the law might have resulted in a declaration of war from the offended party.

While supporters and opponents of Lend Lease testified in crowded hearing rooms in Congress, other meetings of vital importance to Anglo-American relations took place in more private surroundings in the War and Navy Departments. From January through March of 1941,

American and British staff officers met to coordinate joint strategy. The fact they met together to plan wartime operations made them "common-law" allies. In the ABC-1 agreements that emerged from the sessions, a Europe first policy was endorsed and the means for cooperation spelled out.

After Lend Lease and ABC-1, the rest of 1941 was anticlimactic, at least so far as Europe was concerned. A pattern had been established. Step by step, Roosevelt led his insular nation closer and closer to the brink of full-scale intervention. Never moving too quickly, carefully protecting his weak congressional flanks, testing the water before he plunged in, he performed in an effective manner. Critics feel he was laggard in bringing the nation into the war, that he was overly cautious in leading a population ready to follow him almost anywhere. His defenders point out that although he did not lose any important congressional votes during the period of neutrality, his margin on some major issues was excruciatingly thin. This debate over the speed with which the President led us toward war is irrelevant to still other critics who oppose the overall thrust of his policies. For them, Roosevelt acted unconstitutionally time and again, withheld information from the people and Congress, and generally executed dangerous programs that led us into a war in which we did not belong.

No matter how we evaluate his actions, the President did move us in some remarkable directions for a nation still operating under the Neutrality Proclamation of September 1939. For example, in April of 1941 he received permission from the Danish Minister in Washington, whose own country had been occupied by the Germans, to occupy Greenland. During that month, when Hitler extended his war zone further out into the Atlantic, Roosevelt met the challenge with an extension of our Safety Belt around the hemisphere half way across the ocean. Around the same time, we prepared to occupy Denmark's other major possession, Iceland, after the British asked us to lift that burden from their shoulders. All three policies involved a by-then-characteristic unilateral Presidential action. Although the Germans were unhappy, and said so, they did not challenge these incursions for the moment.

Each month brought new provocative policies. In June, because of increased German submarine activity, Roosevelt issued his Declaration of Unlimited National Emergency. The emergency in this case related to the necessity of getting our materials across the Atlantic to the British. The declaration was not enough. We needed a convoy system. However, even though the German sinking of the *Robin Moor* in late May offered an excuse, the President felt that the people would not accept convoy duties that could lead to a shooting war on the high seas. More important, his military advisors were not yet ready to confront the Axis.

The complexion of the war changed dramatically in late June of 1941 when the Nazis invaded Russia. As the pressure on the British eased, it appeared that our policies had paid off. In the days that followed, Roosevelt followed Churchill's lead and began to prepare his public for a new relationship with the Soviets. In a matter of months, we began sending Lend Lease aid to the bombers of Helsinki, as Roosevelt silenced detractors who hoped Hitler would finish off Stalin for us.

Further, in a secret meeting off the coast of Newfoundland in early August, he met with Churchill to discuss the shape of the postwar world as well as plans for military and economic liaison in the months to come. No one at the Atlantic Charter Conference doubted that we would be fighting allies. The question was when and where. More surprising, few voices were raised at home to question Roosevelt about the propriety of conspiring secretly with a belligerent while we were still neutral. Such acquiescence could not be expected on every issue.

Indeed, the wisdom of Roosevelt's cautious policy was painfully illustrated in the congressional debate over the extension of the military draft. The fact that a watered-down bill finally made it through the House by only one vote demonstrated the fragility of the President's congressional support. Although extraneous issues were involved in the debate over Selective Service, if the President had to fight for his life to get that one through, one can imagine his difficulties had he requested war in absence of a direct attack on our territory.

Nevertheless, even before his victory on draft extension, Roosevelt gambled that the country was ready for still another offensive gesture when he inflated the *Greer* incident of early September to justify a new submarine policy. The U.S.S. *Greer* had been shadowing a German submarine for the British for several hours. In frustration, the U-boat commander fired two torpedos in her direction. Although the details were known to Roosevelt, he chose to characterize the affair as wanton German aggression. In his *Greer* report to the nation, he referred to the submarines as the "rattlesnakes of the Atlantic" and announced a "shoot-on-sight" order. Our vessels patrolling the Atlantic could shoot first and ask questions later whenever they sighted a German submarine. He also ordered our navy to convoy British merchant ships from the United States to Iceland. International law gave us no right to shoot on sight or to convoy. The least we might have expected would have been naval retaliation from the Germans in self-defense. They still refused to take up our challenge.

Much of what was left of our neutrality legislation was wiped from the books in November. After spirited debate, Congress abrogated the prohibition against American shipping in the war zone. This was asking for it; there was every reason to expect that we would soon have a replay of World War I.

What else could we do short of declaring war? We were paying for and shipping material to the Allies, convoying their vessels across the Atlantic, shooting at submarines that dared challenge us, and planning war and peace with England.

Though we had gone about as far as we could go, war with Germany was still not on the horizon. With Britain unconquered, and with Russia holding her own, the Nazis could ill afford to provoke a third major fighting enemy. Yet American naval practices were becoming intolerable. Fortunately for the Germans, they were able to settle the matter in the most favorable of circumstances. Just as they were contemplating lashing back at us unilaterally, the Japanese delivered their crushing blow at Pearl Harbor. For that story, we must return to the Pacific where another drama was reaching the climax that had been building for several generations.

THE CLASH OVER CHINA

Of all our interventions in international and civil wars, none seems more defensible than our intervention in Asia on December 8, 1941. After ruthlessly attacking China on two occasions during the 1930s, the Japanese bombed Pearl Harbor without warning. Four decades have passed since that shocking event, the first major foreign attack on American territory since 1815. Today, the story of that attack is much more complicated and certainly a much less one-sided story than might be expected.

From the Japanese point of view, our Open Door policy was brazen effrontery. How could the United States make claims on the disposition of a country more than 6,000 miles away from her shores? When anyone entered the Caribbean, we invoked the Monroe Doctrine. The Japanese respected our rights there—why could not we respect their rights in East Asia?

Although the Japanese pacified Asia in a brutal manner, what was the difference, they asked, aside from body count, between American interventions in Haiti, Santo Domingo, Cuba, Mexico, and other Latin states and their interventions in China? Arguments about the democracy we spread and the stability we maintained were not accepted by the Japanese who enviously watched as United Fruit and Pan American Airlines counted their profits. Claiming that their Greater East Asia Co-Prosperity Sphere was just like the Monroe Doctrine, they also planned to maintain peace and bring prosperity to their benighted cousins. They hoped to develop the area's raw materials, process them into modern products, and sell them back to poorer Asians whose living standards would consequently rise. The Japanese would bring their fellow Asians the know-how and political sophistication that had made them, alone in their region, one of the great powers in the world.

Such a generous approach to Japanese expansion may seem repugnant to those who remember the Rape of Nanking or the prison camp near the River Kwai in Thailand. Looking at the situation from their perspective, however, something we must do in every diplomatic encounter no matter how evil our adversary appears, we had as much right to tell them what to do in China as they had to tell us what to do in Mexico. After all, Japan and Mexico shared the Pacific basin as we shared it with China. Yet as early as 1912, the Lodge Corollary to the Monroe Doctrine warned our fellow Pacific power to steer clear of this continent, even in the peaceful pursuit of trade.

The Japanese of the late 1930s felt that their future depended upon their dominance of East Asia. In order to maintain their economy as well as their relished membership in the Great Power Club, they thought they had to control China and the surrounding territories. It is depressing today to see how mistaken they were in their estimates of what it would take to keep them on top of the pile in Asia. In 1980, without an army, navy, and formal colonies, but with American friendship, they have become the dominant economic power in the Orient and the fourth most important economic power in the world.

An American-Japanese showdown for control of the Pacific had been predicted almost from the time that Admiral Matthew Perry sailed into Tokyo Bay in the middle of the nineteenth century. Certainly by 1895, after "tiny" Japan crushed China in the first Sino-Japanese war of our times, the probability of such a showdown increased. After Japan's upset victory over Russia in 1905, stories of a war between the two young Pacific powers appeared with growing frequency in both countries' media.

Both claimed the Pacific during the same period. In 1898, we secured the Philippines, which we hoped would become a valuable way station for the bountiful China trade to come. Two years later, Secretary of State John Hay announced our guardianship over China in the celebrated Open Door notes. Our own frenetic Asian activity was sandwiched between the two Japanese wars that marked her emergence not just as a regional leader but also as a world power with which all nations had to reckon. At stake was the limitless China market. Although other lands along the periphery of China possessed valuable treasures, the best of them—India, Indonesia, Indochina, Malaya had already been claimed.

The war that broke out in 1941 was probably inevitable. Both Japan and the United States defined their national security in terms of control of China and the Open Door, respectively (some would argue both concepts are synonymous). Although war was headed off time and again through compromises from one or both parties, as long as both clung to diametrically opposed visions of the future in Asia, Japan and the United States were destined to meet on the field of battle. The story of the American-Japanese contest in the Orient is a sad one for diplomatic historians to contemplate. It suggests that some wars, which everyone wants to avoid, are unavoidable and, above all, that in most diplomatic encounters both sides can act rationally and, from their respective points of view, reasonably and still end up fighting one another.

From the turn of the century until 1941, each side in the Pacific contest steadily encroached upon the other's perceived interests. With every forward movement by the Japanese, we saw the Open Door closing another inch or two. With each protest from us, they saw their national development inhibited. Many in Japan, including a good portion of the civilian leadership, were wary about provoking us. They were naturally fearful that an American-Japanese war would be disastrous. We enjoyed economic and military supremacy, even taking into account the logistic advantages Japan had fighting in her own backyard. On the other hand, leading figures in the Japanese armed services, especially the army, were not so pessimistic, and in the Japanese system they were unrestrained by civilian authority.

The Japanese domestic situation posed a serious tactical problem for us. Each time their expansionists challenged our interests, we had to consider the effect our response would have upon their moderates. Unfortunately, whatever posture we adopted could weaken them. We could "hang tough" and alienate our potential friends. A firm response would lead to "I told you so" from the military adventurers—America *was* Japan's enemy. On the other hand, a gentle approach was similarly fraught with danger. A meek response to a military advance would allow Japanese generals to tell their civilian colleagues, "See, the United States is a paper tiger, we can safely proceed in our expanionist program."

This problem is not unique. How to appeal to doves in your opponents' camp always concerns policy makers. A hard line could convert them to hawks, a soft line might bolster the confidence of the real hawks. The policy maker must also be concerned about undercutting the doves by making them appear to be too friendly with the enemy. The dilemma is often insoluble.

A case in point which won us neither friends nor a policy change favorable to our interests was the Manchurian War of 1931–1933. The Japanese conquest of Manchuria was important for American decision makers in the 1950s who saw our tough words, but physical inaction then, as the first appeasement of the decade leading inevitably to world war. The lesson was clear; one cannot appease aggressors. Back in 1931, in the midst of our terrible depression and facing some legitimate Japanese claims in Manchuria, we could only condemn the aggression morally and place ourselves on record as refusing to recognize the new status of the former Chinese province.

The situation was different in 1937 when the Japanese attacked China proper and launched their assault that ended only when the bombs dropped on Hiroshima and Nagasaki in August of 1945. This time, Washington not only condemned Japan but also began sending economic and technical assistance to Chiang Kai-shek whose military organization left much to be desired. Since the so-called China Incident never became an officially declared war, the American government was able to violate the spirit of its neutrality laws and assist the Chinese. They might not have been able to continue their struggle through to 1942 without our political and economic support, especially after 1940 when aid from Russia began to dwindle. All of which raises an intriguing what-might-have-been. As we will see, the chief issue between Japan and the United States was the future of China. The Japanese wanted to establish hegemony over China so that they could freely develop her resources and markets and even settle surplus population. Though they never expected to conquer the entire country militarily, they did hope to place themselves in a position from which they could effectively dominate her political and economic life. Had they been successful, they might have given us some share of the China market, that is, had we been amenable to a deal.

The key to such a deal would have been American withdrawal of support for Chiang Kai-shek. One can imagine the consequences of such a policy reversal. Chiang sues for peace but Mao's communists continue the struggle. Although most of China is pacified, Japan becomes mired in a protracted guerrilla war that might still be going on today. Whatever the outcome of such a war, we had to "win." If the Japanese eventually wiped out the Maoists, an unlikely proposition, communism in China would have been a dead issue, at least for our generation. Had they not been able to extinguish the movement, the Japanese would have become so enmeshed in an interminable little war that they would not have been able to make trouble for us elsewhere. Alas, such a delicious Machiavellian fantasy was not in the cards.

First of all, American policy makers and population alike were captives of almost two generations of rhetoric about the Open Door and our mission in the Orient. The defense of China was an unquestioned axiom of American policy taken in along with mother's milk and the Monroe Doctrine. We were certain that our future was inexorably linked to the future of China—her surrender to the Japanese could not be contemplated. Never were the basic premises of the Open Door challenged during official debates over policy in Asia in the 1930s. Everyone accepted the grand strategic overview, they disagreed only over tactics. Even though the China trade, upon which the Open Door notes were based, had never panned out, and even though Chiang Kai-shek was a corrupt and inefficient dictator, we would not surrender the historic legacy of John Hay and a generation of American expansionists from the Gilded Age. One looks in vain through the official papers of the 1930s for some prominent leader to say, "Wait a second, just why is China so essential to our security?" The question was never asked. Consequently, a realistic, if amoral deal with the Japanese was not possible.

A DEADLY GAME

Through 1939, we were implicit allies of the Chinese in their struggle against the Japanese invaders. Yet while the American government aided Chiang Kai-shek, American businessmen continued to sell minerals and oil to the Japanese that were converted for use against our Chinese friends. Our embarrassment was lessened in July of 1939 when, in response to growing public pressure, Secretary of State Hull announced that the American-Japanese commercial treaty would be abrogated in six months. After that date, Washington could begin limiting the export of strategic materials to Japan. We hoped our threat of economic embargoes would buoy the Chinese, restrain Tokyo, and make our policy more moral and logical. But we had to tread cautiously because we did not want to provoke the Japanese unduly. The specter of a two-front war haunted our policy makers, especially the military. We did not have enough men and material to go around to wage war against *both* Japan and Germany. Maybe we would be ready sometime in 1942, but no earlier.

Although our military leaders did not know it at the time, their preference for going slow and applying limited economic pressure on Japan almost worked. At least at the beginning of 1940, the Japanese considered retiring from China short of their goals. They had been fighting a long, costly, and indecisive struggle for almost three years. Faced with an interminable war, some of their leaders were prepared to bow out of China as gracefully as possible if they did not win by the end of the year. Germany's unexpected easy victories in the spring of 1940, however, squelched Japanese talk of withdrawal. After the Nazis demolished the western imperialists, Japan would have been foolish to think of peace.

Indeed, Hitler's triumphs paid dividends almost at once. From a truncated Vichy France reeling from defeat, Japan demanded and received certain rights in northern Indochina resulting in the severance of one supply line to Chiang Kai-shek from the south. Awaiting the invasion of their homeland, the British also agreed to a temporary closing of the Burma Road to China in an attempt, they said, to facilitate the search for peace in Asia. Since Japan controlled almost all of coastal China, the closing of two major southern supply routes was a blow to Chiang Kai-shek.

At this point, relations between the United States and Japan took on the coloration of a lethal chess match, as each well-calculated move drew a well-calculated countermove. The game would be a long one. In the spring of 1940, check, let alone check mate, appeared far off. Our gambit was the dispatch of the Pacific fleet to Hawaii where, three days closer to Japan, it remained as a constant reminder of our determination to protect our interests in Asia. Conspiracy seekers later claimed that the President sent the fleet to Pearl Harbor to provide the Japanese with a tempting target in December of 1941.

This relatively unaggressive action was followed by our National Defense Act of June 1940 which, among other things, permitted the President to restrict the exportation of materials vital to our defense. Under provisions of the bill, we immediately embargoed 40 key materials but still allowed Americans to sell scrap iron and oil to Japan. We held the latter items over Japan's head as an inducement to good behavior.

Our use of threats and sanctions to halt aggression failed. From this case, observers have concluded that such a policy is not viable—economic sanctions will never work. Whatever the validity of that generalization, the world was in a different shape in 1940 than it had been in 1931 and 1936 when sanctions were considered by the international community. In 1940, our potential allies were either conquered or bogged down in war; moreover, we never did apply our most severe sanctions against Japan until it was too late. In 1931 or 1936, had the League of Nations embargoed oil to Japan and Italy, respectively, the policy of economic sanctions might have emerged from that decade with a better reputation.

In any event, our policy of escalating sanctions did not deter Japan from taking actions that offended us. After we announced our initial embargo list, she began building bases in northern Indochina; after we banned the shipment of iron and steel scrap in September, she announced her formal entry into the growing Axis family of nations.

The latter offense was serious. The Tripartite Pact, in which Japan, Germany, and Italy promised to aid one another if they were attacked by a country not then at war, helped consolidate American opinion against the Axis. When the three perceived aggressors joined in alliance against the United States, millions in this country who were Asia-firsters became convinced of the danger of the Germans, and millions who were Europe-firsters became convinced of the danger of the Japanese. The alliance gave the impression of a global conspiracy against democracy, when in fact it was never anything more than a marriage of convenience between racist Europeans and honorary Asian aryans. Nevertheless, the existence of the pact strengthened the hands of interventionists in the United States who linked the unholy triumverate in their propaganda.

Tokyo and Berlin were not immediately concerned about how their alliance looked to American citizens. They had been attracted to each other because they wanted to confront the United States with the threat of a two-front war. In addition, the pact augured ill for the British in Asia who would be helpless once the Germans made it across the English Channel. Unhappily for the Japanese, the Germans never came close to invading Great Britain and, more important, the Russian-German Neutrality Pact of 1939 came undone in June of 1941 when Hitler sent his legions into Russia. From that point on, as the Japanese themselves were threatened with a two-front war, the Tripartite Pact lost much of its attractiveness. Things looked even bleaker after the fall of 1941 when the Russians surprised the world by surviving the Nazi blitkrieg, the same Russians who had won a huge tank campaign against Japan along the Mongolian border in 1939.

Of all the issues discussed during the extensive conversations between Japan and the United States throughout 1941, Tokyo was most compromising on the pact. It was one of the bargaining chips Japan tried to use to buy us off or, at least, trade for a deal on China. The three main issues separating us were Japan's membership in the pact, her movements in Southeast Asia, and her plans for China. She was willing to alter her role in the Axis alliance, to go slow in Indochina, but not to pull out of China. For our part, we insisted on her withdrawal from China as the *sina qua non* for an agreement, were interested in maintaining the status quo in the rest of Asia, and least concerned about the pact. This was our private bargaining position. In public, our spokesmen referred continually to Japan's partnership in Nazi aggression and inhumanity. The Pearl Harbor infamy, then, was subconsciously expected by an American populace that came to see little difference between Germans and Japanese.

Through the remainder of 1940, we systematically embargoed more and more strategic materials until only one, oil, remained. We reasoned that a precipitate severance of the oil line would force Japan to attack the Dutch East Indies and bring us into the war. Given our commitment in the ABC-1 agreements to Europe first and our inability at that time to conduct a one-front, let alone a two-front, war, we tried to steer clear of a final showdown. All the same, as 1940 came to a close, Secretary of State Hull opined that the odds for peace were about 100 to 1.

Hull knew whereof he spoke because we were privy to secret Japanese policy papers. In August of 1940, we pulled off one of the great intelligence coups by breaking the Japanese coding process through the employment of a deciphering system called MAGIC. After that date, whatever we could pick up around the world, mainly messages transmitted from Tokyo to diplomats, we decoded and read almost as quickly as they were in Japan's chancellories and sometimes, as was the case with the final peacetime note, even quicker.

We used intelligence obtained through MAGIC with circumspection because we did not want the Japanese to discover our breakthrough. Our diplomats had to react in a believable fashion while reading papers they had already seen in private. They had to know when to act surprised, when to raise an eyebrow, or when to pound the table, as their eyes scanned a document in the presence of a Japanese emissary. Although for some of the less guileful this was no mean trick, Cordell Hull had prepared for his role in one of the best theaters in the world, the U.S. Senate.

TOKYO TALKS PEACE

Ensconced in northern Indochina, the Japanese began the new year with a peace offensive. How serious they were is a difficult question. Although not prepared to compromise on basics, they were willing to try us out, to bend a little, albeit without offering what we considered a meaningful compromise. Several prominent Japanese visited Washington in January and February of 1941 to talk of peace, and a new ambassador, Admiral Kichisaburo Nomura, arrived here during the same period. An acquaintance of President Roosevelt from happier days, Nomura was a liberal, pro-American dove who, unfortunately, was also a diplomatic tyro. The highlight of the peace offensive was the spectacular Walsh-Drought proposals.

Bishop James E. Walsh and Father James M. Drought, two American clergymen stationed in Asia, were asked by Foreign Minister Yosuke Matsuoka to convey a new proposal to American authorities. The oral report the priests brought to Washington was so optimistic that they were sent back to their Japanese friends with instructions to get the offer in writing. In April, they returned with a draft agreement representing quite a concession from the Japanese; a promise to withdraw from China if Chiang Kai-shek agreed both to recognize Japanese control of Manchuria and to accept a coalition government with a pro-Japanese Chinese. The Japanese were never again to offer such a proposal. We did not accept it because we thought that Chiang would never form a coalition government and also because other messages from MAGIC cast doubt on the validity of the Walsh-Drought draft. Nevertheless, all of these events suggested that the Japanese were sincere during the winter and spring of 1941 in their attempts to avoid a final break with the United States.

The Walsh-Drought proposals, an independent strain in Japanese-American negotiations, were among the first things Hull and Admiral Nomura discussed. From late February through December of 1941, the two men met in Hull's Washington hotel suite over 40 times. As historian Herbert Feis has written, "There, in the air, which like all hotel air, seems to belong to no one, they exchanged avowals of their countries' policies. And there, among furniture, which like all hotel furniture, is neutral, they sought formulas which would make them friends." All of their discussions came to naught. Hull insisted on a Japanese withdrawal from China and acceptance of the Open Door, while Nomura promised eventual withdrawal but stopped far short of renouncing the Greater East Asia Co-Prosperity Sphere. Both men honestly tried to avert war. The many meetings seem to belie the notion that once reasonable men sit down together they can settle any difficulties. There was no communication problem here except perhaps when Nomura occasionally found himself out of step with Tokyo.

As negotiations continued in Washington, Japan faced a hard policy decision involving her western flank. Germany's invasion of Russia in June of 1941 affected the balance in Asia almost as much as it affected the balance in Europe. The previous April, the Japanese secured Russian neutrality on paper. Presumably they no longer had to worry about an attack from their old rival in case of war with the United States. On the other hand, if they made the first move and invaded Siberia, they could have applied the knockout blow to the Russians. Despite such a temptation, there was time enough to start up with the Bolsheviks—the first order of business was the Greater East Asia Co-Prosperity Sphere whose development would be aided only tangentially by the defeat of Russia. After all, Japanese armies were still bogged down in China with no end to that war in sight. In hopes of tidying up affairs there quickly, they decided on July 2 (in a policy paper to which we were privy) the following: Instead of moving north they would move south into the lower half of Indochina in order to prepare for actions further south; they would not enter the Soviet war until the Russians were on their last legs (shades of the jackal policy adopted by comrade-in-arms Mussolini); and the Japanese Empire would be placed on a war footing.

After studying the implications of the new Japanese strategy, American decision makers countered the proposed forward moves with two of their own: one covert, the other overt. On July 23, 1941, Franklin Roosevelt finally approved a plan to allow civilian American pilots in American planes with Chinese markings to bomb mainland Japan. Pearl Harbor came too quickly for the plan to be effected. One wonders whether Roosevelt would have gone through with it. What would have happened had Americans been shot down and captured by the Japanese?

The Japanese, and the American population for that matter, never learned of the proposed clandestine air war until the archives were opened in recent years. Our overt response to the Japanese forward move was startling enough. On July 26, Roosevelt froze Japanese funds in the United States and thus effectively cut off trade between the two countries, including the trade in oil. Realizing the seriousness of his action, the President originally planned to allow Japan to obtain some oil through special permits. Inexplicably, his bureaucracy never got the message. When the Japanese made inquiries about purchasing oil, they were rebuffed by relatively junior government officials. This brought matters to a crisis point much quicker than Roosevelt had intended. At this point, Tokyo had a one year's supply of the vital fuel. Without oil, Japan would either have to give up the ghost in China or invade the Dutch East Indies whose government had also frozen Japanese funds.

Our perspicacious ambassador in Tokyo, Joseph Grew, was convinced that the freeze order came too late. The Japanese could never retreat from the program they had laid out for themselves; they would have to find oil elsewhere to lubricate their war machines. As Herbert Feis has written, "From now on the oil gauge and the clock stood side by side. Each fall in the level brought the hour of decision closer." The Japanese could no longer afford to wile away their time shadow boxing in those desultory meetings in Cordell Hull's hotel suite. A final solution to the American problem had to be devised in the weeks or, at best, months to come.

Although they should have expected it given what they perceived in the past to be unreasonable American actions, the Japanese were offended by the freeze order. After all, what had they done? With a bit of bullying, they convinced the Vicy French to permit a peaceful occupation of southern Indochina. For this, Roosevelt burnt the last economic bridge behind him? Of course, the Americans only used the new Indochina move as a rationale for a harder line that had already been decided.

Our policy appeared even more incomprehensible given political events in Tokyo in early July. First, the Emperor had intervened in an unprecedented manner on July 2 to urge a peaceful policy on his ministers. More important, on July 16 the most anti-American member of the cabinet and an architect of the Tripartite Pact, Foreign Minister Matsuoka, was pushed out of power. What else could the Japanese have done, short of withdrawing from China, to make clear their pacific intentions?

Undaunted, they tried another tack. Never excited about the prospect of war with the powerful United States, Prime Minister Fumimaro Konoye held off his impatient army with a new grand gesture. He proposed a summit conference with Roosevelt, a face-to-face meeting at which both leaders would try to solve the major issues separating them. We knew that if we rejected Konoye's overture, the peace faction in Tokyo would suffer a blow from which it might not recover. Ambassador Grew advised that Konoye, who was sincere, should be given a chance. The Prime Minister even tentatively approved the four principles that Hull had presented as a basis for negotiations three months earlier. Konoye suggested he might agree to the maintenance of the territorial integrity of all nations, the principle of noninterference in other nations' affairs, equality of commercial opportunity throughout the world, and the maintenance of the status quo in the Pacific.

Roosevelt was at first enchanted with the idea of a summit conference. A proponent of personal diplomacy and confident in his own ability as a negotiator, the President began half seriously considering meeting spots—maybe Alaska or Hawaii. However, Asia was Cordell Hull's domain. He had been minding that store while Roosevelt dabbled in Europe. Hull argued long and hard and eventually successfully against the meeting, suspecting that it would not have been beyond his chief to make some unprincipled deal that would have slighted our interests in China. Furthermore, Hull and his many allies contended that Konoye was a captive of his military, that he would not or could not offer us anything reasonable, and that in the past he had behaved less than honorably.

There are those who compare our failure to grant Konoye's request for a summit to McKinley's closing out of diplomatic options in the spring of 1898. Had Roosevelt met Konoye, the Japanese might have offered a face-saving, peace-keeping compromise we could have matched. What was to be lost by meeting him? At worst, we might have gained a few more months before a Japanese attack; at best, a firm commitment from them to retire from Indochina and portions of China proper. In other words, we might have been able to wangle more than half a loaf from our adversary, who was doing the best he could to avoid war with us. But even three-quarters of a loaf would have violated the principles that Hull and others had long argued were a *sina qua non* for an agreement. Principle number one was the independence and territorial integrity of China—the Open Door.

On October 16, Prince Konoye fell from power. His replacement, General Hideki Tojo, was not a friend of the United States, and he was not as nervous about an ultimate severance of relations with us. Still, Tojo had received a bad press here. As spokesman for the army earlier, he had been a leading hawk in the Konoye Cabinet. As a civilian prime minister now, he promised to do the Emperor's bidding and the Emperor wanted to continue negotiations. Konoye's final deadline for a settlement with the United States had been October 10. With the support of the doves, Tojo extended the deadline to December and immediately prepared a new peace plan. This time, it was clear that the deadline would not be extended unless the impasse was broken.

At an Imperial Conference on November 5, Tojo and his colleagues gave compromise one last chance. Naturally, their definition of compromise and ours were not identical. All the same, they decided to forward a new proposal to the United States. If no accord was obtained by November 25, the army and navy would begin their preparations for movement against the West. The proposal, later called Plan A, included economic equality for all in China and around the world, the retention of Japanese military units in North China, Mongolia, and Hainan for a necessary period (25 years according to Nomura), withdrawal of the rest of the troops from China within 2 years after the conclusion of peace, the end of American aid to Chiang, the evacuation of Indochina after the peace, and some modifications in Japan's role in the Tripartite Pact.

Plan A was clearly unacceptable to us and represented Japan's maximum demands. Foreign Minister Shigenori Togo recognized this and insisted that the Cabinet send along something more attractive, the so-called Plan B. Plan B was a *modus vivendi* to tidy things over for a while. It included the maintenance of the status quo in the Pacific, a promise to withdraw from southern Indochina when the war in China was over, American assistance in reopening trade with the Dutch East Indies, shipment of American oil to Japan, and the final point, the kicker that made the otherwise reasonable proposition ultimately unacceptable. "The government of the United States undertakes to refrain from such measures and actions as will be prejudicial to the endeavors for the restoration of general peace between Japan and China." Despite the final point, Tokyo was serious about Plan B and hoped it would serve as the basis for discussion of a temporary agreement to delay war.

Not only did we have an advance preview of A and B but we also knew of the plans sent to Japanese army and navy units beginning: "The Japanese Empire is expecting war to break out with the United States, Great Britain, and the Netherlands. War will be declared on X day. This order will become effective on Y day." Nomura's copies of the various informations included the following covering comment:

> Both in name and spirit this offer of ours is indeed the last. . . . This time we are showing all our friendship; this time we are making our last possible bargain . . . the success or failure of the pending discussions will have an immense effect on the destiny of the Japanese Empire.

Tokyo was not fooling.

Unbeknownst to the Japanese, we, too, had been drawing up guidelines for the approaching crisis. On November 5, the date of the Imperial Conference, the Joint Chiefs presented a program that called for the retention of the ABC-1 priorities, hoped that war could be avoided unless Japan attacked vitally important territories (i.e., British or Dutch colonies, Thailand, New Caledonia and the Loyalty Islands, Portuguese Timor), the maintenance of all possible aid to Chiang Kai-shek, and an admonition to refrain from provoking the Japanese. The Joint Chiefs did not want war yet, especially a two-front war. They would sit tight, keep their fingers crossed, and wait for Japan to make a move. Interestingly, the Joint Chiefs advocated war even if American territory was not attacked. One wonders whether Roosevelt could have convinced Congress to declare war to defend the British Empire.

On November 7, the next to last Japanese offer, Plan A, was presented to Hull and Roosevelt by an anxious Admiral Nomura. As he expected, it was rejected out of hand. To assist in the important negotiations over Plan B, the Japanese dispatched a second envoy, Ambassador Saburo Kurusu, who never hit it off with the Americans, even though he had an American wife. On November 20, he and Nomura offered the *modus vivendi,* Plan B, to Hull. We knew this was the last chance to avoid a break in relations and thus took the proposal more seriously than the first.

Undoubtedly, the provision for the freezing of the status quo in the Pacific would have been difficult to enforce. We also would have found it impossible to refrain from taking any action prejudicial to peace in China. Nonetheless, we did work up a counterproposal calling for a reopening of trade between the two countries, Japanese withdrawal from the pact, no further Japanese movement south, and American assistance in bringing about a just peace in China. On the surface, such an American Plan B was not too distant from Japan's. In 1946, the imprisoned Tojo claimed that had Roosevelt forwarded his Plan B to Tokyo, it would have been accepted. Had war been averted, even only for a few months, it might not have ever come, for a few months plus inclement weather in the Pacific would have taken us into the spring of 1942, and by then, the Japanese might have concluded that Hitler could not win in Russia. This conjecture rests upon Tojo's analysis. We cannot evaluate it because our planned *modus vivendi* was never submitted to Tokyo.

The domestic forces opposing a *modus vivendi,* led by Hull, were strengthened by the Allied response to the proposition. The Dutch, with much to lose, approved of it, but the British were lukewarm. As Churchill commented in his note of qualified acceptance, "What about Chiang Kai-shek? Is he not having a very thin diet? Our anxiety is about China. If they collapse our joint dangers would enormously increase." The Chinese themselves mustered their considerable influence in Washington to help nip an American Plan B in the bud.

Armed with the unified support of the China lobby, Hull came down strongly against the *modus vivendi.* Left alone, Roosevelt and his nervous military advisors might have tried it out. Ultimately, Hull's moral and practical arguments won the day, despite the fact that we knew that our rejection of Japan's *modus vivendi* meant the end of negotiations and, perhaps, war.

To make matters worse, instead of answering their Plan B with one of our own, Hull responded with a Plan A, our maximum terms. Not understanding what Hull was up to, the Japanese interpreted his 10-point, take-it-or-leave-it proposition as confirmation of what they had expected all along; they could not make deals with the United States. Hull never meant his plan to be a serious negotiating paper. He merely wanted to set the record straight. His final statement of American policy called for a nonaggression pact in Asia, a neutralization of Indochina, Japanese evacuation of China (the Japanese thought he meant Manchuria as well and were furious), an end to extraterritoriality in China, support from all principals for Chiang Kai-shek, a return to the old trade relationships, an end to our freeze order, stabilization of Japanese and American currency, Japanese withdrawal from the pact, and the creation of a new Far Eastern Concert. After dispatching the message to Tokyo, Hull dramatically told Secretary of War Henry L. Stimson, "I have washed my hands of it and it is now in the hands of you and [Frank] Knox [Secretary of the Navy], the Army and the Navy." Alerts were sent out to our military installations as we awaited the Japanese forward movement we knew not where.

There was one final peace proposal: 24 hours before the attack on Pearl Harbor, Roosevelt sent a personal plea to the Japanese Emperor to refrain from taking any action that would bring so much misery and suffering to the peoples of the world. He offered no new plans, merely good will. By the time the Emperor received the message, his army and naval units were in position for attack on several fronts throughout the Pacific.

Many Japanese accepted the final breakdown of negotiations in November with an air of resignation. They did not want war with the United States but they also wanted China. Although army officers thought themselves invincible, their navy counterparts were more realistic. Some planners of the Pearl Harbor attack considered it a desperate gamble that would probably fail. Even if it did take us by surprise, they knew they could never fight a long war against the United States. Facing the growing strength of the expansionists around them, the Emperor and many of the civilian cabinet members finally saw war as the only option available to maintain both domestic peace and international power. Although they could understand how the United States might misconstrue Japan's foreign and military policy, they felt that we had let them down when we failed to seriously consider their attempts to seek a compromise. From our point of view, the Japanese Empire was an aggressor nation, and as we learned from Munich, one could not compromise with aggressors. And that—especially for Hull and eventually Roosevelt—was that.

On December 6, Nomura and Kurusu received the first 13 points of a 14-point statement they were to present to the American government the next day. The document outlined the Japanese case against the United States and led, almost anticlimatically, to a 14th point severing diplomatic relations. We expected as much because we knew that Hull's 10-point statement had crushed all hopes for a negotiated settlement. Over the preceding week, we had noted a variety of Japanese naval and military movements but somehow lost track of part of their fleet, those aircraft carriers and their escorts stealthily making their way across the Pacific toward Hawaii. When the 14th and final point of the Japanese message arrived in Washington on the morning of December 7 and was decoded and translated in both Japanese and American decoding rooms, we still did not know what Japan's military plans were. We did not have to wait long to find out.

Owing to delays in decoding and translation in the Japanese Embassy, Kurusu and Nomura were late for their appointment with the Secretary of State. They did not present their indictment until 2:20, a full hour after the first bombs had fallen on Pearl Harbor. As the chastened envoys left the office of a furious Cordell Hull, Japan and the United States were already locked in mortal combat, combat to settle the destiny of the Japanese Empire, once and for all. . . .

WAR WITH GERMANY, AT LAST

At the epochal December 7 Cabinet meeting, Secretary Stimson suggested that the Germans be included in our declaration of war. After all, he argued, not only were they responsible in part for their ally's reprehensible actions but also we would soon be at war with them anyway. Of course, since they had still not attacked us, a good number of Americans would have opposed entry into the European war through the backdoor of Asia. Roosevelt's Day of Infamy speech was therefore directed against Japan exclusively.

The congressional response to Roosevelt's request for war was predictable. Only one Representative dissented. In an amazing historical quirk, Jeannette Rankin, who had voted against war in 1917, had been returned to the House in 1940, after an absence of 22 years. With tears pouring down her face, she voted no and remained true to her pacifist's faith. As in 1918, she was denied her seat in the subsequent congressional election. Clearly, had Germany been slipped into Roosevelt's request for a declaration of war, other Congressmen would have joined the lonely Congresswoman Rankin in dissent.

That omission of Germany posed a serious problem. According to our joint military plan, we were supposed to devote the major effort to Europe while we fought a holding action in Asia. Without a declaration of war against Germany, we would have had to commit more and more troops to the Asian theater since Japan would have been our only *official* enemy. Hitler might have waited six months or a year before declaring war against us. By that time, we would have been oriented militarily toward an Asia-first strategy and so deeply involved there that we would have been unable to operate effectively in Europe.

Why did Hitler make it so easy for Roosevelt? This has been one of the unsolved riddles of World War II. We know that he was pleased with Japan's attack. His subsequent declaration of war meant a two-front war for us and a diffusion of our formidable strength. Had he waited too long, we might have made short work of the Japanese and then been able to concentrate everything we had against him, or so he might have reasoned. When Hitler did declare war on December 11, he did not mention the pact as a *casus belli,* but based his case on the fact that "from initial violations of neutrality [we] had finally proceeded to open acts of war against Germany." His charge was not far from the mark. Given his failure to invoke the pact, we cannot argue that he went to war because there was honor among thieves.

Psychological variables also play a role. The Germans had recently suffered their first setback of the war when the drive east came to a halt in the snows of Russia. Perhaps, Hitler may have reasoned, a declaration of war against the United States would serve as a morale booster. Similarly, he allegedly claimed that a great power did not wait for war to be declared against it; it acted first. He also may have reasoned that his declaration of war against the United States might produce a Japanese declaration of war against the Soviet Union.

Most probably, the explanation for Hitler's declaration involves all of the above factors, especially the fact that we were just about in the war anyway. In early December, without foreknowledge of Pearl Harbor, the Germany Admiralty was preparing to retaliate against the United States on the high seas. Since we were shooting at them and convoying vital goods to the British, they concluded that they might as well risk fullscale war, which had to come some day, by unleashing their submarines. Hitler did not have time to formally approve a change in his naval strategy before December 7, and after December 11 such a half measure was irrelevant. The probable alteration in German naval policy, in the works on the eve of Pearl Harbor, demonstrates that even without the Japanese attack, we might have been at war with Germany before the year was out. It would not have been easy for Roosevelt to go to war over German submarines again, but a handful of sinkings by Hitler, who was hated much more than the Kaiser had been, might have convinced most of Congress and the public that the time had come to get into the fray. In any event, German and Japanese American policies were running in parallel directions in the late fall of 1941. Hitler's unprovoked declaration eased our anxieties. Had he called off his submarines and kept his mouth shut, who knows what would have happened to ABC-1, the war in Asia, and especially the future of Europe? As Bismarck once remarked, the Lord looks after fools, drunkards, and the United States of America.

NATIONAL SECURITY AND WORLD WAR II

Of all of our examinations of American wars and national security, World War II poses the most difficult problem. Those who have grown up believing that Hitler was the scourge of the earth and that his Japanese allies were little better cannot question our entry into the war. Everyone knows that we had to fight to save civilization from the barbarians. Distinguished scholars such as Charles Beard were dismissed as deluded, senile, or even fascist for their attacks on the wisdom of our interventionist policies from 1939 to 1941. Images of German concentration camps and the brutality in Japanese prisoner of war camps make it almost impossible to deal with World War II on a rational basis. Yet we have dismissed such questions from our previous analyses and must try to do so again, even in the case of war against Hitler.

First of all, the direct military threat posed by Japan and Germany in 1941 was not a serious one. Obviously, Pearl Harbor more than justified a war declaration but such an attack would not have occurred in 1941 had we been more willing to acquiesce in Japanese plans for China. In the short run, there was no way for Japan to invade or occupy any part of our territories east of the Philippines. Moreover, she was not interested in American conquest, at least in the 1940s. As for Pearl Harbor itself, Japan merely destroyed our fleet and withdrew. She did, of course, invade the Philippines, a much easier logistic task, but the taking of our archipelago was not essential to the success of her Greater East Asia Co-Prosperity Sphere. The Philippines, our Achilles heel according to the Republican Roosevelt in 1907, were occupied because they were our base in her territory. Had we not been at loggerheads over China, Japan would not have taken the islands. Even in the heady days of early 1942, most Japanese strategists realized that they could never compete militarily against the United States over the long haul. One can thus envision a cold-blooded deal in which we gave them their head in China in exchange for a guarantee of our properties in Asia.

But what would have happened after the Japanese had subdued China? Would they then have looked toward California? We know that even in the 1930s, Japanese jingoes talked of controlling all of the

Pacific including our West Coast. Such bravado was not taken seriously by those responsible for the destiny of the Japanese Empire. In any event, we had plenty of time to wait to see what they had in store for us since they would have had to conduct a protracted guerrilla war against the Chinese communists. That they had the capability of occasionally bombarding our shores or even launching balloons carrying small bombs across the Pacific goes without saying. But why would they want to start up with us if they did not possess the wherewithal to cross the Pacific and land an effective invasion force? Given their logistic problems, even taking into account technological developments over the next generation, we can argue that both in the short and medium run, Japan was not a military threat.

The Germans posed a more plausible challenge. By 1941, they had reached the Atlantic. Hitler's dreams of world conquest, as documented by his second *Mein Kampf,* knew no bounds. He could operate with more impressive resources and in a smaller ocean than his Asiatic ally. At the time in question, however, even had he not been bogged down in Russia, he did not possess the technical capability to invade a defenseless Latin American country. It took us three years to prepare the amphibious invasion of France, an invasion that involved less than 50 miles of water. An invasion of the United States in the early 1940s was out of the question, despite Hitler's fantasies.

It is true that they were ahead of us in atomic bomb research in 1941. We did not know much about this at the time or what atomic power would mean for the balance of terror in the world. Had they finished work on their first bombs in 1944, which was possible had Hitler not diverted resources away from that project, they might have terror-bombed us with the sort of devices we used on Hiroshima and Nagasaki. Moreover, as we were later to discover with their V rockets, they developed the most advanced delivery systems of the day, systems that presaged intercontinental ballistic missiles. With rockets and atomic bombs in Hitler's hands, would we have been safe? All of this, of course, was science fiction in 1941 to American strategists. Many things could have happened to Hitler before he obtained the means to rain terror on us from the skies. Furthermore, on the eve of our entry into war, he had more serious things to worry about than an aerial attack and invasion in the Western Hemisphere.

Undoubtedly had the Axis powers emerged victorious from their wars in Europe and Asia, they would have eventually threatened our territories and developed adequate capabilities to do so, an attack 10 or 20 years in the future. Should we fight a preventive war now because 10 years from today a country harboring malevolent feelings toward us will be in a position to conquer us?

Although the Germans and Japanese clearly posed the most serious threat to our military security up to that time, we had enough breathing space to wait until the dust had settled from World War II. In 1941, they presented no immediate or intermediate military problem.

The United States had less to fear from the Axis on economic grounds. In 1940, Ambassador to England Joseph P. Kennedy suggested an informal division of the globe into five spheres—German, British, Russian, Japanese, and American. Each major power was to be supreme in its own sphere where it would develop an autarchic economy. Since there were enough economic spoils to go around for everyone with major power status, there would be no need for conflict.

At the time Kennedy offered his scheme to an unimpressed Washington, Germany controlled most of Central and Western Europe and might have been able to seize a few of the choice colonies of the British and French. Clearly, Hitler enjoyed a more favorable economic position than did the Kaiser a generation earlier. Once (and if) he settled his European affairs, we might have been squeezed out of markets and denied vital raw materials.

During the 1930s, however, foreign trade constituted only 3% of our gross national product. Given the Depression, this was not to be sneezed at, yet it is not an impressive figure. Moreover, some of that trade was with countries such as Canada and Cuba that would never be controlled by Berlin. As for raw materials, we might have had some problems with rubber and tin, but when confronted with shortages during the war, we were able to develop serviceable synthetic substitutes. All of the foregoing assumes a Germany bent on warring upon us economically, something not necessarily in the cards, especially if a Kennedy-type plan could have been worked out. But if worse came to worse, our economy could have suffered. As in the case of World War I, we must ask, how much of a drop in gross national product or living standards merited a war?

The economic threat was even less credible in Asia. At bottom, we were contending with Japan for what had proved to be a phantom Chinese market. Prior to the war, trade between Japan and the United States flourished while the dreams of John Hay and his crowd had never materialized. We had every reason to suspect that a friendly Japan would maintain the mutually advantageous trade with us indefinitely. We could do without the Asian market she might have ended up controlling.

It is true that the war production and war trade did seem to solve our economic problems in 1939. The New Deal had failed—the recession of 1937 put us back almost to where we had been in 1933, although the psychological climate had changed for the better. Without a war, our artificially stimulated economy might have faltered again. Did we need a war to combat economic instability and maybe even political unrest? Even if we did, the contradictions of American capitalism did not justify going to war in 1941.

What then about our honor? Did not the continued military success of both the Germans and Japanese represent an indirect assault on our honor? John Hay had announced our support of an independent China in 1900. In succeeding decades that pledge was repeated by Woodrow Wilson, Herbert Hoover, and Franklin Roosevelt. Although such promises were honored more in the breach than in the observance, some Americans considered an attack upon China to be almost an attack on their own country. The complete loss of China to Japan would have been unacceptable to those Americans who had been involved for so long in her educational, religious, and business enterprises. How many Americans are we talking about here? Most likely, those prepared to die for China were few and far between. Everyone would have clucked their tongues about the fate of their little yellow brothers and might have thrown a few coins into the collection box. Few were prepared to do much more to save China. Had Roosevelt himself asked for war with Japan over China, in the absence of an attack on our territories, he would have been laughed out of the Congress. As for other nations, they had never taken our Open Door proclamation seriously, so any unwillingness to put our money where our mouth was would have been shrugged off. Our fellow great powers knew that prudence called for some sense of proportion in international relations and anyone could see that China was not essential to our security.

Even more than Japan, Germany's repressive system and conquest of democratic Europe, if unchecked, threatened to undermine our image of ourselves as the defender of freedom throughout the world (although not in our own South). Yet republicanism had taken a beating many times before without jeopardizing our international status or even self-esteem. Up until 1941, our role as democracy's champion involved merely holding the torch for everyone else to see and refraining from joining in Old World contests between tyrants and free men. One wonders if we could have remained aloof once we learned of Hitler's death camps, although Stalin's death camps of 1937 and 1938 never came close to sparking sentiment for a war against the Soviet Union.

Neither the Germans nor Japanese were violating our legal rights to any significant degree in 1941 nor did they offer any indications that they planned to do so in the immediate future. We had no real *casus belli* based upon honor or rights until Pearl Harbor. And, as we have seen, the Pearl Harbor attack could have been avoided had we been willing to make an amoral settlement with Tokyo.

DISCUSSION QUESTIONS

1. The author makes a similar argument for both Europe and Asia. Where is he most persuasive? Could a stronger argument be made to justify American intervention against Germany than Japan?
2. The author contends that neither strategic threat to American security nor moral outrage are plausible explanations for American entry into World War II, but he leaves us with no explanation of why it did happen. Were American leaders simply inept in their assessment of the national interest, and if so, why? Are there other possible grounds for war than strategic and moral ones?
3. What lessons can the present learn from the past about American foreign policy? Is it possible that any "lesson" is merely a rhetorical device for justifying a current policy decision?

10

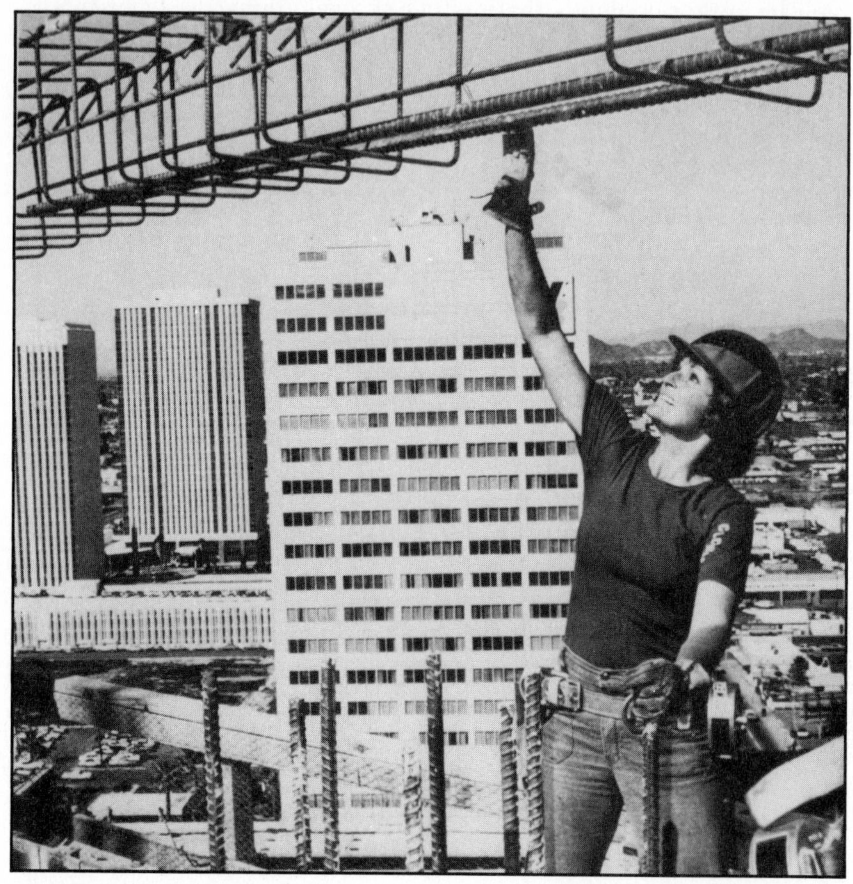

FROM PARTNER TO PERSON: THE WOMAN MOVEMENT, 1945–1975

SHEILA M. ROTHMAN

Throughout our history Americans have looked to the family as the cornerstone of society. Late seventeenth-century Puritan ministers, no less than late twentieth-century politicians, bemoaned the decline of the family as the training ground of spiritual, moral, and social values. To that alleged decline many critics have attributed the rise of social disorders ranging from simple discourtesy to violent crime.

Numerous contemporary cultural leaders have charged that central to the dissolution of the modern family are recent changes in the personal and societal roles of women. After all, they query, who is more important in the lives of children, who more vital to the happiness of breadwinner husband, who more necessary as bearer of moral and ethical values in the society at large than woman—woman as wife, as companion, as mother? But, charge the critics, the modern woman has abandoned those time-honored roles. She has become wage-earner, career professional, lesbian, and feminist—in short, everything contrary to traditional American womanhood. In transition from partner to person, say the critics, modern woman has selfishly asserted her own needs above those of society.

Such an attitude, Rothman reminds us, ignores historical pressures at work on both family and women in American society from the 1930s to the present. Labor force requirements during World War II, the massive movement of young families to suburbia in post-war years, the impact of the civil rights movement during the 1960s, changes in the psychology of education and measurements of social expectations, new laboratory-based experiments in human sexual responses and a new "pop" psychology of sexual advice books, confused and confusing governmental policies about health care and abortion—these and other alterations in the fabric of the recent American past have crafted new designs for the role of woman in society. Having donned a new garb of personal expectations and social responsibilities, the modern woman nonetheless is a product of history.

—STANLEY K. SCHULTZ

No sooner did the model of wife-companion take hold than two catastrophes, the Great Depression and World War II, brought two remarkably contradictory experiences to American women. The Depression drove them out of the job market, the war propelled them back—and in unprecedented numbers. But women and policy makers alike understood that both experiences were atypical, departures from the regular course of things. Normality returned in 1945, and then the conceptions of the 1920s reemerged and took on a second life. For the next fifteen years women attempted to realize the precepts of wife-companion, an effort that turned out to be, in many cases, acutely frustrating and embittering.

THE INTERREGNUM OF DEPRESSION AND WAR

To a country struggling with the most massive unemployment rates in its history, the notion that any woman might wish to work outside the home, or that single women who had traditionally been employed in schools, offices, stores, and factories might want to continue to work promoted widespread objections. The point was to "Get the Men Back to Work," as the slogan went, to spread the few available jobs as widely as possible. Official policies tended to discriminate rather openly against women in the labor force. Already in 1932, a "married persons" clause affected all federal civil service workers; whenever a reduction in personnel was necessary, the first employees to be dismissed were those who had spouses holding another federal position. Although the law did not specify that the husband was to keep his job and the wife to lose hers, more than three-quarters of those dismissed under the act were women. New Deal legislation perpetuated these practices. Men received preferences for Works Progress Administration (WPA) jobs; single women, even those lacking all other resources, were at the bottom of the lists. Women in other positions, such as teaching, did no better. It seemed patently unfair to allow the wife and daughter of an employed man to work while an unemployed man could not feed his family.

During the 1930s, the federal government funded day care centers for the first time. But these institutions certainly did not intend to bring women into the job market. Administered by the WPA in very ad hoc fashion (the centers were typically located in the basements of public schools), they represented a limited effort to employ a few of the women teachers that school boards had dismissed and, even more

PARTNER TO PERSON: THE WOMEN MOVEMENT, 1945–1975 From *Woman's Proper Place: A History of Changing Ideals and Practices, 1870 to the Present* by Sheila M. Rothman. Copyright © 1978 by Sheila M. Rothman. Reprinted by permission of Basic Books, Inc., Publishers. Pages 221–247, 249–250, 253.

important, to provide some of the children of the poor with hot meals. Day care under the New Deal maintained its traditional reputation as a last resort, an appropriate setting only for those in need.

If the Depression kept most women at home, World War II sent them into the factories. With men on the front lines and war supplies in acute demand, the nation had little choice but to employ women in all sorts of positions that had never before (and perhaps never since) been conceived of as appropriate for women. In Republic Steel, for example, the women were in the front offices typing, and in the foundry, next to the furnaces, rolling the steel. (In one government-sponsored propaganda film, "Women of Steel," a reporter asked a worker if the heat were intense, to which she replied, ever so quaintly, yes, but not much hotter than in the kitchen.) Yet at the very same time that the federal government pleaded with women to take war jobs, it made eminently clear that work for them was an emergency measure and a temporary expedient. When peace returned, they were to return to their homes. (Thus, the Women of Steel told reporters in one breath that they loved the jobs, and then, in the next, that they would give them up as soon as the men came back from the war.) In all events, wages climbed, patriotic duty called, and work, as one federal agency concluded, was "tempting to even the most home-loving mother."

Once large numbers of women with children entered the labor force, agitation for some kind of day care program mounted. The War Manpower Commission told employers that women with young children should be hired only "at such hours and on such shifts that will cause the least disruption of family life." The guidelines, however, were impossible to enforce, and hard-pressed manufacturers were not likely to ask women about their household situations. The Roosevelt administration next looked to local communities to provide facilities for the care of children, but few of them wanted to incur the expense. Finally, in 1943, the federal government did intervene. Under the provisions of the Lanham Act (for funding construction of wartime facilities), it provided appropriations for day care; yet, in every way this was a stop-gap measure. The actual administration of the program became enmeshed in bureaucratic warfare, with different agencies battling for control. The Federal Works Administration (concerned only with construction) won out over the Federal Security Agency (dominated by the Children's Bureau), but little good came of that result. It was not only that the FWA ignored altogether the quality of the programs, but in addition the number of centers actually built remained very low. As of February 1944, only some 66,000 children were enrolled in federally-supported facilities, and by the spring of 1945, the number just reached 100,000. The centers met less than 10 percent of the need.

That the centers were so scarce and so poorly run reflected and promoted a sense of their temporary character. Social attitudes towards day care reinforced these judgments. The Children's Bureau, for example, was not at all eager to see day care become a permanent program. Its 1942 Conference quickly decided that day care facilities should not be constructed immediately adjoining defense plants—for then they might become *too* convenient, outlive the emergency, and encourage women to stay at work. So, too, wartime conferences on the family were filled with complaints not about the paucity of day care centers, but about the fact that mothers were actually using them. Readers of one of the most prestigious social science publications, *The Annals,* learned that mothers who resorted to day care "forget what it may mean to take little children from their beds in the early morning and hurry them off. They forget that there are many children who have a dangerous feeling of insecurity when they are away from their mothers from dawn to dark. . . . In this tug of war between children and jobs, the children are losing." Critics charged mothers with being "war work deserters," for neglecting their children and not providing "adequate care and supervision." There were even fears that desertion might become habit-forming: "Once having left the children to their own devices, and finding that it can be done over and over again, the mother may develop much satisfaction . . . from evading her accustomed responsibility." Given these judgments, it is not surprising that federal funds for day care were cut off as soon as hostilities ended, another piece of legislation that, fortunately, no longer seemed necessary.

With the war's end, traditional occupational patterns among women reasserted themselves. Of course, working women did not disappear from the labor force; in fact, between 1940 and 1950 their numbers rose slightly, from 27 percent to 31 percent of all women. But the major increase came in spheres of work that were stereotypically women's (particularly office work) and not in manufacturing (where dramatic gains had been made during the war) or in the professions (which remained closed to women). No less important, older ideas about women's work were not challenged (as they really had not been during the war, either). The post-World War II period did not witness agitation for equal pay or equal rights; there was no sense that married women with children should be working. The war was not so much a transforming experience as an interruption, after which women returned to pursue an inherited role.

UNDERMINING THE MODEL OF WIFE-COMPANION

Immediately after 1945, a massive increase took place in suburban developments. Although such communities had been planned and promoted ever since the 1850s, in the late 1940s an unusually large number of Americans began to put a suburban home at the core of their preferred life style. Between 1950 and 1960, nearly two-thirds of the increase in population in the United States occurred in the suburbs; over this decade, the population in 225 major cities rose 8.7 percent and in their suburbs, 47 percent. Some very practical considerations helped to promote this change. The federal government, fearful of a return to depression conditions, underwrote the construction of homes in the suburbs. Low-interest mortgages were generally available, and veterans had added inducements—until 1972 they could purchase homes with a $1 down payment. At the same time, the federal government undertook a massive highway construction program, thus enabling people to commute to work from communities lacking adequate public transportation networks. But these points merely explain why it was possible for families to live in the suburbs. They do not clarify why a suburban home became the first choice for the American family.

In fact, the appeal of suburbia to women was intimately linked to the ideology of the wife-companion. By opting for the comfort, roominess, and seclusion of a suburban home, a woman announced her preference for an essentially private existence. The very distance of the suburbs from the city isolated her from the problems of urban life, the very problems that had so involved the Progressives. Promoters advertised their developments as "escapes" and retreats from the crime, noise, and dirt of the city—and most of those who made the retreat were content to give up a public commitment.

Sociological studies of the suburbs point to the highly self-conscious character of this decision. In carrying out his research on Levittown, New Jersey in the early 1960s, Herbert Gans asked women to list their "principal aspiration" for moving to this new community. The overwhelming majority (78 percent) told him of their desire to enhance the conveniences and the qualities of family life. They had come for "comfort and roominess for family members in a new home"; for "privacy and freedom of action in an owned home"; for "furnishing and decorating the home"; for "better family life," or, simply, for carrying out the "normal family role, being a homemaker." Only a handful of women anticipated a more active life of any sort outside the home. Only 8.0 percent came for a "better social life"; less than 1.0 percent came to be "active in civic affairs"; and less than 0.5 percent looked to involvements "in churches or clubs." To move to Levittown was to make a commitment to the family, not the community.

Just as an intense concern for the quality of family life brought these women to the suburbs, so this attitude organized their day-to-day world there. Suburban houses looked inward; architects noted that the typical design focused the home within "its own private garden with service facilities (kitchen, etc.) facing the road." The privacy promised to encourage a close and deeply emotive tie between husband and wife. The spacious master bedroom, generally set apart from the rooms of the children, was well-suited to a highly sexual relationship. And wives anticipated spending many evenings alone with their husbands, not with family or friends; in Levittown a woman would often not visit a neighbor whose husband was at home, probably, as Gans concluded, "because of the belief that a husband has first call on his wife's companionship." Social life tended to consist of couples visiting each other informally. If bridge was invented in the 1920s, it reached new popularity in the 1950s. So, too, the suburbs promised to offer children their own private space. Each child would have its own bedroom, in accordance with the best psychological principles; and it seemed safe to play unsupervised in a suburban development. Ostensibly there was no need for an iron fence and a trained matron to keep out corrupt street influences.

Public life in the suburbs represented a variation on the 1920s theme of country clubs and bridge clubs. The women of Levittown organized associations to facilitate casual contact with like-minded people, to pass the time in pleasant and congenial fashion. The clubs did not set out to provide a new community with facilities, to establish a neighborhood center or a library or a teenage athletic team. It was the local lawyer, and not the women, who saw to it that a library was built in Levittown; it was the school superintendent who organized the PTA, and the chief of police who led the drive for a Levittown Youth Sports Association. The women did not even bother to investigate Levittown's public schools. "They were sure," Gans reported, "that the new schools would be as satisfactory as their new neighbors." Suburban women did not share the commitments of their Progressive predecessors. They had much more in common with the feminists new-style of the 1920s than the reformers of the 1900s.

For all the rewards and personal satisfactions that the suburbs promised, some women were soon discovering that the other side of privacy was loneliness and isolation. Gans detected some of this at Levittown. It was only women (albeit a minority of women) who reported loneliness; women suffered disproportionately from emotional illnesses and committed all the suicides. But what was hinted at in Levittown was dramatically articulated and confirmed in the encounters between Betty Friedan and a group of her former Smith College classmates. Friedan was better able than any other critic to uncover and to express the malaise that all too frequently existed for suburban women. She interviewed her 1942 Smith classmates 15 years after graduation and then, "like a reporter on the trail of a story," supplemented their accounts. The story that then emerged in *The Feminine Mystique* (1963) was the gap between the rhetoric of the wife-companion and a reality that was empty and frustrating.

Freidan discovered that the wife-companion ideal appealed to women in all social classes. "The suburban housewife," she wrote, "was the dream image of the young American woman and the envy, it was said, of women all over the world. . . . She was healthy, beautiful, educated, concerned about her husband, her children, her home. She had found true feminine fulfillment. As a housewife and mother, she was respected as a full and equal partner to man in his world." But Friedan was just as certain that the image was a sham. Translating the precepts into practice had disastrous consequences.

Point by point, Friedan exploded the myth of "the feminine mystique." Her informants, she reported, found suburban life a nightmare. "A film made of any typical morning in my house would look like an old Marx Brothers' comedy," recounted one woman. "I wash the dishes, run the older children off to school, dash out in the yard to cultivate the chrysanthemums . . . help the youngest child build a blockhouse, spend fifteen minutes skimming the newspapers so I can be well-informed. . . . By noon I'm ready for a padded cell." Suburban housewives had become prisoners in their own homes, not enjoying privacy but suffering solitary confinement. "Many women," Friedan informed her readers, "no longer left their homes except to shop, chauffeur their children, or attend social engagements with their husbands." Preoccupied by an endless routine of household chores, they had lost self-respect. "The problem," as one woman put it, "is always being the children's mommy, the minister's wife and never being myself." As a wife-companion she could only find fulfillment vicariously, through the achievements of others.

On the basis of these responses, Friedan launched a two-pronged attack: the suburban housewife was both an inadequate mother and an inadequate wife. Devoid of purpose in her own life, she was incapable of giving her children a sense of competency and autonomy. The young, charged Friedan in tones reminiscent of Watson, were not only infantile but "incapable of the effort, the endurance of pain and frustration, the discipline needed to compete on the baseball field or get into college." And she predicted a dismal future for them; an endless number of emotional difficulties would plague them throughout adulthood. The curse of a lack of self-direction and self-satisfaction in the mother would be visited on the children.

The wife-companion was a failure not only in the nursery but also in the bedroom. Friedan's respondents regularly reported that sex was the only thing that made them feel alive and gave them an identity. And she took that to mean that lacking any other outlet, they attached disproportionate importance to sexual intimacy. Their emphasis on sexual fulfillment was destructive. Men, able to achieve satisfaction through careers, found sex a diversion; for wives, sex was a vocation. Under these circumstances, women made sex into a "strangely joyless national compulsion." Friedan quoted one marriage counselor to confirm her point: suburban wives "made such heavy demands on love and marriage [that] . . . sometimes literally almost nothing happens."

Their all-consuming passion disturbed their husbands, the proof to be found in the increase in male-initiated divorce actions. The rise reflected "the growing aversion and hostility that men have for the feminine millstones hanging around their necks."

The villains ultimately responsible for so grim a state of affairs, argued Friedan, were the experts who had foisted this role on women. The psychologists and Freudian analysts had misled women. Without much understanding of either Watson or Freud, and without any sense whatsoever of the historical antecedents of the role of wife-companion, she insisted that "the feminine mystique derived its power from Freudian thought." In terms that were far less novel than she imagined, Friedan declared: "It is time to stop exhorting mothers to love their children more, and face . . . the fact that most of the problems now being treated in the child guidance clinics are solved when mothers . . . no longer need to fill their emotional needs through their children. It is time to stop exhorting women to be more feminine when it . . . depersonalizes sex and imposes an impossible burden on their husbands." Children would not require psychological and psychiatric counseling if their mothers were happy. Sex would prove fulfilling if women made it one of many sources of pleasure.

But then Friedan did go on to make a new point, new at least to the world of Watson and Freud. The way for women to escape their predicament was not for them to devote themselves more fully to their husbands (as Watson intimated), or to bring their children and themselves still more quickly to a child guidance clinic and therapist's office (as psychiatrists suggested), but to gain satisfaction in work. "The only way for a woman, as for a man, to find herself, to know herself as a person is by creative work of her own. There is no other way." Indeed, since Friedan was speaking to college graduates and college students, she urged them not merely to take a job (for earning money or killing time) but to pursue a career (for finding fulfillment). Work was no longer a tactic to improve women's marital choices or an insurance policy to protect her in widowhood. Rather, it was to be at the center of a woman's existence, her primary source of identity. With little notion of the implications of such a message to women who had not passed through Smith, Friedan concluded that a career was "a new life plan for women"—the answer to *all* problems confronting *all* women.

Even as Friedan was writing, married women, particularly those with children, were entering the job market in unprecedented numbers. In 1940, only one-quarter of American women worked; by 1974, 46 percent worked. And the increase was not the result of more single or divorced women joining the labor force, but of more married women, and married women with children, entering it. "In 1940," as two Bureau of Labor statisticians calculated, "almost half the women in the labor force were single and only 30 percent were married; in 1970, about 20 percent were single and 60 percent were married." In 1948 (when such statistics were first collected), one-quarter of women with school-age children (between 6 and 17) were employed; by 1972, over one-half of them held jobs. Even more dramatic was the rise in employment among women with preschool children (below the age of 5). In 1948, mothers of preschool children made up 10 percent of all women workers; in 1960 they were 19 percent. In fact, by 1974, one out of every three mothers with a preschool child was at work.

For all their consistency, these statistics must still be interpreted cautiously. Just as the census may have understated the numbers of married women working in 1900, it may well be exaggerating the number now. The problem rests, of course, with the census taker's reliance on the individual respondent for information. Hence, the statistics may demonstrate not changing habits but changing norms. Since mothers with preschool children now believe that they *should* be working, they may be telling the census taker that they *are* working. Also, many more women than men are employed part-time; only 41 percent of women workers in 1970 were full-time workers. Nevertheless, it remains the case that the composition of the labor force is undergoing a fundamental, even revolutionary, change. Before very long, the overwhelming majority of women, whatever their family situation or household responsibilities, will be at a job.

How are we to understand this new situation? What was it that brought married women with children into the labor force in such large numbers? One critical element was the rapid post-war growth of service industries that dramatically expanded the number of white-collar jobs. If men quickly assumed the best-paying managerial positions, still numerous clerical and office posts became available for women. In 1950, women held only 4.3 percent of all managerial positions; in 1973, after more than 20 years of job expansion, they held 4.9 percent. Yet during the same time the number of women in clerical and office jobs increased. In 1950 women held 27 percent of these positions; by 1974, 34 percent. So there were more openings for women, albeit of a very special sort. While men had greater opportunity to enjoy careers, women had greater opportunity to take jobs.

Labor analysts in the post-war period not only perceived existing vacancies in service industries but also predicted critical labor shortages in the future. To ward off this coming crisis, they adopted a very novel stance; they urged employers to hire and train women for managerial positions. At the same time, they encouraged women with college degrees to return to the labor force and assume these jobs. Thus, the women's magazines that had traditionally carried articles by psychologists declaring that woman's place was in the home were now carrying articles by labor experts insisting that woman's place was in the office. Arthur Fleming, at one time Secretary of Health, Education and Welfare, was in 1962 a contributing editor to *Good Housekeeping*, and he used his position to publicize the new message. "The number of trained women workers," he contended, "must increase 25 percent between now and 1970 as compared with 15 percent of men—if we are to capitalize on our opportunities for economic growth." Given the low birth rate of the Depression years, the earlier age at which women now married, and the increased length of time that they spent in school, many of the vacancies in the labor force would have to be filled by married women with growing children. Therefore, Fleming, like Friedan, urged mothers not merely to go to work but to pursue careers. He paid lip service to the needs of the family but was far more concerned with the needs of an expanding post-war economy. Thus, in the early 1960s educated women received the same advice from two very different sources: whether for reasons of personal fulfillment (as in Friedan) or for public well-being (as in Fleming), they were to join the work force. Leaving the home took on an altogether novel legitimacy.

WOMEN AS A MINORITY

Just when the isolation of suburban life and expanded opportunities in the labor force were beginning to undermine the model of the wife-companion, a new definition of proper womanhood, a notion of woman as person, began to filter through American society. This was a view of woman as autonomous, energetic, and competent. Woman was not to be defined by her household role, by her responsibilities as wife or mother; she was in no way to be limited by any special gender characteristics. This new definition of womanhood emphasized the similarities between the sexes, not the differences. It rendered the notion of special protection outmoded and irrelevant. In brief, woman as person was fully capable of defending and acting in her own best interest.

This ideal showed surprisingly little continuity with a feminist past. The movement for female suffrage, with its insistence on women's special roles and responsibilities, was irrelevant. Even the 1920s National Woman's Party, which survived to introduce an equal rights amendment into Congress almost every year, offered little in the way of appropriate rhetoric or leadership. New feminist organizations, without ties to traditional women's clubs or women's political organizations, were to set forth the new model and establish its relevance to social policy.

Parts of the impetus to a definition of woman as person may have come from an acute dissatisfaction with the narrow and frustrating quality of life as a wife-companion and from a sense of the new options within the labor market. But part of it also came from the civil rights movement. Although it is commonplace to observe that women's protest followed on blacks' protest, that one effort to advance the position of an oppressed group stimulated another, neither the conceptual nor the political links between the two movements are as obvious or as simple as they may first appear. In fact, there is little historical basis for making such a connection. White middle-class women were not involuntarily wrenched from a native culture and transplanted to an alien society to suffer the degradations of slavery. More, the civil rights movement itself was unwilling to see women's problems as identical to its own. Stokely Carmichael's remarks on the appropriate position for women in the movement—on their backs—is now legendary. But other men in more polite ways said almost the same thing. "Women are not a civil rights issue," the leaders of the NAACP Legal Defense Fund told Muriel Fox and Betty Friedan when they were soliciting support for the National Organization of Women. Nor did feminist recruiters receive substantial backing from black middle-class activist women. " 'We don't want anything to do with that bag,' " Friedan remembers them saying. " 'The important thing for black women was for black men to get ahead. And when the black men got the rights they had been denied so long, they would give black women all the equality they desired.' " Sexual discrimination may have been the key issue for white women, but it was not for black women.

Feminists themselves for a long time did not perceive the need for a civil rights organization for women. They did not, for example, take the lead in demanding national legislation that would combat the discrimination that women suffered as it combatted the discrimination that blacks suffered. Curiously, the demand came to be embodied in the law before it was self-consciously advanced by feminist leaders. The federal law that treated the two forms of discrimination in similar fashion was the product of a series of fortuitous circumstances, not of a skillful lobbying campaign. In 1964, Title VII of the Civil Rights Act, outlawing racial discrimination in hiring practices, was the subject of a bitter Congressional battle; conservative Senators were attempting to defeat or to dilute the bill in every possible manner. Howard Smith, a senator from Virginia, in an effort to demonstrate just how ridiculous legislation governing hiring practices was, added an amendment to Title VII forbidding sexual as well as racial discrimination. But the Johnson administration was so determined to see the law enacted that when Congresswoman Martha Griffiths and Senator Margaret Chase Smith threatened to raise a fuss if the Smith clause were omitted, the administration threw its weight into keeping the prohibition against sexual discrimination. While feminists were certainly pleased at this accident of drafting, they had nothing to do with it and they really did not expect very much to come from it. As a result, the clause was not taken seriously by the Congress that passed it, the president who signed it, the administrators who were to enforce it, or the employers who were to obey it.

Although employers dutifully posted signs announcing that their hiring and promotion policies did not discriminate either on the basis of race or of sex, corporations did not in practice treat blacks and women in the same way. Given the power of the civil rights movement at this time, employers did make some effort to alter policies toward blacks. But women did not make gains. Women filed numerous complaints with the Equal Employment Opportunity Commission (EEOC), the enforcement arm of Title VII, protesting unfair treatment. Indeed, it is striking just how quickly individual women turned to the Commission to redress their grievances. (No rhetoric may have linked sexual and racial discrimination, but the women knew at first hand about bias.) Nevertheless, these complaints went unanswered. With no organization ready to pressure the administrative agency, Title VII was meaningless as far as women were concerned.

But not altogether meaningless, for the very presence of the clause in Title VII did inspire a group of "underground" feminists to pursue the issue of sex discrimination. One EEOC staff member did begin to encourage such traditional women's groups as the League of Women Voters and the American Association of University Women to protest the agency's lack of activity on behalf of women. But the organizations ignored him, and Title VII too. They were unable to see any connection between racial and sexual discrimination; middle-class women in salaried positions seemingly had nothing in common with unskilled black laborers. Many of the leaders undoubtedly were reluctant to confront the issue, still believing that women belonged at home. In all events, the established women's organizations did not concern themselves with sexual discrimination. Some of them would catch up and come along later, but they did not lead the movement.

Their reluctance to act was really not surprising. Even Friedan, so aware of the problems of middle-class women, was unwilling until 1966 to form a civil rights-type of organization. At first she was convinced that women did not have "to organize anything as radical as a civil rights movement, like the blacks." It was all a matter of will and energy; once women were committed to careers, employers would recognize their skills and determination and end discriminatory practices. But as Friedan learned more about the unfair treatment that women encountered in the labor force, as more cases filed with EEOC came to her attention, she shifted ground. She began to worry about a "feminist backlash"—if enough women entered the job market, only to be treated as second-class citizens, they would soon beat a retreat to the family and find the same problems all over again. Perhaps a women's civil rights organization was not inappropriate after all.

Dissatisfaction with the EEOC initially prompted Friedan and other feminists to look to the Citizen's Advisory Council on the Status of

Women for corrective action. Originally established by President Kennedy in 1961, the Council had the broad mandate to "examine the needs and changing position of American women to make recommendations to eliminate barriers to their full participation in the economic, social, civil and political affairs of the nation." By the middle of the 1960s, the national Council, and the state Councils that it spawned, had collected voluminous material documenting sexual discrimination; the Council knew well the unwillingness of the EEOC to enforce the sex discrimination clause. The feminists expected support from the Council. Traditionally, federal agencies like the Children's Bureau had drawn up model codes and lobbied for the passage of legislation to correct injustices. But to the feminists' surprise, the Council, at its Third Annual Conference in 1966, refused to allow a public resolution demanding that EEOC treat sexual discrimination like racial discrimination to come to the floor. The Conference officials ruled that the sponsors of the resolution were not official delegates to the meeting and, hence, were out of order.

Behind the Council's refusal to press the issue, to do battle against barriers to women's "full participation" in American society, lay a critical difference between this organization and others like the Children's Bureau or the Women's Bureau. The older bodies were the products of an already-existing coalition; they were the culmination of reform efforts, not their initial sponsors, and they worked to fulfill an agenda that their creators had long before established. Feminists, on the other hand, were trying to capture an already-existing agency and turn it to their own purposes, which was a futile effort. The Council, for all the language of the mandate, was very traditional-minded. Its members came from long-standing women's organizations, service clubs, and religious associations. Not that any of them favored discrimination against women, but the Council was going to move carefully, cautiously, and behind the scenes. Faced with the indisputable fact of massive discrimination against women, it preferred to respond in a low-key manner. So instead of calling in the media and going for the headlines, the Council would petition the EEOC to alter its policies. And when the EEOC ignored its resolutions and refused to give discrimination against women the same attention that it gave discrimination against blacks, the Council did nothing. In effect, the Council disagreed not so much with the aims of the feminists as with their methods—which was another way of saying that the Council would not be a driving force in creating a vigorous public protest movement among women.

It was fitting, then, that the Council's rebuff became the occasion in 1966 for the new feminists to establish their own association. The National Organization for Women (NOW), as the group was called, pledged to "take action to bring women into full participation in the mainstream of American society now," but not the sort of action that the Council took. There was no reason, NOW urged, to "examine conditions"; the extent of discrimination was already documented. Nor was there any cause for merely "encouraging" women's participation in the work force; large numbers of women were already employed and they needed immediate assistance to get better-paying jobs and long-overdue promotions. NOW believed that only by publicizing both the extent of discrimination against women and the unwillingness of government agencies to take corrective action could they generate reform. By moving from politics to the media, from compromise to confrontation, NOW became the first civil rights organization for women.

NOW also found the rhetoric of the civil rights movement to be particularly appropriate and useful. "The time has come," declared NOW's Statement of Purpose, "to confront with concrete action, the conditions which now prevent women from enjoying the equality of opportunity and freedom of choice which is their right as individual Americans, and as human beings." Women in the labor force had to date received "token" appointments; businesses made no "serious effort to advance and recruit" them. "Working women are becoming increasingly—not less—concentrated on the bottom of the job ladder. As a consequence, full-time women workers today earn on the average only 60 percent of what men earn." So, too, women were the victims of inequality in the educational system. They, like blacks, were denied admission to prestigious colleges and professional schools. As a result, "women comprise less than 1 percent of federal judges; less than 4 percent of all lawyers; 7 percent of doctors. Yet women represent 53 percent of the U.S. population." Further, the media, the textbooks, and the law—indeed, all social institutions—portrayed women in stereotypic fashion and presented a "false image." Finally, NOW proclaimed its opposition to "all policies and practices—in church, state, college, factory, or office—which, in the guise of protectiveness, not only deny opportunities but foster in women self-denigration, dependence, and evasion of responsibility."

One must remember that in 1966 the civil rights rhetoric had a very optimistic and Progressive quality that the organizers of NOW found highly appealing. Under the leadership of Martin Luther King, Jr., the movement spoke fervently about cooperation and brotherhood. "My dream," declared King in his 1963 speech from the steps of the Lincoln Memorial, "is a dream deeply rooted in the American Dream. I have a dream that one day on the red hills of Georgia sons of former slaves and the sons of former slaveowners will be able to sit down together at the table of brotherhood." And the women who formed NOW shared a similar vision. Their ambition was to create for American women "an active, self-respecting partnership with men." NOW had no "enmity toward men, who are also victims of the current half-equality between the sexes." Hence in NOW's dream, "a true partnership between the sexes demands a different concept of marriage, an equitable sharing of the responsibilities of home and children and of the economic burdens of their support." In all, NOW assumed that its program would eliminate the causes of "much unnecessary hostility between the sexes."

It would not take very long before this rhetoric would have a naïve ring. Just as the civil rights movement would move from brotherhood to black power, so the women's movement too would shift from partnership to a war between the sexes. But in their origins, both movements believed that their demands were just and in everyone's best interest, and that their success was therefore assured. Whites of good reason and men of good reason would sooner or later promote a new social justice.

Such an identification with the blacks invigorated the women's movement. NOW declared its willingness to offer "active support to the common cause of equal rights for all those who struggle against discrimination and deprivation." This proclamation gave the feminists a very solid sense of purpose. Imagine how it felt for a middle-class woman to have a part in the "world-wide revolution for human rights." This orientation also seemed to reverse some of the traditional lines of influence between middle-class women reformers and the poor, giving feminists a further sense of their own novelty. If the Progressive women had set out to mold the poor in their own image, NOW supporters in the 1960s claimed to be ready to learn from the poor. They adopted their rhetoric and strategy, and predictably, at least some of them began to affect their style of dress and manners. Blue jeans came into fashion, women became "sisters," and first names became the appropriate form of address. And although they had no way of knowing it, women's groups and black groups shared still another similarity—they both became the target of undercover FBI investigations.

But this similarity in style had an even more important consequence for the first feminists. It led them to believe (mistakenly, as we shall see later), that social policies implemented on behalf of middle-class women would, by their very nature, also favor lower-class women. Since feminists viewed themselves as one more oppressed minority, they inevitably assumed that policies designed to improve their own lot would improve everyone's lot. Rather than believing that social class differences would create conflict, they thought that gender similarity promised unity. Identity of sex seemed more important than class divergences. So central was this assumption to the new feminists that they could not imagine a time when the best interest of middle-class women would not fit with the best interest of lower-class women. Their sense of identity with the groups below gave them the self-confidence, deceptive to its core, that social policy could be restructured to the advantage of all women.

The civil rights movement had yet another impact on the women's movement. The drive for school desegregation prompted a major reexamination of learning patterns in American children, a reexamination that would soon alter the understanding of learning patterns among women as well. The proponents of desegregation had not only to overturn the constitutionality of a separate-but-equal doctrine as it applied to school facilities, but also to repudiate a traditional system of classification in the schools that labeled blacks as slow learners. Immediately after the 1954 Supreme Court victory in *Brown*, a group of psychologists (who had successfully pressed the view that the stigma of separateness made it inherently unequal) began to attack established methods of classification. Stereotypes about low levels of academic achievement among black children had to be eliminated before communities would actually go about desegregating their schools. And so psychologists began to reevaluate the accuracy and reliability of the procedure that was at the core of classification systems, the IQ test.

These psychologists maintained that the IQ examination was culturally biased in favor of middle-class children. It tested primarily for "cognitive skills"—in which middle-class children excelled—and did not measure "adaptive behavior" skills—an ability to survive in a difficult and hostile environment in which black children excelled. This limitation was critical because the test was unable to predict which children would succeed in the world beyond the classroom. In fact, this group of psychologists argued that success in adult life had so little to do with a person's IQ that the examination should be altogether abolished.

This was not the first reconsideration of the dependability of the IQ test. It had been under scrutiny ever since its widespread use in the United States beginning in the 1920s. Before the 1950s, however, analyses of the IQ had the purpose of refining the test. They presupposed the value of the procedure, looking only to make the measurement still more accurate and discriminating. Both psychologists and educators had assumed that the ideal school was made up of a series of "special classes," and that the model classroom contained a student body that was homogeneous in intelligence. The ultimate purpose of the IQ was to match the child to the right setting, and the better the test, the more appropriate the classification.

The new psychologists brought altogether different assumptions to the field. They were seeking a mix of heterogeneous children. In their ideal classroom, learning occurred as frequently from social interaction as from books; an unclassified school, therefore, would benefit both the child and the wider society. The IQ, as their novel experiments demonstrated, was a barrier to implementing such a program. The test scores appeared to be self-fulfilling prophecies; teachers who were told that a child "showed great promise" subsequently paid him more attention and graded him higher. In other words, social expectation was the major variable determining a child's level of achievement in school.

This new type of psychological research had a serendipitous effect on the women's movement. While some researchers were examining the differences in school performance between blacks and whites, others began to look at the differences between boys and girls. Again, it seemed that social expectation was the critical element in determining outcomes. The intellectual capacities of the sexes were identical, but their patterns of learning were not. Girls achieved more than boys in elementary school but began to slip behind in high school; by college, women were not only achieving less than men but were even rating men's potential to achieve higher than their own. The key to the puzzle was societal values. As girls matured, they fell victim to cultural judgments that brains and beauty did not mix, that learning was a man's business, that a woman who was too smart would become an old maid.

One set of experiments that psychologist Matina Horner carried out revealed that women tended to fear success precisely because it did not fit with a properly feminine image. "The high, if anything increasing, incidence of fear of success imagery found in our studies," reported Horner, "indicates the extent to which women have incorporated society's attitudes . . . that competition, success, competence, and intellectual achievements are basically inconsistent with femininity." Rather than contradict the norm, women tended to "compromise by disguising their ability and abdicating from competition in the outside world." The implication of Horner's research for the women's movement was clear: to promote a new image that made success compatible with womanhood.

The primary target of the ensuing campaign was not the IQ test but psychoanalytic doctrines—the writings of Erik Erikson, Bruno Bettelheim, Helene Deutsch, and Freud himself. All of them, feminists argued, had elevated socially determined roles into biological truths; all of them had cloaked myth in the garb of science. Thus, they quoted Erik Erikson's dictum that a mature woman's fulfillment had to take account of the fact that "somatic design harbors an 'inner space' destined to bear the offspring of chosen men, and with it, a biological, psychological and ethical commitment to take care of human infancy"; and they then asked how Erikson knew this. So, too, they quoted Bettelheim's contention that "we must start with the realization that, as much as women want to be good scientists or engineers, they want first and foremost to be womanly companions of men and to be mothers." And they wondered what made him so certain of this. Such notions, the feminists insisted, reflected not scientific findings but "the cultural consensus." To psychoanalysts, one feminist noted, "a woman's *true* nature is that of a happy servant . . . and they back it up with psychosexual incantation and biological ritual causes." In similar fashion, "psychologists and psychiatrists embrace these sexist norms of our culture . . . [and] do not see beyond the most superficial and stultifying conceptions of female nature."

The Freudian idea of woman as an inherently passive mother and companion received its fullest expression in the writings of Helene Deutsch. Her immensely influential two-volume work, *The Psychology of Women,* was almost a twentieth-century restatement of the nineteenth-century view that God first made a uterus and then built woman around it. Deutsch linked psychology to sexuality and sexuality to social functioning. Women, she argued, defined their lack of a penis as a psychological and sexual defect and, in an effort at compensation, tried to substitute the clitoris. But the clitoris was merely an "inferior organ," one "so rudimentary that it can barely be considered an organ"; clitoral masturbation inevitably proved unsatisfactory, incapable of gratifying "the active and aggressive instinctual impulses." The result of this sexual frustration was an abdication—the normal woman gave up aggressive drives and turned instead to a feminine—that is, passive—role. In one of the clearest statements of the view that anatomy was destiny, Deutsch concluded, "Thus the inadequacy of the organ can be considered a biologic and physiologic cause of psychological sex differences." Neurotic women, obsessed by the lack of an organ, became aggressive and homosexual. The well-adjusted woman, at peace with her biology, became passive, receptive, and masochistic.

The critical attack on Deutsch came from the laboratory. The experiments of Dr. William Masters and Virginia Johnson demonstrated the absurdity of defining women's role as inherently passive in a sexual sense. The primary contribution of Masters and Johnson was to present an altogether new image of female sexuality. The title of their book, *Human Sexual Response,* conveys the principal finding that basic similarities marked the anatomy and physiology of male and female sexuality, "that direct parallels in human sexual response . . . exist to a degree never previously appreciated." With the aid of sensors and cameras, they measured and photographed women's, and men's, responses to sexual stimulation; and their findings, from changes in heartbeats to color flushes, informed a startlingly ignorant medical profession of the most elementary facts. There was no difference between vaginal and clitoral orgasm; female sexual responses were at least as intense as the male's, perhaps even more. A normally functioning woman, they reported, "within a short period after her first climax, will in most instances be capable of having a second, third, fourth and even fifth and sixth orgasm before she is fully satisfied."

Under these circumstances, it was absurd to describe a clitoris as an inadequate organ. And it was equally absurd to label men sexually active and women sexually passive.

At least one woman psychiatrist skillfully explored the implications that Masters and Johnson's findings had for psychoanalytic theory. Dr. Mary Jane Sherfey dedicated *The Nature and Evolution of Female Sexuality* to Masters and Johnson, and the book was a world apart from Deutsch's *Psychology of Women*. Combining new findings in biology (which demonstrated that insofar as embryonic growth was concerned, males developed from females and not the other way around) with the new data on sexual responsiveness, Sherfey presented a woman who was anatomically whole and sexually active. While carefully noting that an "Adam from Eve" view did not establish female "superiority," she did destroy the notion that anatomy dictated men's dominance in the marketplace and women's passivity in the home. Sherfey also suggested that a conflict of interest marked the relationship between men and women as, indeed, it marked the relationship between women's self-expression and social order. The act of intercourse, for example, was not necessarily the most satisfying form of sexual stimulation for the woman. More, the woman's multiorgasmic capability might well have to be tamed, indeed repressed, in order for society to cohere. Sherfey, still very much within the psychoanalytic framework, was adding another dimension to the discontents in civilization.

The findings of Masters and Johnson also helped to expand the concept of sexual normality. A wide range of stimuli, it seemed, produced satisfying sexual responses. And this premise was critical to the viewpoint of the latest, and incredibly popular, addition to the shelf of sexual advice books, Alex Comfort's *The Joy of Sex*. The title's play on *The Joy of Cooking* and the book's organization into main courses, relishes, and condiments reflected the notion that one can follow instructions in the bedroom to achieve gourmet sex as easily as one can follow instructions in the kitchen to achieve gourmet cuisine. Everyone has the necessary equipment, and the recipes, while important, are easy to follow. No barriers need block the attainment of sexual pleasure.

In sum, all of these elements, from suburban and workplace realities to the diverse influences of the civil rights movements, contributed to the formulation of a new definition of woman. They not only rendered the concept of the wife-companion obsolete but offered another one in its stead: woman as active, energetic, fully competent, and capable of self-definition as a person in sexual and in social terms. Woman's essence was no longer to be found in a household role but in her own achievements.

FAMILY LIFE AS A ZERO-SUM GAME

The first appearance of the new definition of woman was not intended to disrupt family life. The writing of Betty Friedan, the first Statement of Purpose of NOW, the findings of Masters and Johnson, and even the recipes in *The Joy of Sex* did not imagine that an active and liberated woman would war on her husband or her children. On the contrary, they all believed that woman as person would be a better wife and mother. Her energy and activity would make the home a more interesting, more exciting, and more satisfying place.

To Friedan, the ideal feminist was both a working wife and a mother. Liberated women were "not battleaxes or manhaters," and she noted with pride that "there are men in our own ranks." Indeed, Friedan's new woman would command a respect from men that her predecessors had not. "The officials we interviewed," she reported, "treated us as attractive women, but without the glint of contempt that so often belies men's flattery of women. Because we were and are serious about real equality . . . they treated us with real respect." The relevant "other" for Friedan remained the man. The goal was to gain equality with him.

So, too, Masters and Johnson translated their laboratory findings into a sex therapy program in order to enhance marital life. They offered their treatment only to couples who had agreed in advance to remain together for five years. Alex Comfort's books also insisted that a variety of techniques would help keep sexual interest alive over a long married life. In fact, married couples enjoyed the best sex: "One needs a steady basic diet of quiet, night-and-morning matrimonial intercourse. . . . The more regular sex a couple has, the higher the deliberately contrived peaks—just as the more you cook routinely, the better and the more reliable banquets you can stage." Even the unconventional section on "foursomes and moresomes" urged readers to share sex only with other couples committed to maintaining their own marriages.

But despite this initial conservatism, the women's movement was soon issuing far more radical proposals. Amazing as it may seem more than ten years later, the organizers of NOW in 1966 believed that ending sexual discrimination in the work force and establishing a national network of day care centers would immediately accomplish the social and economic equality of American women. Their facile optimism reflected a very limited experience. And no sooner did a national organization for women come into being than their education began. NOW's existence prompted women from all over the country to recount the discriminations that they had experienced. NOW became a sounding board for grievances that went deeper than anyone had ever imagined or could even immediately comprehend. Constituents, in other words, taught the NOW leaders about the real nature of women's experience in the world, and constituents then went on to radicalize the reform agenda.

Unable to anticipate the complexity of a program that would bring equality to women, NOW's first leaders were unable to control the rank and file. Once constituent pressure began to direct organizational policy, the women's movement became (and to this day has remained) essentially leaderless. Some of NOW's founders withdrew when new goals conflicted with their personal beliefs. The others who stayed, like Friedan herself, were forced to accept policies that they had never anticipated or even favored. In fact, the very passive title of Friedan's autobiography, *It Changed My Life*, is an honest indication that she was swept up in the current created by the movement—that in NOW, members directed leaders.

Through this dynamic, NOW's list of demands rapidly expanded. Within a few years it was spearheading the fight for the passage of the Equal Rights Amendment to the Constitution, leading an attack on abortion laws, organizing specific programs to equalize educational opportunities for women, demanding important changes in marriage, divorce, and rape laws, and agitating to end discrimination against lesbians. In each instance, it was constituent pressure that brought the organization into these issues.

In 1967, just one year after NOW's founding, the priority that organizers had first given to the enforcement of Title VII gave way to a commitment to pass an equal rights amendment. It was by no means a universally approved strategy. To some labor union officials, particularly the United Auto Workers (who were actually helping to pay NOW's mailing costs), an equal rights amendment would abolish special protective legislation that they, like the Progressives before them, believed to be in the best interests of blue-collar workers. For others, an equal rights amendment raised the prospects of NOW becoming identified with the National Woman's Party—and they wanted to keep the new feminist organization distinct from an old, tired, and ineffectual one. But these views did not carry; pressure from NOW constituents overrode the objections. "As I listened and watched the women all over the hall who spoke," recalled Friedan, "I saw that very few were opposed to taking a stand on the ERA." The old-line National Woman's Party members made a quick alliance with younger delegates. "When those very old suffragettes sitting in the front row got up to speak on the Equal Rights Amendment," continued Friedan, "I saw that they *spoke to* those very young women who had never heard of it before and were kindled by it as they had not been by narrow job issues."

And no wonder. An equal rights amendment promised in one grand sweep to eliminate not only job discrimination but *all* discrimination.

The younger women in NOW had little desire for special protection. Committed to a view of woman as competent—fully capable of acting in her own best interest—they were far more comfortable with equal rights than with particular privileges. Better to have an amendment that would offer a legal basis for abolishing all forms of discrimination than to perpetuate a system that treated women as children.

NOW's decision at the same 1967 convention to campaign on behalf of abortion on demand also took the organization in a direction that its founders had not anticipated. Perhaps the social class and income of the Smith alumnae allowed them easier access to medical abortions than most women had; or perhaps it was a dirty secret that they would not share with an interviewer. But Friedan, along with other NOW officers, seemed amazed at the diverse types of women who enthusiastically advocated a liberalized abortion policy. "The women speaking up passionately for it," Friedan noted, "were not only the young women from everywhere, but the square, middle-aged housewife types from Indiana and points south." Once again, the firsthand knowledge of NOW's members, and not the ideas of its leaders, wrote the platform.

And so it was with lesbian rights. Friedan, always intent on keeping the organization at least within range of middle-American values, feared that the "lavender menace" would wreck NOW. Convinced that lesbians were trying to capture NOW for their own purposes, Friedan did manage to force many of them out of the organization. Nevertheless, the determination of most members to speak for the rights of all women in all situations overrode Friedan's objections. Although few NOW members were homosexual (in a recent survey, 8 percent reported themselves homosexual and 9 percent bisexual), they empathized with the discriminations that these women suffered. Thus, NOW resolved at its 1971 convention that a "woman's right to her own person included the right to define and express her own sexuality and to choose her own life style; therefore, we acknowledge the oppression of lesbians as a legitimate concern of feminism."

Around the issues of equal rights, day care, abortion, and discrimination against lesbians, NOW left the precepts of educated motherhood and wife-companion for a model of woman as her own person. In a very short time, it rejected and renounced as harmful to women the social policies built on these inherited assumptions. Progressive special protection was one more form of discrimination. Even Sanger's version of "voluntary motherhood" had merely given to women the option to space their children; the feminists of the 1960s demanded that women have the freedom to choose *not* to become mothers—or even wives. The new women reformers had a wide tolerance for various forms of sexual expression. Behavior that before had been labeled sick or corrupting was now protected and sanctioned under a right to privacy. Only women themselves, and no one else, could define and implement their own best interest.

The adoption of these planks not only marked off the feminists of the 1960s from their predecessors but also pointed to a critical shift in the women's movement itself. NOW had begun in 1966 as a civil rights organization; by 1971, it was a women's liberation organization. This shift altered both its agenda and underlying assumptions, particularly its notion that the interests of men and women were ultimately compatible. Friedan and her allies had never thought in terms of competing interests or trade-offs. Ostensibly, programs that benefited women would benefit men. But as such issues as abortion and lesbian rights became prominent, and as the efforts to implement them began, the old view gave way. Friedan complained in 1970 that Kate Millett's *Sexual Politics,* which made sexual warfare the moving force in history, was "genuinely dangerous to the movement." Friedan was convinced that "no serious, meaningful action emerges from a sexual emphasis. There is simply talk, anger, and wallowing. It is also based on a highly distorted, oversimplified view of our society, men and women, family relations, relations to children." But Friedan notwithstanding, beginning in the 1970s a conflict model, not a consensus model, pervaded the women's movement.

The issue of liberalized abortion most dramatically revealed how competing interests affected family relationships. Abortion on demand might be in the best interest and within the rights of women, but it was not necessarily in the best interest of husbands or of society in general. Even its most passionate supporters recognized that a pro-abortion policy did entail benefits to some at costs to others, that trade-offs were inevitably involved. If a woman had the right to abortion, did her decision require the consent of her spouse? What about those cases where the woman's desire to abort a fetus conflicted with her husband's desire to have a child? Did the fetus have rights apart from the mother's? When, if ever, did a fetus take on a life of its own—after three months? six months? only after delivery? Did society have an interest in preventing abortion? Would the right to abortion inevitably lead to infanticide for deformed babies or euthanasia for the senile? Conversely, did the poor have the same right to abortions as they had to medical treatment? The federal courts resolved some of these issues, generally dismissing husbands' claims and those of the poor but disallowing all restrictions on women's prerogatives before the fetus was three months old. The very language and passion of the debate, however, illustrated all too vividly the deep character of the controversy. For the first time, it appeared that women's interests, family interests, and societal interests were in conflict.

The debate over abortion provided one context for the emergence of the children's rights movement. The doctrine of woman as person implicitly suggested that maternal roles might not be consistent with women's needs—and then the case of abortion made the conflict explicit. An early and important statement on children's rights appeared in a small book written by three psychoanalysts: Joseph Goldstein, also a professor of law at Yale, Anna Freud, the director of the Hampstead Child Therapy Clinic in London, and Albert Solnit, a professor of pediatrics and psychiatry at Yale. Aptly entitled *Beyond the Best Interest of the Child,* the tract contended that the traditional notion that courts should promote the child's best interest had been a masquerade, cloaking policy decisions that were ultimately made in the parents' best interest. Just when the women's movement was asserting that the role of mother could conflict with the welfare of women, these authors were arguing that the natural mother—or, for that matter, the father—would not necessarily promote the welfare of the child. Moreover, just when the movement was insisting that women's rights should be enhanced regardless of the costs to others, these authors were insisting that children's rights should be enhanced regardless of the costs to others.

Goldstein, Freud, and Solnit argued the case in only one aspect—child custody proceedings. Previously, custody decisions had automatically favored the biological parent: the right of a mother to her child was almost always held paramount over that of foster parents and usually over that of a father. It was time, declared Goldstein and the others, to revise this policy; a genuine concern for the child should promote custody decisions that favored the "psychological" parent. Carefully avoiding the use of the term "mother," they referred only to the parent, and in their definition, the fit parent was the one who was actually satisfying the child's psychological needs. "Whether any adult becomes the psychological parent of a child," they announced, "is based on the day-to-day interaction, companionship, and shared experiences. The role can be fulfilled by a biological parent or by an adoptive parent or by any caring adult—but never by an absent, inactive adult, whatever his biological and legal relationship to the child." The critical consideration was to respect the child's attachment to his psychological parents. "An absent biological parent," the authors maintained, "will remain or tend to become a stranger."

Thus, in that terrible and tragic case when Dutch Jews returned at the end of World War II to reclaim children left for safekeeping in non-Jewish households, the children's rights doctrine would have reversed the Dutch Parliament's flat decree in favor of the biological parents and instead upheld the psychological parents. "More interests will tilt the scale toward leaving well enough alone, than toward allowing the biological parents to prevail." What seemed cruel and heartless from the perspective of the parent was, in fact, in the best interest of the child. . . .

Given such disparities, it becomes less difficult to understand the steady decline in the American birth rate over the past decade. It was not merely that the technology of birth control (through the advent of the Pill) facilitated family limitation; rather, more women were reluctant to assume the responsibility of rearing several children. In the mid-1970s the birth rate reached an all-time low of 1.8 children per family (and there is every indication that the figure will not climb substantially higher in the near future). This did not mean that more women were choosing to remain childless; instead, women were postponing having children until later in life and then having fewer children than ever before. This pattern was perfectly consistent with career or job interests—with getting a start in a position, interrupting work for a brief stint at motherhood, and then returning sooner rather than later to the work force. As these figures (and Fraiberg's laments) make clear, women's decisions no longer gave mothering its traditional primacy.

By the same token, the individual needs of women no longer seemed compatible with one lifelong marital relationship. Not that women stopped or were supposed to stop marrying; although the divorce rate climbed (doubling over the past ten years), so did the number of remarriages. Rather, an expectation of impermanence now seemed normal within a marriage. If the experts of the 1920s counseled women to find fulfillment in an intensive and all-consuming intellectual and sexual relationship with one man, their counterparts in the 1970s told them that fulfillment was not a unitary, once achieved-always achieved state, that different stages demanded new relationships. In the 1950s, as in the 1920s, diamonds were "forever". . . .

Running through all this literature, from Goldstein to Fraiberg to Sheehy, is a contemporary definition of family life as a battleground among members, each trying to gain his or her own personal victory. It is an unusual perspective, one that is particular to our own times. For generations social critics predicted the demise of the family, but their predictions were by way of a lament, an effort to recall family members to their proper duties, to enhance maternal, paternal, and filial responsibility. Many contemporary social critics also predict the demise of the family, but they are far from certain as to how to rescue it, even whether to rescue it. A few observers like Fraiberg have attempted to revive a traditional ethic, to remind mothers that their grandmothers knew best, that folk wisdom has its strengths. But others insist upon the futility of such an endeavor; grandmothers do not set (and never really have set) the fashion. The more popular response is to take up the cause of one or another family member and set out the strategy that will most effectively realize that member's best interest. Since the family is a battleground, every member should have, and now does have, its own Clausewitz. Hence, women should anticipate divorce as a rite of passage; men should know that when they want to settle down their wives will want to climb mountains; children should understand, or at least have lawyers who understand, that their own interests will not necessarily be furthered by parental decisions.

Whatever the precise nature of the advice, one assumption is common to all of it: family life is a zero-sum game. Some interests must be sacrificed to others. What is good for wives is not necessarily good for husbands and what is good for mothers is not necessarily good for children. Where our predecessors saw harmony, we see discord. Where they saw mutuality of interest, we see conflict of interest. And as we move from the private sphere to the public, the sounds of discord grow more intense. The political arena does not take second place to the family as a battleground for competing interests.

DISCUSSION QUESTIONS

1. How did World War II affect the lives of women? In what ways were women's attitudes and beliefs different in 1950 than they were in 1940? In what ways were they the same?
2. What was the "feminine mystique," and what did the women's liberation advocates of the 1960s see was wrong with it?
3. The author ends on a rather discouraging note, calling the American family a "battleground for competing interests." It is now a little more than ten years since she reached that conclusion. Do you think it is still a valid description of the American family? Or has the family adjusted to the new roles taken up by women?

11

THE VIETNAM SYNDROME

PHILIP L. GEYELIN

More than a decade after it ended, the Vietnam War remains very much with us. Historians and military strategists have poured through the records of that conflict seeking to learn what went wrong and why. Politicians and diplomats have drawn "lessons" from the war, and they have used those "lessons" in foreign policy decision-making, in much the way the "lesson" of Munich guided the early decision-making of the Cold War.

Exactly what those "lessons" are, however, remains unclear. In the following essay Philip Geyelin argues that the "Vietnam Syndrome" contains two quite different "lessons"—or perhaps the same "lesson" perceived by people with radically different mind-sets. Some interpreters of the Vietnam experience stress that it demonstrates the limits of American power and the general futility of intervention. Translated into policy, Geyelin argues, such views have had a paralyzing effect on American action. Others—and these include President Reagan and his advisers—perceive the war as simply the right policy pursued in the wrong way. They feel the only mistake the United States made was failing to do whatever it took to achieve victory. Such thinking induced them to build a defense establishment large enough to guarantee victory in any future confrontation.

Geyelin finds neither extreme satisfactory. He thinks that because of its position as a world power the United States must pursue an activist foreign policy, one in which military intervention remains a viable option. But he would use intervention discreetly and only as part of a diplomatic initiative designed to get at the root of the problem.

Geyelin ends with a plea for an understanding of what happened in Vietnam, and he appears to think that deriving "lessons" from the war—the "Vietnam Syndrome"—merely hampers that understanding. He is no doubt right, but he may have to live with the syndrome nevertheless. After all, we have yet to cast off the "Munich syndrome."

—NORMAN K. RISJORD

Having chosen a cliché for a subject, I should probably define it. The dictionary says a syndrome is "a number of symptoms occurring together and characterizing a specific disease or condition." So the "Vietnam syndrome," presumably, is a general tendency to see in this or that situation conditions and characteristics that remind us of Vietnam. For many this is another way of saying that they remind us of something to be avoided at all costs. But the Vietnam War is not that easy to categorize. It was, obviously, not good. But neither was it in all respects bad. Ronald Reagan was not wrong when he called it a noble cause, if by that he meant that by and large good intentions paved the road to the roof of the U.S. embassy in Saigon in 1975. So what we have here is a collection of analogies, mostly subjective, that together constitute the Vietnam syndrome. The problem is how to distinguish between those Vietnam legacies—those effects on public opinion and on the performance of public officials, those conscious and unconscious reflexes—that inhibit useful undertakings, and those lessons that can put us on the right path, or steer us away from the wrong one. All of us can argue over which are good and which are bad. I shall discuss my own list and in the process offer my opinion of where we may suffer at the hands of so-called Vietnam syndrome, and where we either have profited or might hope to profit from what we can learn from this tormenting chapter in United States history.

DAMAGING LEGACIES

I begin with those particular reflexes and responses to the Vietnam experience that lead in directions which are unconstructive and unlikely to contribute to effective public policy. I start with what appears to be a general debilitating and excessive distrust of government—of its policymakers, and of their policy. This distrust was compounded, of course, by Watergate. But Watergate was Son of Vietnam; it derived directly from Richard Nixon's desperate efforts to deal with the crippling impact of public dissent on his war effort. This was the first purpose of the "plumbers," the enemies list, the telephone taps, and all the rest—to strangle dissent. One cannot forget that line from a U.S. officer in Vietnam as he described to a group of reporters a village in ruins: "We had to destroy the village in order to save it." Watergate was Richard Nixon's way of saying that you had to destroy the American system in order to save it.

THE VIETNAM SYNDROME From Philip L. Geyelin, "The Vietnam Syndrome," in James F. Veninga and Harry A. Wilmer, eds., *Vietnam in Remission* (College Station: Texas A & M University Press, 1985), pp. 76–89. Reprinted by permission.

So we can trace to both Vietnam and Watergate what has clearly been a tendency to turn away in disillusionment from Washington and all things establishmentarian. We see it in the presidents we have elected since Vietnam—in a conscious or subconscious reaching out for candidates who have never been to Washington, except in the most casual way, people who for just that reason could have no clear connection one way or another with Vietnam. First we reached out to Plains, Georgia, and when we didn't like the results, we reached out to Beverly Hills.

Dean Acheson, the quintessential establishment man, was also a wise man, and he used to say that some awful fate condemned the United States to put people in the White House with no experience in foreign policy. Nixon was actually the most recent exception to that rule. Lyndon Johnson and Gerry Ford knew Washington, but even they did not claim a background or even much interest in foreign policy. Jimmy Carter and Ronald Reagan did not even know Washington. We find in their election some vestige of the Vietnam syndrome—some reflection of a public disillusionment with the performance of those who held office in the Vietnam years that has translated itself into a general distrust of almost anybody laying claim to past experience in statescraft.

The "Vietnam syndrome" syndrome is frequently found among those in policymaking or opinion-making positions today who supported the Vietnam War, who think our only failure was in not pursuing the war flat-out with whatever it took. This is a familiar political reflex—a "we were right the first time"—cast of mind among those who cannot accept the possibility that the Vietnam War established limits on American power and ability to influence events. It shows itself in many ways, including a quick rush to judgment at the first bright flicker of jingoism in American public opinion. Iran, it was said at the time of the hostage crisis, was to be, in the words of William Hyland, a former senior member of Kissinger's national-security staff, a "watershed," for "it closes the Vietnam syndrome." But with Hyland, as with Zbigniew Brzezinski (who was saying the same thing privately as Jimmy Carter's national-security advisor), I suspect the wish was father to the thought.

But the wish was powerful and it still is. It found its loudest voice in the jungle yells of Al Haig at his confirmation hearings in the early days of the current administration. His "Me, Tarzan" approach to foreign policy is shared by Ronald Reagan and his associates and followers as well.

A recent *Dallas Times Herald* column mentions a speech by Thomas Reed, the number-three man in the National Security Council who, when making a speech, is making it on good authority. Reed argued that "there is nothing wrong with winning." People had likened him to Prime Minister Margaret Thatcher and Israel Defense Minister Ariel Sharon, he said, and he considered that to be "pretty good company." Now that is a terrible way to talk about a nice iron woman who did nothing more than blunder into a war and beat up the Argentines.

But even assuming that Margaret Thatcher likes the association with Sharon, I am not certain that he is the role model for which we are looking. Of these efforts to overcompensate for Vietnam losses, one can only say they are no less helpful to coherent and realistic foresight policy than the collapse of public confidence in government.

The flip side of "we were right the first time" is the quick conclusion that in just about every respect we were wrong. From this flows an instinctive reluctance to get involved, as they say on the street—to get involved even when a superpower like the United States has the same responsibility and obligation to get involved in certain circumstances as that of a citizen witnessing a crime.

The instinctive shying away from the threat of the use of force—from even the first hint of a potentially escalating entanglement—is as understandable as it is crippling to the pursuit of legitimate security interests. Much has been made of the way we got into Vietnam, of the landing of the first combat troops by Lyndon Johnson in March, 1965. We tend to forget that in April of that year Lyndon Johnson landed over ten thousand American troops a lot closer to home in the Dominican Republic. We also tend to forget that, as a consequence of their presence, Ellsworth Bunker, working for nearly a year, negotiated a settlement of that political conflict and that we have had two peaceful democratic transfers of government in the Dominican Republic since that time. That's one example of a careful combination of carrot and stick having a tremendously useful effect. Likewise, in 1958, when four different revolutions were underway in Lebanon, the U.S. Marines landed and within ten days Robert Murphy, a special envoy of the president, had negotiated an agreement that ended that crisis and gave Lebanon peace for at least another seventeen years.

This is really what the elusive and subtle concept of deterrence is all about. It can work. But to make it work, diplomacy has to be reinforced by the credible threat of the use of force. John Foster Dulles got himself into a lot of trouble talking about "the necessary art" of going to the brink. But no one complained when John F. Kennedy did it with arguable success in the Cuban missile crisis. One way to measure this aspect of the Vietnam syndrome is to ask what the public response would be today if the president of the United States suddenly deployed a naval blockage—an act of war—in a situation involving a comparable threat to U.S. security.

One can find some part of the answer in the initial reaction of Congress in 1982 to the very thought that U.S. Marines might be dispatched to Lebanon, this time in the company of French and Italian troops, for the strictly limited purpose of escorting Palestine Liberation Organization (PLO) militiamen out of Beirut. Right across the political spectrum, from Barry Goldwater to Ted Kennedy, the members of Congress rose up to demand what was going on. Kennedy said the safety of marines should be "guaranteed." Senator Richard Lugar, a conservative Republican, was "deeply concerned with any proposal that would put American military personnel in a situation where there is a strong likelihood they will be fired upon and would have to defend themselves." Senator Dodd, a liberal Democrat, said "I don't believe that you can achieve the kind of assurance that I would insist upon." Congressman Jim Leach said that is "a mistake of tragic proportions." These statements provide an interesting commentary on the mood of Congress—and its reading of public opinion. The president did not bow entirely to reaction—he merely assured the Congress that the United States Marines would be withdrawn "if they were shot at." I don't wish to play the warmonger, but the Middle East is surely central to U.S. security, and successful extraction of the PLO forces from Beirut and a peaceful end to the Lebanon war was surely in the national interest. It was vital that the United States be in a position to offer the services of its troops to that multinational force. The French and Italians were not holding back, yet the first reflex in Congress from the chairman of the House Foreign Affairs Committee was to raise serious questions about whether the president was about to violate the War Powers Resolution.

This brings me to the congressional Vietnam syndrome. It is reflected not only in the War Powers Resolution, which defined the conditions under which the president can commit American forces to a hostile environment, but also in the Clark Amendment, which says what we can and cannot do in Angola, and there is a general inclination for congressmen to elbow their way into the most intimate aspects of the conduct of diplomacy. Here we see a tendency to find in situations where there is a prospective U.S. military involvement those "symptoms and characteristics of a specific condition"—which is to say, the Vietnam War—where analogy doesn't apply. The practical effect of the congressional uproar over the marines in Lebanon is a good example. Under that pressure the administration was almost certainly too hasty in its removal of the marines from the scene. Reluctantly, resisting, the French and the Italians also left. Not long thereafter the Israelis sanctioned the entry of Christian militia forces into the refugee camps, Shatila and Sabra, with the horrible consequences familiar to all of us. You can't prove that this tragedy would have happened if the multinational force had remained, but it is a reasonable supposition. In any event, the inescapable conclusion was that the three-nation force had to return in the interest of shoring up the authority of the new Lebanese government.

And yet, in fairness, one has to put oneself in the place of a member of the Congress. The Tonkin resolution was shouted through the House and the Senate under the lash of President Johnson in 1964. Even those present members of Congress who were not there at the time remember that on that historic occasion the legislative branch was out for lunch. Only a brave few asked the right questions, and they were cut off by assurances from the floor manager of the bill in the Senate, William Fullbright, that the president had not the slightest intention of using that authority to land American troops for combat purposes in Vietnam.

But the resolution they so readily accepted became the legislative justification, regularly cited by Lyndon Johnson and Richard Nixon, for the policy of the United States in Vietnam for years to come. That is the stuff of which congressional syndromes are made. It is the stuff, I might add, of the congressional cut-off of military aid to South Vietnam in the middle of 1975. It is said that this lost the war for the South Vietnamese, and perhaps it did. It is also said that this aid cut-off violated a secret written agreement between Nixon and Thieu made in connection with the 1973 peace agreement.

But that is just the point; this was a *secret* commitment from Nixon—the fine invisible wire that held that flawed peace treaty together. It had to be a secret agreement because the president knew perfectly well what would happen if he had come before Congress and said that in order to make this agreement work we must commit ourselves, not only to continued military aid, but conceivably to a return to Vietnam as well. It was out of the question. It also reflected ignorance of the basic flaw in his own strategy—the limits imposed by the workings of an open society. Or perhaps it is contempt for the political process. As late as 1973, Secretary of Defense James Schlesinger was publicly threatening that we might have to return to Vietnam, so it wasn't just Nixon. Yet we could not conceivably have returned to Vietnam under the terms of congressional legislation then in effect. It was an utterly empty threat that could not possibly have deterred the North Vietnamese. For that matter, Nixon's secret letter to Thieu was certainly no way of deterring the North Vietnamese. I do not doubt a casual relation between what the Congress did and what the North Vietnamese then felt free to do, but one must consider the context in which Congress acted.

One cannot ignore the media Vietnam syndrome: once bitten, twice shy. There was a tendency to favor the government in the early days with a certain amount of trust—what the former director of the FBI, Patrick Gray, once described as "a presumption of regularity." It comes as no surprise that this presumption no longer exists. Here again, there is a syndrome at work, sometimes to excess, a tendency to assume the worst, to question everything, to seek out the soreheads in government and to give them a voice. This tendency on the part of those in the news business is complemented, I might add, by a genuine change in the attitude of those engaged in the policymaking process. Gen. Maxwell Taylor, the former ambassador to Saigon, took note of this in a recent article in the *Washington Post* on the missile crisis. He argued that "A President today cannot count on either the privacy or the loyalty that Kennedy enjoyed. He would be dangerously exposed to the vicious practice of leakage by government officials as a means of sabotaging the course of action of which they disapprove."

I don't know exactly how much of this to attribute to a Vietnam syndrome, but I think that the state of mind of policymakers is part and parcel of the collapse of confidence—the withholding of trust—that is evident with the public, Congress, and the press. It is an internal disintegration of discipline that has something to do with the fierce divisiveness engendered by Vietnam. It has something to do as well with an absence of the sort of collegiality at work in earlier administrations and better times. Part of this may well have to do with that turning away from professionals to amateurs, from the old-boy network of the eastern establishment to new players with no reverence for the older traditions. The difference is more quantitative than qualitative. Great issues of policy have always been aired by calculated leaks. But the new generation of journalists, and some who are old enough to have participated in the Vietnam experience, cannot forget that for a considerable period the media too easily accepted the government line and that an awful lot of the time the government line was misleading.

Where else do we find symptoms of this so-called syndrome? I suspect it is to be found in the resistance of nearly 500,000 young men in this country who this year [1982] defied the law requiring them to register for the draft. This is not like the 1960s protest. Over 90 percent of those eligible today have registered. But this action says something about a lingering antiwar, anti-military-service sentiment on the part of young people. It says even more when you consider that all they are being asked to do is to register; that we are almost alone, except for the British, among the nations of the North Atlantic Treaty Organization in not conscripting; that we are making do with a volunteer army that in no way reflects a cross-section of our society; that not even "the great communicator" with his ambitious plans for rapid deployment forces dares suggest that the burden of manning those forces be shared not just by those willing to volunteer their services, but by all eligible, able-bodied young men.

One can also include the nuclear-freeze movement as a product of what might be called the consciousness-raising effect of Vietnam. The nine nuclear-freeze propositions on the ballots in the congressional elections of 1982 did not escape the notice of Congress as it approached the defense budget.

The Vietnam syndrome cuts two ways. For some it has an inhibiting, restraining effect, for they see the war as a calamity, caused in large part by an overly ambitious, overly militant approach to the world. For others, Vietnam is merely an example of doing the right thing the wrong way and therefore an argument for a bigger, better-equipped U.S. defense force committed to act, not by graduated response in a limited war and creeping escalation, but by fighting to win. These entirely contradictory readings of Vietnam constitute the final negative element of the syndrome—continuing conflict and confusion over what the war was all about. The overhanging question marks are nowhere better illustrated than in the struggle in Washington over the design of the Vietnam Veterans Memorial. The struggle is a metaphor on the war itself.

The small group of veterans who started the project, led by Jan Scruggs, an ex-infantryman who was wounded in Vietnam, symbolized the extraordinary quality of those who call themselves "the survivors." They quarreled heatedly over the design and the very nature of the memorial, but they finally reconciled their differences in the way that precisely defines the two faces of the Vietnam syndrome. A young Yale University architectural student won the contest for the design of the memorial. Protest over the design's stark and muted statement quickly followed. It is a V-shaped black marble wall sunk below ground level, bearing the names of those who were killed. To this was added a rather more conventional monument—a statue of three members of the armed services and an American flag. It doesn't fit together aesthetically, yet it somehow strikes me as exactly the right way to solve an almost insoluble problem. It is a monument to dichotomy; in the form finally agreed on, it is an important statement. It invites, it nearly commands, a continuing questioning about Vietnam, a continuing quest for the right lessons. It commands us to regularly test our foreign policy against the Vietnam experience.

POSITIVE LEGACIES

What I have outlined thus far has dealt with the least constructive aspects of this testing. But some legacies of the Vietnam War are positive and of great value, and I would put at the head of the list of such legacies the Vietnam veterans themselves. For the best part of a sabbatical year, I did research for a possible book on Vietnam veterans. They number 9 million, if we are talking about those who served in the Vietnam era; 2.7 million, if we are talking about those who served in the theater; and 1.6 million, if we are talking about those actively engaged in combat. In the course of dozens of interviews I reached one simple conclusion: there is no stereotype. And I made some friends.

Paul is a children's therapist in Buffalo, New York. He was badly wounded in Vietnam. He told me this story. He and five of his fellow soldiers stationed in Germany were sitting around one night arguing about Vietnam and whether they ought to go there. Five of the six eventually volunteered to go to Vietnam. Of those five, three were killed in action. One came home a double amputee. My friend Paul, after long rehabilitation, has been restored to health. He said that at least once a month he and the double amputee, who has a good job and a happy life in Philadelphia, get a call from the comrade who stayed in Germany. This man had had great success for a time as an advertising executive in Los Angeles, but he was guilt-ridden and became an alcoholic. When I tried to reach him in California, he was in a detoxification program.

One cannot neatly categorize the victims; they run a wide gamut. Bob Muller, the head of the Vietnam Veterans of America, was shot in the chest leading a charge up a hill as a captain in the Marine Corps. He is paralyzed from the waist down, but he and his wheelchair have been in every corner of this country trying to build his organization.

Dean Phillips is a young lawyer in the Veterans Administration. He was a highly decorated paratrooper in Vietnam as a noncommissioned officer. He developed, in the course of his career, a certain irreverence for authority. When they tried to give him his second Silver Star he contrived—I can't imagine how—to roar by the reviewing stand in a jeep at the very moment when he was supposed to be arriving for the ceremony, and "mooned" the assembled officers on the stand. He later joined Vietnam Veterans against the War and threw his medals over the fence in the Washington protest march. He is now wearing a three-piece suit at the Veterans Administration. But, more important, Dean is disturbed in a different way. He worries about our foreign policy. At the time of the Iranian crisis, he volunteered for the reserves. He went down to Fort Bragg. He took the training, and he went back to jumping. I asked him why he was putting himself through all of this and he said that while he was on duty in the reserves the enlisted men he saw in the volunteer army reminded him of the Vietnam draftees; young, disproportionately minority-group members and high-school dropouts. He said if they were ever going to be sent to another war, he wanted to be with them.

Angel Palmadino is the director of the Veterans Outreach Center in Manhattan. I met him at a conference under the auspices of an organization called World without War. There were veterans, journalists, and some very establishment people in the audience, such as William Bundy and Ellsworth Bunker. After a good deal of discussion, Angel took the floor. He is a short, chunky Chicano with black hair down to his waist. As he spoke he did a kind of whirling-dervish dance around the room, waving his arms, and shouting. He talked about the troubled veterans he meets at the outreach center, "young guys who went to fight a war when they were eighteen and didn't know what they were doing" and got screwed. But he went on to speak of the generation of Vietnam veterans, now in their thirties, some of them lawyers, doctors, and in the upper echelons of American society. "So it is not a question of America coming around to us, no, no, no," Angel said. "Patriotism," he said, "we got it . . . we are men . . . and a lot of us are hurting bad . . . but we are going to save each other . . . America, if you want to be a part of it, come on. If you don't, look out—because we are going to set some policies in the future. . . . The sixties generation is the hope of America and I am the cream of the crop and you remember that when you leave this stinking room." He concluded: "If there is going to be another war, I am going to tell my sons that they are going to go when I decide. But it had better be a good war. In fact, if it's that good, I am going."

That's Angel. It's also not a bad summation of the human legacy of Vietnam that is likely to play an increasingly powerful and positive role in the social and political scene. Besides the human legacy, another positive development coming out of the Vietnam War—perhaps the most important one—is an acute awareness that was not there in the Vietnam years of the need to consider, in making foreign policy, the consent of the governed. I have spoken to the excesses of oversight by Congress. I am talking now of the necessity for a reasonable degree of public debate and public support.

It is interesting that this lesson is one which McGeorge Bundy has himself accepted. In his days as the president's national security advisor in the White House he was a model of secrecy and discretion when a journalist wanted to know what was going on. But never mind, in a speech nine years ago talking about American policy in the Middle East, Bundy was critical of precisely the kind of governmental noncommunication that characterized the conduct of the Vietnam War. Cryptic press conferences and back-channel conversations with journalists will no longer do the job, he said. A lot needs to be said, and no policy that requires public support can be sustained without such exposition.

But if that is what Bundy is preaching as a professor now, he is touching on a critical point. For this is not just a fundamental constitutional principle—it is a matter of basic strategy. Vietnam has at least created, if not disposed of, the question of whether limited war, a whole new concept, can be effectively conducted in an open society. The awful irony here is that the intentions of these brightest and best that have been so put down were admirable. They designed what they thought was a way of keeping the war from expanding, of shortening it if possible, and avoiding the awful risk that Professor Rostow has spoken of—an escalation to the level of nuclear exchange. That was the theory of graduated response.

The other part of it was that the government had to make it believable to the people in Hanoi. It had to make them believe that they would go on forever, if it wanted them to stop way short. And that was where the policy collapsed—because that is a game of poker, a game of trying to drive the other guy out of the game. And for that, one needs a poker face. But a democracy cannot keep a poker face, and this is why Nixon needed the "plumbers."

There is other, more conspicuous evidence of a Vietnam syndrome usefully at work. At the beginning of the Reagan administration the plans for El Salvador invited a Vietnam analogy. We were going to increase military aid, we were increasing the number of advisors, we were training the El Salvador army in the fine arts of "search and destroy"—and they were using that term. There was every reason to suspect that the same progression that had taken place in Vietnam was beginning in El Salvador: American advisors, first staying in their camps, then going out on operations, then being armed, and then being authorized to shoot. The plan had escalation written all over it. But Congress moved in significantly with a Vietnam veteran, David Bonior, from Michigan, the leader of the twenty-member Vietnam caucus in the House. They insisted on an accounting of what was intended. They asked for information in advance—to know how far the administration wanted to go, what the terms were, and how human rights would be protected.

A FINAL NOTE

It is obvious that the Vietnam syndrome is a matter of opinion, is in the eye of the beholder. Some read the lessons in radical terms and others refuse to read them at all. But the lessons must be read with care in a way that does not paralyze the necessary conduct of foreign policy in the interest of national security.

I would venture one further counsel. Reflections on the Vietnam experience concentrate logically and understandably on what actually happened. The effect in many instances is to lead people to the conclusion that the right thing now is to do exactly the opposite. We stare long and hard at the road that was taken, without perhaps addressing ourselves, to borrow from the title of a poem by Robert Frost, to "the road not taken," or, more precisely, to the several available roads not taken. Not all these roads would have led in exactly the opposite direction.

History is not too generous in its disclosure of alternatives, but one should note the principal purpose of collecting the Pentagon Papers, as explained to me by the man who ordered it, Secretary Robert

McNamara. He said that future policymakers and historians could not possibly understand Vietnam without knowing not only why decisions went the way they did, and what alternatives were rejected, but also what was never even considered. For that purpose, you needed everything. You needed the comprehensive record. Sadly, the Pentagon Papers did not accomplish that mission. Because of a series of mishaps, the project took on a different form and was never completed. But McNamara was on the right track. In order to return to where we were before we got lost, it is important to search the lessons of Vietnam—to examine the thinking of the early 1960s. And, perhaps, to consider what Jack Kennedy was saying at that time.

I do not wish to invite an argument over whether President Kennedy would have pursued the same policy as Lyndon Johnson—surely he was as gung ho as anyone could have been in the early stages. He invented the Green Berets. But I would argue that toward the end, two months before he was assassinated, he was showing evidence of disenchantment. In September, 1963, he was saying there were limits on what the United States could do for any country. He was publicly critical of the Saigon government. "I don't think that unless a greater effort is made by the government to win popular support that the war can be won out there. In the final analysis it is their war and they are the ones who have to win it or lose it. We can help them, we can give them equipment, we can send our men out there as advisors, but they have to win it, the people of Vietnam against the Communists." You can read a lot or a little into that, but on its face it suggests an alternative that wasn't chosen.

Undoubtedly, we can find as many different lessons in the Vietnam experience as there are different people participating in this symposium. We cannot hope to fully understand the Vietnam War, or even to agree about it, through a weekend symposium. We may not understand it for years. But on one point I think we all agree: We owe it to those who have sacrificed themselves in good faith, believing with good reason in the rightness of their sacrifice, to try to understand it.

DISCUSSION QUESTIONS

1. Explain the "lessons" that constitute the "Vietnam Syndrome." What, in the author's view, is wrong with those "lessons?"
2. What, according to the author, are some of the "positive legacies" of the Vietnam War? Can you think of others?
3. To what extent was President Reagan's policy toward Central America governed by the "Vietnam Syndrome?" What "lessons" will be derived from the linkage of arms sales to Iran with secret aid to the "contras" in Central America?

12

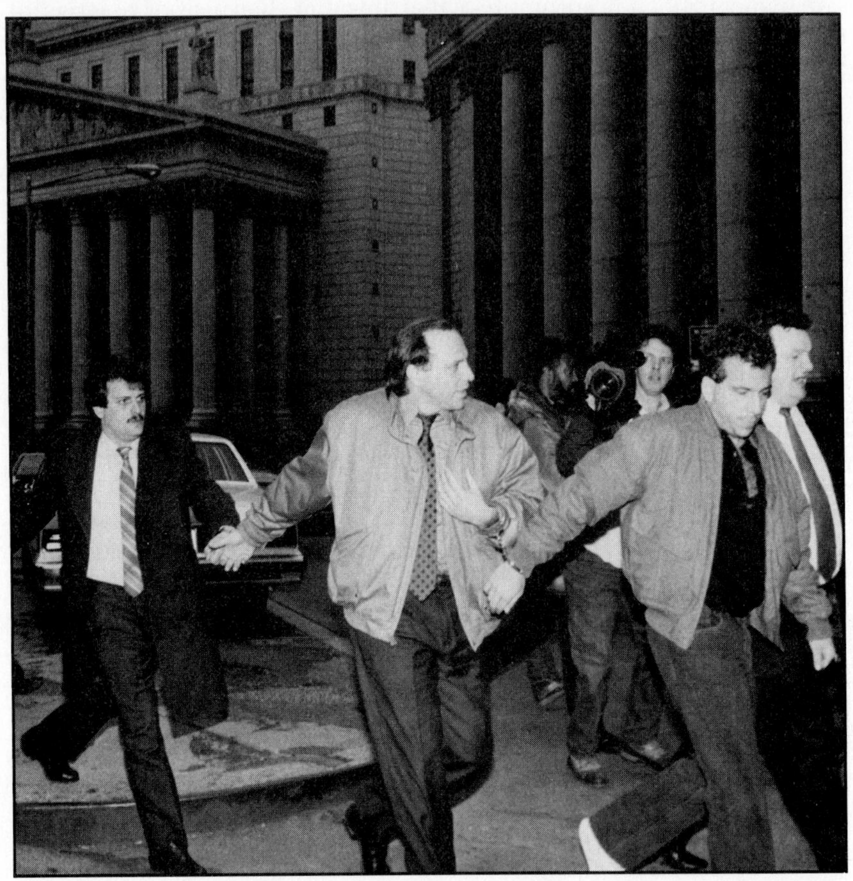

THE NEXT AMERICAN FRONTIER

ROBERT B. REICH

In 1981 the nation's premier industry was in deep trouble. General Motors failed to turn a profit for the first time in more than sixty years, Ford issued no dividends to stockholders, and Chrysler went to Washington for a loan so it could stay in business. Japan had become the world's leading auto maker, and the United States, once the world's leading advocate of free trade, found itself forced to impose restrictions on Japanese auto exports. As one American industry after another sunk into second, third, or fourth place in world competition, scholars, journalists, and politicians began to wonder what went wrong.

Robert Reich argues that the root of the problem is to be found in corporate boardrooms, not in obstructive government or obstinate labor. This nation, which had pioneered modern techniques of management in the late nineteenth century, had become trapped in corporate bureaucracy. In the global economy that emerged in the 1960s, nations with a supply of cheap labor borrowed American production techniques and squeezed American products out of the market. Some of the developed nations, such as Japan, remained competitive by adopting flexible systems of production that made maximum use of the skills of management and labor.

Americans have been slow to adopt these flexible systems. Instead, corporate executives have sought personal security and business profit in what Reich calls paper entrepreneurialism. They concentrate not upon manufacturing goods that can compete in world markets, but upon securing financial gains that improve profit statements. Financiers and lawyers now dominate corporate boardrooms, displacing those who had matured in the production or sales departments. A corporate head is regarded as successful if he or she shows a quarterly profit, but, as Reich points out, the pursuit of short-term gains is sacrificing the long-term future of American business.

In the years that have passed since Reich wrote this article in 1983, the American economy enjoyed an economic recovery, Chrysler repaid its loans to the federal government, and Ford and General Motors have undertaken major rebuilding programs. One of the best selling books of the mid-1980s was *In Search of Excellence,* a study of the success American businesses were having after adopting the flexible systems advocated by Reich. Even so, today we drive more Japanese cars than ever before, and the nation's international trade deficit is frightening. Worse still, the paper entrepreneurialism of corporate mergers is more frenzied than ever. The need to restructure American business organizations remains one of the most important items on the national agenda.

—DIANE LINDSTROM

The worldwide recession that began in 1981 will end eventually. Some say it already has ended. But the underlying problems of the American economy will not come to an end with the next upturn in the business cycle, unless American industry undertakes some basic changes in its organization of production. Unemployment will remain high. Millions of jobs in the nation's basic industries will never return. And the American standard of living will continue to decline.

Between 1920 and 1970, business, labor, and government hewed to a set of organizing principles—originally called "scientific management"—in which tasks were simplified, ordered according to pre-established rules, and carefully monitored. These principles were put into effect by a new class of professional managers. High-volume, scientifically managed industry, producing standardized goods, generated vast economies of scale and levels of wealth unparalleled in history.

The management era ended for America around 1970. Its decline began, ironically, just as many Europeans were coming to view the mastery of high-volume production as the "American challenge," which Europe had either to emulate or to succumb to. Gradually the economic cycles began to follow a downward trend, and over the next decade America's industry was progressively idled.

The proportion of U.S. manufacturing capacity employed in production, which had reached 86 percent in 1965, averaged around 80 percent during the 1970s, and fell to less than 70 percent by 1982. Only 3.5 percent of the labor force was jobless in 1969, but thereafter unemployment climbed persistently, reaching almost 11 percent last year. By the 1980s, the core industries of the management era—steel, automobiles, petrochemicals, textiles, consumer electronics, electrical machinery, metal-forming machinery—were in trouble.

Productivity growth slowed from an average yearly increase of 3.2 percent between 1948 and 1965 to an average of 2.4 percent between 1965 and 1973. The rate of growth then dropped to 1.1 percent between 1973 and 1978, and in 1979 American productivity began actually to decline. Meanwhile, productivity growth in Japan and several Western European nations stayed relatively high. After 1965, American real incomes slowed their long climb. Between 1965 and 1981, the average U.S. worker's real wages declined by one fifth. The American engine of prosperity had stalled.

Standardized production had brought America unparalleled wealth. True, our national well-being was interrupted by a depression and by periodic recessions. But these were interruptions, nothing more. Standardized production always restored prosperity, consistently exceeding previous levels, consistently achieving more efficiency and greater volume.

As the trusted formula has ceased to work, America has been ready to embrace any explanation but the most obvious: the same factor that once brought prosperity—the way the nation organizes itself for production—now threatens decline. Everywhere America has looked, it has seen the symptoms of its economic impasse, but it has been unable to recognize the actual causes because the roots of the problem are so deeply embedded in our business enterprises, labor unions, and government institutions.

Government regulation served as a convenient rhetorical scapegoat in the 1980 presidential election, but offers no real explanation. Environmental laws indeed require firms to invest in new equipment, but those requirements have imposed only modest costs. During the 1970s, the U.S. steel industry spent an average of $365 million annually to reduce pollution and improve worker safety—about 17 percent of its annual capital investment during the decade. Of this cost, 48 percent was subsidized by state and local governments through industrial-development bonds. Spending by European steelmakers was of an equal magnitude. During the same period, Japanese steel manufacturers spent substantially more for these purposes.

Safety regulations also add some costs to operations, but the reduction in accidents has meant savings in time and expense that go far to offset these extra costs. Overall, capital expenditures on pollution control and safety combined have never exceeded 6 percent of industrial investment, and can be blamed for at most around a tenth of the slowdown in productivity.

Nor do government deficits explain any major part of the problem. There is no evidence that deficits have been nearly large enough to discourage private investment and economic growth substantially. Indeed, through much of the 1970s, the governments of West Germany, Japan, and France maintained a much larger public debt in proportion to the national economy than did the U.S. government.

Inadequate capital formation has not been the problem either. Between 1965 and 1980, even in the face of inflation, the country continued to invest about 10 percent of its gross national product in plant and equipment; for the period between 1977 and the present, the rate is more than 11 percent, and early last year it reached 11.7 percent—its highest level since 1928. Indeed, investment in *manufacturing* as a percent of the total output of goods increased substantially—from 10.8 percent between 1960 and 1964 to 14.8 percent between 1973 and 1978. This level of manufacturing investment was not significantly below that of America's foreign competitors.

Other proposed explanations also have failed. U.S. investment in research and development declined from 3 percent of gross national product at the start of the 1970s to 2 percent at the start of the 1980s.

But this decline stemmed mostly from the slowdown in publicly financed defense and space programs, which affected American industry only indirectly. In any event, the decline in America's productive growth actually began in the late 1960s, well before any cutback in research expenditures. Nor can responsibility be placed on escalating energy prices. The oil shock affected all nations, many of which, including Germany and Japan, were much more dependent on imported energy resources than was America. Even more to the point, America's economic decline pre-dated the oil embargo, in 1973.

Nor can the blame be put on the inevitable drop in output from America's mines, on the slowdown in the movement of American labor out of agriculture, on the entrance of women and young people into the labor force, or on unfair trade practices by foreign manufacturers. Even taken together, these explain only a small part of our gradual, steady economic decline relative to other leading industrial nations. They overlook the worldwide reorganization of production and America's failure to adapt to it.

The central problem of America's economic future is that the nation is not moving quickly enough out of high-volume, standardized production. The extraordinary success of the half-century of the management era has left the United States a legacy of economic inflexibility. Thus our institutional heritage now imperils our future.

America's relative decline has been rooted in changes in the world market. Prior to the mid-1960s, foreign trade did not figure significantly in our economy. Only a small proportion of American-made goods were traded internationally; an equally small amount of foreign production entered the United States. This situation changed dramatically.

In 1980, 19 percent of the goods Americans made were exported (up from 9.3 percent in 1970), and more than 22 percent of the goods Americans used were imported (also up from 9.3 percent in 1970). But even those figures understate the new importance of foreign competition. The most telling statistic is this: By 1980, more than 70 percent of all the goods produced in the United States were actively competing with foreign-made goods. America has become part of the world market.

American producers have not fared well in this new contest. Beginning in the mid-1960s, foreign imports have claimed an increasing share of the American market. By 1981, the United States was importing almost 26 percent of its cars, 17 percent of its steel, 60 percent of its televisions, radios, tape recorders, and phonographs, 43 percent of its calculators, 27 percent of its metal-forming machine tools, 35 percent of its textile machinery, and 53 percent of its computerized machine tools. Twenty years before, imports had accounted for less than 10 percent of the American market for each of these products.

America's declining share of the world market has been particularly dramatic in capital-intensive, high-volume industries. Since 1963, America's share of the world market has declined in a number of important areas: automobiles, by almost one third; industrial machinery, by 33 percent; agricultural machinery, by 40 percent; telecommunications machinery, by 50 percent; metal-working machinery, by 55 percent.

The globe is fast becoming a single marketplace. Goods are being made wherever they can be made the cheapest, regardless of national boundaries. And the most efficient places for much mass production are coming to be Third World countries.

The International Labor Office estimates that every year between 1980 and 2000, 36 million people will enter the world labor force, and 85 percent of them will be from developing nations. The newly integrated world market will put many of them to work at America's old specialty of high-volume, standardized production.

Over a period of only fifteen years, many of the world's developing countries have begun to specialize in capital-intensive production. Their production costs are lower than those of the United States, both because their workers are content with lower real wages and because some of these countries have better access to cheap materials. Moreover, the demand for many standardized commodities has been growing faster in developing nations than in industrialized nations, whose citizens already possess these products; and it is often more profitable to manufacture them within these growing markets than it is to ship them there.

One important trend is often overlooked: the hourly output of workers in the newly industrialized nations is catching up to the output of American workers, simply because they are beginning to use many of the same machines. Developing countries have been able to buy (from international engineering and capital-equipment firms) the world's most modern steel-rolling mills, paper machines, and computerized machine tools. The growth of large-scale retail outlets in industrialized nations has given developing countries an efficient way to distribute their wares. Korean television manufacturers, for example, have gained a sizable share of the U.S. television market by selling to no more than a dozen large American department-store chains.

By the mid-1970s, Korea, Hong Kong, Taiwan, Singapore, Brazil, and Spain were specializing in simple products—clothing, footwear, toys, and basic electronic assemblies—that required substantial amounts of unskilled labor but little capital investment or technology. Between

1970 and 1975, Korea's exports of textiles increased by 436 percent, Taiwan's by 347 percent, and Hong Kong's by 191 percent.

Japan's response was to shift out of these simple products into processing industries, such as steel and synthetic fibers, that required substantial capital investment and raw materials, but used mostly unskilled and semiskilled labor and incorporated relatively mature technologies that were not subject to major innovations. Between 1966 and 1972, the Japanese steel industry increased its steelmaking assets by more than 23 percent a year. As its own steel needs began to level off in the early 1970s, Japan increased its exports of raw steel. It invested in more than fifty finishing facilities in developing countries in order to expand its market share.

By the mid-1970s, Korea, Hong Kong, Taiwan, Singapore, Brazil, Spain, and Mexico had followed Japan—shifting their export mix toward the basic capital-intensive processing industries. All told, these developing countries increased their share of world steelmaking capacity from 9 percent in 1974 to 15 percent by 1980.

As less-developed countries moved into steel production, Japan reduced its domestic steelmaking capacity and became a major exporter of steel technology—engineering services and equipment. Japan moved its industrial base into more complex products, such as automobiles, color televisions, small appliances, consumer electronics, and ships—industries requiring considerable investment in plant and equipment as well as sophisticated new technologies.

At the same time, Malaysia, Thailand, the Philippines, Sri Lanka, India, and other poorer countries were taking over the production of clothing, footwear, toys, and simple electronic assemblies. Workers in these countries earned, on average, no more than $25 a month.

By 1980, Korea, Hong Kong, Singapore, Brazil, Spain, and Mexico had increased their production of complex products such as automobiles, color televisions, tape recorders, CB transceivers, microwave ovens, small computers, and ships. Korea already has the largest single shipyard in the world; and with its salary rates averaging only one third those of major Japanese shipyards, Korea may surpass Japanese tonnage in five years.

Almost all of the world's production of small appliances (whether Panasonic, Philips, General Electric, Sony, Zenith, or an obscure brand) is now centered in Hong Kong, Korea, and Singapore. Components and product designs are bought from major companies; financing is arranged through Japanese, U.S., and European banks; and distribution is handled through large retailers, such as Sears, Roebuck, or through the established distribution channels of large Japanese or American consumer electronics companies.

The trend is becoming clear enough. First, America's basic steel, textile, automobile, consumer electronics, rubber, and petrochemical industries (and the other high-volume industries that depend on them) are becoming uncompetitive in the world. Second, now that production can be fragmented into separate, globally scattered operations, whole segments of other American industries are becoming uncompetitive. Whatever the final product, those parts of its production requiring high-volume machinery and unsophisticated workers can be accomplished more cheaply in developing nations.

Automation, far from halting this trend, has accelerated it. Sophisticated machinery is readily moved to low-wage countries. Robots and computerized machines further reduce the need for semiskilled workers in high-volume production (except for workers with easily learned maintenance and programming skills). For example, robots in the automobile industry are replacing workers at more semiskilled jobs, such as welding and spot welding, than unskilled jobs. Meanwhile, automated inspection machines are reducing the cost of screening out poor-quality components—thereby encouraging firms in industrialized nations to farm out the production of standardized parts to developing nations.

What began in the 1960s as a gradual shift became by the late 1970s a major structural change in the world economy. Assembly operations were being established in developing countries at a rapid clip, and America's manufacturing base was eroding precipitously. The recession of the past two years has stalled growth around the globe and plunged several developing nations into near bankruptcy. But it is important to distinguish these short-term phenomena—brought on by a temporary oil glut and high interest rates—from long-term trends that have been growing for two decades and surely will resume.

Other industrialized nations have faced the same competitive threat. Since the mid-1960s, European industries have faced an ever-greater challenge from low-wage production in developing countries. And since the late 1970s, Japan has been challenged as well. Japan is no longer a low-wage nation—the real earnings of Japanese workers are approaching those of their European and American counterparts.

Japan, West Germany, France, and other industrialized countries have sought to meet this challenge by shifting their industrial bases toward products and processes that require skilled workers. Skilled labor is the only dimension of production where these countries retain an advantage. Technological innovations can be bought or imitated by anyone. High-volume, standardized-production facilities can be established anywhere. But production processes that depend on skilled labor must stay where the skilled labor is.

The fate of British industry over the past twenty-five years illustrates this new reality. Britain has consistently led the world in major technological breakthroughs, such as continuous casting for steel, monoclonal antibodies, and CAT-scan devices. But because British businesses lacked the organization and their workers lacked the skills necessary to incorporate these inventions into production processes quickly enough, the British have reaped no real competitive advantage from them. These inventions were commercialized in Japan and the United States.

Industrialized countries are therefore moving into precision castings, specialty steel, special chemicals, and sensor devices, as well as the design and manufacture of fiber-optic cable, fine ceramics, lasers, large-scale integrated circuits, and advanced aircraft engines. Emerging industries such as these hold promise of generating new wealth and employment as their markets expand.

Some of these products or processes require precision engineering, complex testing, and sophisticated maintenance. Others are custom-tailored to the special needs of customers. The remainder involve technologies that are changing rapidly. All three are relatively secure against low-wage competition.

These product categories—precision-manufactured, custom-tailored, and technology-driven—have a great deal in common. They all depend on the sophisticated skills of their employees, skills that are often developed within teams. And they all require that traditionally separate business functions (design, engineering, purchasing, manufacturing, distribution, marketing, sales) be merged into a highly integrated system that can respond quickly to new opportunities. In short, they are premised on *flexible systems* of production.

Flexible-system production has an advantage over high-volume, standardized production whenever solving new problems is more important than routinizing the solution of old ones. The unit costs of producing simple, standardized products such as cotton textiles, basic steel, or rubber tires generally decline more with long production runs than with improvements in the production process. Manufacturers of these products therefore do well to emphasize large capacity, cheap labor, and cheap raw materials rather than flexible systems.

This does not mean that industrialized countries must abandon their older industries—steel, chemicals, textiles, and automobiles. These industries are the gateways through which new products and processes emerge. Rather than abandoning these older industries, other industrialized countries are seeking to restructure them toward higher-valued and technologically more sophisticated businesses—specialty steel, special chemicals, synthetic fibers, and precision-engineered automobiles and auto components. As this adjustment occurs, they can allow the lowest-skilled standardized segments of their production to migrate to developing countries.

Of all industrialized countries, Japan has made the most rapid shift from standardized production to flexible-system production, and rather than forsaking its older industries has accelerated their evolution. Japanese auto makers are experimenting with a variety of fuel-saving materials. They are developing complex manufacturing systems, and have reduced to eighty-four hours the amount of labor required to produce each car (in contrast to 145 hours per car in America). By the same token, Japan's production of high-quality polyester-filament fabrics, requiring complex technologies and skilled labor, now accounts for 40 percent of its textile exports. Japan has substantially reduced its capacity to produce basic steel, basic petrochemicals, small appliances, ships, and simple fibers, while dramatically expanding its capacity in the higher-valued, more specialized segments of these industries. To accomplish this transformation, it has applied such innovations as process-control devices, fiber-optic cable, complex polymer materials, and very large-scale integrated circuits. Japanese companies are also packaging some standard products—copiers and typewriters, for instance—within technologically complex product systems, such as office communications and computer-aided manufacturing, which require custom design and service. In Japan's flexible-system enterprises, the distinction between goods and services is becoming blurred.

Japan has reduced its capacity in the capital-intensive, high-volume segments of its basic industries by scrapping plant and equipment, by simultaneously investing in new high-volume capacity in Korea, Taiwan, Singapore, and Brazil, and by retraining workers for higher-skilled jobs.

West Germany and France are having more difficulty shifting their economies, but each country is making progress. Although the current recession has slowed industrial adjustment in both nations, Germany nevertheless has reduced its basic steel, chemical, and automobile-making capacity somewhat, and has shifted more of its production into specialty steel, pharmaceuticals, and precision machinery.

Even Taiwan and Korea are seeking to shift into flexible-system industries. Korea is now establishing a semiconductor research-and-development association, jointly funded by government and industry. Taiwan is building a science-based industrial park at Hsinchu.

For the United States, however, the shift has been slow and painful. The country has been far less successful than other industrialized nations in increasing its manufacturing exports to cover its increasing import bill. Recently, Japan and the nations of Western Europe have been selling America more manufactured goods than America has been selling back to them.

Sales of grain and coal and revenues from services have helped ease America's trade imbalance. But these enterprises alone cannot guarantee our economic future. The most accessible coal will have been mined within the next few years; additional coal will be more costly to retrieve, not only in terms of machinery and equipment but also in damage to the environment and injuries to workers. Nor can grain exports be relied upon indefinitely; improvements in agricultural production will spread to the areas of the globe with favorable climate and soil conditions, and our soil will gradually become depleted.

Nor can we rely on services. The nation's service exports depend on the vigor of its future manufacturing base. Approximately 90 percent of America's income from services consists of the investment income of its manufacturing firms and, to a lesser extent, of individuals. But this income has declined significantly since the mid-1960s. In 1965, America received 3.6 times as much investment income as it paid out to foreign firms and individuals in dividends and royalties, but by 1978 the ratio of investment income to payments was 1.8 to 1. As foreign firms continue to gain strength relative to their American counterparts in merchandise businesses, this pattern will continue.

These trends pose a troubling question. If it is true that the economic future of countries lies in technically advanced, skill-intensive industries, why have American firms failed to respond by adopting the new products and processes?

The answer is that the transition requires a basic restructuring of business, labor, and government. A reorganization of this magnitude is bound to be resisted, because it threatens vested economic interests and challenges established values. The transition has been easier for Japan and for some continental Europeans, both because they never fully embraced high-volume, standardized production and because they have historically linked their economic development with social change.

As America has forfeited world industrial leadership to Japan, American business leaders have become obsessed with Japanese management. The business press daily praises Japanese practices such as the informal worker groups know as "quality circles," said to encourage commitment, soften workplace conflict, and improve product quality. American management consultants advise business executives to convert to less abrasive forms of management, such as "Theory Z," hailed as the key to Japan's success.

The infatuation with Japan's management technique obscures the point that flexible-system processes cannot simply be grafted onto business organizations that are designed for the production of standardized goods. Flexible-system production is rooted in discovering and solving new problems; high-volume, standardized production basically involves routinizing the solutions to old problems. Flexible-system production requires an organization designed for change and adaptability; high-volume, standardized production requires an organization geared to stability.

American business leaders are responding to the superficial novelty of Japanese management without acknowledging the underlying differences in the organization of production. They hope to upgrade their management techniques while retaining intact the old structure. Yet the answer lies not in new techniques but in a new productive organization, requiring a different, less rigidly delineated relationship between management and labor.

The basic premises of high-volume, standardized production—the once-potent formula of scientific management—are simply inapplicable to flexible-system production. The distinct principles of flexible-system production are understood—perhaps intuitively—by many small, upstart companies in America producing new micro-electronic products and computer software or creating advertisements and films. They are also understood by a few highly successful larger companies—IBM and Hewlett-Packard, for instance. The same principles dominate many Japanese manufacturing and trading companies, and European producers of such items as precision castings, computerized machine tools, and customized telecommunications equipment.

The tasks involved in flexible-system production are necessarily complex, since any work that can be rendered simple and routine is more efficiently done by low-wage labor overseas. Thus no set of "standard operating procedures" locks in routines or compartmentalizes job responsibilities.

Skill-intensive processes cannot be programmed according to a fixed set of rules covering all possible contingencies. The work requires high-level skills precisely because the problems and opportunities cannot be anticipated. Producers of specialized semiconductor chips or multipurpose robots, for example, must be able to respond quickly to emerging and potential markets. Delicate machines break down in complex ways. Technologies change in directions that cannot be foreseen. The more frequently products and processes are altered or adapted, the harder it is to translate them into reliable routines. Again, if problems and opportunities could be anticipated and covered by preset rules and instructions, production could be moved abroad.

Finally, workers' performance cannot be monitored and evaluated through simple accounting systems. In flexible-system production, the quality of work is often more important than the quantity. As machines and low-wage labor overseas take over those tasks that demand only speed and accuracy, workers' skill, judgment, and initiative become the determinants of the flexible-system enterprise's competitive success. Moreover, in devising and manufacturing such complex items as customized herbicides, titanium alloys, or computer-software systems, tasks are often so interrelated that it becomes impossible to measure them separately; since each worker needs the help and cooperation of many others, success can be measured only in reference to the final collective result.

For these reasons, the radical distinction heretofore drawn between those who plan work and those who execute it is inappropriate to flexible-system production. When production is inherently nonroutine, problem-solving requires close working relationships among people at all stages in the process. If customers' special needs are to be recognized and met, designers must be familiar with fabrication, production, marketing, and sales. Salespeople must have an intimate understanding of the enterprise's capability to design and deliver new or customized products. Flexible systems can adapt quickly only if information is widely shared within them. There is no hierarchy to problem-solving: solutions may come from anyone, anywhere. In flexible-system enterprises, nearly everyone in the production process is responsible for recognizing problems and finding solutions.

In high-volume, standardized production, professional managers, staff specialists, and even low-level production workers typically get much of their training before joining the organization, and seldom venture far from a fairly narrow specialty. They move from one organization to another, but they remain within that single specialty.

By contrast, in flexible-system production much of the training of necessity occurs on the job, both because the precise skills to be learned cannot be anticipated and communicated in advance and because individuals' skills are typically integrated into a group whose collective capacity becomes something more than the simple sum of its members' skills. Over time, as the group members work through various problems, they learn about each other's abilities. Like a baseball team, they practice together to increase their collective prowess. Their sense of membership in the enterprise is stronger and more immediate than any abstract identification with their profession or occupational group. They move from one specialty to another, but they remain within a single organization. The Japanese have been more successful than Americans in devising the newest generation of large-scale integrated circuits, because production entails complex and interrelated tasks that can only be perfected by a relatively stable team. Rapid turnover in U.S. companies has hindered this organizational learning.

The high-volume, standardized enterprise is organized into a series of hierarchical tiers. Flexible-system production suggests a relatively "flat" structure: in most firms that stake their success on specialized or technically based products, there are few middle-level managers, and only modest differences in the status and income of senior managers and junior employees. The enterprise is typically organized as a set of relatively stable project teams that informally compete with one another for resources, recognition, and projects.

Finally, because flexible-system production is premised on ever-changing markets and conditions, it is less vulnerable than high volume production to shifts in demand. Its machines and workers are not locked into producing long runs of any single standardized good. For this reason, flexible-system enterprises have less need to diversify into several lines of business as insurance against declining demand in any one. Flexible-system producers thrive on instability. Too much stability, and they would gradually lose their market to high-volume, standardized producers in low-wage countries.

In all these respects, the organization of high-volume production is so fundamentally different from that of flexible-system production that the transformation is exceedingly difficult. Because the roles, experiences, training, and expectations of professional managers and workers in high-volume production differ so sharply from those that flexible-system production calls for, neither group is prepared to adapt smoothly to such a transformation. In fact, they are likely to resist it.

That is what has happened. Because America's blue-collar workers often lack the skills and training necessary for flexible-system production, they have clung to the job classifications, work rules, and cost-of-living increases that brought them some security under standardized production. By the same token, because America's professional managers are ill equipped to undertake the necessary shift from high-volume production to flexible systems, they have resorted to various ploys designed to maintain or increase their firm's earnings without new productive investment. "Paper entrepreneurialism" of this kind merely rearranges industrial assets, while wasting the time and abilities of some of America's most talented people.

Paper entrepreneurialism is the bastard child of scientific management. It employs the mechanisms and symbols developed to direct and monitor high-volume production, but it involves an even more radical separation between planning and production. Paper entrepreneurialism is a version of scientific management grown so extreme that it has lost all connection with the actual workplace. Its strategies involve generating profits through the clever manipulation of rules and numbers that only in theory represent real assets and products.

At its most pernicious, paper entrepreneurialism involves little more than imposing losses on others for the sake of short-term profits for the firm. The others are often members of the taxpaying public, who end up subsidizing firms that creatively reduce their tax liability. The others are sometimes certain of the firms' shareholders who end up indirectly subsidizing other shareholders. Occasionally, the others are unlucky investors, consumers, or the shareholders of other firms. Because paper gains are always at someone else's expense, paper entrepreneurialism can be a ruthless game. It can also be fascinating, and lucrative for those who play it well.

When the management era began to collapse, in the late 1960s, professional managers, seeking to limit the damage, turned to the tools they had at hand. The ideology of management control was so deeply ingrained that the instinctive reaction of professional managers was typically to define, even more precisely than before, the rules and working relationships within their firms, seeking thereby to solidify their control. But because the environment was changing so rapidly—with the entrance of new foreign competitors, new products, new manufacturing processes, and the opening of new global markets—the rules and controls had to be extraordinarily elaborate. They became even more intricate as the pace of change accelerated.

To coordinate the increasingly complex tasks of production, managers introduced complex techniques of "matrix management," through which employees reported to several different managers for different dimensions of their work. (An employee engaged in, say, the marketing of refrigerators in South America would report to three managers—in charge of marketing, refrigerators, and South American sales, respectively.)

When the matrices became too complicated, resulting in endless conflicts and confusion, organizational-development consultants were called in to design and coordinate "project teams." When this team structure had so muddled personal accountability that employees began to engage in buck-passing and bureaucratic gamesmanship, managers added still more controls: budget reviews, computer-based management-information systems, narrative reports on operations, monthly "flash" reports, formal goal-setting systems, and detailed performance-evaluation and incentive-compensation systems.

These ever-more elaborate systems of managerial control brought with them additional layers of staff to devise the new rules and procedures, to design and monitor systems of performance appraisal, to referee the inevitable confusion over responsibility, and to mediate conflicts. Between 1965 and 1975, the ratio of staff positions to production workers in American manufacturing companies increased from 35 per 100 to 41 per 100. In certain industries, the jump has been even more dramatic. In electrical machinery, the ratio increased from 46 staff jobs for each 100 production jobs to 56 per 100; in non-electrical machinery, from 43 to 59; in chemicals, from 66 to 78. Companies with 2,500 or more employees have had a higher proportion of staff positions relative to production workers (44 per hundred in 1972) than companies with fewer than 500 employees (32 per hundred). The largest companies have the highest ratio of staff to production workers. By 1979, half of the employees of Intel—the microprocessor manufacturer—were engaged in administration. When an engineer wanted a mechanical pencil, processing the order required twelve pieces of paper and ninety-five administrative steps. It took 364 steps to hire a new employee.

This sudden proliferation of staff positions within American firms is particularly striking by comparison with firms in other nations. In the typical Japanese factory, for example, foremen report directly to plant managers. The foreman in the typical American factory must report through three additional layers of management. Until very recently, Ford Motor Company had five more levels of managers between the factory worker and the company chairman than did Toyota.

Bureaucratic layering of this sort is costly, and not only because of the extra salaries and benefits that must be paid. Layers of staff also make the firm more rigid, less able to make quick decisions or adjust rapidly to new opportunities and problems. In the traditional scientifically managed, high-volume enterprise, novel situations are regarded as exceptions, requiring new rules and procedures and the judgments of senior managers. But novel situations are a continuing feature of the new competitive environment in which American companies now find themselves.

The typical sequence now runs something like this: A salesman hears from a customer that the firm's latest bench drill cannot accommodate bits for drilling a recently developed hard plastic. The customer suggests a modified coupling adapter and an additional speed setting. The salesman thinks the customer's suggestion makes sense, but he has no authority to pursue it directly. Following procedures, the salesman passes the idea on to the sales manager, who finds it promising and drafts a memo to the marketing vice president. The marketing vice president also likes the idea, so he raises it in an executive meeting of all the vice presidents. The executive committee agrees to modify the drill. The senior product manager then asks the head of the research department to form a task force to evaluate the product opportunity and design a new coupling and variable-speed mechanism.

The task force consists of representatives from sales, marketing, accounting, and engineering. The engineers are interested in the elegance of the design. The manufacturing department insists on modifications requiring only minor retooling. The salespeople want a drill that will do what customers need it to do. The finance people worry about the costs of producing it. The marketing people want a design that can be advertised and distributed efficiently, and sold at a competitive price. The meetings are difficult, because each task-force member wants to claim credit for future success but avoid blame for any possible failure. After months of meetings, the research manager presents the group's findings to the executive committee. The committee approves the new design. Each department then works out a detailed plan for its role in bringing out the new product, and the modified drill goes into production.

If there are no production problems, the customer receives word that he can order a drill for working hard plastics two years after he first discussed it with the salesman. In the meantime, a Japanese or West German firm with a more flexible, teamlike approach has already designed, produced, and delivered a hard-plastics drill.

As the bureaucratic gap between executives and production workers continues to widen, the enterprise becomes more dependent on "hard," quantifiable data, and less sensitive to qualitative information. Professional managers concentrate on month-to-month profit figures, data on growth in sales, and return on investment. "Softer," less quantifiable information—about product quality, worker morale, and customer satisfaction—may be at least as important to the firm's long-term success. But such information cannot be conveyed efficiently upward through the layers of staff. Even if such qualitative information occasionally works its way to senior executives without becoming too distorted in the process, it is often still ignored. Information like this does not invite quick decisions and crisp directives.

Even quantifiable information becomes distorted as it moves up the corporate hierarchy, because it must be summarized and interpreted. Distortions do occur intentionally. Lower-level managers, dependent on senior managers for rewards and promotions, naturally want to highlight good news and suppress bad news. In reporting their costs, for example, they may seek to outmaneuver the accounting department (which determines how overhead costs are distributed among units) by shifting some overhead to another unit. Since lower-level managers are competing with other managers for scarce investment resources, they are likely to present overly optimistic estimates for the projects they seek to fund. Their forecasts may underestimate costs, overestimate market demand, and leave out certain expenses altogether. The planning systems that process these estimates become arenas for organizational gamesmanship.

Professional managers at the top of American firms have come to preside over a symbolic economy. The systems of management control that they initiated in the late 1960s in efforts to maintain profitability have become more intricate and elaborate as the global market has grown less predictable, requiring additional layers of managers and staff specialists. As the bureaucratic distance between senior managers and production workers has increased, the rules and numbers in which senior managers deal have become more and more disconnected from the everyday processes of production—distorted by excessive reliance on "hard" data, by communication failures, and by gamesmanship.

Paper entrepreneurialism relies on financial and legal virtuosity. Through shrewd maneuvering, accounting and tax rules can be finessed, and the numbers on balance sheets and tax returns manipulated, giving the appearance of greater or lesser earnings. Assets can be rearranged on paper to improve cash flow or to defer payments. And threatened lawsuits or takeovers can be used to extract concessions from other players. Huge profits are generated by these ploys. They are the most imaginative and daring ventures in the American economy. But they do not enlarge the economic pie; they merely reassign the slices.

The conglomerate enterprise is one manifestation of paper entrepreneurialism. Before the late 1960s, American business enterprises generally expanded only into lines of business related to their original products. They moved into markets where their managerial, technical, and marketing skills could be applied anew, giving them a real competitive advantage.

The conglomerate enterprises that mushroomed during the 1970s—multibusiness giants such as Gulf + Western, LTV, Textron, Litton, United Technologies, Northwest Industries, and ITT—are entirely different. They have grown by acquiring existing enterprises, often in wholly unrelated fields. Gulf + Western, for example, owns Paramount Pictures, Consolidated Cigar (one of America's largest cigarmakers), Kayser-Roth (a major apparel-maker), A.P.S. (an auto-parts supplier), one of America's largest zinc mines, Madison Square Garden, Simon & Schuster (publishers), Simmons (mattresses), the Miss Universe and Miss U.S.A. pageants, and a large sugarcane plantation. ITT (the world's eighth-largest corporation) owns Wonder Bread, Sheraton Hotels, Hartford Insurance, Avis Rent-a-Car, Bobbs-Merrill Publishing, and Burpee Lawn and Garden Products.

Conglomerate enterprises rarely, if ever, bring any relevant managerial, technical, or marketing skills to the new enterprises they acquire. Their competence lies in law and finance. Their relationship to their far-flung subsidiaries is that of an investor. Indeed, many conglomerates function almost exactly like mutual funds, except that the staff at conglomerate headquarters presumably has slightly more detailed information about their subsidiaries than mutual-fund advisers have about the companies within their portfolios.

Some conglomerates have come a step closer to mutual funds by becoming minority owners of a variety of other companies. Gulf + Western actually maintains a $536 million portfolio of stocks in sixteen companies. Financial advisers within conglomerates like these decide which stocks to purchase or sell according to precisely the same criteria that financial advisers to mutual funds employ. Like the mutual fund, the conglomerate organization does not create new wealth or render production more efficient. It merely allocates capital, duplicating—though awkwardly—the functions of financial markets.

The paper advantages of conglomeration extend beyond speculation and risk-spreading, however. Dexterous tax and accounting manipulations can extract paper profits from economically senseless acquisitions. Whenever a firm's stock-market price falls below its book value (the assumed market value of the firm's total assets, if they were sold off bit by bit), another firm can post significant gains on its balance sheet simply by acquiring the undervalued firm and consolidating the two sets of books. Thus, the acquiring firm's earnings increase with minimal effort. As the American economy has declined, the stock of many companies has fallen to less than book value in this way. The stock market is not being irrational; companies like these are probably worth more disassembled than they are as continuing operations. But conglomeration does not redeploy these assets; it merely displays them more attractively on a new, consolidated balance sheet.

If the acquired firm has lost money in recent years, so much the better. The conglomerate that acquires it can use the losses to reduce its tax liability. Even if the assets of the acquired firm are purchased for more than their stated value in the acquired firm's books, the game is still on—the acquiring company has a higher basis for depreciating its new assets for tax purposes. (The 1982 tax law has made this route somewhat more treacherous.) U.S. Steel's purchase of Marathon Oil Company, for example, saved the steelmaker about $500 million in taxes in the first year and will save at least $1 billion more over the productive life of Marathon's Yates oil field, since tax laws let the oil field be valued for tax purposes at a higher cost than the property represented in Marathon's books. Because U.S. Steel can take new depletion deductions against this high-valued property, the Yates reserves are worth far more to it than they were to Marathon, which had already extracted what it could of the oil field's tax-deduction potential. The field's tax benefits were renewable through transfer, even if the oil was not.

Conglomeration has been proceeding at a breakneck pace. By 1972, 33 percent of the employees of America's manufacturing companies were involved in lines of business totally unrelated to the primary businesses of their companies. In 1977, American companies spent $22 billion acquiring one another. In 1979, they spent $43.5 billion.

That year, sixteen firms, each worth more than $500 million, were gobbled up, including Belridge Oil ($3.65 billion, bought by Shell Oil); C.I.T. Financial ($1.2 billion, by RCA); and Reliance Electric ($1.16 billion, by Exxon). All records were shattered in 1981, when $82 billion was spent on acquisitions. Du Pont paid a staggering $7.5 billion for Conoco; Fluor, $2.7 billion for St. Joe Minerals; and Gulf Oil, $325 million for Kemmerer Coal. The pace continued last year with U.S. Steel's purchase of Marathon Oil for $5.9 billion.

Despite widely advertised concern over a capital shortage and calls for corporate tax breaks to spur new investment, firms bent on acquisition have seldom been deterred by price. Corporations have been paying premiums of 50 and even 100 percent over the market value for the stock of the companies they seek to acquire. Even during the "go-go years" of the late 1960s, when "funny money" fueled a short-lived merger explosion, premiums rarely exceeded 25 percent.

All this has been accompanied by some of the heaviest bank borrowings in history. Du Pont borrowed $3.9 billion to buy Conoco, at an interest rate close to 20 percent. Texaco negotiated a loan of $5.5 billion from an international consortium of banks led by Chase Manhattan. Fluor Corporation borrowed $1 billion to buy St. Joe Minerals—a debt equal to Fluor's entire revenues for the first quarter of 1981.

As late as the early 1960s, "unfriendly" takeovers were virtually unheard of. Since then, they have become a standard strategy of paper entrepreneurialism. Fear of a takeover bid haunts America's corporate boardrooms. In a 1981 survey of chief financial officers in America's 480 largest industrial firms, 49 percent thought that their companies were vulnerable to a takeover, even of the remaining group, 38 percent said that they had developed formal plans aimed at thwarting takeover bids. The fear is well founded. Of the 249 firms that have faced unfriendly takeover attempts within the past three years, only fifty-two have successfully withstood the assault and remained independent.

The fear of takeover has generated an array of paper-entrepreneurial strategies. Many targets of takeover bids, fleeing acquisition by a company unfriendly to their present managers, are running into the arms of another, more congenial firm. When WUI, an international telecommunications firm, learned that Continental Telephone Corporation was on its trail, it sought to be acquired instead by Xerox. Some target companies seek immunity by pre-emptively buying companies in the would-be acquirer's own industries, so that antitrust laws block the acquisition attempt. Daylin, Inc., defending itself against W.R. Grace's recent tender offer, sought to purchase Narco Scientific, Inc.—a maker of equipment in a product line so similar to Grace's that Grace would be barred from taking over Daylin. One of the more bizarre—

and expensive—defense strategies is for a target company simply to reduce its cash reserves and thus become less attractive to potential predators. This may explain J. Ray McDermott & Co.'s $758 million acquisition of Babcock & Wilcox, and Kennecott Copper Corporation's $567 million purchase of Carborundum.

Increasingly, target companies are paying would-be acquirers high premiums to buy back blocks of stock that the acquirers have amassed. As a lawyer experienced in such tactics recently explained to *The Wall Street Journal*, "Look, I now have 7 percent or 8 percent of your stock. I'm not going after your company. But if you don't buy back the block from me at a premium, I know five or six guys who are interested and could take you over." This is the corporate equivalent of a demand for ransom. And paper entrepreneurs are generating large earnings from such threats.

Even if the target company refuses to pay the ransom, its stock typically shoots up when Wall Street learns that a takeover may be afoot. Thus the paper entrepreneur can generate earnings simply by selling the block of stock in the open market. Bendix recently made $75 million after taxes by buying and then selling back 20 percent of the outstanding stocks of Asarco. Gulf + Western announced in September of 1980 that it had made open-market purchases of large blocks of stock in two companies: a 7.4 percent interest in Oxford Industries, Inc., and a 10.4 percent interest in Robertshaw Controls Company. Two months later, both Oxford and Robertshaw bought back their shares, for a total of $2.1 million more than Gulf + Western had paid for them.

The largest gains from conglomeration lie in their potential for opening access to ready cash at low or no cost, while simultaneously avoiding or deferring income taxes. Financial conglomerates offer particularly rewarding possibilities along these lines.

Consider, for example, Baldwin-United—a company that until 1968 was known for the Baldwin piano, which it had been making since 1891. Piano sales were growing slowly, and the pressure from foreign competition was increasing. So Baldwin purchased a bank, twelve insurance companies, a savings-and-loan company, some mortgage-banking companies, America's largest mortgage-insurance company, and America's two largest trading-stamp companies. Many of these companies have been cheap sources of cash. The insurance companies have provided low-cost funds in the form of premiums; the savings-and-loan company has brought in deposits at low, passbook rates; the mortgage-banking and servicing companies have transferred billions of dollars in mortgage and real-estate tax payments from borrowers to lenders, while holding the funds for up to several weeks in the process; and the trading-stamp companies sell stamps to merchants, who give them to customers, who are unlikely to redeem them for months or years, if ever. Baldwin has further enlarged its earnings by avoiding or deferring taxes on these cash flows. Baldwin's mortgage-banking acquisition had unrealized losses in its loan portfolio, which Baldwin then used against its overall earnings; Baldwin also deducts the commissions it pays to its brokers in the year paid, which occasionally generates large tax losses. With these ample deductions, Baldwin has been able to redeem the bonds that its mortgage-insurance company bought, with tax impunity. As a result of all these financial and tax ploys, Baldwin's return on equity has increased from 13 percent to 31 percent since 1968, and its earnings per share have grown at a 20 percent annual rate.

Conglomerates offer no particular efficiency in allocating capital to its best use. Investors who wanted to buy into a particular bundle of industries could simply have bought stocks separately. American investors gain nothing from having the bundle prepackaged in the form of a diversified conglomerate. Indeed, conglomerates undermine the efficiency of America's capital market by eliminating investors' option to buy into Bobbs-Merrill alone, for example, without taking stock in all the rest of ITT's hodgepodge of businesses.

Nor, as we have seen, do conglomerates serve any useful industrial purpose. Unlike earlier multidivisional firms, which featured some complementarity among operations, modern conglomerates are typically little concerned with the actual economic functions of the various subsidiaries, beyond the interest a landlord might take in a sharecropper's labors.

Nor, as we have seen, do conglomerates serve any useful industrial purpose. Unlike earlier multidivisional firms, which featured some
ployed. Workers typically are left to fend for themselves.

Thus modern conglomerates are economically sterile. Their only effects are to facilitate paper entrepreneurialism and to spare managers the need to stake their careers on anything so risky as a single firm trying to make products. The growth of conglomerates illustrates managers' discretionary power to serve their own goals, and reveals how far economic change since the end of the management era has separated managers' incentives from socially productive results.

Paper entrepreneurialism does not rely solely on acquisitions, of course. Every month or so, another innovative paper ploy is unveiled. For example, many companies are now engaging in an expensive and financially empty exchange of new stock for old bonds. It works like this: A company that sold long-term bonds when interest rates were lower—and, thus, so was the yield, or "coupon," the bond had to offer—still carries the debt on its books at the original face value, even though the outstanding bonds are in fact being traded on the market at a discount because they yield less per dollar of face value than new financial assets. (That is, the books may show debt of $10 million even though the market value of the bonds has fallen to $7 million.) This debt bothers the firm's managers, who want the balance sheet to seem as unencumbered by indebtedness as possible.

So investment brokers have gone into the business of buying up old bonds at their (low) market value and offering to return them to the issuing firm in exchange for new shares of common stock. By buying back its old bonds, the company can claim to have "retired" a deceptively large chunk of debt, based on the financially irrelevant face value of the bonds, and so managers are willing to pay the broker handsomely for engineering the swap.

The company makes a precisely offsetting trade—a certain market value of stock for an equal market value of bonds. The cost: millions in brokers' fees and premiums. The only result: some gullible investors may be led to believe that the company has suddenly become less burdened by debt, and therefore more valuable. And the ruse is tax-free, treated as a non-taxable corporate reorganization so long as the broker handles the mechanics. Since August of 1981, more than a hundred such exchanges have swept at least $2 billion in debt from corporate balance sheets. Even U.S. Steel managed to use this ploy to report a profit for the depressed second quarter of 1982, despite its sizable losses in the steel business. Like other gimmicks, this one will go out of fashion in a year or two, when investors and the Internal Revenue Service catch on, and another innovation will replace it.

Paper entrepreneurs also display their virtuosity in "creative" accounting. In 1978, for example, when slumping car sales began to push Chrysler Corporation deeper into the red, forcing the auto maker to halt production at many plants and cut its dividends by 60 percent, the company still managed to project a fourth-quarter profit. Thanks to a little-noticed actuarial adjustment, Chrysler had merely changed the assumed rate of return on its employee-pension portfolio to 7 percent from 6 percent, reducing pension costs and adding about $50 million to its profits. This alteration was likely to escape the eyes of analysts and auditors, who are seldom trained in pension matters. Chrysler did nothing illegal. Indeed, it disclosed in a footnote to its annual report that it had made the actuarial change, although it did not state any figures.

Other methods of "earnings management" abound: showing certain transactions as collateral borrowings rather than as sales; overstating or understating inventories; failing to account fully for the effect of inflation on the value of inventories or profits; overstating the value of good will gained from a merger or acquisition; and understating the price paid for an acquisition. For example, GE paid about $2 billion worth of stock to acquire Utah International in 1976, but "pooling-of-interest" accounting rules let GE show a price of only $548 million on its balance sheet. Utah International's $196 million profit in 1977 looked much better on $548 million than it would have on $2 billion.

None of these ploys is illegal. Nor do they violate generally accepted accounting principles, which give firms wide latitude in reporting their earnings. Given the complexity of modern business practices and the uniqueness of each firm, more rigid accounting rules might actually lead to greater distortions. And that is the point. The set of symbols developed to represent real assets has lost the link with any actual productive activity. Finance has progressively evolved into a sector all its own, only loosely connected to industry. And this disconnectedness turns business executives into paper entrepreneurs—forced to outsmart other participants, or be themselves outsmarted.

All of this paper entrepreneurialism takes place against a background of mounting lawsuits. Professional managers in companies targeted for takeover are suing their predators. Shareholders are suing managers. Acquiring companies are suing the officers of the companies they have acquired. Purchasers of futures contracts are suing sellers who cannot meet the payments. The number of business lawsuits stemming from breach of contract, antitrust, or alleged "wasting" of corporate assets has increased fourfold since 1965.

One must be clear about the problem of paper entrepreneurialism in America. Paper entrepreneurialism does not directly use up economic resources. Every economy needs some paper entrepreneurs to help allocate capital efficiently among product entrepreneurs.

The problem is that paper entrepreneurialism has replaced product entrepreneurialism as the most dynamic and innovative occupation in the American economy. Paper entrepreneurs produce nothing of tangible use. For an economy to maintain its health, entrepreneurial rewards should flow primarily to products, not paper. As Lord Keynes recognized nearly fifty years ago, "When the capital development of a country becomes a by-product of the activities of a casino, the job is likely to be ill-done."

Ours is becoming an economy in which resources circulate endlessly among giant corporations, investment bankers, and their lawyers, but little new is produced. Financial resources are kept liquid in order to meet the next margin call, to enter the next position, or to exploit the next takeover opportunity. They are not applied in earnest to any single undertaking, for fear that they will soon be needed for something else. There is scant investment in new products or processes, because such endeavors tie up resources for too long.

In 1979, RCA Corporation complained publicly that it lacked the $200 million that would be needed to develop a video-cassette recorder, although recorders are the fastest-growing appliance of the decade. RCA thereby ceded the video-cassette market to the Japanese. But RCA had no qualms about spending $1.2 billion to buy a lackluster finance company that same year. In 1979, U.S. Steel decided to scrap its plan for building a new steel plant. Instead, it began building a cash reserve to acquire some other, more promising company, such as Marathon Oil.

While business leaders are otherwise engaged, America's industrial base remains wedded to high-volume, standardized production. Flexible-system production does not fit well into large conglomerate enterprises. The enterprises are too diffuse and fragmented to generate team spirit, too unwieldy and bureaucratic to accommodate novel approaches to new problems. Real-product entrepreneurs bridle at the red tape. Employees are discouraged from choosing unorthodox solutions. It is often difficult, from the mire of conglomerate headquarters, to identify unique customer needs. Big companies also tend to wait for markets to develop; they are not equipped successfully to pursue the markets that do not yet exist. Exxon's plunge into the "office of the future" has been an unmitigated disaster. The company is losing money at a rate that would bankrupt almost anyone else—in 1980 alone, its office-equipment division lost $150 million on sales of $270 million. Industrial giants such as Monsanto, Ford, and Sylvania, which tried several years ago to develop their own commercial semiconductor operations, failed miserably and withdrew from this rapidly changing market. Other large companies—RCA, TRW, Westinghouse—have not done much better.

But perhaps the greatest cost is in human talent. Today's corporate executives spend an increasing portion of their days fending off takeover, finding companies to acquire, conferring with their financial and accounting specialists, and responding to depositions in lawsuits, instead of attending to their products. Indeed, approximately 40 percent of the chief executive officers of America's largest firms have backgrounds in law or finance and rose to their present positions from company legal or financial staffs. This is in sharp contrast to the past. In 1950, only 13 percent of America's key chief executive officers had legal or financial backgrounds. Most came up through the ranks from market, engineering, or sales.

Increasingly over the past fifteen years, the most sought-after jobs among business-school graduates have been in finance and consulting, where the specialty is rearranging assets and shuffling corporate boxes—and from where bright young MBAs have their best shot at becoming corporate executives. Only 3 percent of Harvard Business School's 1981 graduates took jobs in production and 18.6 percent in sales and marketing, while 21.6 percent went into finance. Young people seeking quick affluence without much risk have turned to the practice of law, where America's highest-paying entry-level jobs are found. In a recent survey, 24 percent of Harvard freshmen said they were planning a career in law; only 7 percent were going into science. In 1982, New York City's largest law firms were paying their young recruits, fresh out of law school, $48,000 a year. In 1980, the median income for partners in New York's largest law firms was $242,685, up 50 percent from 1975. Law firms can afford to pay these exorbitant salaries because legal fees keep rolling in.

Between 1940 and 1960, only about one American in 600 was a lawyer. Between 1971 and 1981, the number of practicing attorneys increased by 64 percent. America now has more than 590,000 lawyers—one for every 400 citizens. Over the same decade, however, there was only a 15 percent rise in the number of engineers, and a 25 percent rise in the number of laborers. Only about one of every 10,000 citizens in Japan is trained in law, while one out of twenty-five Japanese citizens is trained in engineering or science. More than 65 percent of all seats on the boards of Japanese manufacturing companies are occupied by people who are trained as engineers; roughly the same percentage of seats on American boards are taken by people trained in law, finance, or accountancy. Thus, in Japan, many problems that arise in business are viewed as problems of engineering or science, for which technical solutions can be found. In present-day America, the same problems are apt to be viewed as problems of law or finance, to be dodged through clever manipulation of rules or numbers.

Increasingly, professional education in America stresses the manipulation of symbols to the exclusion of other sorts of skills—how to collaborate with others, to work in teams, to speak foreign languages, to solve concrete problems—that are more relevant to the newly competitive world economy. And more and more, the career ambitions of America's best students have turned to professions that allow them to continue attending to symbols, from quiet offices equipped with a telephone, a Telex, and a good secretary. The world of real people, engaged in the untidy and difficult struggle with real production problems, becomes ever more alien to America's best and brightest.

Paper entrepreneurialism is both cause and consequence of America's faltering economy. Paper profits are the only ones easily available to professional managers who sit isolated atop organizations designed for a form of production that is no longer appropriate to America's place in the world economy. At the same time, the relentless drive for paper profits had diverted attention and resources away from the difficult job of transforming the productive base. It has retarded the transition that must occur, and made change more difficult in the future. Paper entrepreneurialism thus has a self-perpetuating quality that, if left unchecked, will drive the nation into further decline.

DISCUSSION QUESTIONS

1. What does Reich mean by flexible production methods and paper entrepreneurialism?
2. Most of Reich's examples of America's economic decline come from heavy industry, such as steel and automobiles. Can you think of forms of enterprise in which Americans continue to excell? What makes these "industries" different? Does the fact of American excellence in some fields (computer science for instance) suggest that Reich ought to modify his blanket indictment of American business?
3. Why has international competition become so important in the last two decades? Should we be so concerned about the economic success of other peoples? Is the world economy a "zero-sum game" in which for every winner there must be a loser?

A 8
B 9
C 0
D 1
E 2
F 3
G 4
H 5
I 6
J 7